EVALUATING
DEVELOPMENT
EFFECTIVENESS

World Bank Series on Evaluation and Development
Robert Picciotto, Series Editor

Evaluation and Development:
The Institutional Dimension
edited by Robert Picciotto and Eduardo Wiesner

Involuntary Resettlement:
Comparative Perspectives
edited by Robert Picciotto, Warren van Wicklin,
and Edward Rice

Evaluation and Poverty Reduction
edited by Osvaldo N. Feinstein and Robert Picciotto

Making Development Work:
Development Learning in a World of Poverty and Wealth
edited by Nagy Hanna and Robert Picciotto

Managing a Global Resource:
Challenges of Forest Conservation and Development
edited by Uma Lele

Evaluation and Development:
The Partnership Dimension
edited by Andres Liebenthal, Osvaldo Feinstein,
and Gregory K. Ingram

Evaluating Development Effectiveness
edited by George Keith Pitman, Osvaldo N. Feinstein,
and Gregory K. Ingram

George Keith Pitman
Osvaldo N. Feinstein
Gregory K. Ingram
editors

EVALUATING DEVELOPMENT EFFECTIVENESS

World Bank Series on Evaluation and Development

Volume 7

Transaction Publishers
New Brunswick (U.S.A.) and London (U.K.)

Library of Congress Catalog Number: 2004041242
ISBN: 0-7658-0254-6 (cloth); 0-7658-0810-2 (paper)
Printed in the United States of America

Library of Congress Cataloging-in-Publication Data

Evaluating development effectiveness / George Keith Pitman, Osvaldo N. Feinstein, and Gregory K. Ingram, editors.
      p. cm. — (World Bank series on evaluation and development ; v. 7)
    "This book is based on papers prepared for and presented at the 5th World Bank Conference on "Evaluating Development Effectiveness: Challenges and the Way Foward," held on July 15-16, 2003, in Washington D.C. The conference was organized by the Operations Evaluation Department (OED) of the World Bank ..."—Acknowledgments.
    Includes bibliographical references and index.
    ISBN 0-7658-0254-6 (cloth : alk. paper) — ISBN 0-7658-0810-2
    (pbk. : alk. paper)
    1. World Bank—Congresses. 2. Economic assistance—Developing countries—Evaluation—Congresses. 3. Technical assistance—Developing countries—Evaluation—Congresses. 4. Economic development projects—Developing countries—Evaluation—Congresses. I. Pitman, George Keith, 1945- II. Feinstein, Osvaldo Néstor. III. Ingram, Gregory K. IV. World Bank. Operations Evaluation Dept. V. Series.

HG3881.5.W57E926 2004
338.91'072—dc22

2004041242

Contents

Acknowledgments

This book is based on papers prepared for and presented at the Fifth World Bank Conference on "Evaluating Development Effectiveness: Challenges and the Way Forward," held on July 15-16, 2003, in Washington, DC. The conference was organized by the Operations Evaluation Department (OED) of the World Bank, under the leadership of Gregory Ingram, Director General, Operations Evaluation; Nils Fostvedt, Director (acting), OED; Osvaldo Feinstein, Manager, Partnerships and Knowledge Management, OED; and George T. Keith Pitman, Senior Evaluation Officer, OED.

Patricia Marisa Nixon made a distinguished contribution as the Conference Coordinator, Richard Wall facilitated the Conference, and Rachel Weaving edited the proceedings. Julius Gwyer and Alex McKenzie were responsible for the conference website and Maria Mar and Tom Yoon provided IT support. Special thanks also go to Yvonne Playfair-Scott, Betty Bain, Princess Moore-Lewis, Adala Bruce-Konuah, Helen Joan Mongal, Juicy Qureishi-Haq, Romayne Pereira, and Soon-Won Pak for their unstinting support.

Finally, debt is owed to the speakers, session chairs, panel discussants, and other participants of the conference. We are particularly indebted to the distinguished chairs for their vital contributions: Nils Dabelstein, Ryokichi Hirono, Finn Jonck, Michael Klein, Frannie Leautier, and Robert Picciotto. And the conference debate was enriched by the contributions of the panel of discussants drawn from leaders in the field of development evaluation: Robert Boruch, Marco Ferroni, Sulley Gariba, David Goldsbrough, Colin Kirk, Uma Lele, Nancy MacPherson, Ruth Meinzen-Dick, Martin Ravallion, William Stevenson, Rob van den Berg, and Eduardo Wiesner.

George Keith Pitman
Osvaldo N. Feinstein
Gregory K. Ingram

Foreword

Concern that development aid should show results has reached an all-time high. In both donor and aid recipient nations, governments and the national and international agencies through which they work face new demands for accountability to citizens on how aid is used and what it accomplishes.

The international agreements reached in Monterrey and Johannesburg in the last two years indicate two sides of a bargain: for developing countries and transition countries to practice good management and good governance, and for donor countries to provide increased development assistance, capacity-building, and more open trade. But when we get down to the details of how the bargain is working, we find a debate in progress, focusing on development results. Leaders of the wealthy countries will provide more resources for development—if it can be shown that existing resources are being well used. And individual countries will receive additional aid—if they can show they are making progress against agreed yardsticks, including the Millennium Development Goals.

The Millennium Development Goals, endorsed by all UN member countries, are a prominent example of the new concern for results. The World Bank, like other international financial institutions, must now report to its members on progress towards these goals and on how its specific interventions are helping to achieve them. We have committed ourselves to focus the attention of managers and staff on results, starting from the inception of our strategies, operations, and partnerships. The World Bank is also helping interested client countries implement a results perspective in their poverty reduction strategies. We have launched a pilot program of results-based country assistance strategies, and are also implementing results-oriented approaches to our sectoral strategies. The World Bank is moving from the project-by-project approach to program- and country-level approaches, which focus not only on our own outputs and impact but also on the country's results. Assistance for capacity building in client countries is an essential part of this results agenda.

Many of the participants from thirty-five countries that were invited to this Fifth Annual Evaluation Conference face similar demands from their own managements to demonstrate the results of development spending. Questions of measurement—of the assessment of countries' progress and of the role of aid in that progress—are now the subject of discussion at the very highest levels.

The focus on results puts tremendous importance on evaluators and on the tools that evaluators use. Today, the Operations Evaluation Department of the World Bank faces a much more complex task than in its early days, when it would assess the outcome of a particular project against the goals that were delineated when the project was approved for financing. Now the evaluation task addresses not merely the results of a particular project, but the contribution of that project and other parts of the development enterprise to the achievement of the Millennium Development Goals. Another challenge for evaluators, with the growth of inter-agency partnerships for development, is to develop cooperative approaches to the evaluation of increasingly collaborative development ventures.

As we adapt and develop our evaluation tools and systems, we need to learn and to share insights, not only at the cutting-edge of methodology but also, on the basis of practical experience, about what has worked and not worked for evaluators in different contexts and with different perspectives, and about how best to help our client countries build their own evaluation capacity. I hope that the insights in this volume will help to advance the understanding of what makes for effective development, and thence to achieve the faster development progress that we all seek.

James D. Wolfensohn
President, World Bank

Overview

Gregory K. Ingram

Views about the ends and means of development continue to change, and this implies that approaches to development evaluation should also change. The past few years have seen an increasing emphasis on the results of aid programs by donors and lenders who seek to convince taxpayers that aid funds are well used, and by recipient countries who want to ensure that funds they are borrowing produce sufficient benefits to enable them to repay the loans. Expectations about results are now embodied in the Millennium Development Goals, a set of specific and time-bound targets for performance indicators. This focus on results has increased the demand for evaluation and for evidence of the effectiveness of development programs.

The papers in this volume address the challenges of evaluating development effectiveness and the performance of development agencies, as well as how to improve the quality of evaluative evidence, the use of evaluation findings, and the treatment of uncertainty in evaluations. They take stock of recent advances in the measurement of progress in achieving development effectiveness and in the evaluation of development interventions.

Authors throughout the volume emphasize that there is ample scope for improving monitoring and evaluation activities and products, whether those of aid donors, recipient countries, nongovernmental organizations, or researchers. They are also in broad agreement on a set of immediate challenges faced by development evaluation, including:

- moving from the project (micro) level to higher (macro) levels of aggregation such as the sector level, the country level, the agency level, and the global level;
- carrying out joint evaluations across development agencies and including participation from aid recipients and nongovernmental organizations; and
- clarifying the objectives of development interventions from design through implementation in order to improve their evaluability.

Director-General, Operations Evaluation, World Bank.

On the methodological front, the authors emphasize the importance of transparency in evaluation methods, the promise of randomized experiments as a tool in assessing development effectiveness, and the need to take account more formally of the uncertainty that is inherent in evaluation findings.

Transparent methods. Participants at the World Bank's Fifth Evaluation Conference,[1] from which this book is derived, were pluralistic in their views about evaluation methods. Some agreed with the view of Frances Stewart that simple, evidence-based evaluation methods are best, and that more complex methods tend to play a major role in determining results. Yet great interest was also expressed in methods based on structural models of behavior—such as the model used by John Newman and his co-authors to evaluate a malaria control program in Bolivia—that go well beyond the logical framework in common use. The unifying element of these varying views was agreement that any method or model used must be transparent.

Randomized experiments. As described in several of the papers in this volume, randomized experiments are beginning to be applied to assess development effectiveness. Experience to date indicates that this tool is best used at the micro or project level and that it is unlikely to be useful to evaluate national policies or policy-based lending. At the micro level, while randomized evaluation has drawbacks (e.g., participant attrition, spillover effects), it is the least impaired evaluation method. It does not address accountability directly, but produces knowledge about what does and does not work. It produces results in terms of sample averages and does not readily yield other parameters containing information about the effects of recipient characteristics on outcomes. Conference participants concluded that randomized experiments should be used more often in development evaluation, to complement other useful instruments in the evaluator's tool kit. In practice, however, few development organizations currently have incentives that promote randomized evaluation approaches.

Uncertainty in evaluation. A range of uncertainty in evaluative evidence and conclusions is inherent in all evaluation methods, including randomized experiments, yet evaluations typically do not address this uncertainty in a formal way. Evaluation findings and conclusions essentially represent decisions made under uncertainty about the effectiveness of projects, policies, or other interventions. While many analytical methods have been developed to address decision making under uncertainty, they have not been much applied to evaluation. Andrew Briggs' paper shows, in an analysis of the cost-effectiveness of alternative treatments for the same illness, how the uncertainty about the results from randomized health trials can be formally quantified. The use of these methods, based on Bayesian approaches common in the literature on decision theory, offers a way to quantify the uncertainty and thereby improve judgments that are based on evaluative evidence.

Development, and Development Evaluation, is Changing

The first three papers assess current evaluation practice in the context of changing development thinking and present cautionary tales for those doing development evaluations. Frances Stewart explores the stability or consistency of evaluation results. While agreeing that objective-based evaluation is sensible in the new results-based development environment, she observes that donors, recipient country governments, and nongovernmental organizations are likely to have different objectives for development programs. For example, while the donor community has been concerned with domestic issues in aid-recipient countries, UNCTAD and the South have been concerned with generating improved global terms of trade and distribution of resources. Such differing objectives can lead different actors to different evaluative conclusions based on the same evidence about program outcomes.

Other characteristics of evaluators may also affect evaluation results. One is the evaluators' academic discipline. Economists are often more interested in quantitative measures linked to changes in welfare, such as increased income, while other social scientists are often more interested in whether people affected by a development intervention feel that they are better off because of it. Stewart asserts that evaluators internal to an agency tend to hold more things constant—especially agency policy—than do external evaluators, who are less constrained in their thinking and experience.

The characteristics of the evaluation itself also can affect evaluation results. For example, evaluations carried out at different times for the same project may produce contradictory results; a project that seems successful when first implemented may fail later, and an initially problematic project may eventually succeed. In addition, Stewart observes that evaluation method is often a key determinant of evaluation results. In the interest of transparency, she has a strong implicit preference for using the simplest method consistent with obtaining reliable evaluation results.

Given the need for evaluations to move from the micro to the macro level, White reviews how well evaluators are doing with macro-level evaluations, and finds that there is much room for improvement. Many attempts to prepare evaluations at the macro level aggregate the results from micro-level evaluations and are therefore meta-evaluations, yet very few of them are built on the precepts of meta-evaluation. In addition, White notes that little meaningful attention is paid to risk or uncertainty in either micro or macro evaluations, and that creating plausible counterfactuals at the macro level is necessary but much more difficult than at the micro level.

Killick moves the focus from the details of evaluation approaches and methods to the application of evaluation results. He sees an ongoing shift in aid instruments, away from projects towards programs and sectoral approaches, but not as the result of evaluation evidence. Killick points out how little is known about the full transaction costs of different types of aid instruments, including the costs to recipient countries. Where there are consistent evaluation results—such as the finding that conditionality in aid operations is rarely successful—they are often little used by policy makers. He points out a limitation in evaluators' ability to influence policy: to get a policy changed, he believes, it is not normally enough to show that the current policy is poor; it is also necessary to identify a feasible alternative. But evaluation is not policy formulation, and evaluators are often ill equipped to propose alternative policies. Even so, when evaluation results are used, they can inform the policy dialogue with advantage.

Evaluating the Performance of Development Agencies

Evaluating the performance of development agencies is a specific type of macro-level evaluation, and the papers on this topic support several of the points made by White. Leeuw and Cooksy review the annual summaries of evaluation results produced by three development agencies: DFID, UNDP, and the World Bank. While those summaries vary in quality, the authors find them to be more akin to descriptive compilations of audit results than to syntheses of substantive findings on what works and why. They believe that these annual summaries should deal more specifically with the problems of attributing development outcomes to agency operations or interventions, and that the theories that underlie major programs, projects, and strategies should be articulated, to assist in determining what works (or not). In addition, the summaries need to more frequently break out of their retrospective evaluation view and develop the implications of their findings for the future.

Lindahl reports on a long-term retrospective of SIDA's aid portfolio, which showed that the longest-lasting projects and programs tended to be the worst performers. Echoing Killick's comments on the use of evaluation findings, Lindahl hypothesizes that the reason lay more with political comfort than with evaluation results. He speculates on how this pattern can be avoided, and whether competitive mechanisms could play a role in bringing forth alternative approaches.

Nongovernmental organizations are part of the changing context of development, and have become much more active both as advocates for development and as implementing agencies in delivering services to the poor. They are also beginning to evaluate some of their own activities and their overall impacts. Kruse reviews several early evaluations done by nongovernmental organizations of their own activities. These evaluations found that many of the NGO projects reviewed did not reach the poorest (households in the bottom deciles of the income distribution), and that few were sustainable. Kruse judges the evaluations to be relatively weak in providing evidence and supporting data on project impacts; he recommends the use of multiple perspectives in order to make more objective the interpretation of impact.

Two papers focus on new methods for evaluating country-level programs. Like many aid agencies, the World Bank has moved the strategic focus of its operations from the project level to the country level, and the objectives for its country programs are set forth in country assistance strategies. In addition, many countries are now setting out visions for their own development, often embodying these in poverty reduction strategy papers. The country focus of development operations is forcing development evaluators to carry out evaluations at the country level.

Newman and his co-authors present a structural model based on systems dynamics for monitoring and evaluating a country-level malaria control program in Bolivia. This is a rich model that combines scientific information about disease vectors (mosquitoes) and the spread of malaria with program information on interventions. It supports the exploration of "what if" scenarios, which can be used as counterfactuals in analyzing the impact of the actual malaria control program that was implemented. The model can also be used as a management tool to adjust program interventions in real time. While it has many parameters and is complex, it is transparent.

Johnson and Lamdany present an objectives-based methodology for assessing World Bank country programs. Taking the Bank's country assistance strategy as the statement of the Bank's objectives in the country, the paper describes an evaluation method that triangulates three different perspectives— bottom-up, top-down, and comparative—on country program performance. The first of these perspectives aggregates the performance rating of individual operations to the country level; the second assesses country performance on the basis of macro-level performance indicators; and the third compares the country's macro-level performance with that of other comparator countries. This method and its variants have been applied to more than sixty country-level evaluations to date.

Improving Evaluative Evidence

A source of challenge for many evaluators is the need to compare what actually happened with a particular operation, policy change, or intervention with what would have happened without it. The "without" alternative, or counterfactual, is difficult to specify in many cases. Formal experimentation offers one clear way to define the difference between the two alternatives, and social experiments are a small but growing activity in development evaluation. In addition, in some cases natural experiments occur, and data from them can be analyzed as for designed experiments. In the development arena, most social experiments randomly select people or groups who will be subject to the policy or treatment, and those who will not (the control group).

Duflo and Kremer review several examples where randomized experiments (or appropriate natural experiments) have been analyzed to reveal the effect of policies or interventions. They observe that this approach is most applicable at the micro or project level where the observational units are persons, households, or firms. Randomized experiments cannot be used to evaluate most adjustment or policy-based lending that has a regional or national impact because experiments cannot be done across regions or nations. Experience to date has demonstrated the feasibility of micro-level randomized experiments in development evaluation. The experiments are costly, but no more so than other evaluation approaches that collect and analyze sample survey data. Randomized experiments have fewer limitations than most other evaluation approaches, but they can be compromised if participants drop out of the experiment or the experience of participants receiving the "treatment" changes the behavior of those not receiving it. Duflo and Kremer would like to see much wider use of randomized experiments, with the approach being built into perhaps one out of ten development projects.

A practical challenge is that most project task managers face much stronger incentives to implement a project than to evaluate it. Predictably, few task managers are motivated to produce the public good of evaluation results from randomized experiments associated with their projects unless incentives change. Duflo and Kremer discuss the possible roles of NGOs and international organizations in promoting and implementing randomized experiments, whereas Ravallion argues that external technical support in evaluation must retain a primary focus on governments if it is to have a major impact.

Rawlings reviews recent World Bank experience in supporting randomized experiments. While agreeing that randomized experiments are the least impaired of available evaluation methods, she notes that the result they produce is a sample average. The determinants of success or failure are unclear from such experiments, and there are no other parameter values. She is therefore also supportive of impact evaluations, partly because these provide more information about the determinants of outcomes. But she sees debates about the virtues of randomized experiments relative to other competing evaluation methods as somewhat beside the point when many projects lack even rudimentary monitoring data on their outputs and outcomes. She would give priority to monitoring activities that produce tailored streams of data to inform policy decisions and project management. And, given that randomized experiments often raise ethical concerns, Rawlings notes that the essential elements of randomized experiments can be realized in other ways. For example, when budgets, information constraints, or limited operational capacity prevent programs from reaching all eligible people at the same time, randomization has been used as an equitable way to allocate scarce goods or services. In such cases, randomized experiments become a byproduct of the method used to allocate resources, and have been used to provide evaluative evidence about the programs. In his comments, Boruch highlights the value of systematic reviews of randomized trials in order to learn from them.

Evaluating Sustainability and Its Likelihood

The sustainability of development interventions is about the resilience of net benefits over time. White elaborates this definition and raises concerns that current approaches to assessing sustainability lack rigor, fail to take uncertainty into account, and give insufficient attention to institutional factors. Platteau's paper provides a sobering account of the difficulties of determining the sustainability of social interventions. Conversely, Briggs's paper shows how approaches commonly used in decision theory can be applied to analyze the uncertainty of project outcomes. A feature common to both approaches is that they require a data-rich environment, which could have significant cost implications for evaluation.

Like many of the previous authors, Platteau emphasizes that donors must allow enough time—often longer than a typical project or evaluation time frame—for institutional development and collective action to mature. And maturity requires that beneficiaries become empowered to make their own decisions. Platteau's findings illustrate the practical difficulties of poverty targeting and the need for an evaluation process during the project's life cycle, involving the intended beneficiaries.

Briggs' paper demonstrates the use of probabilistic approaches to assess the cost-effectiveness of alternative medical treatments for the same disease and examines their potential application to World Bank project analysis to determine the likelihood that project benefits will be sustained. His approach uses Bayesian statistical models to trace how the probability distribution of input variables determines the probability distribution or uncertainty of the outcome. Taking his analysis one step further, Briggs postulates that the Bayesian modeling approach could be applied to typical cost-benefit analysis of development projects or even to more complex interventions. He also argues that Bayesian models can be used not only to quantify uncertainty but also to help determine whether a decision should be made immediately, or whether it should be delayed while more information is collected through further evaluations.

Using Evaluation Findings to Improve Development Effectiveness

Two papers supplemented by a panel discussion look at ways in which evaluation results can be applied to improve development effectiveness.

Gariba's paper reports how evaluation has enhanced country-led development in Ghana. While many of the monitoring and evaluation efforts are still nascent, performance-based disbursement is being used to trigger a multi-donor budget support program under the HIPC initiative. A government-led multi-stakeholder sector working group has increased local ownership and control of donor expenditures. Introduction of a scorecard for public service agencies, with results published in newspapers, has changed the behavior and service standards of public utilities, and provoked the formation of a Ghana

Anti-corruption Coalition that has compelled Parliament to establish a public enquiry into judicial corruption. Gariba highlights the role of parliaments in translating the demand for accountability into a demand for evaluation.

Wiesner's paper proposes that evaluation findings should be used to regulate public expenditure on projects and programs. Adopting such an incentive will, he believes, stimulate demand-driven evaluation. Wiesner argues that unless projects or sectoral programs are subject to a hard budget constraint, evaluation will be virtually powerless to change policies.

The panel discussion addressed the hypothesis that successful evaluators should induce reform. Among ways of achieving this were delivery of user-friendly and credible results; a better focus on tangible intermediate outcomes that help program managers; designing evaluations to increase learning; and creating demand for evaluation products. Many participants argued that these improvements will occur only if managers are held accountable for their results and if evaluators are held accountable for improving the relevance of their evaluations.

Note

1.   Participants are listed at the end of this volume.

Part 1

Challenges in Evaluating Development Effectiveness

1

Evaluating Evaluation in a World of Multiple Goals, Interests, and Models

Frances Stewart[1]

Evaluating development efforts is potentially extremely important, since it can affect what happens subsequently—in terms not just of minor adjustments to project design but also of major changes in the direction of development efforts. In principle, evaluation is also an important aspect of the accountability of public institutions (as it is for NGOs and the private sector, too), and should help the institutions themselves improve their efficiency.

Big changes in the direction of development efforts typically result not just from evaluation but from political pressures exerted by a variety of actors. Yet evaluation can usefully inform and make more effective such pressures. Examples of such changes, all involving evaluation as one important input, are the changing attitudes and actions towards the financing of large dams, the recognition (in the 1980s) of the need to incorporate poverty considerations into adjustment policy, the incorporation of environmental issues into development goals and policy, and the growing movement towards corporate social responsibility.

Evaluation sounds as if it is a straightforward technical issue, like auditing. In fact it is complex, involving many methodological questions and value judgments, and indeed it can be highly political in a number of ways. This paper explores the importance of the methodological decisions and values involved in any evaluation—showing how different decisions on these issues can lead to radically different evaluations with highly significant consequences for subsequent action.

The values and political elements involved in any evaluation should be acknowledged—which leads to the conclusion that it is not possible to argue that any single method is *right*. Rightness depends on goals and assumptions

Professor of Development Economics, Oxford University.

about development processes. Both depend on values, and these in turn often reflect the interests of those conducting the evaluation.

The issue of evaluation poses a dilemma. On the one hand, actual evaluations can and do alter action and people's lives. Consequently, it is important to get them right. Yet defining development goals and understanding processes of development, both necessarily incorporated in evaluation, are complex, evolving, and value-laden, so there *is* no right method, rather a set of methods and evaluations depending on the values adopted.

1. Methodological Issues

I call these "methodological" issues, which sounds as if they are technical matters—such as whether it is preferable, for example, to use present value or internal rate of return methods in evaluating projects. Such technical issues are important and interesting, but I am primarily concerned with bigger questions. Let me start with a very straightforward approach to evaluation. The rest of this paper will show why evaluating development efforts is not so straightforward.

Figure 1.1 represents the simplest approach one could take. Let A be "development efforts" and B the development outcome. Then evaluating development efforts consists in assessing the ratio of B/A. Project evaluation comes closest to this. It is assumed that there is a certain cost of inputs that can be measured, and a stream of output resulting from the project—also measurable—and then, with an appropriate discount rate, B and A can be measured and the ratio B/A arrived at.

Even in the project context there are problematic issues, notably in choosing prices that reflect social costs and benefits to measure inputs and outputs, measuring externalities including environmental effects, choosing a time discount rate, deciding whether to weight according to the income distribution

Figure 1.1
A Straightforward Approach to Evaluation

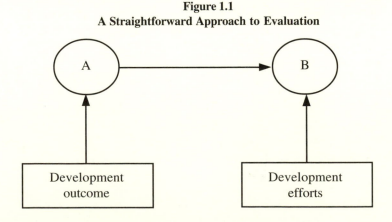

among those affected, and so forth.[2] Dealing with many of these issues in fact involves many of the methodological questions I discuss below.

One reason why current evaluation is much more complex than the B/A approach is that the idea that "development efforts" consist simply of investment in projects has long since gone. Most development efforts today have much more ambitious objectives than, for example, supplying electricity efficiently or building a road. For example, according to World Bank president, James Wolfensohn, an overriding objective is to achieve the Millennium Development Goals (MDGs): "Together, we have set 2015 as the deadline for our results. We must now, together, move beyond words and set deadlines for our actions. We have said we are mutually accountable. It is time to deliver." This seems to be a far cry from the efficient production of electricity.

In selecting evaluation methods, many issues arise that affect the nature of the evaluation and very often the outcome. Decisions made concerning each of these issues are never purely technical but reflect values and interests. Very often, different types of evaluators make different decisions. The most important decision, before making any evaluation, is to define the goals of development that will provide the benchmark of achievement or outcomes for the evaluation. This choice includes the selection of development goals to which development efforts are directed, and whether the goals themselves should be subject to evaluation.

Second and closely related, but an important independent source of differences that can radically alter the evaluation, is how we *measure* the achievement of selected goals, both with respect to precisely which indicator is chosen to measure goal achievement and with respect to whether the concern is with absolute achievement or with the value-added that is to be attributed to specific development efforts. And if the concern is to measure value-added, a source of major differences is the method used to arrive at a measure of value-added.

Third, the time period over which the assessment is made is another variable that can transform apparent success into failure, or conversely.

These three questions all concern how we assess *outcomes*. Fourth, there is the question of how we define the development efforts themselves (that is, *whose* and *which* development efforts are being assessed). The ways in which all these questions are dealt with are likely to be affected by who is making the assessment, which raises the question of who *should* be conducting particular evaluations.

We shall discuss the issue of who the appropriate evaluators are later in the paper, but it is helpful to identify the major types of evaluator at this stage, because the nature of the evaluator is such an important determinant of the many choices made during evaluation.

- One important distinction is between internal evaluation (i.e., within the institution responsible for the development efforts being assessed) and external evaluations (from outside the institution), since internal evaluators generally share the values and objectives of the institution, while external evaluators may not do so. One can overemphasize this distinction, because external evaluators may be closely allied with the responsible institution, for a variety of reasons, including common ideology and interests and the desire for continued association with the institution, while internal evaluators can be at relatively arms length in their relationship with the institution being evaluated, as the World Bank's Operations Evaluation Department (OED) appears to be.

- Within the "external" category, official evaluation may be carried out by international agencies, Northern governments, Southern governments, Northern or Southern NGOs, or by "beneficiaries" of development efforts.[3] As we shall see, since these agents tend to have different interests and values, insofar as interests and values are important in determining how evaluation is conducted, the nature and outcome of the evaluation is likely to differ according to who is conducting the evaluation.

- The disciplinary perspective of those carrying out the evaluation is another important distinction with a bearing on the nature and conclusions of evaluation. For example, while economists tend to make certain assumptions about motives and behavior, anthropologists and sociologists investigate such motives and behavior, so that the former tend to find that imperfect incentives and markets explain development failures, while the latter are more likely to point to institutional elements.[4] Political scientists have another perspective, often evaluating programs according to whether they have gained political support, their implications for democracy, and the implications of democracy for reform (Nelson and Waterbury, 1989; Healey and Robinson, 1992).

Multiple Development Goals

The selection of goals greatly influences how one evaluates efforts, and the results of these evaluations, as I shall illustrate below. There is no universal agreement on development goals. At any one time, particular institutions and/ or individuals tend to have different development goals (contrast those of the International Labor Organization (ILO) and the World Bank today). In addition, goals accepted by different agents change over time in a major and not always unidirectional way. Taking the World Bank, which generally reflects/ leads a consensus of major bilateral donors, a crude representation of goals followed is presented below:

- 1950s, 1960s: projects/infrastructure
- 1970s: Basic Needs
- 1980s: stabilization and structural adjustment; Washington Consensus
- 1990s: growth/poverty reduction/environment
- 2000+: Millennium Development Goals.

The evolution of goals is a product of several factors. One is that unforeseen problems often arise in the context of *success* in achieving other objectives. Evaluation, so long as it is not strictly tied to the initial objectives of the institution, should reveal these problems. In practice it is difficult and, I believe unusual, for internal evaluations to change the goal posts in the middle of an evaluation—particularly if this involves qualifying what seems like a successful outcome. Hence, it is normally external evaluators who draw attention to these issues. Subsequently, the initial institution may take up the new goals. An example is the early development efforts of the World Bank and others broadly focused on promoting economic growth through the development of infrastructure. At this time, World Bank evaluation was mostly in terms of the efficiency of the infrastructural projects. But broader evaluation of these efforts by the International Labor Organization and others suggested that while growth had occurred it left in its wake various other problems, such as unemployment and unsatisfied basic needs (ILO, 1976). Consequently, the ILO took up employment as an objective, and subsequently the ILO, followed by the World Bank, proposed the fulfillment of Basic Needs as an overriding strategy (Streeten et al., 1981). Similarly, in the 1980s, most of the World Bank's evaluations of adjustment focused on success or failure in terms of stabilization, but UNICEF evaluated adjustment efforts in terms of poverty, and a focus on poverty reduction was subsequently incorporated in the objectives of the international financial institutions (World Bank, 1988; Cornia et al., 1986).

A second reason why goals evolve is that the initial goals are *not* achieved. In looking for causes of failure, particular problems are identified, and new goals emerge to deal with these problems. For example, some World Bank evaluators attributed the failure of growth-oriented adjustment in Africa to a failure of implementation due to lack of "ownership" and to problems with "governance," and dealing with these became new World Bank objectives.[5] In contrast to the first case, this source of goal change is more likely to arise from internal rather than from external evaluation.

A third source of change in goals arises from exogenous (or seemingly exogenous) developments, such as HIV/AIDS, adverse movements in the terms of trade, or rising incidence of violent conflict, that require changing goals, or a new sub-goal within an accepted goal (such as a focus on conflict prevention within the general goals of promoting growth and poverty reduction). These developments could be picked up by either internal or external evaluation. In general, internal evaluators are more likely to look for reasons for failures that do not call into question the design of the policies, while external evaluators are more likely to question the policies themselves.[6]

An example is provided by the World Bank Operations Evaluation Department's evaluation of poverty reduction in the 1990s. In accounting for rather modest success, OED points to:

...continuing population increases and economic growth that failed to meet expectations, a shortfall that was aggravated by the uneven distribution of growth in many regions. Further fueling the escalation in numbers were the economic transition in Eastern Europe and Central Asia; financial volatility and its impact...; the AIDS pandemic; civil war; and a chain of natural disasters... (Operations Evaluation Department, 2000)

In contrast, many external evaluators have suggested that besides such factors, the policy reforms themselves may be at least partially responsible for weak performance on growth and poverty, including excessively deflationary macro-policies (e.g., Stiglitz, 2002), trade liberalization leading to job destruction (Lall and Pietrobelli, 2002), and rising inequality (Berry, 1998).

Two other types of exogenous change can lead to changing goals. One arises from changes in the political complexion of the governments of major donors, as well as of recipient countries. The swing from Basic Needs to stabilization and adjustment from the 1970s to the 1980s, and then the return to a focus on poverty reduction and human development in the 1990s, were partly due to the changing political complexion of the U.S. government. Similarly, political changes in recipient countries can influence their goals. The Dependency movement and the New International Economic Order (NIEO) evolved as poor countries gained political independence yet believed they faced unfair terms in the world market place. Goals also change as regimes switch from authoritarian to more democratic forms, or from "reform" orientation to populism. Another near-exogenous source of change is associated with intellectual developments, especially where these are widely taken up by the epistemological community—for example, Friedman's monetarism or Sen's capability approach. Keynes famously said that "practical men, who believe themselves to be quite exempt from any intellectual influences, are usually the slaves of some defunct economist" (Keynes, 1936). I am reluctant (despite being an academic) to give such emphasis to intellectual developments as the origin of major changes, because I believe ideas are mostly lying around waiting to be picked up when the political/institutional time is ripe. For example, import protection preceded List, and Keynesian policies preceded Keynes, while an emphasis on human-oriented goals preceded Sen's capability approach, and the Physical Quality of Life Index preceded the Human Development Index. Thus, in contrast to Keynes' view, I would argue that dominant ideas are mostly the product of politics and interests.[7] While the exact development of and form taken by ideas can be regarded as exogenous, the fact that certain ideas come to prominence at certain times owes more to politics and institutional factors than to the ideas themselves.

Although probably the evolution of goals listed above would be broadly accepted (as in Picciotto, 2002) as the dominant bi- and multilateral consensus about development during successive decades (though one could question the exact timing), the old ideas and goals are never completely abandoned.

In every case, the old goals persist for some time, through a process of institutional and intellectual inertia. In some cases, the goals persist more or less unaltered and are taken up side-by-side with new ones. We would need detailed documentary evidence to show how far one set of goals had displaced others over the years. However, casual observation points to considerable but varying persistence. For example, for the World Bank throughout its existence, infrastructure development has remained an important element of policy; although the promotion of Basic Needs came near to disappearing in the 1980s in the Bank's rhetoric, quite substantial expenditures on basic needs persisted; stabilization and adjustment goals have remained dominant objectives for both the World Bank and the International Monetary Fund (IMF), probably as strongly in the 1990s and 2000s as in the 1980s, while new goals have added to rather than replaced them. This means that to determine the goals against which evaluations are made is quite a complex task, not only because goals regularly change over time, but because at each point of time there are multiple goals even within a single institution.

It has already become apparent that the evolution of goals described above was by no means uncontested. At any one time, many institutions have multiple goals, but there are also differences (often quite sharp) between institutions or agents in accepted goals and in the weighting among them. For example, during the 1970s, a major objective of Southern-dominated institutions and individuals was the promotion of the New International Economic Order, and the focus on providing Basic Needs was regarded as a diversion. Indeed, Galtung regarded these two strategies as "on a collision course" (Galtung, 1978); in the 1980s, UNICEF and others, including nongovernmental organizations and some borrowing governments, attacked the near exclusive focus of the international financial institutions on stabilization and the neglect of economic growth and poverty reduction (Cornia et al., 1986); in the 1990s, the UNDP focused on promoting Human Development, and enhancing capabilities, while the World Bank and others focused on economic growth and poverty reduction (as exemplified by the UNDP *Human Development Report* of 1990 and the World Bank *World Development Report* of the same year). Differences can also be seen in the attention given to redistribution as distinct from economic growth (contrast the World Institute for Development Economics Research and the World Bank); and the emphasis on conditions of work as compared with so-called labor market distortions (contrast the ILO and the World Bank). Throughout, UNCTAD and the South have been concerned with generating improved global terms of trade and distribution of resources, while the donor community has almost exclusively emphasized domestic issues in aid-recipient countries.

The changing development agenda, multiple goals at any one time, and lack of consensus about goals and their weighting, pose major issues for evaluation because the evaluation of any particular development effort can alter radically according to the goals against which the efforts are judged. In the case of infrastructure projects, evaluations have altered as poverty reduction, environmental issues, and population displacement have come to the fore—which is one reason why some donors have greatly reduced their support for this sort of investment (Wade, 1997). To take another example: do we regard recent development efforts in China as successful because they generated high growth and poverty reduction, or as unsuccessful because they were accompanied by rising inequality, massive migration, and lack of political freedom? The point is that all good things do not go together; different groups differ not only on what is desirable, but also, to a greater extent, on priorities and the weighting of accepted goals. These differences lead to differences in evaluation.

The contrast between country ranking according to GDP per capita, UNDP's Human Development Index (HDI), or life expectancy provides an illustration. Changes in country ranking according to achievements in particular development goals provide an indication of how evaluation is likely to vary according to goals. Taking all countries together, the correlation among the rankings is high, but for the countries of greatest concern—those with low human development—it is much lower. In comparisons between the Human Development Index and per capita incomes as criteria for ranking, more than a third of countries change their ranking by fifteen places or more (Table 1.1).

In another illustration of probable differences in evaluation arising from the selection of goals, Figure 1.2 and Figure 1.3 show how the ranking among the highest Human Development Index countries and the lowest differs according to a wider range of indices of progress.

Table 1.1
Spearman Correlations between Some Development Objectives, 2000

Countries	Human Development Index/GNP per capita	Human Development Index /Life expectancy	Life expectancy/ GNP per capita
All countries	0.923	0.755	0.629
Developed	0.753	0.348	0.005
Developing and transition	0.894	0.694	0.524
Low HD	0.562	0.745	0.384

Sources: UNDP (2002); World Bank (2002).

Figure 1.2
Performance Ranking of Top Ten Human Development Index Countries

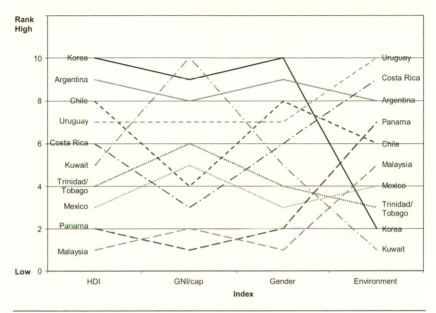

Note: Omits very small countries and those with incomplete data.

The existence of multiple and contested goals has several implications for evaluation. First, multiple evaluations are possible according to the selection of goals and their weighting. Second, evaluation is likely to differ according to who does it, because interests shape values and goals (or the weighting among them). Third, evaluating the goals themselves and their weighting can itself be an important aspect of evaluation, which can lead to major changes in development efforts.

Some evaluation efforts, including many internal evaluations, are set up in a way that excludes an evaluation of the goals, on the basis that it is not up to the evaluators to change the goal posts. But this approach could miss the most important dimensions, like assessing the quality of Nero's violin playing rather than the well-being of Rome. In contrast, a good deal of independent evaluation, notably that of some leading NGOs, is mainly concerned with evaluating the goals to which particular development efforts were directed. In fact, the most important contributions of independent evaluators have been to draw attention to the need to change goal posts. Consequently, it should not be surprising that external and internal evaluations frequently disagree.

The conclusions of any evaluation depend on the particular goals used by the evaluators, and are not necessarily correct or relevant in relation to differ-

Figure 1.3
Performance Ranking of Bottom Ten Human Development Index Countries

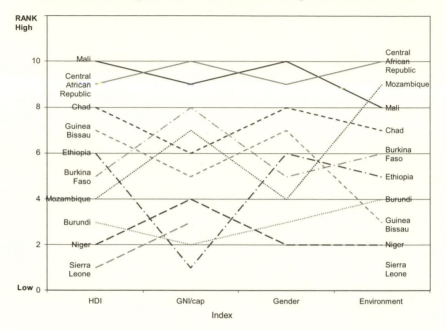

ent goals. Evaluations become problematic therefore if claims are made that go beyond this: that certain policies have been shown to be successful, without specifying the assumed goals by which the evaluation was made. General claims of success (or failure) are only legitimate in cases where the policies or programs got positive results in relation to any set of goals, or the weighting of them. Few evaluations in fact fully specify the goals they are using; very few specify the weighting of such goals; and almost none systematically evaluate according to a range (let alone a comprehensive range) of goals and weightings. Yet statements are often made implying that the results are correct, without delineating the goals. For example, Cassen et al. argued that "Aid works," although they failed to provide systematic evidence on its effects on poverty or human development (Cassen, 1986). Dollar and Kraay have famously asserted that "Growth *is* good for the poor," defining "good for the poor" as any increase in the money incomes of the poor (Dollar and Kraay, 2001), so that growth in which the incomes of the poor rose by one-twentieth of those of the rich could still count as being good for the poor.

The case of *Adjustment with a Human Face* (Cornia et al., 1986) illustrates how goal selection affects evaluation. This book criticized adjustment efforts of the international financial institutions because of their argued consequences for poverty. Poverty consequences were ignored by many evaluations because

poverty reduction was not part of the goals of the international financial institutions at the time.[8] Among evaluations of large infrastructure projects, for
example dams and airports, some authors find negative consequences, because they put heavy weight on negative environmental consequences and
the displacement of peoples, while those who support the projects point to
positive growth and poverty reduction effects. The recent debate about developing a new airport near Mexico City is a clear example.

Measuring the Success of Development Efforts

Even where there is agreement on the broad goals and their weighting,
different methods of measuring development outcomes can lead to big differences in evaluations.

Choice of outcome indicator. I will illustrate this by the case of poverty.
While there is widespread agreement on the goal of poverty reduction, a range
of problems about defining and measuring poverty can greatly affect the outcome of evaluation.[9] Different decisions about these elements can change the
estimated numbers of people in poverty in a country hugely: according to one
estimate from 17 to 77 percent (Szekely et al., 2000). Then there is the question of whether one should measure monetary poverty (i.e., income or consumption poverty) or other types of poverty, including capability poverty,
participatory measures of poverty, and social exclusion. Our research in India
and Peru has shown that about half the people classified as in poverty according to monetary measures are not in capability poverty, and conversely (Table
1.2) (Ruggeri-Laderchi et al., 2003).

A similar lack of overlap was found when comparing the people whom
communities recognized as poor, in a well-being ranking exercise, with those
classified as poor according to monetary or capability measures:

Table 1.2
Individual Overlaps in Types of Poverty

Capability poverty measured as		Education		Nutrition/health	
		child	*adult*	*child*	*adult*
% of CA-poor not in monetary poverty	India	43	60	53	63
	Peru	32	37	21	55
% of monetary poor not CA-poor	India	65	38	53	91
	Peru	93	73	66	94

CA: capability.

Source: Ruggeri-Laderchi et al. (2003).

- In India, only about half of those ranked as "low well-being" were also monetarily poor.[10] Even the highest monetary decile had 34 percent of individuals ranked as "low well-being." In Peru, in the rural area studied, 48 percent of the monetary non-poor were identified as poor according to the well-being ranking, while 39 percent of the extremely poor, by well-being ranking, were *not* monetary poor. In the urban area studied, 49 percent of the monetary non-poor were ranked as poor while 44 percent of those ranked as poor were not monetary poor.
- In Peru, a lack of overlap also appeared between self-perceptions of poverty and monetary poverty. In the rural area, 29 percent of the self-declared poor were non-poor according to the monetary indicator, while among the monetary poor, 42 percent did not believe themselves to be poor. In the urban area, 40 percent of the self-declared poor were not monetary poor, and 42 percent of the monetary poor did not state that they were poor.
- Low levels of congruence were also found between capability poverty and poverty by well-being ranking. For example, in Peru, in the rural area, 43 percent of the capability poor (nutrition) were non-poor according to the ranking, and 33 percent of those ranked as poor were not capability poor for the same dimension.

Taking social exclusion as the basis of assessment leads to yet another classification, as well as to different policies. This means that the success/failure of development efforts with respect to poverty reduction is likely to vary greatly according to how poverty reduction is measured.

Use of intermediate indicators. A second issue concerns the chosen measure of achievement: the final outcome or some intermediate one. It may seem obvious that one should measure the final outcome. But because policies only target intermediate variables and those are often easier to measure and monitor, and also because there are multiple influences on the final outcome beyond those efforts being evaluated, intermediate variables are frequently evaluated, even if they have only a loose connection with the ultimate objective. For example, in the Basic Needs approach one could measure health expenditure, health service access, or health outcomes. However, although health outcomes are what is aimed at, there is very little agreement on how to measure them: some evaluators use child nutrition or child mortality rates as a measure of health outcomes, which does not necessarily reflect on adult health; others focus on adult perceptions of health or ill health, but this tends to be inversely related to income, because rich people tend to report greater ill health than poor people; the Body Mass Index (BMI) is probably the best indicator of adult health but it is rarely available and it only relates to physical health. Many evaluations of health performance, therefore, use health expenditure or health personnel, neither of which has a unique stable relationship with health outcomes. Targeting the wrong variable can not only lead to false evaluations, but also distort efforts as these are devoted to achieving success in the variables that are targeted. The use of intermediate variables as targets is currently dominating UK medicine with such distorting consequences, it is claimed.[11]

In the macroeconomic field, similar issues arise—for example, with respect to whether the budget deficit and/or inflation rates should be used as indicators of successful macro-policies. The tendency is to use these variables, along with economic growth, as indicators of success in macro-policies.[12] Yet, only if a firm and invariable connection can be established between inflation and the growth rate and poverty reduction (assuming these are the accepted goals) is it appropriate to use the inflation rate as an indicator. In fact, no invariant connection has been established, particularly below inflation rates of 40 percent, although some put the threshold much lower (Gunter, 2002).[13]

The assumptions connecting intermediate variables with final outcomes are then critical. These assumptions are often value-laden, and generally depend on particular models and methods.

Value-added and the counterfactual. Probably the most difficult and important methodological issue is that of assessing how far any observed result is the effect of a particular development effort. To do so it is necessary to come to some view about the counterfactual—what would have happened without the development effort. The use of a counterfactual can completely alter the assessment: what appears to be weak performance, for example, rising poverty or falling growth, can turn out to be positive if the counterfactual looks worse than what happened. Hence, the counterfactual is critical. Certain (sometimes implicit) assumptions about the counterfactual are made in project evaluation as well as macro-assessments, but here I focus mainly on the macro level.

By its nature a counterfactual is not observed, and in arriving at a counterfactual assumptions become critical. There are problems with *all* the methods for estimating counterfactuals in assessments of macro programs. Before/after methods are obviously flawed because the previous situation may not have been sustainable, and new exogenous developments might have changed the course of events in any case. Comparison of countries with or without particular programs also has its problems, because there are particular reasons that lead countries to have programs. As a result of these difficulties, computable general equilibrium models have become a popular way of arriving at such counterfactual, but their conclusions depend critically on the underlying models and the closure rules (De Maio et al., 1997). In particular, neoclassical models tend to produce more positive evaluations of adjustment reforms than structuralist models. This is because most neoclassical models assume substitutability between factors and in use of resources, with short or no time-lags, so that resource underemployment is not an issue, while structuralist models, in contrast, tend to assume limited substitutability and long time-lags in the redeployment of resources that can lead to substantial unemployment over the short to medium term.

Such methodological issues become more important the more extensive the intervention. Although project evaluation does rely on a host of assumptions, careful use of sensitivity analysis can make a range of evaluations of a single project fairly straightforward.[14] But when it comes to macroeconomic policy change, because much more is being changed (generally including financial flows as well as policy), conducting sensitivity analysis to allow for the many underlying assumptions underpinning the counterfactual is more complex—and indeed is rarely done. The task becomes nearly impossible when the intervention is as extensive as the implementation of the Comprehensive Development Framework—because a change as big as this may not just involve economic variables but also institutional, legal, and cultural ones.

In my view, it is never correct to take a single counterfactual, because of the dependence on partially supported assumptions and the models adopted. In many cases, when one varies the models and assumptions underlying the counterfactual, one will often end up with conclusions that differ radically in sign as well as magnitude. Examples are the very different conclusions coming out of the evaluation of the impact of adjustment on growth and poverty by Taylor (1993), who takes a structuralist view of the economy; Sahn et al. (1997), who adopt a neoclassical model and broadly assume full employment; and the varying models of the OECD evaluations (Bourguignon et al., 1991), whose conclusions differ according to the models used.

Actual performance. I would also argue that looking at actual performance remains very important. This sounds rather simple-minded and unscientific. How can one attribute particular effects to certain development efforts, unless one can say what would have happened without them? My answer is that most development goals are framed in absolute terms: that is, reducing poverty, improving human development, and so on. If these absolute improvements do not occur—for whatever reason—then the development efforts have failed even if the use of counterfactual analysis denies this. It is absolute performance that affects people's lives. Failure in absolute performance therefore points to inadequate development efforts. The efforts may have been inadequate because they failed to foresee and deal with new developments, and/or because they did not tackle the problems that worsened the situation (e.g., terms of trade or debt), or because the policies were not implemented for political or capacity reasons, or because the policies were misconceived. But whatever the reason, they were a failure, and any evaluation should clearly show this.

Failure to assess development efforts in terms of absolute performance can lead to a quite unjustified complacency about such efforts when in fact things are going badly but this is concealed by the counterfactual. For example, an early IMF analysis of the distributional impact of IMF policies argued that their programs generally favored the poor, while being quite explicit that "the alternative to a Fund-supported program is an important measure of the redistributive impact of programs" (IMF, 1986, p. 36). At this time, income distribution was worsening and poverty rising in most Fund-supported countries.

The use of counterfactuals in evaluations of adjustment has permitted a continuous stream of positive evaluations, mainly Washington-based, despite two decades of adjustment experience in which African per capita growth has hovered below or around the zero mark, while in Latin America growth has been way below the achievements of the 1960s and 1970s and the poverty record has been very poor. Yet assessments of the adjustment efforts continually call them a success, albeit sometimes a qualified one, and the same set of policies are still being introduced. World Bank (2001) states, "On average they [reforms] have delivered lower inflation and higher growth," yet a little earlier on the same page, it states that "This does not mean that the developing world as a whole enjoyed rapid growth as a result of the reforms of the 1980s and 1990s. Indeed, growth in the developing world has been disappointing, with the typical developing country registering negligible growth" (p. 64).

Similar complacency is indicated by replies to a questionnaire to staff of the UK Department for International Development (DFID) on how DFID should alter its policies in light of the fact that most countries were not on track with respect to meeting Millennium Development Goals. The overwhelming response was that DFID should *not* change anything, even though the Goals are clearly posed in absolute and time-bound terms, so that any failure to realize them should be quite apparent and not concealed behind an assumed counterfactual (Black and White, 2003).

Time period. The time period over which assessments are made is another factor that can alter evaluations. Most evaluations are carried out after a rather short time, for obvious bureaucratic reasons. This can fail to capture important effects. In his brilliant book evaluating projects, Hirschman pointed to a "hiding" hand, which often meant that apparently failed projects turned out to be successful because of unexpected events, normally taking time (Hirschman, 1967). A short time perspective combined with ignoring externalities can then lead to the wrong conclusions.

An example comes from the steel industry in Turkey. In-depth analysis of decisions in this industry showed a history of failure on almost every front. Yet ultimately the industry became internationally competitive as well as promoting industrialization in Turkey (Szyliowicz, 1991; Duruiz and Yentürk, 1992). Similarly, in Thailand, import-substitution efforts were criticized as failing to generate substantial learning effects (Adulbhan et al., 1972; Bell and Scott-Kemmis, 1985; Westphal et al., 1990). This was shortly followed by Thailand's rapid export growth. More generally, import substitution efforts are typically assessed without allowing for the learning effects that eventually enable countries to switch into a successful export strategy. Failure to take a longer time perspective biases evaluations and decisions against the inclusion of learning effects, which can be critical elements in successful industrialization (Chang, 2002; Lall, 1987). Another type of long-term effect is changes in social processes and institutions, which constitute critical aspects of anthropologists' evaluations but are rarely considered in most official evaluations, with their short time perspective.

Long-term external (and other) effects are not, of course, always positive. In Ghana's Volta dam project, for example, the expected externalities and linked projects broadly failed to materialize. The point here is that evaluation requires a long perspective to incorporate such effects, positive or negative, and that failure to provide this perspective biases the evaluation against projects and programs with long-term learning and linkage effects.

The importance of taking a long time perspective is illustrated by work that we have been doing on human development (HD) and economic growth (EG) (Ranis et al., 2000). Despite the fact that there are strong connections between HD and EG (EG providing the economic resources for promoting HD, and HD the human resources that promote EG), taking a long-term perspective—1960-92—we show that country achievement varies significantly both at a point in time and over time, according to whether one takes human development or per capita income as an indicator of success. In addition to providing further evidence of the importance of goal selection for evaluation and policy implications, by taking a long-term perspective we come to important conclusions on sequencing that would be unlikely to emerge from the much shorter period (maximum ten years) that is typical of evaluation.

The two-way causality between economic growth and human development leads to the potential for both virtuous and vicious cycles of development (some countries doing well on both goals, ending up in a self-reinforcing virtuous cycle, and some badly on both, ending up in a reinforcing vicious cycle). The challenging question is how countries can move from vicious to virtuous cycles. By looking at countries in ten-year periods, we show that *no* country that promoted economic growth without also promoting human development succeeded in moving into the virtuous cycle category. Indeed, where countries do temporarily achieve good economic growth despite poor human development, they invariably fall back into the vicious category. In contrast, countries that promote human development without economic growth can then move into the virtuous cycle category (Figure 1.4).

This long time perspective throws into question the usual view on sequencing—that is, that getting the economic fundamentals right is the first priority, even if it means sacrificing human development. This research suggests that this sequence will not lead to sustained growth, and that if a trade-off has to be made, human development should get priority over the economic fundamentals. Ongoing econometric work on the determinants of sustained growth supports this conclusion (Boozer et al., 2003).

The Nature of Development Efforts

It is obviously essential to define the development efforts one is evaluating. Here it is clear that different agents/interests select different efforts to evaluate.

Generally, donor evaluation has been primarily concerned with a particular subset of donor policies, although this subset of instruments (or development efforts) has changed and been extended along with the changing goals (indeed some of the goals imply or are closely associated with certain instruments). In the early years of evaluation, as noted above, development efforts were mainly taken to be the financing of and technical assistance for large infrastructure projects. Initially development efforts to promote basic needs were identified with expenditures on BN, but it was subsequently recognized that development efforts needed to go beyond this to other important elements that determined BN, including income growth and distribution (Streeten et al., 1981). From the early 1980s, macro and sectoral adjustment loans became a major component of development efforts, and these were the prime target of evaluations in the 1980s. However, as the sphere of donor policy discourse and intervention has widened—in response to widening goals and

Figure 1.4
Patterns of Development Observed over 1960-92

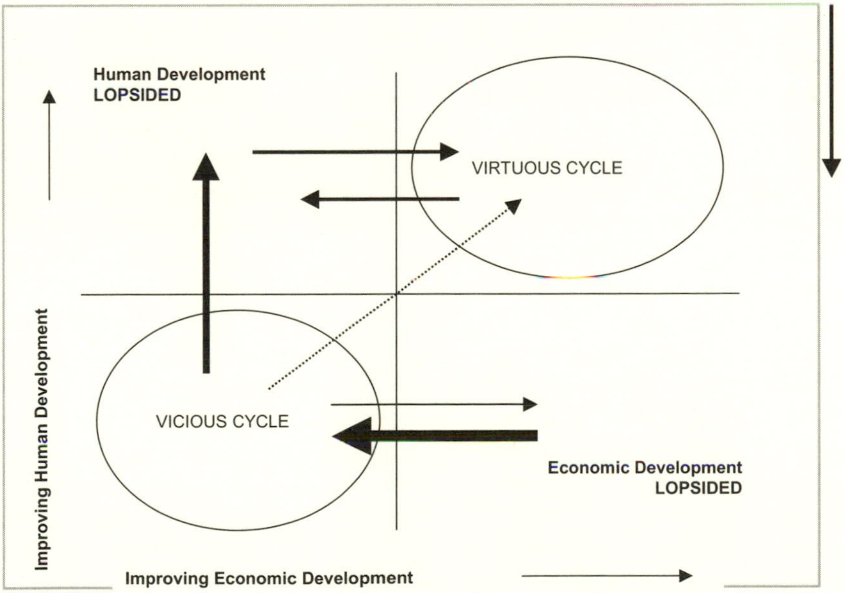

Source: Based on Ranis et al. (2000), Figure 3.

to the less than totally successful impact of previous policy conditionality—donor development efforts have widened their range to include social safety nets and other policies to reduce poverty, environmental projects and policies, and governance projects.

The Comprehensive Development Framework (CDF) represents the most extensive definition of development efforts from a donor perspective. It propounds a holistic, comprehensive approach to development, shaped by a long-term vision. In interpretation, however, the content appears rather similar to a combined package of the previous structural adjustment, governance, and basic needs efforts—that is, besides short-term macro policies, longer-term structural and social considerations are to play a part, including expanding and improving education and health facilities, maintaining infrastructure, and training a new generation of public officials (OED, 2003). The novelty is the requirement that "recipient countries should lead aid management and coordination through stakeholder partnerships" (ibid., p. 5), which means that the *process* of determining programs and policies becomes part of the development effort. Indeed, OED's first evaluation of the CDF has focused on process rather than outcome (OED, 2003).

The most obvious way in which all these instruments, including the CDF, represent only a subset of "development efforts" is that they exclude many influences that rich countries exert on poor countries—for example, trade policies and terms of trade, non-aid capital flows, intellectual property rights, debt repayments, and interest rates. It is noteworthy that almost all donor assessments of the MDGs have put Goal 8 (which concerns rich country obligations) into a secondary class, and made no attempt to see how far countries are on track with respect to this goal. And discussion of the environmental goal has put all the onus on developing countries, although most environmental problems originate in rich countries (Black and White, 2003).

In contrast, NGO (and to some extent UN) evaluations, as well as those of some Southern governments, while not ignoring the donor efforts discussed above, focus primarily on the impact of rich countries on poor. Some titles of OXFAM publications illustrate: *Rigged Rules and Double Standards* (2002); *For Richer for Poorer: An Oxfam Report on Western Connections with World Hunger* (1986); *The Coffee Report: Mugged - Poverty in Your Coffee Cup* (2003). *Patent Injustice: How World Trade Rules Threaten the Health of Poor People* (2002). UNCTAD reports have focused on similar issues, especially in UNCTAD's early years (Zammit Cutajar, 1985; United Nations Conference on Trade and Development, 1992).

Again this leads to differences in evaluation. Take Zambia for example. Both donors and NGOs would agree that development efforts have not been successful. But while donors have focused on weak governance, poor institutional performance, and uneven implementation as important causes, NGOs have pointed to the sharply worsening terms of trade, limited trade access, the debt problems, and inappropriate policies (Mwanza, 1992; World Bank, 1994b; White 1997; Kayizzi-Mugerwa, 2001). Such differences are paralleled in more general analysis of development efforts in Sub-Saharan Africa (e.g., World Bank, 1989; World Bank, 1994a; Stewart et al., 1992; Cornia et al., 1994; Engberg-Pedersen, 1996).

2. Who Does the Assessment?

It should be clear from this discussion that evaluation depends on who does the assessment, since agents differ with respect to goals, methods, and definition of development efforts—all of which are critical to determining the evaluation outcomes.

As noted earlier, possible agents of assessment are the lenders, including the multilateral and bilateral international financial institutions, the borrowers (themselves heterogeneous in conditions and values), the beneficiaries (i.e., those within the borrowing countries who are directly affected by, or are the target of, development efforts), NGOs (international or local), or more generally "civil society" in borrowing and/or lending countries.

Arguments can be advanced in favor of each of these agents carrying out the evaluations, and there are also objections to each one.

Lenders

From some perspectives, these could be considered the appropriate agents of evaluation, at least of their own efforts. One perspective is that since they are financing the efforts, they have some right to determine goals and evaluate their impact. Moreover, the financiers have to answer to their own constituents (donor governments in the case of international financial institutions, and electorates/parliaments in the case of governments), who might refuse further support if their own objectives were not reflected in those of the lenders. Further, where the aim of the evaluation is to assess the efficiency of the lending institution itself, it would seem appropriate to do this assessment using the goals in place when the lending took place, and not some independent set of goals.

However, there are strong objections to lenders being the sole evaluators, as this generally includes determining the definition of development efforts as well as the choice of goals, thus potentially overriding countries' rights of self-determination. The objection is especially forceful where the goals are far reaching, affecting many aspects of the recipient's economy and governance, such as with the Comprehensive Development Framework. If development efforts are evaluated in terms of the lenders' goals, and the latter conflict with those of borrowers (or beneficiaries), then "success' in development may be asserted even though the country/beneficiary regards the efforts as a failure. This at best constitutes only partial success.

Similar arguments apply to methodology. Although methodological issues seem to be technical issues, unaffected by who conducts the exercise, this is often not the case, as argued above. The methodology selected often implies a particular result, or at least gives a bias towards one, and may differ according to who performs the evaluation.

Recognizing the fact that externally imposed programs have been associated with poor implementation, donors themselves have accepted that national ownership of programs is needed. Indeed, this forms an important aspect of the CDF.[15]

Recipient Governments

There is a common presumption that governments are the legitimate representatives of aid-recipient countries and hence that they should define their own goals and evaluate success/failure. But some regard this presumption as depending on the nature of the borrowers—with less legitimacy for undemocratic and corrupt governments. Rawls, for example, regards non-democratic governments as unqualified to enter into any global compact (Rawls, 1999). To complicate matters, many governments of recipient countries are in democratic transition: "semi-democratized states in which domestic politics tends to be patronage-based, with fragmented party systems and weak civil societies" (Booth, 2003, describing some Africa cases where PRSPs have been introduced). Among the donor community—partly because of this transitional state—there appear to be pervasive doubts about governments in newly democratic countries, with suspicion of corruption, and of unwillingness and lack of capacity to go along with donor-defined goals (an attitude, in part, reflecting the general distrust of government that forms part of the prevalent philosophy of many donors). Whatever the motive, it has led to the idea among donors that program ownership should involve beneficiaries and civil society as much as governments.

Beneficiaries

These are the subgroup in the country supposedly benefiting from the development efforts and they are therefore in a good position to help define goals and evaluate the impact of policies on them. Yet there is a circularity of argument here, since defining this group itself presupposes some targeting of development efforts—which implies that goals have already been decided. Moreover, many development efforts affect large numbers of people, who are difficult to identify and whose views are hard to elicit. For example, *Voices of the Poor* (Narayan et al., 2000) assumes that only the poor are legitimate targets of development efforts and only their voices should be heard, while the exercise reveals problems in getting representative views, and those conducting such an exercise unavoidably influence the interpretation of views. Moreover, Platteau (chapter 13 in this volume) argues that community priorities and terms of reference are so far from those of the donors that they are not effectively expressed or communicated in consultation exercises. Finally, poor beneficiaries are generally not in a position to contribute to the more technical aspects of evaluation.

NGOs and civil society. The CDF/poverty reduction strategy paper (PRSP) exercise has turned to nongovernmental organizations and civil society, together with national governments, to generate country ownership of poverty reduction strategies and their evaluation. But NGOs have little political legitimacy, being an arbitrarily selected and heterogeneous international and domestic set of organizations, some of which are strongly influenced by the donors who supply much of their finance. "Civil society" is a broader (and open-ended) concept, potentially covering all actors outside the government, including workers' organizations, private sector groups, community organizations, and NGOs (Whitehead, 2002). As such, it is not possible to define a representative sample nor to derive a representative view emanating from it. From the perspective of democratic political legitimacy, it would seem better for civil society to contribute to the formation of the policy of democratically elected governments, as in advanced democracies, rather than playing an independent role. Aside from this, in practice the PRSP exercise thus far has confined consultation to a subset of civil society and a rather narrow range of issues, mainly focused on the social sectors, generally leaving out macro policies altogether, while many independent assessments of PRSPs to date question the extent of participation and ownership (Bretton Woods Project, 2001; Catholic Relief Services, 2001; Booth, 2003; Stewart and Wang, 2003). Examples of CDF processes suggest a wider consultative exercise, although still raising problems of representativeness as well as implementation (Deneulin, 2003; OED, 2003).

Independent Evaluations

Numerous groups, including UN agencies, prominent NGOs, and academics, conduct independent evaluations. In some ways such independent agents have less legitimacy than the previous categories, being neither lenders nor recipients/beneficiaries. Yet their independence means that they are able to question goals and methodologies in a way that is not open to other agents. They have played an important role in changing goals and policies on a range of issues. A notable recent example is the Jubilee 2000 coalition, which led to the HIPC debt reduction initiatives.

No "Right" Answer

Which agent is the appropriate one to set goals and conduct evaluations partly depends on the purpose of the exercise. While it is perfectly legitimate for any institution to conduct its own evaluations against the goals it has set for itself—and indeed important for the achievement of institutional efficiency—it must be recognized that these assessments do not necessarily have wider legitimacy.

In general, however, the principle that is broadly contained in the CDF,[16] that countries should determine their own goals, seems the right one. Outsiders surely do not have the right to determine goals. For Western democracies most people would agree that democratically elected governments (central or local as appropriate) are the appropriate decision makers, influenced and constrained by their own civil society actors. This argument may need to be modified somewhat in the context of the fragile, imperfect, transitional democracies of poor states. But I would argue that the aim should be to permit the same democratic freedom to recipient countries as we expect in the West, and any modification should be in processes not in the actual decision making.

Where does this leave outsiders? *Not* ideally as partners, as is proposed in many donor initiatives. Partnership gives outsiders an excessive role in determining goals, impossible to justify on democratic principles, especially as any such partnership is bound to be unequal. Accepting the principle of democratic decision making, the role of outsiders should be to advise, when requested, and to check that the books are reasonably likely to balance before making loans so that lending makes financial sense. Evaluation, like goal setting, then becomes primarily a task for recipient governments, with support from outsiders.

Nonetheless, a political case can sometimes be made for partnerships and joint evaluations, where this seems the best way of getting political commitment from both sides to the outcome. In such cases, recipient and donor endorsement of third party evaluations can sometimes be effective, bearing in mind the issues just raised.

Yet recipient governments, as well as donors, are constrained by interest groups, by external pressure, and by bureaucratic logic. Hence, for imaginative leaps and truly critical appraisal, one must look to the independent evaluator. No one is compelled to follow these leaps but they provide options and opportunities that are absent in the narrower vision of official evaluation.

3. Conclusions

- Development is a hugely contested area. There are few or no "right" answers. Yet many evaluations of development efforts suggest there are.
- There is room for many approaches at one time, reflecting different goals and ideologies of evaluators.
- "Joint" evaluation is not a solution because it either conceals and confuses, or suborns some of the participants, even though there may be an occasional political case for joint evaluation, preferably by independent evaluators with endorsement from different parties.

- Evaluating the goals of development efforts is a critical part of evaluation.
- Donors must be evaluated as much as "recipients."
- The current fashion for "results-based" or "evidence-based" processes sounds plausible, and indeed must be better than non-evidence or results-based processes; but it still leaves open most of the questions discussed above, that is, on the choice of goals, indicators, and methodology.
- Interests are involved in the choice of objectives and methodology in both donor community and recipients. Different policies serve different interests, and different agents have an interest in "proving" the success of particular efforts. This is relatively easy to do because of the complexity of the issues. Just as financial auditors can give an OK to firms that cheat, so sophisticated methods, including econometrics and social accounting matrices, can "justify" bad policies. Hence, evaluation must be undertaken by people representing a range of interests, and alternatives should be taken seriously.

Defining development and understanding processes is an evolving and political/ideological arena. Yet it has real consequences for people, many of whom are very poor. So it is important. Evaluation will always be work-in-progress, and contested. Nonetheless, in my view, while recognizing the contested nature of any evaluation, sticking to a bottom line indicator of improving the conditions of the worst off is a good starting point, with no counterfactuals or excuses.

Notes

1. I am grateful to Michael Wang for research assistance and to Amrik Heyer, Gustav Ranis, participants at the conference, and the conference editorial team for helpful comments on a previous draft.
2. Little and Mirrlees (1974); Kirkpatrick and Weiss (1996); Van de Walle et al. (1998).
3. Of course, which of these agents are "external" depends on the development efforts being evaluated.
4. For example, Easterly (2001) concludes that failed incentives account for growth failures, while Putnam (1993) points to weak social capital. Sociologists and anthropologists have emphasized the need to evaluate social processes with radically different implications for evaluation outcomes, e.g., Long (2001).
5. See, for example, World Bank (1997).
6. For example, a box in the World Bank's *World Development Report 2000/1*, entitled "Why do reforms sometimes fail?" gives three answers, none related to the policies themselves: incomplete financial sector reforms in East Asia; grand corruption in Russia; and inadequate public investment and excessive bureaucracy in Sub-Saharan Africa.
7. This is much closer to Marx's view of intellectuals as part of the superstructure of the economy. Cole et al. have suggested that "economists are slaves to some defunct politician." Cole et al. (1991).
8. A survey of twenty-three evaluations of adjustment policies that took place between 1978 and 1993 showed that none explored the poverty impact of adjustment. Stewart (1995), pp. 40-41.

9. These include the choice of poverty line; which prices to use; assumptions to be made about intra-household distribution, equivalence scales and economies of scale of household consumption; and how to allow for the depth of poverty and its duration.
10. For India, the participatory data comparisons involving the monetary approach could only be done on urban data due to problems with estimation of home-grown consumption in rural areas.
11. "The government's obsession with waiting times and performance targets is making 'honest people dishonest,' damaging patient care and leading to fiddled figures on how well the NHS is doing" according to the Chairman of the British Medical Association, *Financial Times,* July 1, 2003.
12. For example, World Bank (2000), p. 63, referred to a decline in inflation rates as an encouraging indicator of success in reform.
13. According to Gunter, there is broad agreement that "high and volatile inflation has negative impacts on growth and poverty, but no agreement on the impact of moderate inflation."
14. See Briggs (chapter 14 in this volume) for methods of doing this.
15. "Change driven by domestic interest is usually more acceptable and more sustainable than change induced by external sources." OED (2003).
16 . "The country needs to be in the driver's seat, owning and directing the development agenda with the support of all other actors." OED (2003), p. 69.

References

Abdulbhan, P., R. M. Bell, and V. N. Poubejara. (1972). "Transfer and Utilization of Technology in Manufacturing Industry in Thailand." Paper presented at the International Seminar on Dissemination of Technology, Korean Institute of Science and Technology, South Korea (November).

Bell, R. M., and D. Scott-Kemmis. (1985). "Report on a Study of Technology Transfer and the Accumulation of Technological Capacity in Manufacturing Industry in Thailand." Working Paper 1, Sussex University, Science Policy Research Unit.

Berry, A., ed. (1998). *Poverty, Economic Reform and Income Distribution in Latin America.* London: Lynne Rienner.

Black, Richard, and Howard White. (2003). *Targeting Development: Critical Perspectives on the Millennium Development Goals.* London: Routledge.

Booth, D. (2003). "Introduction and Overview to Special Issue: Are PRSPs Making a Difference? The African Experience." *Development Policy Review* 21 (2): 131-159.

Boozer, M., G. Ranis, F. Stewart, and T. Suri. (2003). *Paths to Success: The Relationship between Human Development and Economic Growth.* New Haven, CT: Economic Growth Center, Yale University.

Bourguignon, F., J. de Melo, and C. Morrison. (1991). "Poverty and Income Distribution during Adjustment: Issues and Evidence from the OECD project. " *World Development* 19 (11): 1485-1508.

Bretton Woods Project. (2001). "PRSPs are just PR, Say Civil Society Groups." http://www. Bretton Woods project.org/topic/adjustment/a23prspstats.html.

Cassen, R. (1986). *Does Aid Work? Report to an Intergovernmental Task Force.* Oxford: Clarendon Press.

Catholic Relief Services. (2001). *Review of the Poverty Reduction Strategy Paper Initiative.* http://www.imf.org/external/np/prspgen/review.

Chang, H. -J. (2002). *Kicking Away the Ladder.* London: Anthem Press.

Cole, K., J. Cameron, and C. Edwards. (1991. *Why Economists Disagree: the Political Economy of Economics.* London: Longman.

Cornia, G., R. Jolly, and F. Stewart. (1986). *Adjustment with a Human Face*. Oxford: Oxford University Press.

Cornia, G. A., and G. K. Helleiner. (1994). *From Adjustment to Development in Africa: Conflict, Controversy, Convergence, Consensus?* Basingstoke: Macmillan.

De Maio, L., R. van der Hoeven, and F. Stewart. (1997). *Computable General Equilibrium Models, Adjustment, and the Poor in Africa*. Oxford: Queen Elizabeth House.

Deneulin, S. (2003). *Sen's Capability Approach as a Guide to Action*. Oxford: Queen Elizabeth House.

Dollar, D., and A. Kraay. (2001). *Growth is Good for the Poor*. Policy Research Working Paper No. 2587. Washington, DC: World Bank.

Duruiz, L., and N. Yentürk. (1992). *Facing the Challenge: Turkish Automobile, Steel and Clothing Industries' Responses to the Post-Fordist Restructuring*. Istanbul: Mydan Sokak.

Easterly, W. (2001). *The Elusive Quest for Growth*. Cambridge, MA: MIT Press.

Engberg-Pedersen, P., and Center for Udviklingsforskning (Denmark). (1996). *Limits of Adjustment in Africa: The Effects of Economic Liberalization, 1986-94*. Copenhagen and Oxford: Center for Development Research (Copenhagen) in association with James Currey.

Galtung, J. (1978). "Grand Design on a Collision Course," *Development* 20.

Gunter, B. G. (2002). *Towards Poverty-Reducing Macroeconomic Policies*. Washington DC: New Rules for Global Finance Coalition.

Healey, J. M., and M. Robinson. (1992). *Democracy, Governance and Economic Policy: Sub-Saharan Africa in Comparative Perspective*. London: Overseas Development Institute.

Hirschman, A. O. (1967). *Development Projects Observed*. Washington, DC: Brookings Institution.

International Labor Organization. (1976). *Employment, Growth and Basic Needs: A One-World Problem*. Geneva: International Labor Organization.

International Monetary Fund. (1986). *Fund-Supported Programs, Fiscal Policy and Income Distribution*. Washington, DC.

Kayizzi-Mugerwa, S. (2001). *Explaining Zambia's Elusive Growth Credibility Gap, External Shocks or Reluctant Donors? From Crisis to Growth in Africa?* London: Routledge.

Keynes, J. M. (1936). *The General Theory of Employment, Interest and Money*. London: Macmillan.

Kirkpatrick, C. H., and J. Weiss. (1996). *Cost-Benefit Analysis and Project Appraisal in Developing Countries*. Cheltenham: Edward Elgar.

Lall, S. (1987). *Learning to Industrialize: The Acquisition of Technological Capability by India*. Basingstoke: Macmillan.

Lall, S., and C. Pietrobelli. (2002). *Failing to Compete: Technology Development and Technology Systems in Africa*. Cheltenham: Edward Elgar.

Little, I. M. D., and J. A. Mirrlees. (1974). *Project Appraisal and Planning for Developing Countries*. London: Heinemann Educational.

Long, N. (2001). *Development Sociology: Actor Perspectives*. London: Routledge.

Mwanza, A. M. (1992). *The Structural Adjustment Program in Zambia: Lessons from Experience*. Harare: SAPES Books.

Narayan, Deepa, et al. (2000). *Voices of the Poor: Can Anyone Hear Us?* Washington, DC: World Bank.

Nelson, J. M., and J. Waterbury. (1989). *Fragile Coalitions: The Politics of Economic Adjustment*. New Brunswick, NJ and Oxford: Transaction Publishers.

Operations Evaluation Department, World Bank. (2000). *Poverty Reduction in the 1990s: The World Bank Strategy.* Washington, DC: Operations Evaluation Department, World Bank.

———. (2003). *Toward Country-led Development: a Multi-partner Evaluation of the Comprehensive Development Framework.* Washington, DC: Operations Evaluation Department, World Bank.

Picciotto, R. (2002). "Development Cooperation and Performance Evaluation: The Monterrey Challenge." In *OED: The First Thirty Years.* Washington, DC: Operations Evaluation Department, World Bank.

Putnam, R. D. (1993). *Making Democracy Work: Civic Traditions in Modern Italy.* Princeton, NJ and Chichester: Princeton University Press.

Ranis, G., F. Stewart, and A. Ramirez. (2000). "Economic Growth and Human Development. " *World Development* 28 (2), pp.197-220.

Rawls, J. (1999). *The Law of Peoples* with *The Idea of Public Reason Revisited.* Cambridge, MA and London: Harvard University Press.

Ruggeri-Laderchi, C., R. Saith, and F. Stewart. (2003). "Does It Matter that We Don't Agree on the Definition of Poverty? A Comparison of Four Approaches." *Oxford Development Studies* 31 (3), pp. 243-274.

Sahn, D. E., P. Dorosh, and S. Younger. (1997). *Structural Adjustment Reconsidered: Economic Policy and Poverty in Africa.* Cambridge: Cambridge University Press.

Stewart, F. (1995). *Adjustment and Poverty: Options and Choices.* London: Routledge.

Stewart, F., S. Lall, and S. Wangwe. (1992). *Alternative Development Strategies in Sub-Saharan Africa.* London: Macmillan.

Stewart, F. and M. Wang. (2003). *Do PRSPs Empower Poor Countries and Disempower the World Bank, or Is It the other Way Round?* Oxford: Queen Elizabeth House.

Streeten, P., S. Burki, M. ul Haq, N. Hicks, and F. Stewart. (1981). *First Things First: Meeting Basic Human Needs in Developing Countries.* New York: Oxford University Press.

Szekely, M., N. Lustig, J. A. Maija, and M. Cumpa. (2000). *Do We Know How Much Poverty There Is?* Washington, DC: InterAmerican Development Bank.

Szyliowicz, J. S., and St. Antony's College. (1991). *Politics, Technology and Development: Decision-making in the Turkish iron and Steel Industry.* Basingstoke: Macmillan in association with St. Antony's College, University of Oxford.

Taylor, L. (1993). *The Rocky Road to Reform.* Tokyo: United Nations University.

United Nations Conference on Trade and Development. (1992). *Technology Transfer and Development in a Changing International Environment: Policy Challenges and Options for Cooperation.* New York: United Nations.

United Nations Development Program. (2003). *Human Development Report.* Oxford: Oxford University Press.

———. (2002). *Human Development Report.* Oxford: Oxford University Press.

Van de Walle et al. (1998). "How Dirty are 'Quick and Dirty' Methods of Project Appraisal?" Washington, DC: World Bank Development Research Group.

Wade, R. (1997). "Greening the Bank: The Struggle over the Environment, 1970-1995." In D. Kapur, J. Lewis, and R. Webb, *The World Bank: Its First Half-Century*, vol. 2. Washington, DC: Brookings Institution.

Westphal, L., K. Kritayakirana, K. Petchsuwan, H. Sutabutr, and Y. Yuthavong. (1990). "The Development of Technological Capability in Manufacturing: A Macroscopic Approach to Policy Research." In R. E. Evenson and G. P. Ranis (eds.), *Science and Technology: Lessons for Policy Development.* London: Intermediate Technology Publications.

White, Howard. (1997)."Zambia in the 1990s as a Case of Adjustment in Africa," *Africa Development Review* 9 (2), pp. 56-87.

White, Howard, and Geske Dijkstra. (2003). *Beyond Conditionality: Program Aid andDevelopment.* London: Routledge.

Whitehead, L. (2002). *Democratization: Theory and Experience.* Oxford: Oxford University Press.

World Bank. (1997). *World Development Report 1997.* Washington, DC: Oxford University Press.

_____. (1988). *Adjustment Lending: An Evaluation of Ten Years of Experience.* Washington, DC: World Bank.

_____. (1989). *Sub-Saharan Africa: From Crisis to Sustainable Growth.* Washington, DC: World Bank.

_____. (1994a). *Adjustment in Africa: Reforms, Results, and the Road Ahead.* Washington, DC: World Bank.

_____. (1994b). *Zambia Poverty Assessment,* Main Report Vol. I. Washington, DC: World Bank.

_____. (2001). *World Development Report 2002. Building Institutions for Markets.* New York and London: Oxford University Press for the World Bank.

_____. (2002). *World Development Report 20003. Sustainable Development in a Dynamic World.* New York and London: Oxford University Press for the World Bank.

Zammit Cutajar, M. (1985). *UNCTAD and the South-North dialogue: the First Twenty years: Essays in Memory of W. R. Malinowski.* Oxford: Pergamon.

Floor Discussion

Participant: I interpreted Professor Stewart as saying that a country should determine its own goals, constrained by globally agreed human rights. Yet the state of globally agreed human rights may not be consistent with improving the condition of the worst-off. Should we not consider a more specific definition for helping the poor, for example, using the Millennium Development Goals (MDGs) as the criteria against which to evaluate countries' progress against poverty?

Stewart: The difficulty is that there are huge problems in interpreting the MDGs in practice. For example, can we say that the MDGs are achieved when the world as a whole is achieving them but many individual countries are not? And can we say the goals are achieved in a particular country when, nationwide, the country has halved the level of poverty, but still has huge pockets of people who are getting worse off? I believe that aid-recipient countries should determine their own goals, but "constrained by human rights," because there are cases where such countries are deliberately violating human rights. Given the problems in operationalizing the MDGs, I think it would be better to define more carefully what we mean by human rights—that is, which universal human rights we require a country to observe, so as to temper the excesses of some governments—rather than to adopt the MDGs as the criteria for evaluating countries' progress. Also, if a developing country has goals that don't necessarily fit into the MDGs, I think it is legitimate in pursuing them.

Participant: Would you say that we in industrial countries emphasize too much the political side, as compared to developing countries, which tend to emphasize the economic side, in dialogues on development issues?

Stewart: Yes. Because policies in some developing countries have not been all that effective, the tendency in industrial countries has been to see politics as the obstructing agent, rather than to look at the effects on developing countries of the economic policies that are in force in industrial countries. There is a tendency in the West to feel that we know how a democracy should be run, and that this gives us the right to overrule policymakers in imperfect democracies in developing countries. Yet Western democracies, too, are very imperfect, and we wouldn't take at all kindly to the view that other people could come in and overrule our decisions because they felt that our implementation was poor.

Participant: I'm struck by an issue that Frances Stewart raised: whether to evaluate value added or to attempt a much more composite evaluation of overall impacts. If we do not evaluate value added, and we attempt to measure absolute impacts, what would the evaluation enterprise be if, at every step, we seek comprehensiveness?

Stewart: I think one must look at the absolute outcome as well as at value added. When you evaluate value added, almost invariably your results reflect the methodology you used rather than what actually happened; thus you can only really be sure of your results if you have obtained the same ones using a whole range of methodologies. If every methodology that you use produces the same results, then focusing on value added obviously has a lot of legitimacy. But you must always look at the absolute as well: at the bottom line, what's really happening to people. For example, if the development objective is to improve the conditions of the poor, or to achieve the MDGs, it's not good enough for evaluators in the year 2015 to say, "Though the objective has not been met, that's all right, because our evaluation methods show that without these development efforts, the objective would be even further off than it is now."

Participant: Partnerships between rich and poor countries tend to dominate the language of development evaluation today. The inequality of these partnerships between rich and poor countries suggests that the values that underpin the evaluation conceptions are likely to be those of rich countries. Could you comment on the process of establishing independent indicators if partnerships are part of the game?

Participant: As regards the goals of developing countries, I would like to have more comments about how to incorporate values in evaluation, because goals and values are very related.

Stewart: As to partnerships and the way in which values influence perceptions about goals and their achievement: values are hugely influenced by the way in which the world economy as a whole, and particular economies and particular communities, change. And these values, in turn, change the way development is perceived and the way development goals are perceived and the way people behave. The values question certainly arises in partnerships. Especially in an unequal partnership, it's very difficult for the less powerful partner not to espouse the values of the more powerful partner.

Participant: Context dynamics are very crucial in evaluation, particularly as regards donor demands versus country needs. In some African countries, for example, the World Bank is making demands, and the country is showing its needs to the World Bank, and making clear that "your demands are actually not on par with our needs." So the question is, "How to achieve the right balance?"

Participant: How do we avoid the situation where evaluations are dominated by donor organizations and biased toward their concerns and therefore their results are rather narrowly accepted? Here independent monitoring groups offer the advantage of greater objectivity and credibility than evaluations driven by donors.

Participant: Peer reviews are another relevant option here. In the Development Assistance Committee of OECD, we do peer reviews of members' development cooperation policies and programs. These techniques are not only relevant for the OECD/DAC members, but more broadly. For example, the New Partnership for African Development is trying to develop a process of peer reviews in the African context, and we are collaborating with them in that effort.

2

Challenges in Evaluating Development Effectiveness

Howard White

The World Bank's mission statement is headed, "Our dream is a world free of poverty." The aim of the UK Department for International Development is "To eliminate poverty in poorer countries" and that of the German Development Agency GTZ is "To improve the living conditions and perspectives of people in developing and transition countries." And so on. The Millennium Development Goals (MDGs) are a set of bold promises to poor people around the world. The challenge faced by evaluators is to make credible statements as to whether the activities supported by these agencies make a positive contribution toward their stated goals and so draw lessons to contribute to more effective development.

The nature of this challenge has changed as the development paradigm has evolved, and with it the activities of donor agencies. Stand-alone projects, notably those in infrastructure, can be evaluated using the techniques of cost-benefit analysis that were developed in the 1960s and early 1970s, partly at the World Bank.[1] The shift away from growth as the measure of development was mirrored by a shift in how effectiveness was evaluated. This shift was partly driven by the mistaken view that social sectors were less amenable to economic cost-benefit analysis.[2] It was also driven by a desire to focus directly on non-economic outcomes. The latter was certainly the driving force as the development agenda broadened to encompass rights issues such as gender equality. It was felt that cost-benefit analysis could not possibly capture these things,[3] so that a more qualitative approach was required. By the 1980s, qualitative approaches had come to dominate the evaluation studies conducted for development agencies.[4]

Senior evaluation officer, Operations Evaluation Department, World Bank.

The move toward qualitative approaches was reinforced by an emphasis on process. Process evaluations generally focus on the way in which a project was managed, including aspects such as donor coordination, institutional development, and management systems. These are important issues that may be overlooked in a narrow economic study. And it is usually fair to say that "process projects," whose primary focus is often institutional development, are too far removed from final development outcomes to quantify their impact on the latter.[5]

But the new focus on results in the context of the MDGs demands more than qualitative studies alone can give us. Qualitative methods cannot answer the question, "To what extent are agencies' interventions bringing about progress on MDG-related indicators?"

Quantitative approaches have reestablished themselves at two levels. The first is in measuring agency performance: how well is a particular donor doing? The second is in project-level interventions. Rather belatedly, the development community has been adopting randomization in program design to facilitate evaluation. And where this is not possible, recent econometric developments allow the construction of more satisfactory controls than had hitherto been possible. However, the vast bulk of evaluation work is carried out without the use of these techniques.

This paper discusses techniques in three areas of contemporary relevance: measuring agency performance and other studies that aggregate across evaluations; evaluation methods at the project level; and sustainability analysis. In each of these areas it is argued that much evaluation work is carried out well within the "evaluation possibility frontier," which is explored in the following section.

1. The Evaluation Production Function

The argument of the evaluation production function consists of data and techniques, with a positive first differential for each.[6] Figure 2.1 and Figure 2.2 show the combinations of data and technique yielding evaluations of a given quality. In Figure 2.1, a degree of substitutability in production is assumed; for a given budget constraint (the budget for the evaluation), P1, the optimal combination of data and technique can be derived. However, the shortcoming of this analysis is that while data are study-specific, techniques once acquired can be used in subsequent evaluations, which brings down the price of technique (it shifts the bottom end of the budget constraint rightwards along the X-axis). The shift in the budget constraint is greater, the greater the spending on technique in the initial evaluation.

The implications are that optimizing quality on an evaluation-by-evaluation basis will result in an overspending on data and an underinvestment in technique. If quality is maximized over more than one evaluation (i.e., a multi-period optimization), then the resource allocation shifts in favor of techniques, especially in the first of the studies.

Figure 2.1
**Evaluation Production Isoquants (with substitutability
in production coefficients)**

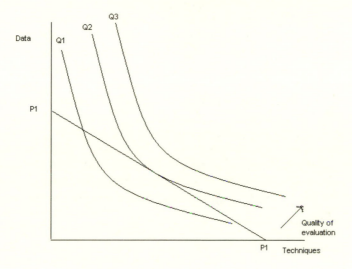

Figure 2.2
Evaluation Production Isoquants (with fixed coefficients)

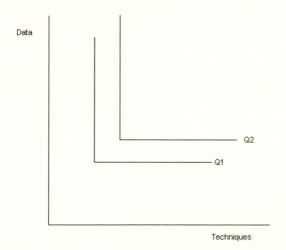

It might be thought that substitutability between data and technique is somewhat limited.[7] This view is taken to the extreme of fixed technical coefficients of production in Figure 2.2. Here the optimal combination is always a corner solution, and if the optimal combination is achieved then increases in both data and technique are required to improve evaluation quality. Any resource combination on the vertical segment of the isoquant is inefficient as it entails spending money on data that remain underutilized, given the techniques being applied in the study. And, of course, any additional data collection will add nothing to the study unless there is also some increase in technique. On the other hand, a resource combination on the horizontal segment of the isoquant has an excess of technique given the available data. I suggest that many evaluation studies are on the vertical segment: they are data-rich but technique-poor. This may seem surprising to economists, since much economic analyses develops very nice techniques but without the data to apply them (that is, they are on the horizontal segment).

Evaluations may also be subject to X-inefficiency. That is, they operate within the evaluation possibility frontier. More explicitly, they are not of the quality that could be achieved given the level of inputs available. Examples of X-inefficiency would be a *mis*use of techniques (rather than their *under*use, in combinations that lie on a non-optimal segment of the evaluation isoquant). For example, a rich data set is available and used for multivariate analysis, but model misspecification undermines the results. Table 2.1 summarizes the possible combinations of misuse and underuse of both data and theory. Ideally, a study author can enter "No" in each cell.

Table 2.1
Possible Problems in Evaluation Production

	Data	Technique/theory
Misuse		
Underuse		

2. Aggregating Results across Evaluations

The increased emphasis on results in the context of the Millennium Development Goals has increased the importance of reports that aggregate across evaluations, and the need for these reports to say something about outcomes. Indeed, the MDGs suggest the need for a new sort of report, based on outcomes rather than sectors. The unit of analysis should not necessarily be the sector, but all interventions geared toward achieving a particular MDG.

Inadequate attention has been paid to methodological issues. Below, I discuss the lack of explicit attention to the techniques of meta-analysis in studies that involve the aggregation of agency ratings, and in the following subsection, methods used for the collection and analysis of qualitative data, which frequently fall short of what is possible.

Measuring Agency Performance

Development agencies are accountable through parliament, their boards, and directly to the taxpayers who finance their activities. In addition to annual reports, which usually focus on a fairly descriptive review of sources and uses of funds by sector and region, several agencies produce more analytical reviews of the development effectiveness of their work. The flagship in this area is the World Bank Operations Evaluation Department's *Annual Review of Development Effectiveness* (*ARDE*), which succeeded the earlier *Evaluation Results* in the mid-1990s. In 1999, the UN Development Program launched its *Results-oriented Annual Report* (*ROAR*), and the UK Department for International Development completed its first *Development Effectiveness Report* (*DER*) for the year 2001. These reports are singled out here as they attempt to summarize agency performance based on aggregations of project-level results.

The World Bank's *Annual Review of Development Effectiveness* uses the ratings of projects that have closed during the year to give an overall portfolio rating of the percentage of projects rated as satisfactory, broken down by country and sector. DFID's *Development Effectiveness Report* uses quantitative data from two reporting mechanisms within DFID: the project completion report and the output-to-purpose review, which is equivalent to the mid-term review in many other agencies. These data are also used to show the percentage of satisfactory projects. UNDP's *Results-oriented Annual Report* is different, as it draws its data from a new system of reporting geared toward results-based management; no overall performance rating is assigned, but outputs and outcomes are rated against six goals.[8]

Elsewhere I have discussed the triple-A requirements of such reports: attribution, aggregation, and alignment.[9] *Attribution* is the well-known problem of making a link between what the agencies do and the outcomes they hope to influence. *Aggregation* is whether the agency's reporting system produces data that can be meaningfully aggregated across projects. All three agencies measure project performance using scales that facilitate aggregation (for example, the percentage of projects falling under a certain classification, such as satisfactory). And *alignment* is whether the data collected at the micro level tell us anything about performance as measured against the agency's objectives.

All existing systems of agency performance measurement are lacking in some respects against these criteria. DFID's own *Development Effectiveness Report* itself states that there is "a clear gap between what DFID aspires to achieve, and what it can confidently demonstrate that it has achieved" (p. vi).

The discussion here focuses on just one aspect: the methodology used for aggregations. The reports of each of these agencies aggregate the results of completion reports or other reviews (which here are all called evaluation reports for convenience) to give a summary of portfolio performance. This task is the one faced in conducting meta-evaluation,[10] but the methodology for preparing these reports has not been anchored in the techniques developed for meta-evaluation. Hence it is worth asking if the reports could be improved by a stronger methodology. Leeuw and Cooksy pursue this issue in chapter 4 in this volume. Here I make some initial observations.

Based on Weiss (1998, pp. 238-39), we can identify six steps to meta-analysis: (1) define the problem; (2) collect the relevant studies to be reviewed; (3) screen the studies for quality; (4) standardize the indicators and code them; (5) produce a synthesis measure; and (6) present results.

The problem addressed in each of these reports is to measure agency performance, while the relevant studies to be used are the agencies' own evaluations. Hence all agencies readily handle the first two steps in a common manner.

The third step, screening out low-quality data, may not seem to be needed since the ratings are assigned by the agency itself. But matters are not so straightforward. *ARDE* uses OED's own ratings based on the department's independent review of the Bank's implementation completion reports. DFID's ratings, by contrast, are those reported in the original project completion report, which is completed by DFID operational staff or the contracted project manager.[11] The guidelines that DFID provides for completing a project completion report are sketchy, and there is no independent check on the ratings awarded. UNDP's *ROAR* falls between these two extremes. It uses data reported by UNDP operational staff, and it is hoped that staff training will ensure consistency. But those preparing the ROAR screen the data and reject any that fail to meet a minimum standard.[12]

The fourth and fifth steps are the most complicated in meta-analysis, since indicators from different studies may have been measured in different units, using different sample sizes, and have differing levels of statistical significance. But the data used in donor performance monitoring come from common reporting systems, so that no standardization is required. Moreover, the indicators are not sample estimates, but based on the whole population—for example, in the case of the World Bank, all projects closing in a given fiscal year. So the indicators can be added together, weighting by size if desired, without the need for statistical adjustments. This would not be the case if it were decided to use a sample of project ratings, rather than those from the whole portfolio.

Step five, the production of a synthesis measure, raises the issue of whether like is being added to like, or if apples are being added to oranges. Adding apples and oranges is to some extent inevitable given the diversity of the portfolio. "Satisfactory" cannot mean exactly the same in a road-building project as it does in a financial sector adjustment credit. In this case comparability means that we are satisfied that common criteria have been applied in awarding the ratings, something that is ensured by well-established guidelines and an independent check. Beyond that, it *is* okay to add apples and oranges if we want to know how many pieces of fruit we have.

For the purpose of quantitative portfolio reviews, then, this brief discussion identifies some, though rather limited, gains that could be achieved from the formal application of meta-analysis techniques.

However, none of the reports is restricted to the synthesis of quantitative ratings data. OED, for example, produces country assistance evaluations and sector studies, and each year OED's *Annual Review of Development Effectiveness* draws lessons from these. Similarly, DFID's Development *Effectiveness Report* reviews progress against the goals set out in DFID's institutional strategy papers.[13] Meta-analysis also requires the aggregation of qualitative data, which the following discussion suggests has proved more problematic.

Country and Sector Studies

Each year the World Bank's Operations Evaluation Department conducts a number of country assistance evaluations and sector studies. Two issues relating to such studies are addressed here: (1) the role of case studies, and (2) summarizing qualitative data.

The role of case studies. Sector and country studies combine a number of approaches. The portfolio review analyzes lending trends in the Bank's portfolio for that sector or country, summarizes ratings-based performance measures, and may analyze aspects of design. The background work for an OED sector study will typically include four to six country case studies, as do many large evaluation studies by other donors (e.g., DFID's poverty evaluation and the Swedish International Development Agency's global evaluation of program aid). The choice of countries is frequently contentious, with critics arguing that nothing can be learned from looking at just four countries when the portfolio covers sixty or more.

OED and other evaluation departments use two well-established defenses of the combined methodology they use for sector and country studies. The first is the familiar debate on a case study approach, which abandons representativeness (breadth) for depth. The depth of engagement in a case study allows an exploration of issues that cannot possibly be uncovered in a desk-based portfolio review (which may be seen as synonymous with a cross-country approach).[14] The second defense is that the study is not based on the case studies alone but uses a mix of methods, combining the data from a number of instruments and approaches.[15] OED uses portfolio reviews, for example, in both sector studies and country assistance evaluations. At the very least these reviews describe trends in the size and composition of the portfolio (for example by region or subsector) and an analysis based on OED ratings. But they may be more comprehensive, studying the evolution of project objectives and design over time.[16] In the portfolio review in OED's study of social funds,[17] design features such as the use of outreach, targeting mechanisms, community contribution, and maintenance arrangements were codified based on a desk review supplemented with task manager interviews. The theory-based approach used in this evaluation suggested the importance of some features for successful operations, such as comprehensive outreach and community-level arrangements for maintenance. Four country case studies were undertaken to provide material with which to test the importance of these factors, and their results helped identify the most critical design features. The portfolio review showed how social funds had evolved, acquiring better design features over time.

Summarizing qualitative data. The second defense of OED's mixed-method approach to country and sector evaluations is that it summarizes the results from qualitative work, such as country case studies, or from different evaluations. Both quantitative and qualitative data should be analyzed in a way that yields a good summary. But both can be analyzed in a way that distorts the data, so a systematic approach is required to avoid this.

As is well known, mean-based quantitative statistics can give a misleading summary. For example, in a rather bizarre week in Washington earlier this year it snowed at the beginning of the week, with the temperature 15 degrees below the usual average for April. But by the end of the week it had reached 15 degrees above average. So it can safely be said that the average temperature that week was equal to the usual April average! This statement is true but misleading; it is not a good summary of the data. Regression coefficients are also a mean-based statistic, and failure to inspect the data can give misleading results if influential points "distort" the slope of the line or if an incorrect functional form is used.[18]

Equally, techniques should be used to ensure that qualitative data are summarized in a way that reveals, rather than distorts, the patterns in the data. The failure to use a systematic approach may lead to "cherry picking." For example, suppose six country case studies are conducted as part of an evaluation study. One of the study questions is whether decentralization increases the feeling of autonomy of local government officials.[19] The study design has not included structured questionnaires but unstructured interviews with officials in five districts in each country. It may well be possible to write that: "decentralization increases the feeling of autonomy of local government officials; for example, one local official in Malawi commented that "the changes have made a real difference, I really feel in control of what I do now'." But it may be that no one else in Malawi made a similar comment, and nor did any official in any of the other five countries. Such a misrepresentation of the data is an example of data mining (searching the data until you find the evidence you are looking for)—though we should recognize that this is hardly something of which quantitative analysts are innocent.[20]

Well-established methods are available for the systematic analysis of qualitative data; they include content analysis and computer programs (e.g., QSRNudist) for conducting such analysis.

Yet this is an area where many evaluations either fall within the evaluation possibility frontier or devote inadequate resources to technique. It is rare to find evidence that qualitative data have been collected and analyzed in a systematic way.[21] For example, in a multi-county study, it is not sufficient to have common terms of reference. More detailed guidance is required on the range of data to be collected and the sources to be used. And these data need be presented in such a way as to allow a systematic summary.

Where there are a small number of country case studies I believe that a tabular summary can suffice. Returning to the decentralization example, suppose we are interested in three questions: (1) does decentralization increase the feeling of autonomy of local government officials? (2) does decentralization increase the perceived accountability of local government among local communities? and (3) does decentralization result in an increase in spending on community-level facilities? In all six countries, data have been collected on these issues through, respectively, (1) interviews with local officials, (2) focus group and key informant interviews in communities and, (3) budget analysis from five districts in each country, supplemented by the key informant interviews at community level. A table can then be constructed with the structure shown in Table 2.2.

The cell summarizes the evidence from that country for that question. Given a systematic approach to data collection, no cell should be left blank. Reading across the rows gives an overall impression of the weight of the evidence. This evidence should be reported in a way to show that all the data are being summarized: "In five of the six countries no evidence was found that decentralization had increased feelings of autonomy of local officials, and in the sixth country (Malawi) only one official mentioned a positive effect." In the executive summary it would suffice to say that "the evidence collected by the study did not support the view that decentralization increased the feeling of autonomy amongst local officials." If the exception is to be mentioned at all, it should not be in a way that gives it undue emphasis.[22] The systematic recording of data can also help avoid misreporting findings.

Table 2.2
Schema for Summarizing Qualitative Data

	Country a	Country b	Country c	Country d	Country e	Country f
Question 1						
Question 2						
Question 3						

The misrepresentation of data by cherry picking is sometimes formalized in the best practice approach, which focuses the analysis on an acknowledged outlier. Studies may focus on desirable processes and impacts. But they frequently do not document how exceptional is this best practice or examine the conditions that explain why best practice has been achieved in one case but not others. At its worst, focusing only on best practice can result in an entirely unrealistic approach to project and program design. There is, of course, some merit in looking at best practice. But such analysis must involve looking at the conditions required for best practice and their replicability. There is also a case for looking at worst practice—don't we want to learn from our mistakes? To put it another way, we want to know what works and what doesn't. In order to learn that, we must look at cases that have not worked.

3. Micro-Level Evidence of Development Effectiveness

The term impact evaluation has been used with several different meanings. The four most common, which are not mutually exclusive, are:

- Rigorous analysis of the counterfactual;
- A focus on outcomes;
- Evaluation carried out some years after the intervention has ended;
- Country or sector-wide studies.

A review of OED's 108 impact evaluation reports listed in the World Bank's document database[23] shows that all these different meanings of impact have been used.[24]

In the results-based climate of today, impact evaluations focus on outcomes. In any study they conduct, evaluators should be concerned with the requirement to take account of the counterfactual. Within this context an increasing number of studies, many from the World Bank's research department, have presented a counterfactual analysis of outcomes. These studies typically rely on advanced econometric techniques, which are being promoted in some quarters as the model to adopt for all evaluations, and certainly for evaluations with an impact focus. But such techniques may not always be appropriate, so there is still a need to develop rigorous alternative approaches.

Technical Innovations for Measuring Impact: Randomization and Propensity Score Matching

At the micro-level the problem of attribution is embodied in the construction of a counterfactual: what would outcomes have been in the absence of the intervention? Common ways of addressing this issue are:

- Before versus after comparison of outcome indicators for those benefiting from the intervention (commonly called the treatment group).

Since this method does not control for other factors affecting outcomes, it is not usually regarded as giving credible results.

- Comparison of outcomes with those in a control group. This approach requires a control group whose outcomes were similar to those of the treatment group prior to the intervention and which has subsequently been subject to the same shocks and trends as the treatment group.

- The double difference method, which combines the previous two, by comparing the change in the outcome in the treatment group with the change in the control group. This method is preferred because it eliminates constant unobservable differences between the treatment and control groups.

The problem is, of course, to identify a credible control group. One way of doing this is to allocate program resources in a random manner. In that way, program beneficiaries are a random sample of the population as a whole, and their outcomes can be compared with those of another randomly drawn sample of non-beneficiaries (the control group).[25] Randomized design has been widely used in medicine and is increasingly used in social interventions in developed countries. Its use in developing countries is more recent, as reviewed in the papers by Rawlings (chapter 9) and Duflo and Kremer (chapter 10) in this volume.

Where randomization is not possible (or may have been possible but the intervention was not designed that way)[26] then the comparatively recent technique of propensity score matching allows the construction of good controls.[27] The objective here is to match each individual in the treatment group with a person in the control group, producing pairs of individuals or households who are as similar to one another as possible. The data on which we wish to match the individuals or households are a set of observable characteristics that are unaffected by participation in the program. Thus, baseline data are a first requirement. But even with just, say, five characteristics, matching becomes difficult and ultimately arbitrary when several dimensions are being used to make the match. As Rosenbaum and Rubin (1983) showed, we can match by the propensity to participate in the program, where this propensity is the predicted probability of program participation based on the observed characteristics.[28] Each participant can then be matched with the non-participant who has the nearest "score" and the difference in outcomes in the pair calculated. In practice, results are better when matching with a larger number of members from the control group, such as the nearest five,[29] or when matching each participant with all members of the control group, calculating the mean outcome for the control group using weights that vary according to the similarity in score.

Taken together, these techniques provide a firm basis for saying something about impact. The problem is that they are applicable only to only those types of intervention that can be seen as delivering a treatment to a clearly defined group. The medical analogy is appropriate. Where an intervention is discrete and homogenous, like taking a tablet, then these techniques can be used. But where this is not the case, alternative approaches are needed.

Alternative Approaches to Impact Evaluation

These techniques are not suitable for a wide range of activities that development agencies support, including the policy reforms supported by adjustment lending and the program aid of bilateral donors, or other channels through which policy advice is given, such as economic and sector work.[30] Nor do they apply to technical assistance that is provided to support institutional development rather than to implement specific activities. Nor can they be used to evaluate institutional development activities more generally where these are carried out either at the central level or in a very small number of districts. For such cases, alternative approaches are needed.

Furthermore, match-based comparisons assume that all beneficiaries receive the same treatment. This is not the case in most interventions, and it is helpful to know which parts of project design work and which do not. An example of the problem of heterogeneity is provided in a recent analysis of social funds. This study used household-level data from six countries to conduct regressions of welfare outcomes.[31] A social fund dummy variable was assigned a value of one if the household lived in a community with a social fund intervention in the appropriate sector and a value of zero otherwise. There are three problems in this approach. First, we do not know if "non-social fund communities" have no facility or a facility that has not received social fund support.[32] Hence, we do not know what is the counterfactual. Second, the nature of social fund support can vary in scale and type between facilities. Classroom rehabilitation will have less impact on enrollments than expanding the size of the school by building new classroom blocks, but all are subsumed under the project dummy. Finally, the use of the dummy variable does not allow us to unpack the causal chain to understand why effects are, or are not, being found. Several of the regressions showed an insignificant "social fund effect" and even in a few cases a perverse one. For example, in Zambia health facilities supported by the social fund exacerbate wasting in the recipient community.[33] It is more useful to "open the black box" of the project contained in the use of the project dummy.

The methodology in OED's current program of impact evaluations is based on modeling the determinants of those outcomes given by the objectives, and then linking the outputs of Bank interventions to those determinants.[34] Applying this logic to the study of social funds just mentioned, it would have made sense to model the determinants of the welfare outcomes, where some of these determinants (such as access to and quality of services) could be linked to the social fund intervention. An advantage of this approach is to merge a process-oriented approach with impact analysis. The causal chain included in the logical framework encompasses process issues, such as the dynamic behind policy changes, some of which may be addressed using qualitative techniques.[35]

4. Sustainability

Sustainability is often equated with environmental concerns. But in evaluation, environmental sustainability is just one aspect of sustainability. For example, the OECD Development Assistance Committee glossary states that "sustainability is concerned with measuring whether the benefits of an activity are likely to continue after donor funding has been withdrawn. Projects need to be environmentally as well as financially sustainable."[36] OED defines sustainability as "the resilience to risk of net benefits flows over time," elaborating the definition with the following questions: "At the time of evaluation, what is the resilience to risks of future net benefits flows? How sensitive is the project to changes in the operating environment? Will the project continue to produce net benefits, as long as intended, or even longer? How well will the project weather shocks and changing circumstances?"[37]

However, beyond definitions there is little agreement. A recent review stated that "much remains to be done in terms of [sustainability's] evaluation as an objective."[38] The OED definition makes clear the strong link between sustainability analysis in evaluation and risk analysis at appraisal. In principle it should be possible to use the same techniques for both. However, when we turn to the World Bank's practice in appraising risk, we find it falls far short of best practice.

The World Bank's Operational Policy 10.04 (Economic Evaluation of Investment Operations) deals with both sustainability[39] and risk.[40] The approach it advocates is traditional deterministic sensitivity analysis, that is, varying key assumptions and noting the changes in the return to the project.[41] But, as argued by Belli et al. (2001), this approach is of limited use, since it does not tell us how likely or how large is the variation from our assumed value. In addition, varying one assumption at a time understates the risk if there is a positive correlation between changes in the different variables. The preferred approach is to conduct Monte Carlo simulations, which requires specifying the distribution of all-important variables and the correlation between them.[42] In each simulation the internal rate of return is calculated so that the frequency distribution of the return can be plotted.

Recent papers in health economics have adopted a Bayesian approach to sensitivity analysis.[43] Health evaluations use the incremental cost-effectiveness ratio (ICER), which may be seen as equivalent to the familiar cost-benefit ratio in economics.[44] The ICER compares a new treatment (B) with an existing one (A), or compares pairs of possible treatments. The numerator is the difference in the cost of the treatments, which includes cost savings from health improvements from the new technique. The denominator is the change in some measure of health outcomes, such as quality-adjusted life-years (QALYs). The result is a four-quadrant diagram (Figure 2.3). In quadrant I the old treatment dominates, as it was cheaper and more effective, whereas in the fourth quadrant the new treatment dominates. In quadrant II the new treatment is more effective but also more expensive. It will be preferred if the ratio exceeds some norm on acceptable cost per QALY saved. In the third quadrant the new treatment is cheaper but less effective, which gives ambiguous feelings about what to do.

Deterministic sensitivity analysis can be applied to calculating the incremental cost-effectiveness ratio, as can a stochastic approach that maps its distribution. The problem with the latter is that the ICER is non-bounded for small changes in effects and that equal values of the ICER from the second and third quadrants actually refer to rather different things. The Bayesian approach thus takes prior assumptions about model values to calculate the posterior distribution of the ICER.[45] Specifically, it is possible to calculate the probability that B will be preferred over A (probability in quadrant IV plus probability in lower part of quadrant II). Other studies calculate the probability of the ICER being in each quadrant separately and then map the distribution in that quadrant.

Figure 2.3
Analysis of the Incremental Cost-Effectiveness Ratio

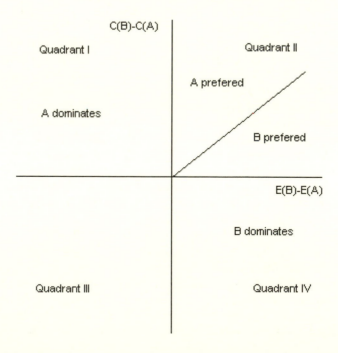

All this is rather far from current practice at the World Bank. World Bank appraisal documents at best follow the Bank's guidelines of conducting deterministic sensitivity analysis. None calculates a risk-based expected return.[46]

Hence there is an established method of tackling sustainability in project appraisal that could equally well be used at the evaluation stage in re-estimating the IRR. However, there are three reasons for not following this route to sustainability analysis.[47] First, its relative technical sophistication may mean that it is only used on a small selection of projects, which would be disadvantaged by this more rigorous analysis compared with other less closely scrutinized projects. Second and more importantly, the method can produce impressive-looking output that may distract users of evaluation reports from the critical step of identifying key assumptions and their attendant probability distributions. Third, such analysis is most amenable to varying assumptions on clearly defined variables, such as price and yields, and it can readily incorporate delays. It is less easy to see how to incorporate the types of risks often identified in project documents, such as "government will not maintain its commitment." As an intermediate step, it is proposed that analysis of sustainability would be best served by more serious attention to risks and their likelihood. When this becomes established practice then it may be time to move to complete the formalization of the approach by linking these risks to variables used in the calculation of the rate of return and producing distributions of those returns.

How should key risks be identified? Belli et al. (2001) suggest that sensitivity analysis can be used to identify which variables matter most. But this approach will only work if a spreadsheet project analysis has been set up. And it will not capture such factors as "lack of government commitment." More appropriate is a theory-based approach similar to a log-frame analysis of project design, which should already incorporate risk. Theory-based evaluation (TBE) seeks to uncover the key assumptions that underlie project design. It asks, "the goal is to improve indicator Y, and the project is delivering input X. What is the causal chain, or set of assumptions, by which the project designers believe that input X will affect outcome Y?" A theory-based evaluation tests these links.

TBE can be adapted to the analysis of sustainability. The theory lays out a set of conditions under which X will lead to Y. If Y cannot be observed—as it cannot in the case of future benefits—then the evaluation can test whether or not the conditions for X to lead to Y are in place. Whereas TBE per se seeks to test these conditions, the analysis of sustainability uses reference to other literature to validate the theory linking X to Y. This approach was adopted in OED's analysis of the sustainability of sub-projects supported by social funds.[48] Based on a review of the literature on project sustainability, conditions were derived that should be met if sub-projects are to be sustainable, and the importance of these conditions was validated through the four country case studies. The portfolio review recorded which projects had the required design features for sustainability and which did not. The study found that social funds were learning the lessons of experience and beginning to adopt the required design features for sub-project sustainability more widely.

Theory-based evaluation enables identification of factors critical for sustainability, but it does not tell us about the probability of different events. It would seem a minimum requirement that identified risks should be labeled as "very likely" to "not at all likely," with some common understanding of the range of probabilities referred to by each label. Where the risks are of a vague sort ("lack of government commitment") the evaluator should be required to spell out in more detail the implications for the project. Table 2.3 provides an example of some reasonably generic factors that might be considered in a sustainability analysis.

5. Conclusion

Evaluation has a crucial role to play in today's results-based culture. Studies must be able to credibly establish the beneficial impact on the poor of official interventions. And they must be able to draw out relevant and applicable lessons for policymakers. Evaluations frequently fall short of their potential, usually because their authors give inadequate attention to application of the most appropriate techniques.[49]

This paper has discussed the following cases of the need for more attention to technique:

- formal application of meta-analysis in studies that aggregate performance (agency-wide performance, and country and sector studies);
- weak analysis of qualitative data, including the prevalence of data mining (cherry picking), sometimes formalized in the best-practice approach;
- paying greater attention to establishing the control in evaluation design, either through randomization where possible or through propensity score matching—both of which imply taking a prospective approach, which is not commonly applied;
- seeking ways to establish impact that "open the black box" and so provide lessons about what works and what doesn't; and
- application of risk analysis to discussions of sustainability.

This is a demanding agenda. But results-orientation is demanding, and the challenge of eliminating world poverty more so. Evaluation units and evaluators in the development community need to ask themselves if they are doing their best to help meet this challenge.

Table 2.3
Possible Factors in Sustainability Analysis

Aspect	Factor	Data
Financial		
Government	Strength of tax base	Historical analysis of revenue variation and factors behind it (e.g. commodity prices).
	Ability to finance	Shortfalls between actual and budgeted expenditure.
	Willingness to finance	Likely government priorities. If government may change, what are priorities of opposition parties?
Communities	Ability to pay	Forecasts of charge as a percent of average income (requires analysis of livelihood of community).
	Willingness to pay	Possible changes in pattern of demand, perhaps because of competing suppliers. Will the project continue to produce benefits of sufficient value? (e.g. prices fall so output not worth as much, so producers won't pay for technical services).
Donors	Continued donor finance	Is it planned?
Institutional		
Government	Capacity	Are the skills required for project implementation or supervision present and will they stay there?
	Existence	If the project is under a special unit, will it continue to exist or are arrangements in place for the take over of functions by exiting government units?
NGO	Organizational viability	Will the organization continue to exist without external project finance?
	Capacity	Are the skills required for project implementation present and will they stay there?
Community	Organization	Are there command-based organizations to be responsible for community level responsibilities? Can these responsibilities be enforced?
	Capacity	Do community members have the required skills, or are mechanisms in place so that they acquire them?

Table 2.3 (cont.)

Technical		
Design	Soundness	Are physical structures sound or do they have structural problems?
Operations & maintenance Environmental	Ability	Do those responsible have the required skill for operation and maintenance?
		Is project depleting stocks of a non-renewable source? Are there adverse environmental consequences of project technology that will undermine its effects?

Notes

1. There were two competing approaches, one from UNIDO (1972) and one developed under the auspices of OECD by Little and Mirrlees (1974). The latter became more widely adopted and was promoted in the World Bank publication by Squire and van der Tak (1975), and in a more applied form in Gittinger (1985). In practice, very simplified methods of cost-benefit analysis, if any, were used. A retrospective of the Bank's experience concluded that cost-benefit analysis had little real influence in the World Bank (Little and Mirrlees, 1990) and a review by World Bank economists concluded that only about one-fifth of project decisions were based on good economic analysis (Devarajan et al., 1996). See also the contribution by Angus Deaton (chapter 12) in this volume.
2. Mistaken since it is precisely the valuation of non-market benefits that provides a motivation for economic rather than financial analysis. Most World Bank appraisal documents for social sector lending state that the rate of return is not applicable. However, Devarajan et al. (1996) show that sectoral shifts do not explain the declining use of cost-benefit analysis in the World Bank, which they attribute to the abolition of a central unit responsible for the quality of appraisals and the increased focus on macroeconomic issues in the 1980s.
3. See Kabeer (1992) for an explicit statement of this position.
4. In the words of a former Director General of OED, "development interventions today are assessed through a multiplicity of techniques, drawing on many disciplines" (Picciotto, 2002, p. 7).
5. This statement needs to be treated with caution. The ultimate rationale for the assistance is poverty reduction. Where the causal chain is long—such as providing technical assistance to a ministry of finance—there seems little point in attempting to establish any direct link between the activity and poverty reduction. But in other cases, such as supporting the decentralization of health service delivery—the chain is short enough to make it desirable to be able to say something about how decentralized delivery affects health outcomes.
6. One may also consider a third input, theory, which in these figures is subsumed under techniques, to facilitate the graphical presentation.
7. Ravallion (1996) suggests some, but limited, substitutability.
8. The six goals are: creation of an enabling environment for sustainable human development, economic and social policies and strategies focused on the reduction of

poverty, environmentally sustainable development to reduce human poverty, advancement in the status of women and gender equality, special development situations, and UNDP support to the United Nations.

9. White (2003).
10. The term meta-evaluation refers to the evaluation of evaluations.
11. The team preparing the *Development Effectiveness Report* reviewed forty-one project completion reports and 123 output to purpose reviews. They found quality to be highle variable, with significant over-grading in project completion reports. However, no corrections were made to the data.
12. United Nations Development Program (2000) p. 63.
13. The institutional strategy papers lay out DFID's vision of the appropriate role of the international agencies with which DFID works, and how DFID may best work with that agency. For each institutional strategy paper there will be an institutional performance review that can be used in an evaluation synthesis, though at the time of preparing the first development effectiveness report only one institutional performance review was available.
14. See Casley and Lury (1987) for a fuller discussion of the role of case studies.
15. See Woolcock and Rao (2002) for a more general discussion of the iterative approach to combining quantitative and qualitative methods in evaluation.
16. As is the case, for example, in OED's health sector review, World Bank Operations Evaluation Department (1999).
17. World Bank Operations Evaluation Department (2002).
18. For example, fitting a straight line to a quadratic relationship can yield an insignificant coefficient even if the true relationship is very strong.
19. This is a hypothetical example; it does not refer to an actual study.
20. For an elaboration of this point see White (2001). Data mining should be distinguished from the perfectly legitimate enterprise of data analysis, a data-driven approach that allows the data to tell their own story rather than being forced into a preconceived view of what they should say (i.e,. a pre-specified model). See Mukherjee et al. (1998).
21. I do not pursue here the very scant use made in some official agencies of participatory evaluation, a particular approach to qualitative data that has wide support amongst nongovernmental agencies.
22. For example, "in Malawi evidence was found that decentralization has increased the feelings of autonomy of local officials, although the evidence was less strong in the other countries." The quantitative equivalent of this Malawi example is either basing arguments on statistically insignificant coefficients or allowing a single influential point to drive the results.
23. Gupta Kapoor (2002).
24. The rather diffuse meaning of impact in these studies was one source of criticism from the Meltzer Commission: "The banks seldom return to inspect project success or assess sustainability of results. The World Bank reviews only 5 percent of its programs three to ten years after final disbursement. These impact evaluations focus on such important, but poorly defined and subjective, measures as improvements in the environment, the role of women, the interaction of societal institutions, income distribution and general welfare. It is difficult to relate Bank activities to these social indicators. Thirty percent of the investigators found that lack of monitoring of project results precluded valid judgments. Though the agencies devote significant resources to monitoring the procurement of inputs, they do little to measure the effectiveness of outputs over time." International Financial Institution Advisory Committee (2000).

25. The unit of observation need not be the individual. It could, for example, be a school, a district or a farmers' group.

26. Randomization is in principle possible for all interventions for which the universe of potential beneficiaries exceeds the number of possible beneficiaries allowed by the program budget (or the possible number in the first phase). There are cases in which all possible beneficiaries are intended to be reached—for example the HIPC initiative, recently evaluated by OED (World Bank, 2003).

27. See Ravallion (2002) for an accessible introduction to the technique.

28. That is, we estimate a logit model for participation, in which the dependent variable is 1 for participants and 0 for non-participants and the regressors are the observed characteristics.

29. In this case, one calculates the mean outcome of the nearest five and compares this mean with the outcome for the participant.

30. There may be rare cases of sectoral policies that can be implemented in discrete geographical units on a random basis, but these would be very much the exception. But if policy change is costless, the moral defense for withholding beneficial treatment from the control collapses.

31. Some of the results from these country studies are presented in *World Bank Economic Review*, August 2000.

32. In some studies the selected communities were those in the pipeline. The rationale for using pipeline communities is that their acceptance for a project should mean they are similar to already accepted communities, but this fact does not solve the problems mentioned here.

33. These results are summarized in World Bank (2002), Annex E.

34. Earlier OED impact evaluations also adopted nonexperimental approaches (the most recent examples are World Bank, 1998 and 2000), and see Gupta Kapoor (2002) for a review.

35. See World Bank (forthcoming) for an illustration.

36. Development Assistance Committee Working Party on Aid Evaluation (2002).

37. *www.worldbank.org/oed/eta-approach.html.*

38. CIDA (2002), p.1.

39. "To obtain a reasonable assurance that the project's benefits will materialize as expected and will be sustained throughout the life of the project, the Bank assesses the robustness of the project with respect to economic, financial, institutional, and environmental risks. Bank staff check, among other things, (a) whether the legal and institutional framework either is in place or will be developed during implementation to ensure that the project functions as designed, and (b) whether critical private and institutional stakeholders have or will have the incentives to implement the project successfully. Assessing sustainability includes evaluating the project's financial impact on the implementing/sponsoring institution and estimating the direct effect on public finances of the project's capital outlays and recurrent costs."

40. The economic analysis of projects is necessarily based on uncertain future events and inexact data and, therefore, inevitably involves probability judgments. Accordingly, the Bank's economic evaluation considers the sources, magnitude, and effects of the risks associated with the project by taking into account the possible range in the values of the basic variables and assessing the robustness of the project's outcome with respect to changes in these values. The analysis estimates the switching values of key variables (i.e., the value that each variable must assume to reduce the net present value of the project to zero) and the sensitivity of the project's net present value to changes in those variables (e.g., delays in implementation, cost overruns, and other variables that can be controlled to some extent). The main purpose of this

analysis is to identify the scope for improving project design, increase the project's expected value, and reduce the risk of failure.

41. Deterministic sensitivity analysis can be either univariate—varying one assumption at a time—or multivariate—varying several assumptions at once (in different scenarios).

42. A Monte Carlo simulation simply means repeating an event with a random outcome many times. The simulations themselves are relatively straightforward on a spreadsheet. The more difficult task is to specify the underlying distribution and the correlation between variables. See the discussion in Belli et al. (2001) Chapter 11 on how to do this.

43. See, for example, Briggs (1999) and his chapter 14 in the present volume.

44. If a "no project" counterfactual is used, as is often the case in cost-benefit analysis, then the values for the comparison in the cost-benefit ratio are zero.

45. As stressed by Briggs in chapter 14 in this volume, model specification is likely to be the most important source of uncertainty.

46. A free text search of the term "expected net present value" in the World Bank's document database, Imagebank, returns only one project appraisal document. In this case the term expected was being used in the lay sense, that is, "given our assumptions we expect the IRR to be this," rather than its more precise statistical meaning.

47. These suggestions apply equally to appraisal and evaluation.

48. World Bank (2002).

49. Not discussed here is the preference for "quick and dirty" studies as many agencies shy away from the higher cost of "longer but clean" studies. However, any cost-benefit calculation will favor the latter.

References

Belli, Pedro, Jock R. Anderson, Howard N. Barnum, John A. Dixon, and Jee-Peng Tan. *Economic Analysis of Investment Operations: Analytical Tools and Practical Applications.* A World Bank Institute Development Study. Washington, DC: World Bank.

Briggs, Andrew. (1999). "A Bayesian Approach to Stochastic Cost-Effectiveness Analysis." *Health Economics Letters* 8, pp. 257-261.

Canadian International Development Agency (CIDA). (2002). "Assessing Sustainability," What We're Learning No. 2. Ottawa: Canadian International Development Agency.

Casley, Dennis J., and Lury, Denis A. (1984, reprinted 1987). *Monitoring and Evaluation of Agricultural and Rural Development Projects.* Baltimore, MD: Johns Hopkins University Press for the World Bank.

Devarajan, S., L. Squire, and S. Suthiwart-Narueput. (1996). "Project Appraisal at the World Bank." In Colin Kirkpatrick and John Weiss, *Cost-Benefit Analysis and Project Appraisal in Developing Countries.* Cheltenham: Edward Elgar.

Development Assistance Committee Working Party on Aid Evaluation. (2002). Glossary of Key Terms in Evaluation and Results-based Management. Paris: Development Assistance Committee, Organization for Economic Cooperation and Development.

Gittinger, John. (1985). *Economic Analysis of Agricultural Projects.* Washington, DC: Economic Development Institute, World Bank.

Gupta Kapoor, Anju. (2002). "Review of OED Impact Studies." OED Working Paper. Washington, DC: World Bank Operations Evaluation Department.

International Financial Institution Advisory Commission (IFIAC). (2000). *Final Report of the International Financial Institution Advisory Commission to the US Congress and Department of the Treasury.* Washington, DC: IFIAC.

Kabeer, N. (1992). "Evaluating Cost-Benefit Analysis as a Tool for Gender Planning." *Development and Change* 23, p. 115.

Little, I. M. D., and J. A. Mirrlees. (1974). *Project Appraisal and Planning for Developing Countries*. London: Heinemann Educational.

_____. (1990). "Project Appraisal and Planning Twenty Years On." Paper prepared for World Bank Conference on Development Economics, April.

Mukherjee, C., M. Wuyts, and H. White. (1998). *Econometrics and Data Analysis for Developing Countries*. London: Routledge.

Picciotto, Robert. (2002). "Development Cooperation and Performance Evaluation: The Monterrey Challenge." OED Working Paper. Washington, DC: World Bank Operations Evaluation Department.

Ravallion, Martin. (1996). "How Well Can Method Substitute for Data? Five Experiments in Poverty Analysis." *World Bank Research Observer* 11 (2), pp. 199-221.

_____. (2002). "The Mystery of the Vanishing Benefits: An Introduction to Impact Evaluation." *World Bank Economic Review* 15 (115).

Rosenbaum, P., and D. Rubin. (1983). "The Central Role of Propensity Score Matching in Observational Studies for Causal Effects." *Biometrika* 70, pp. 41-55.

Squire, L., and H. Van der Tak. (1975). *Economic Analysis of Projects*. Washington, DC: World Bank.

United Nations Development Program (UNDP). (2000). *Results-Oriented Annual Report*. New York: United Nations Development Program.

United Nations Industrial Development Organization (UNIDO). (1972). *Guidelines for Project Evaluation*. New York: United Nations Industrial Development Organization.

Weiss, Carol. (1997). *Evaluation*. New York: Prentice Hall.

White, Howard. (2001). "Combining Quantitative and Qualitative Techniques in Poverty Analysis." *World Development* 30 (3), pp. 511-522.

_____. (2003). "Using the MDGs to Measuring Donor Agency Performance." In Richard Black and Howard White, *Targeting Development: Critical Perspectives on the Millennium Development Goals*. London: Routledge.

Woolcock, Michael, and Vijayendra Rao. (2002). "Integrating Qualitative and Quantitative Approaches in Program Evaluation." Chapter 8 in Francis Bourguignon and Luiz A. Pereira da Silva (eds.), *The Impact of Economic Policies on Poverty and Income Distribution: Evaluation Techniques and Tools*. New York and Oxford: Oxford University Press for the World Bank.

World Bank Operations Evaluation Department. (1998). *India: The Dairy Revolution*. Washington, DC: World Bank Operations Evaluation Department.

_____. (1999). *Investing in Health: Development Effectiveness in Health, Nutrition, and Population*. Washington, DC: World Bank Operations Evaluation Department.

_____. (2000). *Agricultural Extension: The Kenya Experience*. Washington, DC: World Bank Operations Evaluation Department.

_____. (2002). *Social Funds: Assessing Effectiveness*. Washington, DC: World Bank Operations Evaluation Department.

_____. (2003). *Debt Relief for the Poorest: An OED Review of the Highly Indebted Poor Countries Initiative*. Washington, DC: World Bank Operations Evaluation Department.

_____. (forthcoming). *Adjusting Education: An Impact Evaluation of World Bank Support to Basic Education in Ghana*. Washington, DC: World Bank Operations Evaluation Department.

3

Macro-Level Evaluations and the Choice of Aid Modalities

Tony Killick[1]

In recent years, the pendulum of professional opinion about effective aid modalities has swung away from project-based assistance in favor of more programmatic forms, most notably budget support and the associated modality of debt relief. Thus, a recent British policy statement on the subject:

> ...there needs to be a real improvement in the way that assistance is delivered. That means reducing support for stand-alone projects, and increasing support for sector-wide reforms. Where governments have a strong commitment to poverty reduction and strong policies in place, it means moving towards providing financial support directly to recipient government budgets using their own systems. (DFID, 2000, p. 93)

The World Bank has been providing programmatic "policy-based" adjustment credits since the end of the 1970s, but, in low-income countries, the opening of its Poverty Reduction Support Credit (PRSC) window has added a further dimension, not least because—to its great credit—the Bank is beginning to go to some lengths to harmonize the terms of its PRSCs with those of the budget support baskets put together by bilateral and other donors. The introduction of the Enhanced Highly Indebted Poor Countries debt relief scheme (E-HIPC, sometimes known as HIPC II) in 1999 added a further string to the program aid bow.

This shift represents a challenge to evaluators. New issues arise and new needs for evaluation are created. One big issue is the extent to which the shift from project to program support is soundly based on evidence. Another issue

---

Senior research asssociate, Overseas Development Institute, London, and visiting professor, University of Surrey.

is the extent to which those who decide on modalities are actually driven by evidential factors. Do they listen to evaluators? Perhaps to some extent they are unable to because of time lags. The contemporary aid environment is a rather fast-changing one whereas evaluation is retrospective, occasional, and reflects the aid choices of the past rather than the fascinations of the present. Finally, the switch to programmatic support raises questions about the level at which evaluation should be conducted and who should undertake it.

This paper illustrates some of these issues by reference to four topics. In Section 1, starting from the common assertion that program aid is superior to the project-based alternative because it lowers transactions costs, I will raise questions about the state of our knowledge about comparative costs, and about the loose way in which these costs are defined in debates about aid modalities. In Section 2, I will use a recent study by the World Bank's Operations Evaluation Department to argue that, in aid-effectiveness terms, there is probably a rather severe conflict between evidence-based considerations and the heavy weight attached to political factors in the use of aid resources for debt relief. In this case, the evidence is there, but the question is, Who's listening? Section 3 investigates the interactions between work on policy conditionality and the practices of the Bretton Woods institutions, which are another apparent case of the failure of decision makers to take an evidence-based approach. Here the reasons include political considerations but also institutional factors and research time lags.

The logic of the movement towards partnership-based general budget support is that more and more evaluative work needs to be done at the country-wide as opposed to the project- or sector-specific level. This not only has large implications for the types of skill and information required, and for methodologies, but it also raises the less obvious question, Who should undertake such studies? Section 4 draws on a recent exercise in Tanzania to argue that such work will often best be conducted by evaluators who are independent of both donors and recipient governments—so-called independent monitoring groups.

1. Transactions Costs and the Choice of Aid Modalities

Program aid is claimed by its growing number of advocates to be superior for a number of reasons (stronger influence on the policy environment, superior ownership properties, greater aggregate coherence, and so forth) but many of these boil down to the oft-heard claim that a given sum of program aid gives rise to smaller transactions costs than an equivalent amount in the form of traditional development projects. Thus, a recent report on aid relations in Tanzania:

> ...we see program aid as avoiding various of the drawbacks ... of project aid, especially when it takes the form of a pooling of resources and coordination among donors. The

presumption is that, with a much smaller number of reporting points, with no necessity for a multitude of Project Implementation Units, with donors accepting common reporting procedures and standards, with tied procurement virtually eliminated and with much less necessity for enforced project-linked technical assistance activities, transactions costs per dollar of aid received will be much smaller. (Independent Monitoring Group, 2003, p. 37)

That is now the conventional wisdom and I agree with it *as a hypothesis*. Many complaints are leveled against the project approach, which is seen as undermining local capacity development, imposing heavy procurement and reporting requirements because of the large numbers of individual projects, and reducing the value of aid through the imposition of procurement tying. However, the superiority of program aid in this respect remains only a hypothesis because it rests on a presumption of the comparative costs of the respective aid modalities that has not, to my knowledge, been validated in a systematic way. In fact, a literature search revealed only one study, examining aid transactions costs in Vietnam.[2] The language of transactions costs has been used too loosely and would merit a substantial empirical study.

Conceptual Issues

One reason to take a careful look is that some conceptual issues are generally disregarded. The textbook meaning of transactions costs is clear enough: the costs of negotiating, monitoring, and consummating a contractual arrangement. But professional usage is unclear about what the chief categories are in the case of aid-delivery contracts. The following is an attempted classification of the types of transactions costs associated with aid.

Administrative (recipient and donor)
- *Ex ante* identification, appraisal, and preparation of the aided activity;
- Implementation, including any special procurement requirements;
- Monitoring and administrative and financial reporting, including special arrangements to safeguard against misadministration and to secure aid effectiveness;
- *Ex post* evaluation, including tracker, outcome, and impact studies.

To be included in each of the above items are the administrative opportunity costs resulting from absorption of scarce staff time within both donor and recipient agencies, although the presumption is that the burden of such costs is disproportionately high within recipient administrations. And, as a special case, there are the opportunity and other costs arising from "staff capture" as a result of donor inducements to recipient civil servants to give priority to a particular aided activity, or to move across to that activity from regular duties.

Tying (recipient)
- Costs arising for recipients from loss of coherence and national owner-ship as a result of the tying of aid to large numbers of individual projects.
- The higher costs of imports resulting from procurement tying. The World Bank (1998) has estimated that such tying typically reduces the value of aid by about one fourth.
- Costs arising for recipients from losses of national ownership and sov-ereignty as a result of policy tying (conditionality), and perceived increases in political risks resulting from any associated governmental loss of policy freedom.

Fiscal (recipient)
- Erosion of fiscal discipline by the extent of off-budget allocations (associated with project approaches) and the wider consequences of that.
- Fiscal management problems generated by under-funding, requirements for counterpart funding, and the recurrent costs of aided activities.
- Planning problems created by the volatility and unpredictability of different classes of aid, and the macroeconomic consequences of that.[3]

All aid modalities are likely to give rise to a number of these different cost types, but they do not do so equally and it is easy to see from this categoriza-tion why project aid has a bad reputation.

There are questions too about how transactions costs are distributed— between donors and recipients, within the structures of each party, and over time. Take the case of a shift from project to macro-level program aid. Within the donor agency in question, administrative and professional work will shift away from project specialists towards more macroeconomically oriented staff (which is one reason why project staff so often oppose the move to program aid and why this can be a sensitive issue in the internal politics of donor agencies). Since donors often shift their project-related administrative costs on to spe-cially contracted consultants, and this may be less readily done with program aid, a shift to program aid is apt to increase the work burdens of aid agency staff, as well as concentrating more of it in agencies' "macro" departments.

Shifts will also occur within the recipient administration. In crude terms, as a result of aid, more resources—and the associated transactions costs—flow through the budget from the center, "the Ministry of Finance and Develop-ment," whose capacity to bear the brunt of donors' reporting and evaluation requirements becomes a critical variable. Even line ministries may also find themselves with additional burdens, because they must now account through regular budgetary processes for items that were previously off budget (most likely being handled semi-autonomously by project implementation units and the like).

Another consideration is the way comparative transactions costs may change over time. For example, some of the transactions costs associated with program aid are essentially start-up costs, which can be expected to diminish as experience is gained and systems are developed, so that while a shift to program aid may well eventually reduce aggregate transactions costs, the initial effect may be to raise them.[4]

A final complication concerns the fact that at least some of the costs described above are intended to produce benefits. This is most obviously the case with the various administrative measures intended to safeguard against misuse of aid. Similarly, policy conditionality is intended to improve the policy environment and hence aid effectiveness. On the one hand, it obviously does not make sense to view the costs in abstraction from whatever benefits they might generate.[5] Against this, since we are not here talking of costs and benefits that can be reduced to a common quantifiable numeraire, a large element of judgment is involved in any attempt to net them out.

Considerations like this help to explain why researchers and evaluators have in the past shied away from the direct study of transactions costs. As Brown et al. (2000) spell out, there are numerous other difficulties. Several of the costs listed earlier cannot be directly observed. Even some of those that can—for example, some of the fiscal costs—are difficult to quantify. The totality of aid transactions in aid-dependent economies involves large numbers of agencies and individuals, with the result that the information required to get a view of the extent of transactions costs will be fragmented and dispersed. There will also be a variety of perceptions; one man's cost is another's safeguard.

All this is daunting. Clearly, no more than indicative evidence would result from even the most thorough investigation. At the same time, the concept of transactions costs is being used to justify really large changes in the modalities of aid delivery. This suggests that it would be well worthwhile to strip away as much as possible of the conjecture surrounding this topic. At present, our ignorance is such that a statement like "program (or project) aid is preferable because it reduces transactions costs" is little better than saying "I like program (or project) aid." In particular, the empirical study of transactions costs seems worthwhile because there are grounds for questioning the alleged superiority of program aid in this regard.

Costs of Program Aid

First, we should note a major type of cost that is largely unique to program aid: policy tying, or conditionality. Conditionality, assuming it achieves its intended purpose, can be thought of as generating costs because, by requiring governments to undertake policy measures they would not otherwise have chosen—or to do so at a faster pace—they are apt to generate political risks and to reduce governments' ability to manage these risks. Note that the risks are borne almost entirely by the recipient, as distinct from the multilateral lender (or bilateral donor) in question. There is also likely to be a perceived loss of sovereignty and, therefore, of national ownership of policies. Many policy changes also generate adjustment costs of various kinds.

It may reasonably be objected that in contemporary best practice, program aid goes along with a partnership approach designed deliberately as an alternative to extensive policy conditionality. But the Bretton Woods Institutions have not thus far substantially reduced their reliance on conditionality. And far from all of the bilateral donors have adopted the partnership approach as an alternative to conditionality;[6] although some are serious about moving in that direction, most of them probably continue to have faith in conditionality, especially the use of prior actions.

Conditionality, of course, necessitates monitoring and reporting, which brings us to the administrative transactions costs listed earlier. Project aid generates large administrative costs but these are not necessarily larger than those of program aid. This is well illustrated by the elaborate monitoring arrangements that are currently being established in connection with the Highly Indebted Poor Countries initiative (HIPC). Here the task is to ensure that extra monies released through debt relief are spent on the designated priority poverty-reducing budgets. But this task is complex and involves significant costs.

Some bilateral donors also try to track what "their" funds are spent on through the budget, imposing substantial transactions burdens both on themselves and recipient administrations. As White and Dijkstra (2003, pp. 476-77) put it:

> Donor attempts to trace their funds resulted in complicated systems which were anyhow likely to be an accounting fiction. These attempts also led to systems trying to micro-manage the recipient's foreign exchange allocation system which may have been inappropriate…. Some agencies may have been forced to adopt such procedures for domestic political reasons, though a better response would be to educate decision-makers on how program aid works.

More generally, the enhanced levels of dialogue and conditionality associated with program aid generate substantial costs for all parties, but especially for recipient administrations. Especially where sectoral program aid is combined with direct budget support, the tendency to develop rather elaborate mechanisms for dialogue, monitoring, reporting, and *ex post* evaluation is apt to impose substantial burdens. This is particularly so where there is a less than perfect convergence of government and donor objectives, and less than complete trust by the latter of the former.

A further aspect of program aid is the special extent to which it relies on coordination and harmonization in order to reduce transactions costs; the practical difficulties of coordination and harmonization are well known. Since many of the costs of coordination and harmonization fall on the local representatives of donor agencies, they may be discounted as less onerous, although they are real. I would argue that coordination is most likely to be effective where the government is actively involved and "in the driving seat," in which case it bears quite a lot of the costs in question. Of course, in the (more general) case where coordination and harmonization are not very effective, most of the costs of these failures fall upon the recipient country.

Even on a rather narrow view of transactions costs, which equates them to staff time taken, the benefits of a shift to program support are uncertain, as illustrated by the conclusions of a recent evaluation of Dutch program support to the local governance sector in Uganda:

> ...for the Netherlands, the decrease in costs (due to pooled funding, harmonization of procedures, and less time needed in direct program management) is outweighed by the increased time use due to coordination, particularly on the sectoral level. On balance, there may have been hardly any time saving in overall aid management for Dutch assistance ... not least during this initial period of establishing mechanisms of operational coordination.

> For Uganda, the increase in time, particularly due to own program management ... and increased coordination time, surpasses the time savings due to pooled funding and harmonization of procedures. Overall, increased intensity of coordination has led to an increase of transaction costs for Ugandan partners... (Netherlands Ministry of Foreign Affairs, 2003, p. 71.)

Program aid also creates problems for fiscal management. Part of the reason is that budget support tends to be geared to the fiscal cycles of the various donors, and gives rise to patterns of commitments and disbursements that do not fit recipients' cycles of budget preparation and execution. Thus, a recent needs assessment survey recently conducted by OECD-DAC in eleven aid recipient countries found that "donor-driven priorities and systems" was by far the most often mentioned as the most burdensome aspect of dealing with donors.[7] Even more serious, program aid appears to be especially prone to volatility, political interference, and unpredictability. This is well demonstrated by a research paper by IMF staff members, which investigates the volatility and predictability of aid in general, and of program versus project aid.[8] Among their remarkable results are the following:

- Aid is more volatile than domestic fiscal revenues and tends to be procyclical.
- Fiscal planners are highly uncertain of aid receipts and "the information content of commitments made by donors is either very small or statistically insignificant."
- There are much larger prediction errors, and a stronger tendency to overestimation, in program aid than in project assistance. This is partly

because of the application of conditionality but there are other reasons, too.

The hypothesis that transactions costs are proportionately lower with program aid is thus not one whose validity should be taken for granted. Indeed, one study of aid to the health sector (Foster et al., 2000) has suggested that the truth may lie the other way round, a judgment with which Lawson et al. (2002) concur, at least as it relates to the shorter term.

Conclusion

Table 3.1 pulls together some of the suggestions made above. An obvious conclusion is that the greater part of the burden falls on recipients rather than on donors—a factor that would be multiplied manifold if it were considered relative to the resources available respectively to donor and recipient administrations. From the recipient side of the table, it does seem that lower transactions costs may be associated with program aid, particularly on a narrow view of costs that concentrates on the administrative aspects. On a broader view, however, this is less clear. One of the limitations of the exercise is that it treats all types of cost as equally significant, whereas the loss of freedom for political management or macro destabilization is a cost on a different scale from, say, evaluation costs. That apart, the entries under program aid challenge any idea that program aid generates only small transactions costs. But the main point is that the entries in the table are only my guesses, which I dignify by calling them hypotheses. We really don't know.

My comments above are not intended as an attack on program aid. For one thing, there are other reasons for preferring program aid to project approaches. But what I have tried to do is to suggest that the trend in aid share in favor of program aid may not be as strongly based on evidence as is commonly assumed and that, to some extent, the language of transactions costs has been used as a weapon in the rhetoric of debates about the effectiveness of alternative modalities. It is perhaps rather telling that in the OECD-DAC needs assessment survey mentioned earlier, switching to budget support was not among the most often mentioned suggestions for lowering transactions costs.[9] Recipients, it seems, are far from seeing program aid as a panacea.

There is, therefore, a strong case for a serious evaluative study of the whole transactions costs question. Because this would need to be a major effort, such a study would probably lie outside the capabilities and budgets of the evaluation departments of bilateral donors, which leaves the World Bank's Operations Evaluation Department as the best equipped to undertake it, perhaps heading a consortium of donor evaluators.

2. The OED's HIPC Evaluation: Who's Listening?

My second topic raises questions about the capacity of evaluators to induce changes in policies and projects where decision makers appear to place a

Table 3.1

Hypotheses about Comparative Transaction Costs of Program and Project Aid

TRANSACTION COSTS	RECIPIENT		DONOR	
	Program	*Project*	*Program*	*Project*
Administrative				
Pre-investment appraisal, etc	Moderate	Moderate	Moderate	Very large
Implementation	Low	Potentially large	Low	Moderate
Monitoring & reporting	Large	Very large	Large	Moderate
Ex post evaluation	Low	Moderate	Large	Moderate
Tying				
Loss of coherence & ownership	Nil (?)	Large		
Price premium	Nil	Large ("25%")		
Political etc costs of policy conditionality	Potentially large	Low		
Fiscal				
Counterpart fund & recurrent cost problems	Nil	Large		
Volatility/unpredictability, destabilization	Very large	Moderate/large	Moderate	Moderate
Erosion of budget by extra-budgetary aid	Nil	Large		

Note: The identified cost types are those suggested in the text and the suggested extent of costs in each entry should be read as *relative to the investment cost of the aided activity in question*.

low value on evidence-based considerations. I take the provision of debt relief for low-income countries as an example. The OED's recent evaluation of the HIPC debt initiative examines issues of design, implementation, and (in a necessarily preliminary way) effectiveness.[10] While it does not spell out the implications of its findings for the likely developmental effectiveness of the assistance in question, the implications are barely below the surface and are negative. It can be inferred from the report that on balance the HIPC scheme has been bad news for aid effectiveness, for reasons summarized below. I will take the argument further than the OED report chooses to.

Failure of the Additionality Principle

In assessing the effects of the Enhanced Heavily Indebted Poor Country debt initiative, the OED report draws attention to the central importance of the notion of additionality, i.e. the extent to which the resources provided by creditors to finance the E-HIPC scheme are additional to normal and previously planned flows of development assistance. The creditors formally agreed on the principle that these resources should be additional and, had they adhered to this principle, the result would have been a substantial net addition to resource transfers to poor countries. However, the OED report highlights that (1) the E-HIPC scheme contains no specific provisions to ensure that additionality is observed, and (2) the early evidence does not suggest that additionality has been achieved in practice. Indeed, introduction of the original HIPC scheme in 1995 coincided with a very sharp fall in total transfers to HIPC countries, to levels that have not since recovered.

Additionality is an elusive concept, because of the difficulties of assessing the counterfactual, but it can be said that successive HIPC schemes have not prevented a decline in net financial transfers to debtor countries; the financial cost of debt relief has apparently been deducted from intended aid transfers,[11] and actual transfers to these countries have been well below projected levels. It would take a major creditor-by-creditor research effort to be able to estimate the true extent of additionality but the presumption is that, generally and over the longer term, a creditor-donor government will decide how much total assistance it wishes to provide and will then reduce its other aid programs to accommodate the budgetary cost of debt relief.

Inefficient Redistribution of Aid

While aid to the HIPC countries has stagnated, resources have been sharply redistributed away from low-income countries that are not rated as eligible for HIPC relief (Table 3.2).

Is the privileged treatment of E-HIPC recipients consistent with aid effectiveness? The E-HIPC scheme has poverty reduction as one of its principal objectives, but eligibility for HIPC relief is not well correlated with the incidence of poverty. Outside Africa, China, India, Bangladesh, Pakistan, and Indonesia are obvious examples of non-HIPC countries with much poverty.

Table 3.2
Distribution of HIPC Resources

Country status	Percent of total net resource transfers	
	1998	**2000***
HIPC	44	76
non-HIPC	56	24

*Latest available data.

Within Africa, Nigeria stands out as among the excluded, along with Eritrea, Namibia, South Africa, and Zimbabwe—all non-HIPC countries with large numbers of people in absolute poverty. Ranis and Stewart (2001) estimate that, among low-income countries, actual and potential HIPC agreements cover only about one-fourth of all people thought to be living in poverty. Given the failure of additionality, the poor in countries outside the HIPC scheme are subsidizing those who live in HIPC countries, raising questions about the consistency of the scheme with its expressed poverty reduction goal.

There are other reasons to question the desirability of this redistribution among aid-recipient countries, given the failure of additionality. One flows from the use of indebtedness as the prime criterion of eligibility for E-HIPC assistance. Hitherto, the aid-effectiveness literature has shown that aid should be allocated selectively on the basis of the quality (however defined) of prospective recipients' economic and social policies. Inserting indebtedness as an overriding criterion and giving E-HIPC debt relief a privileged status among aid modalities seriously impedes the application of this selectivity criterion. Indebtedness tends to be inversely correlated with the quality of past policies. Although exogenous factors have been important too, the case studies conducted for the OED report showed that poor past fiscal policies and failures to adjust were important reasons for the emergence of unsustainable debt burdens. This confirms earlier results by Brooks et al. (1998), and others before them, showing weak macro and adjustment policies and lack of prudent debt management strategies to be associated with debt difficulties among HIPCs. Thus, the global redistribution of aid may be consistent neither with maximum poverty reduction nor with productive use of the assistance. It may also raise questions of moral hazard, punishing countries with good records of economic management in order to rescue those with less responsible or competent governments.

Such concerns have been compounded, as the OED report makes clear, by the processes that brought the E-HIPC scheme into existence. As is well known, the scheme was a political response by creditor governments under varying degrees of pressure from civil society organizations to be generous at the end of the millennium, as a result of successful mobilization by groups campaigning under the Jubilee 2000 banner. One consequence was that creditor governments not merely agreed to E-HIPC, introducing considerably more liberal terms than the original HIPC scheme, but also committed themselves to a target of getting at least twenty countries into the scheme (at "decision point") by the end of 2000. This target was achieved (actually twenty-two countries) but only as a result of what is now labeled "the Millennium rush," with seventeen debtor countries being accepted as having reached their decision point between July and December 2000.

Inevitably, this could only be achieved by lowering the required standards of policy performance. For this group, the OED report shows worse policy track records, weaker development programs, and poorer past records of using aid productively. Unsurprisingly, a substantial proportion of these "rush" countries have subsequently failed to deliver on policy promises. The pace of new inclusions has since slowed considerably but the report indicates that the most recent entrants into the scheme have particularly poor policy records. It appears that E-HIPC is turning out to be a mechanism for reallocating resources in favor of countries that, taken as a group (and with important exceptions), cannot be expected to make the best use of the scarce resources on offer.[12]

Undesirable Policy Biases

One of the most striking aspects of the E-HIPC scheme, as the OED report points out, is its association, under pressure from NGOs, with a particular and narrow approach to the task of reducing poverty, namely the expansion of spending on social services, to the neglect of wider growth and developmental priorities. This trend in the allocation of aid monies had already been well under way for some time, but the E-HIPC initiative took the bias to a higher level. The report points out that, in the thirteen countries for which data were available, 65 percent of all resources released by E-HIPC debt relief were to be devoted to social services, with 7 percent going to infrastructure, 4 percent to governance, and just 1 percent to structural reforms. This pattern has been associated with a sharp rise in the share of total aid in these countries devoted to the social sectors with an almost corresponding decline in the share of aid used to support production. Moreover, HIPC progress reports indicate that more than half of government revenues will be earmarked for social spending in future years.

To what extent will this concentration on social services act on the causes of poverty? Inadequate access to education and health is certainly a powerful influence on poverty. But poverty has many other causes too, notably the effects of past economic stagnation or decline, inadequate access of the poor to various forms of capital, large and growing inequalities, high demographic dependency rates, gender biases, and various forms of disempowerment and of state failures.[13] Only a few of the causes of poverty have much to do with a neglect of social spending induced by the necessity to service external debts.

The E-HIPC link between debt relief and social service provision pays little heed to what is universally agreed: that much more than money is needed to ensure that social spending will actually raise the living standards of the poor. OED's report draws attention to the pervasiveness of low efficiency, poor service quality, capacity shortfalls, and low utilization within poor countries' social services. In fact, cross-country evidence suggests that spending levels have little influence on educational outcomes, although comparable tests for health provide more mixed results.[14] There is also the problem of skewed access to these services; for example, African evidence suggests that these services are overwhelmingly enjoyed by the more affluent members of the population, with the poorest quintiles receiving much less than a proportionate share.[15]

The concentration on social spending biases attention away from the fundamental need to raise economic growth and remedy structural weaknesses. It is not sufficiently realized on what soft terms the HIPC countries have obtained capital in the past.[16] In 1999, for example, the HIPCs borrowed at 3½ percent interest, on average, with an average maturity of more than twenty years and a 43 percent grant element. Moreover, in the same year, they received grants equal to more than half of their total borrowings, so that the true average terms were actually much softer than those just cited. The equivalent figures for Sub-Saharan African countries were even more favorable. How could countries receiving capital on these terms possibly run into debt-servicing problems? The explanation doubtless varies from country to country. But generally it is to be found in a combination of exogenous shocks; poor past macroeconomic management, worsening the already large problem of capital flight; weak domestic saving, fiscal, and export performance; and low returns to past investments. In turn, low returns can be seen as reflecting often poor public investment decisions, deteriorating terms of trade, obstacles to market access, inflexible export structures, past and continuing policy failings (as already discussed), and low enforceability of property rights.

Excessive indebtedness can exacerbate these disincentives to foreign investors through the "overhang" effect (which discourages investors by adding to uncertainties, not least about future tax levels). In principle, the negative force of the policy biases could be mitigated if the E-HIPC scheme were to reduce the overhang problem, in which case investment and growth could be boosted. There is little controversy that in the circumstances of middle-income debtor countries, such as the Latin American debtors who dominated the debt crisis of the 1980s, the overhang could and did have such an effect. But the applicability of this argument to the small, low-income recipients of HIPC resources, with their many other deterrents to foreign investment, is less clear. The evidence does not show a strong connection between debt stocks and investment levels, and the direction of causality is ambiguous. The OED report suggests that an overhang effect has not been convincingly demonstrated,[17] so it would be unwise to rely heavily on E-HIPC relief for a strong reduction of the overhang effect.

Creditworthiness and debt sustainability, as the OED report makes clear, will best be achieved by measures that strengthen the domestic economy and its underlying institutional bases, and address the above causal factors. Debt difficulties are better seen as a symptom of economic weaknesses than as a cause of them. The current donor preoccupation with social spending diverts attention away from this priority and thus carries the risk that the resources devoted to social spending will not be effectively used, and that the goal of debt sustainability may prove unattainable. Of course, the Bretton Woods Institutions would deny this, asserting that poverty reduction strategy papers should tackle all these weaknesses as part of the anti-poverty effort. But not everything can be done at the same time; attention bias is real. Much stress is now on raising the quantity and quality of social services and this is likely to further increase total consumption relative to saving, when saving and investment are already too low.

Multiple and Conflicting Objectives

The OED report points out that the E-HIPC scheme has been burdened with multiple and potentially conflicting objectives: (1) debt sustainability, (2) acceleration of long-term growth, and (3) reduction of poverty. With enough resources, and in grant form, it might be possible to reconcile these objectives,[18] but the failure of additionality means that this condition is not satisfied.[19]

The tension between these three objectives and the inadequate size of the resource envelope also causes a strong tendency to make highly optimistic export projections for the debt sustainability analyses that underpin the E-HIPC packages. For the twenty-four HIPC countries analyzed by OED, the projected export growth rate was more than twice the historical average for 1990-2000, almost six times the average for 1980-2000, and almost twice as fast as the growth actually achieved in 2000-01. Not surprisingly, Bretton Woods Institution staffs have not been transparent about how these and other key macroeconomic forecasts were derived. Efficiency is bound to suffer if an aid scheme is based on systematically unrealistic assumptions.

Conclusion

The OED evaluation thus draws attention to some serious problems with current debt relief arrangements. Especially if non-additionality continues to dominate, the consistency of the E-HIPC scheme with aid effectiveness is seriously in question.

Some compensating gains can be entered on the other side of the ledger. As Birdsall and Williamson (2002) have argued, aid in the form of debt relief reduces the enormous burden of never-ending debt renegotiations on the (usually few) individuals who can deal with such matters in the public administrations of low-income countries, releasing them for more productive policy analysis. In effect, E-HIPC substitutes untied program aid for tied donor projects and this should reduce transactions costs and enhance local ownership. As the OED report states, E-HIPC also embodies best practice in strengthening institutions and incentives for aid coordination, in seeking in the design of poverty reduction strategy paper (PRSP) processes to strengthen local ownership, and in its greater concern for the social content of agreed policy programs. Moreover, the PRSPs, around which E-HIPC relief is mobilized, have pushed poverty closer to the top of recipient governments' policy agendas and—through their emphasis on participatory approaches—have the potential to engage citizens and civil society much more in policy formation, monitoring, and execution. These are genuine gains, although all parties involved acknowledge that the E-HIPC linkage has seriously degraded quality by inducing governments to rush PRSP processes in order to secure the irrevocable relief that is granted on reaching "completion point."

Hence, the E-HIPC scheme has important positive as well as negative aspects. But the last few pages have surely been enough to show a real danger that E-HIPC is eroding aid effectiveness. At the very least, given the failure of additionality, the desirability of increased debt relief should not be taken as axiomatic. Well-targeted transfers delivered as regular aid by cost-effective means would be preferable to a further absorption of these scarce resources by means of yet more liberal debt relief. The OED report does not argue this but one does not have to read too deeply between the lines to draw that conclusion.

The question for present purposes is, Who is listening and learning? With evaluations of projects and other institution-specific interventions there are, in principle at least, established channels for lesson learning and reasons for believing that examining the past may improve the future. This is less obviously the case with a topic like debt relief, responsibility for which straddles both Bretton Woods Institutions and a large number of creditor-donor governments. The undoubted fact that debt relief is highly political in its motivation further lessens the prospects that evidence will govern future decisions. The OED report, even if actively disseminated, may not carry much weight or even reach those who are influential in these matters. And the Bank's own defensive, stonewalling Management Response to this report is not encouraging.[20]

3. Conditionality: Another Knowledge-Practice Gap?

Another mismatch between known facts and the continuing policies of the aid community generally and the Bretton Woods Institutions in particular relates to the use of conditionality as a means for achieving policy change in aid-recipient countries. Much research, and quite a lot of World Bank (though not International Monetary Fund) rhetoric, emphasizes the limitations of conditionality as an instrument for change. But it can be argued that, at least among low-income indebted countries, governments now face an even wider array of policy stipulations than in the apparent heyday of conditionality in the earlier 1990s.

The issues here are complex and the evidential basis unsatisfactory. But they need examination, because large amounts of public money can be misapplied as the result of reliance on an instrument that fails to deliver the safe-guards it appears to offer.

Doubts about Conditionality[21]

The use of policy conditionality exploded during the 1980s and into the 1990s, as the World Bank became increasingly involved in structural adjust-ment lending, as the IMF extended the range of its own conditions from a fairly narrow macroeconomic focus to a much wider range of "structural" matters, and as various other multilateral and bilateral donors increased their own use of this instrument. From the beginning there was much controversy about the appropriateness of the conditionality designed by the Bretton Woods Institutions, but both they and their critics agreed that these policy stipula-tions were carried out, whether for good or ill.

As the 1990s proceeded and evidence accumulated, however, a growing body of research cast doubt on the efficacy of conditionality. It had long been well known, for example, that a high proportion of IMF programs broke down before the end of their (relatively brief) intended currency.[22] Similarly, casual empiricism suggested that programs of structural adjustment were not work-ing well, at least in many low-income countries. My own work and that of others (listed in endnote 21) began to show the limited impact of Bretton Woods Institution programs and to raise questions that went to the heart of the use of conditionality as a way to achieve policy change. Countries that had received large numbers of successive highly conditional credits were still rated by the Bretton Woods Institutions as having weak, sometimes deteriorat-ing, policies, with little apparent association between programs and policy trends. Programs were often poorly implemented, so that it was not surprising that they produced weak results, but non-compliance with the Bretton Woods Institutions policy stipulations appeared rarely to be punished in any effec-tive or consistent way. When, as was often the case, a conflict of interest was perceived locally between domestic political imperatives and Bretton Woods Institution stipulations, domestic politics usually won. Conditionality relat-ing to governance issues was thus particularly prone to be ineffectual.[23]

The use of conditionality came to be seen as conflicting with a growing consensus about the need for local "ownership" of chosen reforms, and as undermining the credibility, and therefore effectiveness, of the measures that were undertaken. Governments had learned that they would probably suffer no more than temporary inconvenience as a result of failure to implement "agreed" conditions.[24] The Bretton Woods Institutions (and donors) had strong institutional imperatives to keep aid flowing, not least a desire to protect the servicing of past credits, and these imperatives were often reinforced by the staff incentives within these institutions. By providing the appearance but not the reality of safeguarding against poor policy performance, over-reliance on conditionality was blamed for resulting in major misallocations and waste of public monies.[25] Far better, the critics argued, would be greater insistence on local ownership and more selectivity in the choice of governments to be supported.

The World Bank and members of its staff have contributed quite strongly to the negative evidence. In the words of one Bank report (1995, p.1), "adjustment lending has mostly promoted good policies, but got weak program results." An important Bank study of Africa concluded flatly that "Conditionality as an instrument to promote reform has been a failure" (Devarajan et al., 2001). Another Bank report (1998) concluded that conditionality had been ineffectual where reform lacked political support and had been counterproductive in some cases. More examples could be cited but the point is that the Bank appeared to acknowledge as valid the critique of conditionality and to share it.

Institutional Responses

It was reasonable, then, to expect a fairly strong movement away from reliance on conditionality but this has not occurred. Some donors, notably the UK and European Union, have been trying to diminish such reliance, moving instead to greater selectivity and to relationships with recipient governments based more on dialogue, ownership, and partnership.

Within the World Bank, voices are urging movement in the same direction, particularly in connection with the new Poverty Reduction Support Credit (PRSC) facility. But there is a large apparent disconnect between the Bank's own evidence on conditionality and its continuing heavy reliance upon it. The average number of conditions per Bank program rose sharply during the later 1980s, peaked at fifty-eight in 1988-92, and declined in the latter half of the 1990s.[26] The biggest reductions occurred in what the Bank calls "nonbinding" conditions (from 23 to 8) with a smaller proportionate reduction in the more serious "legally-binding" conditions (35 to 28). In any case, the 1998-2000 average was still well above the numbers that prevailed in the earlier 1980s, and even in the later period Bank staff regarded only 37 percent of all conditions as "very relevant" to the attainment of loan objectives. Moreover, the share of adjustment lending has grown to new record levels—64 percent in 2002—and with it the importance of conditionality.[27] There is ample scope for streamlining action by the Bank, comparable with what is occurring in the International Monetary Fund, but there are no strong signals that this is occurring.

In the Fund, a substantial "streamlining" exercise introduced in 2000 aims to reduce the number of "structural" conditions in Fund-supported programs[28] and to focus conditionality more on actions regarded as critical to program success and within the Fund's own core areas of expertise. Early evidence suggests that this exercise has appreciably reduced the number of structural conditions on average, but with wide variations from country to country.[29] It remains unclear to what extent the streamlining exercise should be seen as a response to the weaknesses of conditionality. On one view, it is a rather narrowly conceived efficiency measure, as reflected in the Fund's *Annual Report* for 2001: "the main goal of streamlining was to make conditionality more efficient, effective, and focused..."[30] In his comment on the present paper, Goldsbrough (see Comments in this chapter) argues, however, that streamlining should be viewed more broadly and as concerned with enhancing local ownership. Streamlining seeks to reverse the proliferation of structural conditions, calls for greater clarity in program documents about what constitutes Fund conditionality, and seeks to ensure that, in countries where both agencies are operating, there will be a clear division of responsibility on policy matters between the Fund and the Bank. The exercise is confined exclusively to what the Fund classifies as "structural" conditionality, with no comparable change in the Fund's traditional macroeconomic stipulations. Streamlining, in other words, is a fairly limited exercise and once we lift our eyes from the purely quantitative aspect of conditionality, it is by no means clear that it marks a real move away from reliance on conditionality per se.

A relatively new element in the situation, with potential for reduced reliance on conditionality, is the initiation of poverty reduction strategy papers (PRSPs) as a focus around which the Bretton Woods Institutions and bilateral donors can harmonize their assistance (and also their debt relief under E-HIPC). In principle, PRSPs can be viewed as an attempt to replace old ways of doing business, replacing them with broad-based, locally owned strategies in which policy commitments are self-defined by the responsible governments, subject only to "endorsement" by the Bretton Woods Institution boards.

But though there is real potential here, it is by no means clear that the move towards PRSPs constitutes a move away from Bretton Woods Institution-defined policy conditions. HIPC governments must now concern themselves with further conditionality arising from the Bank's country assistance strategy papers, as well as that specific to the HIPC completion-point arrangements,[31] to say nothing of the stipulations of other multilateral and bilateral donors. Countries that aspire to join the European Union also have the EU's conditionality to worry about. HIPC conditionality alone is potentially both onerous and wide ranging, with its content recently summarized as normally centered on macroeconomic issues, structural reforms, social sectors, and "other poverty reduction requirements," especially governance and budget management issues.[32] Not much is left out there! There are also reports of bilateral donors picking up structural conditions that are being dropped by the Fund as a result of streamlining[33] and of the Fund actually increasing its stipulations for actions in the governance area. It may well prove that the E-HIPC–PRSP arrangements have provided a vehicle for further increasing conditionality, despite all the rhetoric of ownership.

Two other considerations rather reinforce this view. One is the prospect that the more important structural conditions dropped as a result of Fund streamlining will be taken up in Bank credits. According to a Fund staff report on initial experiences with streamlining, the Bank is "strengthening" its conditionality in areas, such as privatization, health system reform, and public sector reform, from which the Fund is scaling back. In a number of cases, the report states, "measures no longer covered by Fund conditionality were incorporated as conditions by the Bank, but in others this was not the case." (IMF, 2001d, pp.17, 34). Eurodad (2003) is more categorical:

> World Bank involvement in the areas where the IMF pulls out is seen as a prerequisite for streamlining and the findings of this paper suggest that indeed the World Bank is taking over conditions left by the IMF in an aggressive manner.

The second consideration concerns the extent of cross-conditionality between the two Bretton Woods Institutions. There has long been *de facto* cross-conditionality from Fund to Bank adjustment programs, but under the arrangements between the Bank and Fund concerning their Poverty Reduction and Growth Facility (PRGF) and Poverty Reduction Support Credit (PRSC) programs the degree of cross-conditionality has been increased at the level of broad performance. The boards of both institutions state that cross-conditionality should not be applied to policy specifics within either program, and that each institution is "separately accountable for its lending decisions..." (IMF-World Bank, 2001, p. 26).

What the above adds up to is a major disjuncture between a rather widely shared perception that conditionality is a flawed instrument and the continuing practices of the Bretton Woods Institutions (as well as donor agencies). Much of the reason no doubt lies with the difficulty of persuading executive boards to move away from conditionality and of presenting alternatives that would satisfy them. Another source of difficulty, as Thomas (2002) has recently argued, may be that a good deal of the evidence on which the critique of conditionality was based relates to the 1980s and early 1990s, since when the record of compliance may have improved and with it the usefulness of conditionality.

Is Compliance Improving?

Both Bretton Woods Institutions can point to some evidence of improvement. OED's reviews of development effectiveness in Bank adjustment lending operations report a rise in "satisfactory or better" outcome scores, from around 60 percent in the 1980s to 86 percent in FY1999-00 (or 97 percent when weighted by disbursements). As regards the Fund, a recent review of the performance of conditions in twenty-four operations found that only 10 percent of conditions were not implemented, while 65 percent were fully implemented,[34] but against this, other Fund evidence suggests that program failure remains a large and growing problem. Recent IMF working papers provide evidence of such difficulties. Mussa and Savastino (1999, Table 2) rate as failures those programs where actual disbursements are less than half of agreed amounts; they show a rising proportion of programs failing this test over the last two decades, after an earlier period of apparently improving outcomes (Table 3.3).

Ivanova et al. (2003, Table 1) similarly show that in 1992-98 only one-fourth of ESAF/PRGF programs were *not* subject to some interruption and that nearly half (45 percent) experienced irreversible interruptions.[35] Similarly, the first report of the recently created Independent Evaluation Office of the IMF, on the issue of the "prolonged use" of Fund resources, shows, both absolutely and proportionately, that prolonged use has been a continuous and rather steeply rising trend, from the late 1970s at least through 2000.[36] This evidence too is consistent with the view that Fund conditionality is ineffectual, perhaps increasingly so.

Econometric analysis by Ivanova et al. (2003) confirms the finding of independent researchers that domestic political economy factors are dominant determinants of Fund program success. Thomas (2003, forthcoming) found that neither heightened effort by Fund staff nor even increased resort to prior actions could substitute for favorable political economy conditions and that they had no significant influence on the likelihood of program implementation. A Fund paper on conditionality policy issues asserted, apparently with approval, that the primary role of Bretton Woods Institutions "is to identify reformers, not to create them" and that "IFIs should have no illusions that their conditionality will appreciably affect the probability of reform."[37] Indeed, the Fund's own Executive Board is on record as stating that "conditionality cannot compensate for a lack of program ownership." These influences have led to a recent Board paper on the strengthening of country ownership in Fund programs.[38]

Table 3.3
Increased Failure Rate of IMF Programs

	Percentage of programs less than 50 percent disbursed
1983-87	29
1988-92	33
1993-97	46

Source: Mussa and Savastino (1999), Table 2.

The Case for an Evaluation

The evidence on the more recent record of conditionality is too mixed and incomplete to permit a firm judgment on whether the earlier-identified weaknesses have been reduced and whether further action is necessary. A major research and evaluation effort, which should at least straddle both Bretton Woods Institutions, could update the evidence and answer some of the many unresolved questions:

- Given new developments, such as the E-HIPC initiative, the increased use of PRSPs, and the IMF's streamlining exercise, what is the overall trend in policy conditionality? Do governments today have greater room for maneuver in policymaking? What difference is IMF streamlining making?
- Have there been decisive changes in institutional and staff incentives that gave priority to new lending over the implementation of past programs?
- Is there evidence of more effective sanctions against non-compliance (other than that which arises from shocks) and of more selective decision making on which governments to support? Has the HIPC initiative made any difference in this respect, by reducing pressures for defensive lending?
- To what extent have the negotiation styles and modalities of the Bretton Woods Institutions changed in order to foster better relationships and greater borrower ownership of the programs supported?

4. Monitoring and Evaluating the Donors

The shift in favor of partnership-based program aid has implications for the level at which evaluation work needs to be undertaken and for who should undertake it. Because program aid supports a government's general program of development and poverty reduction, its evaluation needs to be undertaken at the countrywide level. But if the notion of partnership—and the desire to move to relationships less reliant on the dubious efficacy of conditionality—is to be taken seriously, there are implications also for who should undertake such evaluative work. At present, almost all monitoring and evaluation at the country level is by donors of recipients, raising the question of who will scrutinize the donors. The logic of partnership is that increasingly such monitoring should be jointly conducted or sponsored and cover the performance of all parties, not just recipients. Some donors might claim that their evaluations are already joint, in the sense that terms of reference, consultants, and so forth must be approved by recipient governments, but most will admit in private that this is largely a formality, with little substantive meaning.

There is today increased questioning of the past pattern of aid relationships and more desire to move towards a new paradigm. OECD's Development Assistance Committee has been doing much work to compare experiences and to promote greater harmonization of donor policies and practices.[39] It has also begun to discuss the possibilities of evaluations led by recipient countries. There are fairly strong moves towards establishing aid relationships based on "partnership," which implies co-equality and mutual acceptance of responsibilities. In connection with the New Partnership for African Development (NEPAD) initiative and in collaboration with the OECD, the Economic Commission for Africa has been promoting the idea of mutual donor-recipient accountability and of joint reviews of developmental effectiveness—another manifestation of the same desire for a changed paradigm.

This section draws attention to an experiment conducted in Tanzania and urges wider adoption of the model employed there.[40] So far as is known, this has been a unique experiment, although a more limited version has been employed in Rwanda.[41]

The Tanzanian Case

The history is as follows. An escalating crisis in relations between donors and the Government of Tanzania (GoT) came to a head in early 1995 at a Consultative Group (CG) meeting. Donors suspected large-scale misuse of aid counterpart funds and alleged high-level corruption in the tax-collection system. For their part, the Government saw the donors as excessively intrusive and unrealistically demanding. Trust broke down.

In an attempt to reverse this deterioration, the Danish Government in 1993-94 established an ad hoc Group of Independent Advisers whose broad task was to explore whether and how donor-GoT relations could be improved. The Group was chaired by Professor G. K. Helleiner, a well-known Canadian international economist with long-standing experience in Tanzania, and included four other members—two Tanzanians and two non-Tanzanians. It was important that all members were quite senior and were regarded as independent of both GoT and donors. The Group heard evidence from virtually all donors in the country, from a range of GoT ministries and agencies, and from other interested parties. Its report, in June 1995, criticized both the GoT and donors and presented recommendations for improving the situation. It urged major changes in relationships between the two parties and in the operational cultures of both.[42]

The elections of late 1995 ushered in a new president, Mkapa, who was determined to improve the situation and decided to use the Helleiner report as a basis for doing so. The report led directly to an eighteen-point action program between the GoT and donors to redefine the terms of their development cooperation, including through enhanced GoT leadership in development programming, and increased transparency, accountability, and efficiency in aid delivery. The elaboration of a framework for cooperation culminated in the preparation of a Tanzania Assistance Strategy, published in 2002.

Following the GoT-donor agreement of January 1997, it was agreed to monitor the implementation of the action program and to report on progress to meetings of the Consultative Group in 1997, 1999, and 2000. At the latter meeting, it was agreed that the monitoring activity was beneficial but needed to be institutionalized, and as a result, in February 2002, the GoT and donors jointly appointed an Independent Monitoring Group (IMG) to review progress in aid relationships. The IMG reported to a meeting of the CG in December 2002. Its main message was that the situation had greatly improved since 1995 but that much scope remained for further improvements on all sides. Its many specific recommendations for future improvements included the following:

> Evaluations comparable with that presented in this report should be undertaken every two or three years. These should examine GoT-donor relations in the round, i.e., not be confined to donor performance. They might be given a more specific focus...
>
> We urge that evaluations of government-donor relations similar to our own could usefully be replicated in other aid-dependent countries and recommend that donors suggest to their respective headquarters that they promote the wider use of this type of monitoring activity in other countries. (IMG, 2003)

In terms of replicability, the following features of the IMG are significant:

- The group was again a mix of senior Tanzanian and outside members. It was chaired by a Tanzanian economist who at that time headed the country's leading independent policy research institute. There was one other Tanzanian, a former ambassador, and three external, European-based, members, one of whom (the author of this paper) had also been a member of the original Helleiner group. The group also included a senior Ugandan member. The group had complete autonomy in deciding how to fulfill its terms of reference and in what it said in its report.
- There was a tendering process within Tanzania for a contract to constitute and service the group. This was won by a local think-tank, which provided research, logistical, and administrative back up. It fell to the contractors to identify group members, although various parties made suggestions, and the constitution of the group was subject to approval by the GoT and donors.
- The activity was financed by contributions by various donors into a fund administered by the UN Development Program, which is the lead agency for donor coordination in Tanzania. The local UNDP office oversaw the tendering and contractual processes, but did not provide secretariat services, nor was it represented on the group.
- The TOR for the group required a mix of monitoring and evaluation, although with a greater stress on the former. The Group was asked both to present information on changing aid relationships and to analyze this in order to recommend ways forward.

One other important aspect of the IMG's work should be noted. There had been a tendency locally to think of it as mainly focusing on the policies and modalities of the donors. However, the IMG took a different view:

> An important principle we would urge here is that such exercises should not be confined to monitoring just one side of GoT-donor performance. It has rightly been observed that the GoT is already subjected to intense monitoring by the donors ... whereas such monitoring of the donors as occurs is much less rigorous. The question, "Who will monitor the donors?" is well put. But we would make two points about this: (a) that there is value in reviewing GoT performance independently of the donors because that is likely to yield different insights, and may reinforce the donors in some areas while protecting the government from what may be unwarranted or over-hasty judgments; and (b) that the actions of both parties are likely to be influenced by what is done (or not done) by the other, so that it is not appropriate to judge the performance of the donors except in the context of trends on the government side, and vice versa. (IMG, 2003)

Implicit in the Group's report was a desire that any future such activities should become more evaluation-based, suggesting that future groups might be given somewhat more focused terms of reference, to enable them to achieve greater depth by concentrating on some particular aspect.

Is This a Replicable Model?

One thing to note is that the 1995 and 2002 groups for Tanzania were convened in markedly different circumstances. The first instance was marked by crisis and a breakdown of trust, the task being to find ways of breaking the deadlock and moving forward. The 2002 IMG, by contrast, was convened against the background of general perceptions that much progress had been made and that what was needed was an independent stocktaking, with pointers towards the next steps.

Since the principal new element introduced by independent monitoring is that a searchlight of enquiry is extended to the donors, donors are only likely to agree on such monitoring where their country representatives are willing to open their activities to scrutiny. For the activity to be fruitful, the independent monitors must be able to count on some minimum level of cooperation by local donor agencies, as well as by the government. However, this hurdle may not be high. The 1995 group in Tanzania was initiated and financed by just one donor (Denmark) and was not the result of a collective donor decision, but the group successfully obtained access to all significant donors. The creation of the 2002 group was a more collective decision, facilitated by the existence of an active local development assistance committee and by staff members of the UNDP, though there were dissenting voices and some opposition. Once again, the group was able to talk to virtually everyone it wanted to question. Neither group had problems accessing government officials, although the improvements in the intervening years meant that the intercourse with GoT officials in the second study was much more satisfactory.

A reasonable level of agreement on the desirability of establishing the group in the first place, and existence of forums at which its report can be taken forward, will enhance the possibilities of follow-up action.

One difficulty in the way of wide adoption of the Tanzanian model is the absence of obvious incentives for donors to open themselves up to critical independent investigation. In overcoming the natural reluctance, perhaps the most important ingredient in both Tanzanian studies—and something that is potentially present in all aid-receiving countries—was the existence of individuals minded and positioned to push forward the idea of an independent group. The Danish Ambassador was a crucial player in the mid-1990s; Professor Helleiner and UNDP staff were crucial moving spirits in setting up the 2002 group. Basically, all it needed was a few well-placed individuals from the donor and government sides. There is, as suggested earlier, greater openness now to a search for more satisfactory aid relationships; independent monitoring and evaluation can be used as part of a new model. Others may be unenthusiastic, even hostile, but are likely to want to have their voices heard when a group is actually formed.

What are the key ingredients of a successful group? The following suggest themselves:

- Its members, and particularly its chairperson, should be sufficiently senior and experienced to command respect. Above all, they should be perceived as independent of any particular interest. The group should contain a good balance between nationals of the country in question and of the outside world. Involving a senior official from another country within the same region is an attractive option.
- So far as possible, the group should be so financed as to protect it from suspicion that it would wish to avoid offending its financiers. Similarly, it is better that the group is serviced outside of the government or any donor. The arrangements for the 2002 group in Tanzania were excellent in this respect.
- The group's terms of reference should allow flexibility for enquiries to roam as appears necessary in the light of the information that comes available.
- Preferably mechanisms should be in place that allow the group's recommendations to be considered and acted upon. In Tanzania, the 1995 Group was lucky because of the emergence shortly afterwards of a new reform-minded political leadership. By the time of the 2002 Group, well-organized avenues of dialogue and coordination—most notably a Tanzanian Ministry of Finance with a lively interest in these matters, which had already developed a national assistance strategy and an active and well-led local DAC—had evolved to take forward the Group's recommendations (although it is too early yet to know how much

follow-up there will actually be). Again, the importance of the activist voice should not be discounted.

The above account strongly suggests that the model of the Tanzanian IMG could readily be adopted in other aid-dependent countries. In the context of the conduct of evaluation studies to promote greater aid effectiveness, it points to the desirability of taking the IMG model further as a modality well suited to aid relationships that aspire to develop in the directions of partnership, mutual accountability, and harmonization.

Notes

1. I am grateful for helpful comments on an earlier draft by Howard White and others at the World Bank's Operations Evaluation Department.
2. Brown et al. (2000). In addition, see Annex 3 of OED (1999), which contains a brief discussion of the costs of coordination.
3. Conceptually, this might be thought of as the opportunity cost of the extra volume of reserves it would be necessary to hold in order to smooth out unexpected variations in aid receipts.
4. Lawson et al. (2002).
5. One criticism raised against the conference version of this paper was precisely that I was confusing the costs of program aid with lower-than-expected benefits, i.e., that one needs to think in terms of *net* costs or benefits.
6. See, for example, Lawson et al. (2002).
7. OECD-DAC (2003), p. 103.
8. Buli and Hamann (2001). This paper is, incidentally, an excellent example of how at least some aspects of transactions costs are amenable to rigorous empirical testing.
9. It came only ninth in a list of thirteen ways to improve donor practices. OECD-DAC (2003), p.117.
10. World Bank Operations Evaluation Department (2003).
11. See also Gunter (2001) for a similar finding.
12. For a further argument along these lines, see Easterly (2001).
13. For a survey of the causes of poverty in Africa, see White, Killick, et al. (2001), Part II.
14. The evidence is briefly surveyed in ODI (2003).
15. Castro-Leal et al. (1999).
16. For an elaboration of the following argument, see Killick (2003). I am at this point going beyond the coverage of the OED report. See also Bird and Milne (2003). The source of the following debt statistics is World Bank (2001), pp. 260-61.
17. For a recent examination of the debt-growth connection, see Pattillo et al. (2002). For a large sample of developing countries they find that high levels of debt are associated with lower economic growth, operating through lower factor productivities rather than through investment effects. However, they do not investigate HIPC, or low-income, countries as a sub-sample and are notably cautious in interpreting their results for that group.
18. Although the theory of policy suggests that pursuing three objectives with one instrument is unlikely to be an efficient way of proceeding.
19. Even if it were, there are also problems of design and attention bias, as already shown.

20. In OED (2003), Annex K.
21. The following borrows quite heavily from my own work on conditionality (Killick et al., 1998) but see also Collier et al. (1997); Crawford (1997); Dollar and Svensson (2000); and Mosley et al. (1995).
22. Killick (1995).
23. Crawford (1997) found that in only two out of twenty-nine cases examined was donor pressure effective in inducing political change.
24. Amply justified, in the case of IMF conditionality, by research showing little association between past compliance and future credits. Bird (2002); Dreher (2003).
25. Killick (1998), p. 168.
26. World Bank (2001a) p. 80.
27. Thomas, (2002) p. 2.
28. Which had escalated from an average of two per program in 1987, four in 1994, and fourteen in 1997-99. Goldstein (2000), p.82.
29. Adam and Bevan (2001); Killick (2002); Eurodad (2003).
30. IMF (2001c) p. 45.
31. For example, at a Commonwealth Secretariat-IMF consultation in July 2001, the Tanzanian delegate reported that his government was confronted with no fewer than thirteen specific HIPC completion point conditions, over and above those of the Bretton Woods Institutions.
32. SPA Task Team (2001), p. 9.
33. Debt Relief International (n.d.), para 13.
34. Nestmann and Weder (2002).
35. They also show an apparently more satisfactory 73 percent compliance with program conditions but this figure is hard to interpret because the authors regard this figure as biased upward. For a useful very brief review of other evidence on program effects see IMF (2001a), pp. 45-46. See also Bird (2002) for corroboration of declining IMF program completion rates.
36. IMF Independent Evaluation Office (2002).
37. IMF (2001a), p. 55.
38. IMF (2001b).
39. See, for example, DAC (2003).
40. See also Wangwe (2002) for a more elaborate account and a collection of key documents.
41. In 2000, the Rwandan and UK governments agreed on an independent annual monitoring of the Memorandum of Understanding between them and in 2002 the Netherlands and Swedish governments decided to adopt this model. A monitoring exercise conducted by two independent consultants in October-November 2002 therefore reviewed progress with respect to development cooperation between Rwanda and all three donor countries. (Information kindly provided by DFID, London.)
42. See Helleiner (1995).

References

Adam, C. S., and D. L. Bevan. (2001). "PRGF Stocktaking on Behalf of DFID." Processed. (November). Department of Economics, Oxford University.

Bird, Graham. (2002)."The Completion Rate of IMF Programs." *World Economy* 25 (6).

Bird, Graham, and Alistair Milne. (2003). "Debt Relief for Low-income Countries: Is It Effective and Efficient?" *World Economy* 26 (1).

Birdsall, Nancy, and John Williamson. (2002). *Delivering on Debt Relief.* Washington, DC: Center for Global Development and Institute of International Economics.

Brooks, Ray, Mariano Cortes, Francesca Fornasari, Benoit Ketchekmen, Ydahlia Metzgen, Robert Powell, Saqib Rizavi, Doris Ross, and Kevin Ross. (1998). *External Debt Histories of Ten Low-Income Countries: Lessons from Their Experience.* Working Paper 98/72, Policy Development and Review Department. Washington DC : International Monetary fund.

Brown, A., F. Naschold, T. Conway, and A. Fozzard. (2000). "Aid Transaction Costs in Viet Nam." Processed. (December). London: Overseas Development Institute.

Buli, Aleš, and A. Javier Hamann. (2001). "How Volatile and Unpredictable are Aid Flows, and What are the Policy Implications?" IMF Working Paper WP/01/167. Washington, DC: International Monetary Fund.

Castro-Leal, Florencia, Julia Dayton, Lionel Demery, and Kalpana Mehra. (1999). "Public Social Spending in Africa: Do the Poor Benefit?" *World Bank Research Observer* 14 (1).

Collier, P., P. Guillaumont, S. Guillaumont, and J. W. Gunning. (1997). "Redesigning Conditionality." *World Development* 25 (9).

Crawford, Gordon. (1997). "Foreign Aid and Political Conditionality: Issues of Effectiveness and Consistency." *Democratization* 4 (3).

Dagdeviren, Hulya, and John Weeks. (2001). "How Much Poverty Could HIPC Reduce? (August). Available at www.wider.unu.org.

Debt Relief International. (n. d., 2001?). "Reviewing PRSPs: The Views of HIPC Ministers and PRSP Coordinators." Processed. London: Debt Relief International.

Department for International Development (DFID). (2000). *Eliminating World Poverty: Making Globalisation Work for the Poor.* London: DFID.

Devarajan, Shanta, David Dollar, and Torgny Holmgren. (2001). "Aid and Reform in Africa." Washington, DC: World Bank.

Dollar, David, and Jakob Svensson. (2000). "What Explains the Success or Failure of Structural Adjustment Programs?" *Economic Journal* 110 (October).

Dreher, Axel. (2003). "The Influence of Elections on IMF Program Interruptions." *Journal of Development Studies*. 39(6) : 101-102.

Easterly, William. (2001). "How Did Highly Indebted Countries Become Highly Indebted? Reviewing Two Decades of Debt Relief." World Bank Working Paper 2225. Washington, DC: World Bank.

Eurodad. (2003). "Eurodad 2003 PRGF Research Program: Is the IMF Pro-Poor?" (summary of three unpublished papers). Available through Eurodad website: www.eurodad.org.

Foster, M., A. Brown, and T. Conway. (2000). *Sector-wide Approaches for Health Development: A Review of Experience.* Geneva: World Health Organization.

Goldstein, Morris. (2000). "IMF Structural Conditionality: How Much is Too Much?" (October). Washington, DC: Institute for International Economics.

Gunter, Bernhard. (2001). "Does the HIPC Initiative Achieve Its Goal of Debt Sustainability?" Processed. available at www.wider.unu.edu.

Helleiner, G. K., et al. (1995), *Report of the Group of Independent Advisers on Development Cooperation Issues between Tanzania and Its Aid Donors.* Copenhagen: Royal Danish Ministry of Foreign Affairs.

Independent Monitoring Group. (2003). "Enhancing Aid Relationships in Tanzania." Dar es Salaam: Economic and Social Research Foundation.

International Monetary Fund. (2001a). "Conditionality in Fund-supported Programs— Policy Issues." Processed. (February 20). Washington DC: International Monetary Fund.

_____. (2001b). "Strengthening Country Ownership of Fund-Supported Programs." SM/01/340 (November 13). Washington DC: International Monetary Fund.

_____. (2001c). *Annual Report.* Washington, DC: International Monetary Fund.

_____. (2001d). "Streamlining Structural Conditionality—Review of Initial Experience." SM/01/219 (July 12). Washington DC: International Monetary Fund

International Monetary Fund Independent Evaluation Office. (2002). *Evaluation of Prolonged Use of IMF Resources.* Washington, DC: International Monetary Fund.

International Monetary Fund and World Bank. (2001). "Strengthening IMF-World Bank Collaboration on Country Programs and Conditionality." Processed. (August). Washington, DC: International Monetary Fund and World Bank.

Ivanova, A., W. Mayer, A. Mourmouras, and G. Anayiotos. (2003). *What Determines the Success or Failure of Fund-Supported Programs?* Working Paper WP/03/08. Washington, DC: International Monetary Fund.

Killick, Tony. (1995). *IMF Programs in Developing Countries: Design and Impact.* London and New York: Routledge and Overseas Development Institute.

_____. (1998). *Aid and the Political Economy of Policy Change.* London: Routledge and Overseas Development Institute.

_____. (2002). "The 'Streamlining' of IMF Conditionality: Aspirations, Reality and Repercussions." Report for Department for International Development, London. Processed. (April).

_____. (2002b). "Helleiner on Africa in the Global Economy." *Canadian Journal of African Studies.* 36 (3).

Lawson, A., D. Booth, A. Harding, D. Hoole, and F. Naschold. (2002). "General Budget Support Evaluability Study, Phase I. Final Synthesis Report." Report to UK Department for International Development. (December). Oxford: Policy Management and Overseas Development Institute.

Mosley, Paul, Jane Harrigan, and John Toye. (1995). *Aid and Power: The World Bank and Policy-based Lending*, Volume 1, 2nd ed. London: Routledge.

Mussa, Michael, and Miguel Savastino. (1999). "The IMF Approach to Economic Stabilization." Working Paper WP/99/104.Washington, DC: International Monetary Fund.

Nestmann, Thorsten, and Beatrice Weder. (2002). "The Effectiveness of International Aid and Debt Relief: A Selective Review of the Literature." Paper prepared for the 5th Limburg seminar on financing and development. Processed.

Netherlands Ministry of Foreign Affairs. (2003). "Coordination and Sector Support: An Evaluation of the Netherlands Support to Local Governance in Uganda, 1991-2001." The Hague: Policy and Evaluation Department (June).

Organization for Economic Cooperation and Development, Development Center. (2003). *Harmonizing Donor Practices for Effective Aid Delivery.* Paris: Organization for Economic Cooperation and Development.

Overseas Development Institute (ODI). (2003). *Can We Attain the Millennium Development Goals in Education and Health through Public Expenditure and Aid?* ODI Briefing Paper. (March). London: Overseas Development Institute.

Pattillo, Catherine, Hélène Poirson, and Luca Ricci. (2002). *External Debt and Growth.* Working Paper WP/02/69. Washington, DC: International Monetary Fund.

Ranis, Gustav, and Frances Stewart. (2001). "The Debt Relief Initiative for Poor Countries: Good News for the Poor?" *World Economics* 12 (3) (July-September).

SPA Task Team on Contractual Relationships and Selectivity. (2001). "Comparative Review of I-PRSP Targets and Conditionalities for HIPC Completion Point." DEV/B/2/ FCS D (October). Processed. Brussels: European Commission.

Thomas, Allun. (2004). *Prior Actions—True Repentance? An Evaluation Based on IMF Programs over the 1992-99 Period.* Working Paper (cited by Ivanova et al.). Washington, DC: International Monetary Fund.

Thomas, M. A. (n. d., ca. 2002). "Can the World Bank Enforce Its Own Conditions?" Washington, DC: World Learning.

Wangwe, Samuel M. (ed.). (2002). *NEPAD at Country Level: Aid Relationships in Tanzania.* Dar es Salaam: Mkuki na Nyota Publishers.

White, Howard, and Tony Killick with S. Kayizzi-Mugera and M. A. Savane. (2001). *African Poverty at the Millennium.* Washington, DC: World Bank.

White, Howard, and Geske Dijkstra. (2003). *Program Aid and Development: Beyond Conditionality.* London and New York: Routledge.

World Bank. (1995). "Higher Impact Adjustment Lending." Report of a Working Group to SPA Plenary. (October). Washington, DC: World Bank.

_____. (1998). *Assessing Aid: What Works, What Doesn't and Why.* Washington, DC: World Bank.

_____. (2001a). "Adjustment Lending Retrospective: Final Report." Operations Policy and Country Services Department. (June 15). Washington, DC: World Bank.

_____. (2001b). *Global Development Finance.* Washington, DC: World Bank, pp.260-61.

World Bank Operations Evaluation Department (OED). (1999). *The Drive to Partnership: Aid Coordination and the World Bank.* Washington, DC: World Bank Operations Evaluation Department.

_____. (2003). *Debt Relief for the Poorest: An OED Review of the HIPC Initiative.* Washington, DC: World Bank Operations Evaluation Department.

Comments on the papers by White and Killick

Rob D. van den Berg

I agree with almost everything Howard White puts forward in his paper, but the issue of relevance merits further discussion. The evaluation community to a large extent still looks at relevance as a question of the coherence or consistency of development *inputs* with policy goals. That is, the focus is very much on the *ex ante* relevance of planned activities for policy goals. But in a time of results-based management and budgeting, the focus should be on whether the *results* of our actions are in line with policy goals and the problems that these goals are trying to address. Such a focus on results instead of inputs does not require a new definition of relevance in the Development Assistance Committee (DAC) criteria for assessing aid, but it does call for further support for impact assessment, as White urges.

Tony Killick's paper paints a pessimistic picture of the current state of development aid and raises disturbing questions. Killick argues that too much money is going to the Highly Indebted Poor Countries (HIPC) initiative, concentrating scarce resources in countries that are clearly not performing well macroeconomically. But the evaluation by the World Bank's Operations Evaluation Department[1] shows that HIPC will only succeed if additional money

Director, Policy and Operations Evaluation Department, Ministry of Foreign Affairs, The Netherlands, and chair of the OECD Development Assistance Committee Network on Development Evaluation.

comes in. So money goes from good performers to bad performers, and it is not really enough to help the bad performers. Aid effectiveness in general will probably decline as a result. OED's report is written from an optimistic perspective rather than a pessimistic one. Where Killick argues that HIPC will probably fail, because its success depends on additional money coming in, OED argues that HIPC will probably succeed, provided that additional money comes in. On conditionalities, overoptimistic assumptions, and sky-high ambitions, OED carefully notes improvements that have taken place over the past few years. For Killick these improvements are clearly not enough. He calls for a more in-depth evaluation of program aid and proposes to focus this on the use of conditionalities.

In my view Killick's proposal is not sufficient. His paper compliments OED's HIPC evaluation report by saying that the negative side of the coin can be inferred from the positive side that the report presents. He shows us the negative side and then concludes that an in-depth evaluation of conditionalities would be appropriate. In doing so, he takes the OED position in the HIPC evaluation as his starting point.

I want to go beyond that. To be sure, OED's evaluation of HIPC is excellent, coming up with crucial findings and hopefully helping World Bank management to move in the right direction. Yet it is a report of relatively narrow scope, which should lead us to even more basic questions than Tony has raised.

First, the OED report does not address the cause of the debt situation. This can be compared to the doctor prescribing a medicine for the symptoms rather than the causes of your illness. If you do not know why you are sick, are you sure that the medicine will cure you? Second, more crucially, the report does not address the role of the World Bank in creating the debt situation. The doctor who gives you the right medicine today (debt relief), may have given you the wrong medicine (loans) yesterday. And, in fact, the doctor is looking at you right now, to see whether the right medicine is taking on, so that he can give you some more misguided medicine tomorrow. And is this perhaps a factor in why the doctor is overoptimistic in his assumptions on whether the right medicine will take?

Why did OED not raise these questions in the HIPC evaluation? OED is very independent of management; it reports directly to the World Bank's Board. However, OED is not independent of the Board. What is not clear either from the OED evaluation or from Killick's paper is what role the World Bank's Board has played in the HIPC initiative. That role may be more problematic than we often assume. Who will evaluate the role the Board plays and has played? Is OED mandated to do so? Is there a need for an evaluation on so high a level? In the Netherlands, the Court of Auditors is a high organ of state, independent of the executive branch of government and of Parliament. In a recent evaluation, it criticized the Dutch government for being overly ambitious, with too many policies and not enough means to implement them all.

The role of Parliament was evaluated as well: in fact many of the unrealistic ambitions of the Dutch government could be attributed indirectly (and sometimes directly) to parliamentary initiatives, questions, debates, and so on. My question is: who can play the role of Supreme Audit Institution in the case of the World Bank? At present, nobody.

Are there safeguards in the present setup? Let me point to the democratic deficit in the governance of the World Bank. The Bank's executive directors formally do not represent its members. They do not operate "under instruction," as the permanent representatives of member states in the European Union or other international organizations do. Furthermore, many executive directors represent more than one country. Who evaluates what they are doing?

Why is this important? If it is true that debt relief is based on unrealistic assumptions, is there not a chance that the loans that added to the debts were based on unrealistic assumptions as well? And if so, who is to blame for that? Currently, the recipient country is blamed. It has incurred the debts and should be happy that the International Monetary Fund and World Bank are coming to its rescue. But if the blame lies partly or wholly on the side of the Fund and Bank, these institutions should carry the costs or part of the costs. This means that the missing money should not be found through a debt relief operation, but through additional capital contributions of the members to the Fund and Bank. This raises many disturbing questions, which I cannot go into right now. Suffice it to say that the issue of the World Bank's contribution to debt problems as opposed to debt relief has only been raised by critics of the Bank in the United States, coming from the right side of the political spectrum. Perhaps it is time to raise this issue from other sides as well, so that an answer may be found and the development community may learn from experience.

This leads me to pose three challenges for the evaluation departments of the World Bank and International Monetary Fund:

1. Given the central role that these two agencies play in macroeconomic issues in partner countries, the Operations Evaluation Department of the Bank and the Independent Evaluation Office (IOE) of the Fund should join an initiative recently started by the United Kingdom Department for International Development, with the support of the DAC Evaluation Network, to develop a common framework for (joint or parallel) evaluation of general budget support. I challenge them to do so.
2. OED should follow up its successful HIPC evaluation with an in-depth study of the results of debt relief.
3. OED and IOE should find a way to evaluate independently the governance of their institutions. There are two possibilities for doing so. One is to invite the International OrganiZation of Supreme Audit Institutions to undertake such an evaluation. Another is to undertake a joint evaluation including other evaluation departments in this exercise. I do not agree with Frances Stewart's view (chapter 1) that joint evaluations are not useful. They can be especially useful to provide an independent viewpoint

that any one of the partners may not achieve on its own. Furthermore, the results of a joint evaluation may have more authority and as a result more impact than those of an evaluation by a single agency.

Lastly, let me briefly address my remaining issue with Killick's paper: evaluating the donors. It seems that here Killick argues on the misunderstanding that donors tend to evaluate partner countries. The truth is that donors tend to evaluate themselves. In these evaluations, partner countries are often mentioned as the reason why donors' policies have not been as successfully implemented as they could have been. Given this slight change in perspective, I find the Tanzanian model very interesting. It is not as unique as Tony claims; there have been other initiatives, most notably an evaluation of the donors by South Africa. But I support his call for more of these initiatives.

Note

1.   World Bank Operations Evaluation Department (2003).

Reference

World Bank Operations Evaluation Department (OED). (2003). *Debt Relief for the Poorest: An OED Review of the HIPC Initiative*. Washington, DC: World Bank Operations Evaluation Department.

Comments on the papers by White and Killick

David Goldsbrough

Drawing upon the experience of evaluation of International Monetary Fund-supported programs, I will comment on two aspects of the papers by White and Killick: (1) why there is a wide gap between evaluation evidence and policy practices; and (2) how best to direct the further investments that are needed in evaluation techniques.

Why does there seem to be such a wide gap between the evaluation evidence and practice? I will focus particularly on the policy conditionality issue—what Tony Killick refers to as the Who's listening? question. Here I suspect part of the answer is that it depends on Who's talking. The evidence about the efficacy of conditionality is largely negative and belies the continued leaning toward conditionality by both the Bretton Woods Institutions and donors more generally. An important part of the reason lies in ambiguity about objectives. Take the case of the initiative to streamline Fund conditionality. Killick's paper, quoting the IMF *Annual Report*, says that the objectives of Fund streamlining were relatively limited: to reduce the proliferation of struc-

Deputy director, Independent Evaluation Office, International Monetary Fund.

tural conditions and to improve the Fund's division of labor with the World Bank. Those objectives are essentially to make conditionality more efficient, rather than to change its structure or broad goals. Yet the policy papers that provided the background to the streamlining initiative make clear that there was also a broader objective in mind, of enhancing ownership, and that that objective increased its importance in the context of the Poverty Reduction and Growth Facility (PRGF), which is the Fund's lending instrument linked to poverty reduction strategy papers. The policy documents make an explicit link between streamlining conditionality and ownership.

The lack of clarity about how to pursue these dual goals of "efficiency" (i.e., improved division of labor) and "ownership" simultaneously leads to conflicting expectations. If ownership were paramount, you would expect to see aggregate World Bank/IMF conditionality decline. If narrow efficiency concerns were paramount, then you would not necessarily expect to see aggregate conditionality decline. The lack of clarity about which objective is paramount also means that it is possible for evaluators to come to very different conclusions from the same evidence. This is the "Who's talking?" part of the issue. Internal assessments essentially focus on the efficiency objective. Assessments by civil society of various Fund and Bank activities related to the poverty reduction strategy papers tend to focus on the ownership objective; they may not always meet all of the methodological challenges that Howard White mentioned, but they are essentially coming to rather negative conclusions.

Certainly, the objectives underlying the streamlining of conditionality are less than clear when one tries to evaluate what the two Bretton Woods institutions combined—rather than the IMF alone—are trying to do.

Conditions on structural policy issues included in Fund-supported programs are monitored, and they certainly have started to decline. But we do not have a good database of what has happened to aggregate Bank/Fund conditionality, let alone conditionality involving other donors. Databases within the Fund and the Bank contain relevant data: the Monitoring of Arrangements (MONA) database in the Fund, and a database on conditionality in adjustment lending, the ALCID database, in the Bank. But neither of these is in the public domain, for reasons I have never fully understood, nor are they easily comparable. And they are not being used to think about the conditionality issue in the sense of what the two institutions collectively are doing.

I suspect another reason why policy makers are reluctant to act on the evaluation evidence about conditionality is that it is difficult in practice to carry out the essential corollary of reducing conditionality—that is, to exercise greater selectivity in providing financial assistance to countries. As Killick notes in the context of the HIPC debt relief, it has in fact been very difficult to impose selectivity based on assessments that countries are ready to implement domestically owned adjustment strategies. There are many political pressures.

An evaluation that the Fund's Independent Evaluation Office did of the prolonged use of IMF resources gave very much the same message—that it is quite difficult to decide not to support a country because of its track record, even if the government hasn't changed.[1] What tends to happen, therefore, is that the imperfect tool of conditionality is still leaned upon to try and overcome the problems, despite the extensive evidence that conditionality is a very imperfect tool.

White's paper makes the point that more investment is needed in evaluation techniques, as is more thinking about impact evaluations. Where should we place this investment to get the biggest bang for the buck, particularly in program-type evaluation work? The IMF's experience suggests two messages here. First, in the business the Fund is in, there are limits to what even good techniques can yield in terms of evaluating final impacts (e.g., on growth). Because the chain of events is long, with actions by the Fund, the Bank, or by donors, and because the final results are macro-level results, it is very difficult to assign effects to causes. Attribution is much harder than it is in evaluating an intervention at a more micro or sectoral level. Second, as Frances Stewart has noted, the techniques for defining the counterfactual have methodological limits; there is a risk of getting results from the methodology you have used rather than getting an ultimate assessment of what value has been added. The real bang for the buck is going to be in what White refers to as unpacking the causal chain—that is, in thinking about what types of policies and what types of institutional change affect the final macro outcomes and then thinking about what interventions, by the Fund, Bank, or other agencies, can do to effect those types of changes.

Note

1.   IMF (2002).

Reference

Independent Evaluation Office, International Monetary Fund. (2002). "Evaluation of Prolonged Use of IMF Resources." Available at www.imf.org/ieo.

Floor Discussion

Participant: Evaluation today has to be understood as more than a technical function. But now that multilateral and bilateral agencies have changed the unit of account for their evaluations, from project to program or from sector to country level, are these higher-order evaluations yielding more useful information for their sponsoring organizations? And what do aid recipient countries think: will the methodological improvements lead to more acceptance of the evaluation function and to obtaining more application of the results of evaluations?

Killick: As to whether higher-level evaluations yield better results, I will take the case of country-level evaluations. I believe that internal and external evaluations of IMF programs give a fairly good indication of the uses and limitations of these programs. Some of the uses are powerful; very large sums of money are associated with these programs, and increasingly large sums of money are associated with program aid of various kinds. So we need to get the best possible information about the effectiveness and impact of program aid. Thus, because they give us the kind of knowledge that influences policy, country-level evaluations are extremely important. But they still face the limitation mentioned by Frances Stewart: that the counterfactual is unknowable. So while we clearly need crosscutting evaluations, particularly because these are directly addressed to major questions of policy, we need to be aware of their limitations.

White: We need to build up evaluation capacity in developing countries so that donors and international financial institutions can get out of the development evaluation business. Having aid recipient governments do evaluation is a good way to build their capacity. I also believe that if aid takes the form of programmatic budget support, and recipient governments evaluate it, better decisions will be made on the uses of aid. I believe we should invest very strongly in building up the capacity of governments to undertake evaluations of the sort we're currently doing in the World Bank's Operations Evaluation Department. We may want to exercise some quality control function, but basically, our view should be, "This money was spent by you for your people; please give us a report on how well you think it was used." That report can be produced either by governments or by independent think tanks within those countries.

Participant: We all agree on the desirability of transferring responsibility for evaluation to aid-recipient countries. But this is not just a matter of transferring the capacity: political demand for evaluation is not there. The question is, How do we foster that demand both in the medium and the long term?

Participant: To pick up on a point made by Rob van den Berg, if we evaluate the decisions of the World Bank's Executive Board, do we not evaluate the decisions of the Bank's member states?

Van den Berg: As far as I know, the executive directors of the World Bank do not operate under instruction from their headquarters—unlike, for instance, the permanent representative of a member state in an international organization. Individual executive directors may represent a group of member states. So the question is, Who evaluates what the executive directors are doing?

Participant: A question for Howard White: what evidence do you have that the Millennium Development Goals (MDGs) are being taken seriously?

White: Let me take the example of the UK Department of International Development (DFID), which was one of the first agencies to sign up to the MDGs (in November 1997). Over the following four years, DFID realigned its goals and changed the nature of its operations in accordance with the MDGs. The strategy for each country takes the Millennium Development Goals as its reference point. There has been a big shift in the UK aid portfolio. For example, UK aid to China used to go mainly to the eastern seaboard, for infrastructure and engineering projects; it was mainly financed by what was called the Aid and Trade Provision (part commercial loans, part aid money) and was all tied to British providers. Today the aid and trade provision has been closed; tied aid has been abandoned; and the money all goes to health and education in the central highlands, one of China's poorest areas. In Zambia, the bulk of UK aid goes to health and education, but whereas in the early 1990s, most of it went into teacher salaries in secondary schools and to the university teaching hospital in Lusaka, now it goes to primary schools and rural health centers and urban clinics.

Participant: Clearly, there has been a shift in the assumptions underlying development. Has this shift resulted from a meaningful dialogue between developing and developed nations, or just from a dialogue among donor nations?

Participant: In evaluating the effectiveness of aid we should set aid in context: is there an inconsistency in donor aid policies and other donor policies such as trade? What is then the overall effect on the aid-recipient country?

Participant: What has been the impact of the IMF's Independent Evaluation Office (IEO) on Fund programs and policies?

Goldsbrough: First, I should mention that the constitution of the IEO provides that after its first three years of operation, IEO itself will be evaluated. Second, to give an example of our impact, our evaluation of the prolonged use of IMF resources made a number of recommendations calling for changes in the internal processes of the IMF. These have now been approved by the Board, so systemic changes will take place.

Part 2

Evaluating the Performance of Development Agencies

4

Evaluating the Performance of Development Agencies: The Role of Meta-Evaluations

Frans L. Leeuw and Leslie J. Cooksy

Development organizations such as the World Bank, the Consultative Group on International Agricultural Research, the UN Development Program, and others focus on the goal of reducing poverty in the world. Their work involves enormous investments of money, time, and talent. Because of the size of the investments, both donors and society need to be informed about the effects of these organizations' work. Therefore, these organizations have been investing in evaluation capacity, M&E (monitoring and evaluation), and project and program evaluations, often in rather large numbers. In recent years, more attention has been given to meta-evaluations. Sometimes the term "meta-evaluation" is used to describe a comprehensive study of a development agency's performance.[1] More often, meta-evaluations are evaluations of evaluations.

This paper looks at the concept of meta-evaluation in two ways: first it reviews the use of the term "meta-evaluation," in the field of evaluation in general; then it argues that meta-evaluation is a critical component of the evaluation of development agencies and their interventions.

1. Meta-Evaluation: What is It and Why Do It?

Meta-evaluation is generally defined as a systematic review of evaluations to determine the quality of their processes and findings.[2] Stufflebeam gives a definition that operationalizes the concept of quality: meta-evaluation is the

Chief review officer, Education Review Office, Government of the Netherlands, and professor, Policy and Program Evaluation, Department of Sociology, Utrecht University.

Director, Center for Community Research and Service, University of Delaware.

"process of delineating, obtaining, and applying information and judgmental information—about the utility, feasibility, propriety, and accuracy of an evaluation and its systematic nature, competent conduct, integrity/honesty, respectfulness, and social responsibility to guide the evaluation and/or report its strengths and weaknesses."[3]

The practice of meta-evaluation has been championed by a number of evaluation luminaries, including Chelimsky (1987), Cook and Gruder (1978), Greene (1992), Larson and Berliner (1983), Schwandt and Halpern (1988), Scriven (1991), and Stufflebeam (1981), among others. The importance of meta-evaluation has not diminished, as recent publications show. Stufflebeam (2001) describes meta-evaluation as "a professional obligation of evaluators" (p. 146). A forthcoming volume edited by Schwartz and Mayne (2004) further reinforces the importance of quality assurance in evaluation; they also present suggestions on how to control quality.

Meta-evaluation can be applied to project and program evaluations as well as to policy evaluations and performance studies. Project and program evaluations assess specific projects and combinations of projects or other kinds of interventions, which are classified as programs. Policy evaluation examines packages of programs, projects, and strategies. Performance studies almost always deal with effectiveness at the organizational level. This paper argues that meta-evaluation is a critical component of the evaluation of the performance of development agencies and their interventions.

Although the term "meta-evaluation" is sometimes used to refer to studies that synthesize evidence from previous evaluations and other sources in order to come to an overall conclusion about effectiveness, such studies are more appropriately called "evaluation syntheses" (GAO, 1992). Evaluation syntheses are similar to what an international development organization might call a "desk study"; they are characterized by a reliance on information contained in existing studies. A synthesis that is primarily a qualitative analysis of information across sub-studies has been called a narrative review (GAO, 1992) or a research review (Light and Pillemer, 1984). The quantitative counterpart of a narrative review is meta-analysis—a statistical approach to combining quantitative findings in order to come to a conclusion about the overall effectiveness of a kind of intervention (Glass, 1976; Rossi, Freeman, and Lipsey, 1999). Sometimes a set of evaluations is conducted not only for the information each study imparts individually but also as a source of information for a future evaluation synthesis (Horton et al., 2003). Evaluation syntheses are a common approach to assessing overall impact. However, they are only as good as the evaluations they synthesize. Meta-evaluation is the method that should be used to ensure that the meta-studies (either narrative reviews or meta-analyses) are based on defensible evaluations.

Why Do Meta-Evaluations?

Meta-evaluation results have three commonly discussed uses, discussed in turn in what follows:

- Informing stakeholders' decisions about whether and how to use evaluation findings;[4]
- Informing evaluators' and researchers' decisions about including evaluation findings in evaluation syntheses;[5] and
- Identifying strengths and weaknesses in evaluation practice, including monitoring and evaluation systems, in order to develop evaluation capacity.[6]

Deciding whether and how to use evaluation findings. Schwartz and Mayne (2004) in their forthcoming book, Quality Matters, describe the concern about the quality of evaluation results that underscores the need for meta-evaluation: "While evaluative information has become widely available, relatively little attention has been paid to issues of quality including reliability, validity, credibility, legitimacy, functionality, timeliness, and relevance. Yet evaluative information that lacks these characteristics stands little chance of legitimately enhancing performance, accountability, and democratic governance" (p. 6). Muir (1999) provides evidence to this effect in an article on the use of evaluation findings for education reform policymaking. He assessed 116 evaluation studies—which constituted the evaluative support base for twenty-four common school reform programs—on the basis of their scope, objectivity of measurement instruments, construct validity, internal validity, sample bias, use of appropriate statistical technique, and external validity. He found that "Out of the two dozen programs examined, only three had both an adequate research base and strong evidence of success" (p. 6).

An evaluation in which little attention has been paid to quality may be the result of a poorly trained or unscrupulous evaluator, an evaluation client who is not knowledgeable about criteria and standards defining good evaluation, or both. As Schwartz and Mayne (2004) explain, "Anybody can call themselves an evaluator and bid for evaluation contracts. Purchasers of evaluations and performance reports often lack the expertise to distinguish professional evaluators and competent performance measurers from well-intentioned amateurs or charlatans. They tend to lack the skills to determine whether evaluation and performance measurement products constitute solid work or worthless words and data" (p. 6).

Political pressures are another reason why the quality of an evaluation may be compromised. Observers of program evaluation have long warned that political and commercial pressures on evaluation clients and on evaluators can lead to bias in evaluation reports.[7] Administrators' interests in organizational stability, budget maximization, and the promotion of a favorable image contribute to a general desire to prefer evaluations and performance reports that do not cast programs in a bad light. Public choice theory warns about these and similar developments.[8] Public choice theorists see evaluations as incentive systems that might realize the goals set (such as "more effective policies") but need not do so. Tunnel vision, performance paradoxes, and similar behavioral consequences of evaluation and evaluation systems are examples.

Some contexts have seen a dramatic increase in numbers of evaluations as well as the over-demand and undersupply of good studies. This phenomenon has been observed in the European Union.[9] Though there are a variety of motivations for evaluation,[10] often the demand for evaluation (especially evaluation sponsored by public sector organizations) is driven by the belief that evaluations are a legitimate source of information about an organization and its interventions, providing a sound basis for decisions. However, when there is no effective quality control mechanism and shabby studies are produced, decisions made on evaluative information could have grave consequences. As Tilley (2000) warned, we should be careful about "shooting down" policies and programs on the basis of inadequate studies.

Deciding whether to include evaluations in evaluation syntheses. As described above, one needs to know the quality of an evaluation before deciding whether and how it can be used. One use for evaluations is as information in an evaluation synthesis. Given the goal of coming to an overall understanding of the performance of an organization or intervention, evaluation syntheses clearly need to be based on rigorous, defensible, individual evaluations. Ideally, then, an evaluation synthesis begins with a meta-evaluation of the evaluations that could potentially be included in the synthesis. If the results of the meta-evaluation indicate that there are too few robust studies for a synthesis, the synthesis should not be conducted. When the meta-evaluation has filtered out weak evaluations and there are still enough studies to warrant a synthesis, the meta-evaluation becomes part of the argument for the validity of the synthesis conclusions.[11] As mentioned earlier, it is possible to plan individual evaluations with the goal of synthesizing them later.

Identifying strengths and weaknesses in evaluation capacity. Meta-evaluation results can also be used to identify aspects of the M&E system, or evaluation capacity more generally, that need improvement. For example, if an evaluation synthesis is aborted because none of the evaluations used appropriate samples for the evaluation questions, then training in sampling issues and strategizing about overcoming obstacles to appropriate sampling might strengthen the evaluation activities of the agency. Development agencies could also conduct meta-evaluation specifically for the purpose of assessing evaluation capacity, without any plan for an evaluation synthesis.[12]

2. Criteria for Use in Meta-Evaluation

Shoddy evaluation work results in poorly supported claims of knowledge about a program, which can in turn result in inappropriate use of evaluation results (for example, cuts in or elimination of effective programs; continued or increased support for ineffective programs). When evaluations are being used for such important decisions, they should be able to pass through the filter of meta-evaluation. But what comprises the filter? Usually, dimensions of quality (criteria) are identified and standards of acceptability are defined for each dimension. The Joint Committee on Standards for Educational Evaluation (1994) has produced one of the most thoroughly articulated sets of standards, which has four dimensions:

- *Utility*—an evaluation will serve the information needs of intended users.
- *Feasibility*—an evaluation will be realistic, prudent, diplomatic, and frugal.
- *Propriety*—an evaluation will be conducted legally, ethically, and with due regard for the welfare of those involved in the evaluation as well as those affected by its results.
- *Accuracy*—an evaluation will reveal and convey technically adequate information about the features that determine worth or merit of the program being evaluated.

Thirty evaluation standards are grouped into these four dimensions. Each standard consists of a specific rule, such as, "The program being evaluated should be described and documented clearly and accurately so that the program is clearly identified." The standards selected as measures of quality drive the kinds of information the meta-evaluation can provide. For example, a meta-evaluation that applies the Joint Committee's standards is likely to result in information about the evaluation's utility, feasibility, propriety, and accuracy, as defined by the specific standards.

While these standards are thorough and explicit, there are still problems in using them in practice. For example, in the standard stated above, how clear is clear enough? However, even without a full articulation of the standard, one understands at least that there needs to be some description of the thing being evaluated.

A simpler categorization, developed and applied by Hoogerwerf (1995), Leeuw (1998), Vedung (1997), Van de Vall (1980) and others, distinguishes between criteria regarding the methodology of evaluations on the one hand and criteria regarding the relevance of evaluations and their usefulness for policymaking on the other hand. Only three criteria are distinguished:

- methodological aspects of evaluations;
- strategic aspects of evaluations, focusing on the type of evaluative knowledge produced and its relevance to the problems at hand; and

- utility-focused aspects of the studies.

This is a less detailed categorization than that of the Joint Committee, but it provides more opportunity for tailoring standards within each of the three dimensions of quality. The next section of this paper describes the application of the methodological, strategic, and utility dimensions of evaluation quality to three recent evaluations of the performance of three development agencies.

3. Meta-Evaluation of Evaluations of Development Agencies' Performance

To illustrate the kinds of information obtained from a meta-evaluation, three evaluations were evaluated using methodological, strategic, and utility criteria, to answer the following questions:

- What are the reports' approaches and methods (the methodological criterion)?
- What type of evaluative knowledge is produced (the strategic criterion)?
- Have the reports realized their goals (the utility criterion)?

The specific reports and their purposes are:

- The (draft) report of the United Kingdom Department for International Development (DFID), *How effective is DFID?,*[13] whose goal is to provide "a concise, independent assessment of DFID's overall effectiveness." In the following discussion, it will be referred to as the DFID report.
- The United Nations Development Program's *Development Effectiveness Report: Review of Evaluative Evidence, 2001,* which aims "at helping to achieve the goal to maximize the effectiveness of the support we provide, through an in-depth analysis of UNDP programs and projects" (p. 1).
- The World Bank Operations Evaluation Department's *Annual Review of Development Effectiveness, 2002,* which sets out to "assess, using available evaluation evidence, how the World Bank's country, sector, and global programs are helping clients toward the Millennium Development Goals and other related targets" (p. i).

It should be stressed that our meta-evaluations are limited to the evidence provided in the reports as published.

Meta-Evaluation Results

The results are presented below in sections corresponding to the three meta-evaluation criteria: methodological quality, strategic quality, and utility.

Methodological analysis. A first conclusion is that the methodology of these studies is, though adequate, strongly focused on producing audit-type information (Table 4.1). For example, the reports come to conclusions like "x % of the projects have achieved their goals, or y % of the projects are dedicated to institutional development." This audit-oriented type of knowledge in two of the three reports is probably not the most effective communication strategy if one wants to inform management, field workers, staff, stakeholders, and society at large about the progress made in the field of development effectiveness and organizational performance.

A second concern is the preponderance of recommendations to increase the number and quality of evaluations, relative to recommendations about program quality or organizational performance. But are more evaluations and more M&E systems necessarily better? Studies show that there are "performance paradoxes," in which so much auditing, evaluation, oversight, and inspection are taking place that it leads to less policy effectiveness instead of more.[14] DFID's report is the exception to this concern, with results focused on performance and a discussion about the ability to attribute results to DFID's actions.

Strategic analysis. The strategic analysis of evaluations focuses on the type of knowledge produced that is relevant for helping to realize the goals of policy programs.[15] The goals that are referred to in the three reports all concern topics such as poverty alleviation, sustainable development, and good governance, which have to be realized under different societal conditions. As a result, it is important that knowledge be available on the attribution issue.

Table 4.1
Description of the Methodological Elements of the Reports

Criterion	DFID	UNDP	World Bank
Purpose of evaluation	Assess effectiveness of DFID	Help maximize effectiveness of UNDP support	Assess progress toward goals attributable to World Bank programs
Criteria of success	Quality of process, policy, and resources	Relevance, efficiency, institution building, impact.	Progress toward MDGs
Data sources	1,400 project completion reports; Several larger-scale, independent evaluations; Peer review report	1,500 project evaluations, 160 strategic and thematic evaluations.	331 projects; 18 country assistance strategies; 12 poverty reduction strategy papers; 17 OED evaluations
Time period	1990 – 2000	Late 1980s - 2000	1998 – 2000/01
Types of analyses	Organizational performance: descriptive statistics on inputs, processes, outputs, deliverables. Development effectiveness: Descriptive vignettes, case examples, statistics.	Descriptive statistics of project-level ratings of relevance, performance, and success. Narrative synthesis of strategic and thematic evaluation results.	Descriptive statistics and to a lesser extent case examples.

In addition to relevance and discussion of attribution, the match of the conclusions to the original purpose of the evaluation is another criterion for success. With regard to conclusions, Leeuw (1998; 2003) distinguishes between two types of evaluative knowledge:

- Knowledge about organizational (pre)requisites, conditions, and procedures, such as planning and control devices and management information systems inside the public sector, that are believed to be important if one wants to achieve effective and efficient (public) policies;
- Substantive or explanatory knowledge about mechanisms within society that make policies work (or not) and that are assumed to be relevant for achieving effective and efficient (public) policies. This type of knowledge is focused on what makes policy programs and interventions work and in which contexts. Examples are knowledge about the effectiveness of public information campaigns, why naming and shaming of criminals and schools is an (in)effective way to achieve change, and how subsidies and other incentives-focused tools of governments affect behavior.

Of these, the substantive or explanatory knowledge is what is needed in the three reports that were meta-evaluated. Table 4.2 shows the analysis of the reports on the criteria of relevance, discussion of attribution, and the match between the type of knowledge produced and the goals of the evaluation.

Table 4.2
Description of the Strategic Elements of the Reports

Criterion	DFID	UNDP	World Bank
Relevance: Type of knowledge produced	Compares large numbers of project completion reports to results of independent ex post evaluations to examine policy effectiveness. Analyzes country reports for information about social processes and development like school enrolment, privatization, eradication of polio, etc.	Reports descriptive and audit-oriented focusing on (statistical) characteristics of 1,500 projects and other activities over the years.	Focuses on directions of change in general ways, such as in the conclusion that there appears to be an upward trend with regard to the number of satisfactory outcomes of projects.
Attribution addressed	Yes	Minimally	Yes
Findings related to the evaluation's goals	Mostly: Information is presented within the contexts outlined in the purpose. Concludes that little is known about organizational effectiveness: "It is not possible, on the basis of current performance assessment systems, to provide a complete and confident answer to the question: how effective is DFID?"	Minimally: Does not describe progress regarding development effectiveness and performance in a practical and substantive way. Comes to broad statements of organizational impact (e.g., "UNDP is playing an increasingly prominent role as a source to upstream policy advice.").	Partial: Concludes that country, sector, and global programs "are consistent with the MDG themes." Finds that evaluations of country assistance programs address outcomes in terms of direction of change instead of in the achievement of specific targets. Finds that the linkages between sector strategies and poverty goal have become more explicit over time.

Utility analysis. Table 4.3 presents the analysis of the utility of the three reports. For utility, three major criteria were applied:

- The report provides information on what works, why, and when.
- The report provides recommendations on how to increase organizational performance.
- Program managers, fieldworkers, and other practitioners can use the information.

Recently, Pawson (2002a; b) discussed developments in the field of meta-analysis and meta-evaluation. One of his points of criticism is that most of the current work in the field of meta-analysis "squeezes out vital explanatory content about the programs in action (that is, the programs evaluated that are part of the meta-analysis), in a way that renders the comparisons much less rigorous than the arithmetic appears on paper." More specifically, he points to the following problems:

- *Melding of program mechanisms.* Program mechanisms are the engines behind programs, interventions, strategies, and actions. Most meta-studies bring together or meld programs simply because the latter belong to the same policy domain (poverty, health, justice, etc.). This leads to a big loss in informative content.
- *Oversimplification of program outcomes.* This refers to the point that outcomes are put forward in binary terms like means.
- *The problem of concealed contexts.* Most of the meta-studies discussed by Pawson neglect important social, economic, legal, and cultural differences. One size fits all appears to be the adage.

Table 4.3
Description of Utility Elements of the Reports

Criterion	DFID	UNDP	World Bank
What works, why, and when	Yes: (1) what is <u>not</u> known, (2) what is disputable (e.g., more favorable results from project reports than from in depth studies), and (3) what we know about organizational and policy effectiveness.	Minimally: Focuses on numbers and trends.	Limited
Recommendations	Recommendations not only focused on the future of monitoring and evaluation but also on substantive matters. Summarizes "evaluation lessons."	Recommends increasing attention to evaluating outcomes, and improving the M&E systems.	Recommends that sector strategies provide guidance on how different groups of countries could prioritize specific sectors to increase impact of country programs. Talks about the need for better analysis.
Audience	Headquarters and practitioners	Primarily headquarters	Partial headquarters

If one compares this critique with the analysis of the three reports, these three problems apply rather well. None of the reports does a good job of describing the theories/assumptions that underlie the (thousands of) programs, projects, and strategies. Information about the mechanisms behind these projects, strategies, and actions is therefore not presented. Instead, everything is put under a few very broad umbrellas. These umbrellas serve as organizing principles that make it possible to report about "progress made" in the field of development effectiveness but without telling the reader what type of progress is made, why that is the case, or what are the characteristics of the progress made.

Similarly, outcomes are discussed in terms of broad categories like "sustainability" or "institutional development," making the reports less useful than they would be if they described more specific outcomes; such specific information could be used to make recommendations about the relatively less successful outcomes. UNDP's report seems to be particularly lacking in such information. In addition, the reports give very little information about contexts. While DFID gives, in a few tables, specific information about impacts in specific countries and the Bank provides some contextual information, the UNDP report seems not to address the impact of contexts. Finally, instead of suggesting a more theory-driven approach to (future) evaluations, intentions regarding more and better measurement are formulated. Such recommendations resemble old wine in old bottles.

4. Discussion

The three reports analyzed above describe comprehensive evaluations of the effectiveness of three development agencies. The specific elements of the three quality dimensions (methodological, strategic, and utility) contain stringent expectations. For example, one of the utility standards is that evaluations will be useful to all levels of program staff—field workers, managers, and administrators—not to mention the communities involved in agency projects. This expectation is especially challenging for evaluations that address organizational performance instead of (or in addition to) examining program effectiveness.

This standard and some of the others applied in the above meta-evaluations raise questions about what can reasonably be expected from an evaluation of the performance of a development organization. For example, do such evaluations always need to be useful to all organizational stakeholders? Or can an evaluation be tailored to specific users without affecting its overall quality? In addition to questions about specific standards, the meta-evaluations described in this paper bring up global questions about the selection of criteria and standards for meta-evaluation, such as:

- How should meta-evaluation criteria and associated standards be selected?

- Who should be involved in selecting criteria and standards?
- Are any criteria or standards universally applicable?

These questions call attention to the fact that meta-evaluation is evaluation. Just as there is no single definition of program effectiveness, there is no single definition of evaluation quality. Instead, quality is defined by a mix of tailored and generic standards. For example, a fairly common element in a definition of quality is the expectation that the purpose of an evaluation will drive the evaluation questions and processes. The same expectation holds for meta-evaluation. The purpose of our meta-evaluations was to (1) provide information about the quality of these specific evaluations and (2) illustrate the value of meta-evaluation in the evaluation of development organizations' performance.

Recommendations

We urge the use of meta-evaluation when evaluating the performance of development organizations. Although our assessment of the DFID, UNDP, and ARDE reports may seem harsh, the results indicate areas in which future performance evaluations could be improved. Our specific recommendations are:

- Let auditors do the counting work ("in the latter part of the 1990s x percent of projects addressed sustainability, good governance, and empowerment while in the early 2000s this percentage is y"). Let the (meta) evaluators use theory-driven approaches to look more deeply into the mechanisms of effectiveness.
- Articulate the theories that underlie major programs, projects, and strategies. This gives information on what makes what work (or not). This also makes it possible to collect comparative data on these assumptions.
- Apply up-to-date methodology to do this job. Web-based help tools are available.[16]
- Focus future meta-studies on families of mechanisms across, rather than within, policy domains, comparing the effectiveness of projects and programs that have the same underlying program mechanisms. For example, Pawson (2002) is a meta-study across the domains of health, crime, welfare, employment and education that compares programs that are all based on "incentivization" as the mechanism. He shows what progress of knowledge can be realized if different programs using the same program theory are assessed.

Our recommendations are the result of a systematic assessment of three reports describing evaluations of the performance of development organizations. As evaluators, we must be willing to submit our work to the evaluation and critique of meta-evaluation. It is the only way that our work can improve and, in turn, that evaluation can appropriately inform decisions about agency and program cuts, continuation, and improvement. For those of us who work in organizations with global missions like the reduction of poverty, the sustainable management of natural resources, and peaceful relations among nations, meta-evaluation is one way to ensure that our small piece of that mission—the evaluation of development activities and organizations—is as meaningful as possible.

Notes

1. See, for example, the paper by Kruse (chapter 5 in this volume).
2. See Vedung (1997) for a discussion of other ways in which the term is used.
3. Stufflebeam (2001), p. 185.
4. Greene (1992); House (1987); Schwandt and Halpern (1988); Whitmore and Ray (1989).
5. Cook, Cooper, Cordray, Hartmann, Hedges, Light, Louis, and Mosteller (1992); Dickersin and Berlin (1992); U.S. General Accounting Office (1992); Wortman (1994).
6. Bickman (1997); Cook and Gruder (1978); Horton et al. (2003); Lipsey, Crosse, Dunkle, Pollard, and Stobart (1985); Vedung (1997).
7. Chelimsky (1987); Schwartz (1998); Weiss (1973); Wildavsky (1972).
8. Schwartz and Mayne (2004).
9. Leeuw and Toulemonde (1999).
10. Weiss (1998).
11. See Cooksy (1997a, 1997b) for an example of this use of meta-evaluation.
12. See Mackay and Horton (1998) for an example.
13. Flint et al. (2002). The disclaimer says, "the views contained in this draft are not necessarily those of DFID."
14. Van Thiel and Leeuw (2002).
15. Nutley et al. (2003).
16. Rogers (2000); Leeuw (2003).

References

Bickman, L. (1997). "Evaluating Evaluation: Where Do We Go from Here?" *Evaluation Practice* 18 (1), pp. 1-16.

Chelimsky, E. (1987). "The Politics of Program Evaluation." *Social Science and Modern Society* 25, pp. 24-32.

Cook, T. D., H. Cooper, D. S. Cordray, H. Hartmann, L. V. Hedges, R. J. Light, T. A. Louis, and F. Mosteller. (1992). *Meta-Analysis for Explanation: A Casebook.* New York: Russell Sage Foundation.

Cook, Thomas, and Charles L. Gruder. (1978). "Meta-Evaluation Research." *Evaluation Quarterly* 2 (1), pp. 5-51.

Cooksy, L. J. (1997a). "A Review of Documents Reporting Effects of International Agricultural Research Centers." (Report No.1 from the Review and Synthesis Project). Report submitted to the Impact Assessment and Evaluation Group of the Consultative Group on International Agricultural Research.

_____. (1997b). "A Methodological Review and Analysis of Selected Evaluation Reports by International Agricultural Research Centers." (Report No. 2 from the Review and Synthesis Project). Report submitted to the Impact Assessment and Evaluation Group of the Consultative Group on International Agricultural Research.

Dickersin, K. and J. Berlin. (1992). "Meta-Analysis: State-of-the-Science." *Epidemiological Review* 14, pp. 154-76.

Flint, M., C. Cameron, S. Henderson, S. Jones, and D. Ticehurst. (2002). "How Effective is DFID? Development Effectiveness Report." London: United Kingdom Department for International Development.

Glass, G. V. (1976). "Primary, Secondary, and Meta-Analysis." *Educational Researcher* 5 (10), pp. 3-8.

Greene, J. C. (1992). "A Case Study of Evaluation Auditing as Meta-Evaluation," *Evaluation and Program Planning* 15, pp. 71-74.

Hoogerwerf, A. (1995). "Policy Evaluation and Government in the Netherlands: Meta-evaluation Research as One of the Solutions." In J. Mayne, M. L. Bemelmans, Joe Hudson, and Ross Conner (eds.), *Advancing Public Policy Evaluation: Learning from International Experiences*. Amsterdam: Elsevier.

Horton, D., A. Alexaki, S. Bennet-Lartey, K. Noele Brice, D. Campilan, F. Carden, J. de Souza Silva, L. Thanh Duong, I. Kadar, A. Maestrey Boza, I. Kayes Muniruzzaman, J. Perez, M. Somarriba Chang, R. Vernooy, and J. Watts. (2003). *Evaluating Capacity Development: Experiences from Research and Development Organizations around the World*. International Service for National Agricultural Research (ISNAR), the Netherlands; International Development Research Center (IDRC), Canada; ACP-EU Technical Center for Agricultural and Rural Cooperation (CTA), the Netherlands. Available: http://www.isnar.cgiar.org/publications/eval.htm.

House, E. R. (1987). "The Evaluation Audit." *Evaluation Practice* 8 (2), pp. 52-56.

Joint Committee on Standards for Educational Evaluation. (1994). *The Program Evaluation Standards*. Thousand Oaks, CA: Sage.

Larson, R., and L. Berliner. (1984). "On Evaluating Evaluations." *Policy Sciences* 16 (2), pp. 147-163.

Leeuw, Frans L. (1998). "Doelmatigheidsonderzoek van de Rekenkamer als regelgeleide organisatiekunde met een rechtssociologisch tintje?" In *Recht der Werkelijkheid* (14), pp. 35-71.

_____. (2003). "Managing Evaluations in the Netherlands' Public Sector: Different Types of Knowledge Production, Different Levels of Utilization and Learning." Draft Paper, University of Utrecht, Utrecht.

_____. (forthcoming, 2004) "Managing Evaluations in The Netherlands" and "Types of Knowledge." In Ray C. Rist and Nicoletta Stame (eds.), *From Streams to Studies*. New Brunswick, NJ: Transaction Publishers.

Leeuw, F., and J. Toulemonde. (1999). "Evaluation Activities in Europe: A Quick Scan of the Market in 1998." *Evaluation* 5, pp. 487-496.

Light, R. J., and D. B. Pillemer. (1984). *Summing up*. Cambridge, MA: Harvard University Press.

Lipsey, M. W., S. Crosse, J. Dunkle, J. Pollard, and G. Stobart. (1985). "Evaluation: The State of the Art and the Sorry State of the Science." In D. S. Cordray (ed.), *Utilizing Prior Research in Evaluation Planning*. New Directions for Program Evaluation, no. 27, pp. 7-28. San Francisco: Jossey-Bass.

Mackay, R., and D. Horton. (2002). *Evaluating Organizational Capacity Development in the Area of Planning, Monitoring, and Evaluation*. ISNAR Briefing Paper No. 51. International Service for National Agricultural Research (ISNAR), the Netherlands. Available: http://www.isnar.cgiar.org/publications/eval.htm.

Muir, Edward. (1999). "They Blinded Me with Political Science: On the Use of Non-peer-reviewed Research in Education Policy." *Political Science and Politics* 32 (4), pp. 762-764.

Nutley, S., I. Walter, and H.T.O. Davies. (2003). "From Knowing to Doing: A Framework for Understanding the Evidence-into-practice Agenda." *Evaluation* 9 (2), pp.125-148.

Pawson, Ray. (2002a). "Evidence-based Policy: In Search of a Method." *Evaluation* 8 (2). pp. 157-181.

_____. (2002b). "Evidence-based Policy: The Promise of 'Realist Synthesis'." *Evaluation* 8 (3), pp. 340-358.

Rogers, Patricia J., T. A. Hacsi, A. Petrosino, and T. A. Huebner (eds.). (2000). "Program Theory in Evaluation: Challenges and Opportunities." *New Directions in Evaluation* No. 87. San Francisco: Jossey-Bass Publishers.

Rossi, P. H., H. E. Freeman, and M. W. Lipsey. (1999). *Evaluation: A Systematic Approach.* Thousand Oaks, CA: Sage.

Schwandt, T. A., and E. S. Halpern. (1988). *Linking Auditing and Meta-Evaluation.* Applied Social Research Methods Series 11. Thousand Oaks, CA: Sage.

Schwartz, R. (1998). "The Politics of Evaluation Reconsidered: A Comparative Study of Israeli Programs." *Evaluation* 4, pp. 294-309.

Schwartz, R., and J. Mayne (eds.). (2004). *Quality Matters.* New Brunswick, NJ: Transaction Publishers.

Scriven, M. (1991). *Evaluation Thesaurus*, 4th ed. Newbury Park, CA: Sage.

Stufflebeam, D. L. (1981). "Meta-Evaluation: Concept, Standard, and Uses." In Ronald A. Berk (ed.), *Educational Evaluation Methodology: The State of the Art*, pp.146-163. Baltimore: The Johns Hopkins University Press,

_____. (2001). "The Meta-Evaluation Imperative." *American Journal of Evaluation* 22, pp. 183-209.

Tilley, Nick. (1999). "Evaluation and Evidence—(mis)led Policy." *Evaluation Journal of Australasia* 11 (2), pp. 48-63.

U.S. General Accounting Office (GAO). (1992). *The Evaluation Synthesis* (GAO/PEMD-10-1.2). Washington, DC: U.S. General Accounting Office.

Van de Vall, Mark. (1980). *Sociaal beleidsonderzoek, een professioneel paradigma.* Alphen aan den Rijn: Samson.

Van Thiel, Sandra and Frans L. Leeuw. (2002). "The Performance Paradox in the Public Sector." *Public Productivity and Management Review* 25.

Vedung, Evert. (1997). *Public Policy and Program Evaluation.* New Brunswick, NJ: Transaction Publishers.

Weiss, C. H. (1973). "Where Politics and Evaluation Research Meet." *Evaluation* 1, pp. 37-45.

Weiss, C. H. (1998). *Evaluation*, 2nd ed. Upper Saddle River, NJ: Prentice-Hall.

Whitmore, E., and M. L. Ray. (1989). "Qualitative Evaluation Audits." *Evaluation Review* 13 (1), pp. 78-90.

Wildavsky, A. (1972). "The Self-Evaluating Organization." *Public Administration Review* 32, pp. 509-520.

Wortman, P. M. (1994). "Judging Research Quality." In H. Cooper, H. and L. V. Hedges (eds.), *The Handbook of Research Synthesis*. New York: Russell Sage Foundation.

5

Meta-Evaluations of NGO Experience: Results and Challenges

Stein-Erik Kruse

NGOs used to be like butterflies—small and colorful with a short and intense life. In the last ten to fifteen years, they have grown both in numbers and size, both in the North and the South, into a major force for transformation. In Uganda, more than 3,500 NGOs were registered in 2002 as compared to 1,000 in 1994. In Nepal, the number of nongovernmental organizations (NGOs) grew from 140 in 1989 to 10,500 in 2000. The total number in Brazil is estimated at 210,000 and that in India is around one million. In Norway, NGOs channel 25 percent of the government's budget for development cooperation;[1] close to 100 NGOs receive funding from NORAD while the biggest five absorb the major share and have 50-100 staff.

But have the butterflies made a difference? Have they directly improved people's lives? Do they strengthen civil society as a democratic force and affect the long-term political and socioeconomic causes of poverty? Or have they just been colorful, flapping their wings and representing the hopes for an alternative development pattern? These are questions that evaluations should have answered, but despite the increased and significant investment in NGOs, assessments of their impact have provided only few and often indefinite data.

In a traditional view, there is a proportional relationship between a cause and its effect. But in a non-linear system, a tiny event, or cause, can produce huge, unexpected effects. But in popular science this is often referred to as the butterfly effect—a term borrowed from the meteorological sciences. Butterflies flapping their wings cause tiny changes in air pressure that escalate through feedback processes and may generate a storm on the other side of the globe.

Senior partner and chairman of the Center for Health and Social Development (HESO), Oslo.

This paper looks at what we know thus far about NGO impact—at how successful Northern NGOs have been in generating storms on the other side of the globe. We will also discuss some of the methodological problems involved in evaluating NGO impact. The storm may be real, but how do we know that the wind came from the NGOs? And how do we deal with and evaluate the complex and often non-linear chain of causes and their effects? NGOs are increasingly intermediaries, facilitators, and parts of larger networks where there are complex and often unclear causal relationships. Does the traditional evaluation methodology promoted by the World Bank and official donors capture the depth and breadth of NGO impact or is an alternative NGO evaluation approach required?

This paper does not attempt to provide a comprehensive up-to-date picture of NGO impact. It draws its data mainly from two sources:

- an OECD meta-evaluation[2] of NGO impact.[3] We reviewed a large number of evaluations from OECD countries and carried out several country case studies in the North and South.
- two meta-evaluations of all NGO reviews submitted to NORAD in Norway over two years.[4]

The OECD study is more than five years old and the Norwegian experience is limited in scope compared to NGO evaluations that have been carried out in other countries. There could also be a Scandinavian bias in the observations, with relevant experience in other countries being left out. On the other hand, we believe that some of the findings have broader relevance and remain valid. The methodological issues certainly do.

1. Findings from the OECD NGO Evaluation Synthesis Study

This study was commissioned by what at that time was called the OECD/Development Assistance Committee Expert Group on Aid Evaluation. Its primary purpose was to assess the impact of the NGO development projects as well as the methods used in assessing impact. The information was gathered from evaluation reports commissioned by donors and from data and information gathered through reports and interviews in thirteen case studies in both donor and southern countries,[5] altogether covering 240 projects in developing countries.

The primary focus of the study was on the impact of discrete development projects. Some attempts were made to include projects focusing on capacity building, but the database of such projects was found to be very weak.

A first overarching conclusion, confirmed by data and interviews in all the different case study countries, was that in spite of growing interest in evaluation among the NGOs, there was still a lack of reliable evidence on the impact of NGO development projects and programs. Three reasons were mentioned for this state of affairs: most impact assessments have had to rely on qualitative data and judgments, as a result of inadequate or nonexistent monitoring and baseline data; most impact evaluations have been undertaken rapidly; and most evaluations have focused on recording project outputs, not outcomes or broader impact.

Except in the United States, donor-commissioned studies on the impact of NGO development were found to be relatively new. Such studies have assessed impact against such criteria as: achievement of objectives; impact in terms of poverty reach and the degree of participation; financial and institutional sustainability; cost effectiveness; innovation and flexibility; replicability and scaling up; gender impact and environmental impact; and impact in terms of advancing democracy and strengthening civil society. The absence of much quantitative and historical data meant that wide use had to be made of qualitative judgments.

Were the evaluations external or internal? Most of the evaluations in the sample could be called external. Two generalizations can be made about the donor studies. First, no cases were found of evaluations deliberately undertaken solely by external evaluators and not involving stakeholders at the project level. This does not mean that interaction with all stakeholders consistently took place, however. In particular, shortages of time and money frequently meant that projects were never visited and their assessment had to depend upon written documentation. More often, discussions took place with NGO staff but not with project beneficiaries.

Second, the various studies approached the issue of participation in widely different ways. Though the intention was to involve the beneficiaries, the evaluations differed greatly both in the nature of involvement and in its degree of intensity. Project visits of two to four days were the most common. The usual form of interaction was to use some sort of focus group discussions with open or guided questions.

What other roles did beneficiaries play in the evaluation process? Most commonly, very little. They were not involved in determining the terms of reference of the studies and were not on the evaluation teams. In summary, while involvement with the beneficiaries frequently occurred, it was often in a strained context where hurried answers were sought to hurried questions.

Most often, the donor-commissioned evaluations were undertaken by experienced evaluators, most of whom had expertise in undertaking NGO evaluations and came from outside the NGOs concerned. Men and nationals of the donor country dominated most of the teams. A common practice was for the external evaluator to join with local consultants for joint evaluations, but in most cases, the southern evaluators were in a minority and not team leaders.

The broad conclusions on impact from the synthesis of donor studies were:

- *Achievement of objectives:* 90 percent or more of the projects and programs had achieved their immediate stated objectives.

- *Impact*: Impact on the lives of the poor varied considerably, ranging from "significant benefits" to little evidence of making a difference.
- *Poverty:* All agree that even the best projects were insufficient to enable the beneficiaries to escape from poverty. Most NGO projects reached the poor, but not the poorest,[6] though analysis of the socioeconomic status of the target groups and others appeared to be rare. NGOs also seemed to perform better in traditional social sectors and worse when moving into more technical interventions.
- *Sustainability*: Most studies focused on financial sustainability; more recent ones also examined aspects of institutional sustainability, and a minority looked at environmental sustainability. Most projects examined were found to be financially unsustainable, with poor prospects. In most cases, the poorer the beneficiaries, the less likely a project is to be financially sustainable.
- *Cost-effectiveness:* On the one hand, most studies cited inadequate data with which to judge cost-effectiveness. On the other hand, a number of studies argued that in most projects the benefits exceeded the costs. The study offered some crude comparisons with official aid projects, with the results broadly favorable to NGOs, even though NGOs often underestimated their total project costs.
- *Innovation and flexibility:* Some studies praised the NGOs for their innovativeness; others argued that there is little unique in their activities. Where innovations do occur, they often appear to be linked to close interaction with the beneficiaries and are frequently based on long-term and detailed research.
- *Other factors:* Evidence on replicability and scaling up was sketchy, largely because the evaluations focused on discrete time-bound projects. Most projects tended to reinforce traditional gender roles, though there were clear and impressive exceptions. While some studies indicated that environmental impact was small, some had negative impacts of which many NGOs remained unaware. The studies provided little hard data with which to assess advancements in democracy or in strengthening civil society.

The study did not produce a comprehensive synthesis of impact evaluations undertaken by NGOs, but gathered evidence from the thirteen case studies. It found:

- Growing and widespread support for evaluation among NGOs, while previously there was significant skepticism. There was a call for a more genuine NGO evaluation approach, but less clarity about what this would entail.
- Growing evidence that NGOs were adapting an increasing number of criteria from the donor-commissioned studies. It seemed that NGO evaluations gradually became more similar to donor evaluations. There was less of an NGO-specific evaluation approach to be found in the reports.

- Concerns among several NGOs that evaluations were focusing exclusively on impact. Their fear was that if donors begin to fund NGOs on
  the basis of impact, this will have a detrimental effect on reaching the
  poor and on their innovative and experimental work.
- An important difference between larger NGOs—many of which were
  undertaking regular evaluations—and smaller NGOs—many of which
  were not. Only the largest NGOs had their own evaluation officers.
- A paucity of detailed information about impact, not least because of
  data inadequacies and the focus on recording project outputs.
- Confirmation, from case studies, that NGOs were more successful when
  implementing social projects and delivering services, and less successful when moving into the economic sphere.
- Confirmation of the importance of the wider context in influencing
  project outcome.

The NGO studies were more critical than donor-commissioned studies in
pinpointing weaknesses. Internal evaluations or self-assessments were also
not necessarily less critical than external evaluations.

The study confirmed the need to be extremely cautious in making generalizations about the impact of NGO development activities, not least because the
evaluations revealed wide variations in performance and because the methodology for judging performance was weakly developed and not uniform.

The study concluded that there is a need to enhance knowledge about
defining impact and the importance of impact evaluations and that this is likely
to require not only further work on assessing impact, but also a wider focus of
attention to embrace appraisal, planning, baselines and ongoing monitoring.

The main recommendations of the study were:

- Despite the remaining data gaps, donors should not commission more
  general studies on impact, but more thematic and sectoral studies.
- Future evaluations should pay particular attention to research and longitudinal studies. Typical three to five week evaluation missions are
  inadequate to evaluate and document processes of change and impact.
- Donors should encourage and fund networking and information exchange among NGOs to share data on impact and evaluation methods.
- Donors should provide funds to help strengthen NGOs' own capacities
  to undertake evaluations.
- More work needs to be done to evaluate non-project development
  interventions such as capacity building, advocacy, and development
  education. Northern NGOs still need project evaluations, but also tools
  for evaluating other and broader program objectives.

2. Findings from Norwegian Meta-Evaluation

The purpose of the meta-evaluation commissioned by NORAD was to provide better knowledge about NGO achievements. What we did was to review
all evaluations submitted to NORAD from Norwegian NGOs over two years

and extract what they said about short- and long-term results. To judge to what extent the evaluations were reliable sources of information, we also assessed the quality of the reports.

Each year there were about 100 reports, covering twenty-seven countries and twenty-one different Norwegian NGOs. The total number of NGO projects supported by NORAD each year was around 1,000, so we had a sample of about 10 percent.

The first part of the report summarized results along different dimensions, including:

- The evaluation process (what types of reports, when they were carried out, main focus, etc.).
- The scope of the evaluation (type and number of questions, etc.)
- The evaluation team (size, composition, external/internal, choice of team leader, etc.).
- The evaluation report (language, length, TOR, recommendations and summary included or not, etc.).
- Data collection methods (structured/unstructured, participatory/non-participatory, quantitative/qualitative methods, etc.).
- Sources of information (use of documents, staff, participants, field visits, monitoring data, etc.).
- Types of analysis carried out (discussion of limitations in methods, relevance to national needs and plans, cost-effectiveness analysis, analysis of capacity development efforts, lessons learned and policy/strategy discussions).

Main Findings

Information on long-term outcomes and impact was missing. We did not find enough evidence to assess achievements: 60 percent of the reports did not provide satisfactory information about impact; some reports assessed impact and their assessments were in general positive, but the findings were not based on any systematic collection of data, and were anecdotal and unsystematic. The reports we reviewed were thus of limited value as a source of information about NGO long-term development effectiveness. It should also be added that several reports explained well why such data were hard to collect and could not be presented.

The reports that did assess long-term effects were quite positive. None of these effects was categorized as very satisfactory, but nearly 40 percent of the reports analyzed were rated satisfactory in terms of achievements and none was rated "very unsatisfactory" (Table 5.1).

More and Better Information Was Available about Outcomes, or Short-Term Achievements

Like the evaluations featured in the OECD study, the Norwegian evaluations showed that more specific project objectives were to a large extent

Table 5.1
Achievements in the Projects Studied
(percent)

	LONG-TERM IMPACT	OUTCOMES	OUTPUTS
Very unsatisfactory	0	2	5
Satisfactory	38	68	75
Unsatisfactory	2	5	5
Highly unsatisfactory	0	8	7.5
No response	60	17	7.5

achieved. Two-thirds of the projects had achieved their intended short-term outcomes. The NGOs delivered and they delivered well. Serious deviations from project plans were relatively rare, including "crisis projects" (only 8 percent) or examples of "white elephants." No reports described any form of corruption or misuse of funds. In brief, NORAD got to know quite a lot about the individual projects, and that they were managed well and produced satisfactory outcomes. The reports provided much less information about the projects' long-term effects and broader societal relevance. It should be added that corruption or serious failures may still exist in NGO projects, even if such malpractices were not uncovered in evaluation reports.

Most and Best Information Was Available about Outputs

As expected, the best and most plentiful information was available about the lowest level of results: outputs of services and products. Here, 80 percent of the evaluations reported satisfactory achievements. This meant that Norwegian NGOs delivered what they were expected to deliver in terms of specific project outputs. This information was easy to collect and could be readily retrieved from progress reports and presented in evaluation reports.

This is also the type of information that NORAD and other donors have traditionally asked for. The Danish NGO impact study states, "DANIDA keeps a tight grip on the Danish NGO performance, but tends to stress financial probity and the achievements of outputs and objectives, rather than examining the wider issues of what really happens as a result of project interventions."

More recently, NORAD, like most other donors, has changed its reporting requirements and demands more data and information about results, but it provides less guidance on how to do this.

There Were Still Few Specific and Measurable Targets in NGO Projects

The quality of NGO project plans had improved considerably, but objectives were still unclear and targets often not measurable. At a higher level, NGOs sought "to contribute to," "to improve, increase or enhance," but they more rarely specified in what dimensions changes were expected to occur or by how much. The objectives represented the guiding vision and the NGO intentions, while the actual obligations were perceived by the NGOs to be to deliver at lower levels. It seems clear that the assessment of impact will not improve before objectives and targets become clearer and more measurable.

The Evaluations Themselves Focused on Project Benefits and Not on Broader Political and Socioeconomic Impact and Relevance

Almost all the evaluations were project-focused, though a few were thematic studies or broader program evaluations. Only a few made efforts to open up the project perspective and discuss the work of NGOs in a wider context. NORAD got what it had asked for, but less information about results and strategic analysis of relevance to national needs and plans, poverty reduction strategy papers, and sector programs.

Results Were Described but Not Explained

Most of the evaluations tried to document results. As mentioned, they covered quite well the lower levels in the results chain, but the achievements were rarely analyzed and explained. There was little information to help us understand why some projects succeeded while others failed. What were the factors at various levels explaining NGO performance? The assessments of impact provided interesting information, but there was a need to open up and get an understanding of processes taking place within the "black boxes."

Baselines and Use of Indicators Were Weakly Developed

Few NGO projects had carried out baseline studies to measure change over time. Only a small minority had used indicators for regular monitoring of changes and results. The selection of indicators was not a systematic part of the project design. Financial and activity monitoring was much more common. The use of indicators was not deliberately avoided, but in practice it was not included.

Capacity Development Was Weakly Discussed

Capacity development or strengthening of civil society in the South represents the overall goal for Norwegian NGOs. According to their own vision,

Norwegian NGOs should not only channel funds, but also strengthen administrative and technical capacity among partners. Assessment of the Norwegian NGOs' capacity-building efforts would have provided relevant information about results in this area, but more than 70 percent of the reports contained no such assessment. The collaborations between Northern and Southern organizations were not analyzed or discussed. The reports covering capacity building were largely positive, but how and to what extent the Norwegian NGOs added value—over and above being donors—was not well explained and documented. (Table 5.2.)

The lack of such analysis is easy to explain. The NGOs' evaluation mandates did not include the relevant questions. The responsibility was here with the organizations preparing the mandates and not so much with the evaluators.

Institutional Sustainability: Promising Results

Institutional sustainability covers the Southern NGOs' administrative and technical capacity: their ability to manage and plan, implement, and follow up projects without external technical and managerial support, even if financial support was necessary. About half of the evaluations could report satisfactory institutional sustainability, while 20 percent found a continuing need for external support. This is an indication of successful capacity building and promising changes in the area of technical and administrative capability.

Financial Sustainability: Extremely Weak

Financial sustainability was found to be satisfactory in only 12 percent of the projects. Most of the reports did not assess issues of sustainability. A pic-

Table 5.2
Capacity Development, Institutional and Financial
Sustainability in the Projects Studied
(percent)

	CAPACITY DEVELOPMENT	INSTITUTIONAL SUSTAINABILITY	FINANCIAL SUSTAINABILITY
Very unsatisfactory	0	2.5	0
Satisfactory	20	45	12.5
Unsatisfactory	8	20	30
Very unsatisfactory	0	10	27.5
No response	72	22.5	30

ture thus emerged in which the Southern NGOs increasingly knew what they wanted and were able to do it themselves, but they remained overwhelmingly dependent financially on Northern NGOs. Financial dependence was most prominent within the social sector, but even income-generating or small-credit projects commonly did not have a sound financial basis.

Can We Trust the Evaluations?

To what extent could we trust the evaluations? Did they reflect realities or the views of evaluators? Did the NGOs receive the reports they deserved or were the evaluations too positive, critical, or simply poor in quality? To answer such questions, a quality assessment of the evaluations was also carried out, focusing in particular on the selection and use of methods.

The quality varied widely, but the quality of NGO evaluations had improved considerably; 45 percent of the reports could be characterized as "good," and 30 percent as "adequate" according to a list of quality criteria.[7] Several reports had major weaknesses; more than half of them contained no terms of reference, executive summaries, or questionnaires (instruments). It was also often unclear who had commissioned the evaluations and how the findings and recommendations would be used. The large majority of the evaluators were men. Seventy percent of the team leaders were said to be external, but it was difficult to know how external/internal the team leader and the team were. The NGOs tended to recruit people they knew well in advance.

Sixty percent of the evaluations followed a systematic and structured approach, specifying steps and procedures for data collection and analysis, while in others, the lack of data and the unsystematic collection of information made it difficult to assess the plausibility of findings and recommendations.

Few of the reports contained financial analysis. There were also few efforts to extract lessons learned and provide strategic guidance based on findings from the evaluations. A more thorough discussion of relevance could have led to a discussion about the extent to which objectives and strategies were still appropriate.

NGOs have often criticized what they perceived as traditional donor evaluations, for putting too much emphasis on specific evaluation criteria and for using external teams with a low level of participation by target groups. The sample contained only a few examples of "alternative evaluations," for instance testing for participatory methods. Examples of innovation were rare; Save the Children, for instance, made efforts to involve children in evaluations. There were also examples where NGOs evaluated complex capacity-building projects with systematic organizational assessment instruments.[8] Some NGOs used new tools for evaluating institutional and financial sustainability.

Almost all evaluations (90 percent) used qualitative information, and 40 percent were not based on any systematic quantitative data. The most commonly used methods of data collection were interviews (90 percent), review of documents (70 percent), and observation (60 percent). Seventy percent of the evaluations presented no baseline data and could not use a systematic before-and-after or with-and-without design. Change was primarily assessed through informed judgment.

There was an increased supply of evaluation competence and experience among the Norwegian NGOs, but the interest was limited to a few staff[9] and the demand for evaluations from senior management and NGO boards of directors was still weak. Evaluations had not yet become standard procedure in most organizations. Increasing demand was, however, coming from NORAD as the donor. Long-term evaluation plans became a requirement in applications and NORAD initiated an increasing number of organizational assessments and project evaluations.

3. Methodological Challenges

Assessment of impact is challenging from both a conceptual and practical point of view. What problems do NGOs face when their donors demand greater accountability—in other words, better measurement and documentation of results?

Most NGOs are anxious to improve the quality and quantity of data and information about results, but the road ahead is not straightforward. Experimentation is going on among the NGOs,[10] but with few clear answers on how to proceed. The following are some of the methodological challenges that emerged from the work with the meta-evaluations.

Impact is about Lasting Results

Impact assessment is the systematic analysis of the changes—positive or negative, intended or not—in peoples' lives and in civil society brought about by a given action or series of actions. For NGO activities such information is not easily available. Official aid agencies have developed and started using results-based measurement systems collecting data on a broad range of indicators. A few Norwegian NGOs have tried to develop similar systems, without conspicuous success. They have found it much easier to define indicators than to set up viable systems for collecting reliable data. There is also a sentiment among NGOs that indicators, as the term says, merely indicate and reveal only the tip of the iceberg of what really goes on as a result of NGO programs. There is an expressed need for evaluations that analyze the comprehensive and multiple nature of NGO impact.

The Comprehensive and Multiple Nature of Impact

Most NGO objectives are broad, long-term, and of a multiple nature. They are also becoming more ambitious in the sense that they address broader issues at all levels—local, national, and global—from communities and districts to national and international politics. Norwegian NGOs place their work within a global perspective where they advocate changes in political attitudes and decisions.

This means that the numbers of means and objectives are growing and, subsequently, so is the gap between objectives and their measurement. Donors' expectations that NGOs will provide solid data about long-term results become more and more difficult to meet. How can NGOs collect such information and how can results be aggregated from the community up to national and even international levels? Several NGOs express the view that evaluations are more geared towards measuring the results of discrete projects, and not the "multiple nature of NGO impact."

The higher up the activity in the chain of results, the more difficult it becomes to measure results. How successful is, for instance, Save the Children Norway as an international child's rights organization, in building strong organizations and advocating a broad range of changes at individual, organizational, and system levels?

Most NGOs want to achieve and assess impact at three levels (Figure 5.1):[11]

- standards of living (incomes and services determining level of poverty);
- organizational skills and capacities; and
- policy environment (political empowerment and civil society development).

The first level is about the effects of service delivery, the second one about organizational capacity building, and the third about policy environment, in

Figure 5.1
Three Levels of Impact

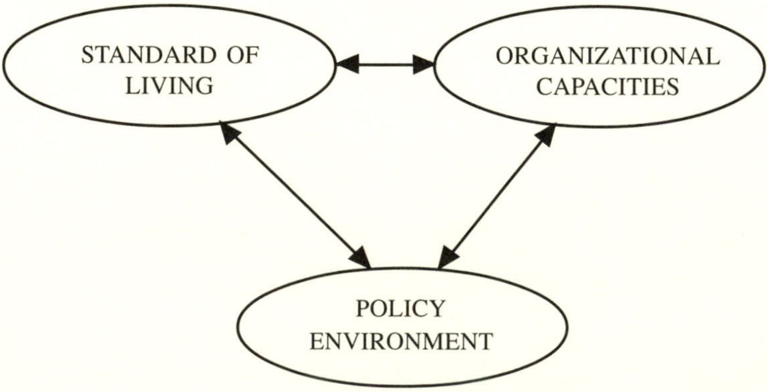

which evaluations seek to capture NGOs' contributions to political empowerment and strengthening of civil society.

At each level, both tangible and intangible results need to be taken into
account. Most evaluations have been focusing only on the standard of living
and not on the policy or organizational levels. The inverted cone in Figure
5.2, developed by the Inter-American Foundation, has been applied in several
countries. It illustrates a comprehensive framework for how NGO impact should
in principle be assessed.

The Increasing Number of Means and Ends along the Impact Chain

We refer here to the stages and levels starting from the time a government
donor allocates funds to a Northern NGO until support reaches national NGOs
in Southern countries. A good example would be the Ethiopian NGOs operating as intermediaries to local community-based organizations that provide
credit or health services to poor villagers. The number of people and organizations involved in the impact chain has increased dramatically. This means in
practice that intentions and funds travel far in order to be translated into action
and eventually results. Several stakeholders shape and reshape objectives.
Inputs from Northern NGOs become small pieces in a big puzzle.

The distinction between means and ends also becomes more blurred. What
is an objective at one level becomes a means at the next. A Northern NGO
defines as its objective to strengthen the capacity of a national NGO. This

Figure 5.2
Comprehensive Framework for Evaluating NGO Impact

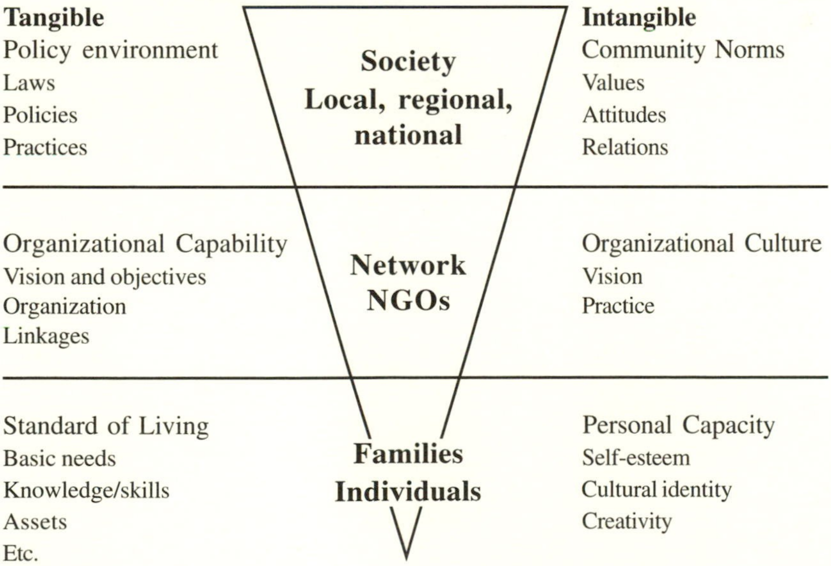

Tangible	**Society**	**Intangible**
Policy environment	**Local, regional,**	Community Norms
Laws	**national**	Values
Policies		Attitudes
Practices		Relations
Organizational Capability	**Network**	**Organizational Culture**
Vision and objectives	**NGOs**	Vision
Organization		Practice
Linkages		
Standard of Living	**Families**	**Personal Capacity**
Basic needs	**Individuals**	Self-esteem
Knowledge/skills		Cultural identity
Assets		Creativity
Etc.		

organization builds the capacity of local capacity-building organizations, which then work with individual farmers. What and where are the results that should be measured and for which the Northern NGO be accountable: at the organizational or at the target group level or both?

The increase in the number of international NGOs providing support to the same national NGOs further complicates the issue of attribution. Finally, external factors often have greater importance for project success and failure than do NGO interventions themselves. There are thin and almost invisible lines and links between NGO projects and people's living conditions.

Figure 5.3 shows the interconnections commonly found in the NGO project flow: the interfaces where one organization's ends become another's means, the factors that influence the flow of resources, and the different points at which performance can be assessed in terms of outputs, outcomes, and impact. Impact evaluation will have its focus at the end of the chain: impact among poor people, the policy environment, and the Southern NGOs themselves. The partnership between Northern and Southern NGOs is meant to lead to capacity building not only of individual community-based organizations, but also of civil society in the country concerned. Hence, impact is both about project benefits for poor people (men and women), organizational capacities, and policy change.

Figure 5.3
Interconnections in the NGO Project Flow

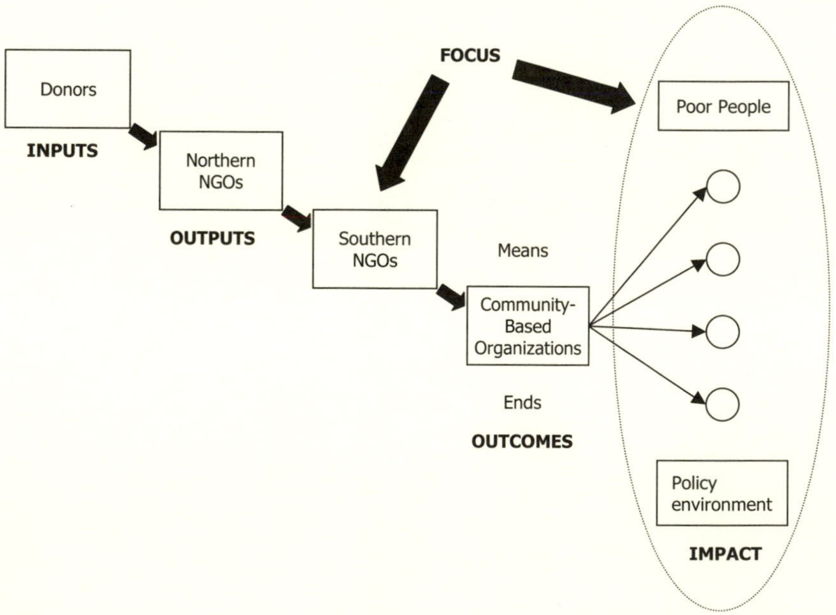

Source: Based on Fowler (1997).

4. A Way Forward: Dealing with Complexity

We started with butterflies and I would like to end with complexity. It is common to point to the complexity of development and well known that social change is multi-dimensional. However, when it comes to defining and measuring results and evaluation methodology, all this wisdom is often forgotten and surprisingly many analysts are stranded in simple deterministic and mechanistic models of the world. Norman Uphoff (1992) points to four fallacies in analytical orientations when analyzing development issues:

- The reductionist fallacy, which is a dominant strategy in many disciplines driven by methods of analysis, meaning to simplify phenomena or relationships, casting them into simple either/or categories, or simplistic scales of measurement.
- The individualist fallacy, treating social or collective phenomena as if they were only reflections of personal interest.
- The materialist fallacy, denying the reality and importance of nonmaterial factors.
- The mechanistic fallacy, regarding things as if they were machines.

Norwegian NGOs are increasingly using a logical framework for project presentations, and this often results in a rather mechanistic and linear input-output-outcome-impact model. The logframe model is also advocated in official M&E guidelines and handbooks.

Logical framework analysis has improved NGO project design and presentation, but sometimes as a substitute for thoughtful reflection and analysis. It might have been necessary medicine for poor logic and order in project presentations, but it has not proved sufficient for capturing a more comprehensive understanding of NGO impact. Uphoff calls for a "post-Newtonian social science that looks beyond reductionist thinking to explore collective action and non-material realities." The methods and assumptions of positivist social science (most often reflected in traditional evaluation guidelines) do not do justice to values, ideas, and motive forces like human solidarity that are so important for NGOs. As these have very real consequences, they deserve more attention than they receive within reductionist frameworks for modeling the social universe.

What then does it actually mean to think of society as a complex, adaptive, and non-linear system? Does it make any difference in the evaluation of, for instance, NGOs? The answer is yes, because while in linear models it is taken for granted that the extent of an effect is similar to the extent of its cause, in a non-linear system, as we saw at the outset of this paper, a tiny event can produce huge, unexpected effects. The use of indicators in measuring change will rarely capture such complex processes of change.

Other features of non-linear systems are cluster effects and qualitative leaps. Put simply, the idea of cluster effects means that all things must be in place before a system changes, and that changes must be understood contextually. It is like the slot machine where you can only win if the three cherries show at the same time. Similarly, NGOs may only perform at their best when several conditions are fulfilled simultaneously and then progress may suddenly be very fast.

The dominant notion in development theory is that social change occurs gradually and incrementally. Growth is measured by steady increases of a few percentage points each year. This cannot be denied, but important changes also occur in leaps and bounds.

So, if we consider that evaluation methodology has to deal with butterfly effects, cluster effects, and qualitative leaps in non-linear systems, does that mean results are impossible to assess? Definitely not, for in fact the social sciences have made a great deal of progress since these models were introduced. But what about approaches and methods for evaluating NGOs? Does the traditional evaluation methodology cover the multiple nature of impact and take care of the often non-linear nature of change?

To a large extent the NGO evaluations have adopted linear and mechanical models, inspired by logical framework analysis, for understanding causal relations. Most of them also follow evaluation guidelines prepared by the official donor. The Norwegian NGO Evaluation Network offers training in participatory evaluation, but also introductions to the Evaluation Handbook from the Ministry of Foreign Affairs.

It would be beyond the scope of this paper to follow up the theoretical perspectives about non-linear change and evaluations. However, our meta-evaluation yields some practical recommendations for the road ahead when it comes to NGO impact evaluations.

Impact Assessment is a Process, Not an Event

Norwegian NGOs still treat evaluations too much as events. Assessment of change in knowledge, attitudes, and behavior and at system level requires time-series data, collected at various points during the implementation of a project. Unless monitoring is built into the project design, such data will never be collected regularly.

Learn by Doing

The most constructive way to learn about impact assessment is to test and experiment with various approaches and methods. A few Norwegian NGOs have tried to develop comprehensive M&E systems, aggregating data from indicators of individual projects to organizational performance. Such experiences have been costly and not very successful. More interesting and pragmatic experimentation is going on among NGOs and donors. For instance, the

Evaluation Division in the Ministry of Foreign Affairs in Norway has initiated a two-year impact study in Ethiopia and Sri Lanka in collaboration with two Norwegian NGOs and their partners, with a focus on participatory learning.

Link Impact Assessment to Project Planning

Impact can only be assessed when a project has matured and change can possibly be observed. Several donors are often unrealistic about time frames and expect to see lasting results after only two or three years, including changes in attitudes and behavior or HIV/AIDS prevalence as a result of small interventions. NGOs need to state more clearly what data they can provide with the time and resources available and what level of change is realistic. The measurement of impact also needs to be discussed and to be part of the project design at an early stage in the planning process.

Assess Impact only for Selected Programs

Assessment of impact requires extra resources and it is not realistic to demand that an NGO should produce impact data for all its projects. For one-time contributions or small projects, impact assessment should not be mandatory.

Reporting requirements should change the further up we come in the results—or impact—chain. All projects require data on inputs, meaning documentation of what is received and how resources are used. Most also require data on outputs, while information about outcomes and impact requires separate data collection systems and should only be gathered for large projects or new projects with innovative features.

Be Clear about Conditions for Measuring Impact

To measure impact, a number of conditions need to be met:

- Clearly articulated and operational objectives.
- Successful and known process of implementation.
- Need for a comparison and a proper evaluation design.
- Sufficient time, technical and financial resources, and funding.
- Agreement on indicators and M&E arrangements.

The Issue of Attribution

The degree to which the context influences change increases, the further up the impact-chain we move. Thus, we may be able to measure change—but change caused by what? It is most often impossible to determine causality precisely, in the sense of attributing changes and impact to specific NGO interventions and measuring their relative contributions to change. Often the best that can be done is to demonstrate through reasoned arguments that a given input leads logically towards a given change, even if that cannot be proved statistically. Donors also increasingly focus on gross effects and not on the net effects of individual interventions.

Another part of the way ahead for impact measurement is simply more and better triangulation of methods, that is, to collect data and information about impact using a broad range of qualitative and quantitative methods. The combination of various methods may lead to a more reliable and valid picture. This is probably the case for both bi- and multi-lateral organizations and NGOs. NGOs need to use traditional evaluation methods, but should integrate those approaches into a broader range of efforts to assess the multiple nature of NGO impact.

By nature of their function, NGOs need to be assessed not only with regard to financial returns or quantitative results. The assessment must also focus on the quality of services provided—and quality is often in the eye of the beholder.

Another promising way forward is to engage multiple stakeholders systematically in the assessment of quality.[12] In relation to project performance, a promising direction for impact assessment appears to lie in applying methods that allow all interested parties to have a say in defining means and ends. The interpretation of impact becomes more objective when multiple perspectives are brought to bear. This is a perspective that brings the planning and evaluation perspective closer together and it underlines the need for a participatory process.

Notes

1. NGOs are estimated to disburse US$ 12-15 billion a year. Edwards and Fowler (2002).
2. Meta-evaluation is here defined as an evaluation of evaluations.
3. Riddell and Kruse (1997).
4. Kruse (1998 and 1999).
5. The case studies covered Belgium, European Union, Finland, France, The Netherlands, Norway, United Kingdom, United States, and the developing countries Bangladesh, Brazil, Chile, Kenya, and Senegal.
6. See, for instance, Riddell (1995), p. 75.
7. With some adjustments we used quality criteria suggested by Kim Forss (Forss, 1997).
8. For example, the Missionary Society has prepared a guideline for "How to Assess Organizational Capacities."
9. Today, still only two of the larger Norwegian NGOs have designated M&E officers.
10. Several interesting examples are presented in Roche (1999).
11. Edwards and Fowler (2002).
12. Edwards and Fowler (2002).

References

Edwards, M., and A. Fowler. (2002). *NGO Management.* London: Earthscan.
Forss, K. (1997). "The Quest for Quality—Or Can Evaluation Findings be Trusted?" *Evaluation* 3.

Fowler, A. (1997). "Striking a Balance: A Guide to Enhancing the Effectiveness of NGOs in International Development." London: Earthscan.

Kruse, S. E. (1998). "Hvilke resultater skaper de frivillige organisasjonene? Erfaringer fra et utvalg evalueringer." Oslo: NORAD (Norwegian Agency for Development Cooperation).

_____. (1999). "Hvilke resultater skaper de frivillige organisasjonene? En gjennomgang av evalueringsrapporter fra norske frivillige organisasjoner." Oslo: NORAD (Norwegian Agency for Development Cooperation).

Marsden, D., Peter Oakley, and Brian Pratt. (1994). "Measuring the Process: Guidelines for Evaluation in Social Development." International NGO Training and Research Center.

Oakley, P. (1999). "The Danish NGO Impact Study. A Review of Danish NGO Activities in Developing Countries." The International NGO Training and Research Center.

Oakley, P., Brian Pratt, and Andrew Clayton. (1998). "Outcomes and Impact: Evaluating Change in Social Development." International NGO Training and Research Center.

Riddell, R. (1995). "Promoting Development by Proxy: An Evaluation of the Development Impact of Government Support to Swedish NGOs." Stockholm: SIDA (Swedish International Development Agency).

Riddell, R., and S. E. Kruse. (1997). "Searching for Impacts and Methods. NGO Evaluation Synthesis Study." Development Assistance Committee of the Organization for Economic Cooperation and Development and Ministry of Foreign Affairs, Finland.

Riddell, R., A. Bebbington, M. Salokoski, and T. Varis. (1994). "Strengthening the Partnership: Evaluation of the Finnish NGO Support Programme." Helsinki: FINNIDA (Finnish International Development Agency).

Riddell, R., A. Bebbington, and Lennart Peck. (1995). "Promoting Development by Proxy: The Development Impact of Government Support to Swedish NGOs," Evaluation Report No. 2. Stockholm: SIDA (Swedish International Development Agency).

Roche, C. (1999). "Impact Assessment for Development Agencies." Oxford: Oxfam.

Uphoff, N. (1992). *Learning from Gal Oya, Possibilities for Participatory Development and Post-Newtonian Science.* London: Cornell University Press.

Comments on the papers by Leeuw-Cooksy and Kruse

Marco Ferroni

Better butterflies than dinosaurs, and better theory-driven (particularly when data are scarce) than informed by prejudice and opinion. In the discussion about development effectiveness, it seems appropriate to ask, What role for evaluation? And, How can evaluation contribute to improving the performance of development agencies (official and NGO; bilateral and multilateral)? These are the questions that the papers under consideration are asking—particularly the Leeuw-Cooksy and Kruse papers, but also, in a different way, the paper by Newman et al. (chapter 11 in this volume).

Principal evaluation officer, InterAmerican Development Bank Office of Evaluation and Oversight.

The Leeuw-Cooksy and Kruse papers point to a large *potential* role for evaluation in the quest for greater agency effectiveness. As to the *actual* contribution in the settings researched, the authors reach sobering conclusions. They identify:

- An undersupply of good evaluation studies (as judged by stated methodological, strategic, and utility criteria) in a field crowded with "superfluous assessments."
- A tendency on the part of evaluators producing audit-like products— bean counting, one might call it, where the "beans" are the evaluated activities' immediate outputs—as opposed to efforts to determine the activities' effectiveness in accomplishing intended purposes.
- A tendency, even on the part of evaluators, to celebrate effort instead of assessing results.
- A lack of theory and analysis of how given realities are meant to be modified by specified interventions. The specification of *results chains* or *structural models* (as exemplified in the Newman paper) is as indispensable for evaluation—for example, to assess "relevance" and to develop plausible narrative regarding attribution—as it is intellectually challenging.
- A lack of independence of evaluation in many settings, and evaluators' aversion to risks—which may make for a quiet life, but inevitably (I submit) undermines the role, utility, and credibility, and thus the potential impact, of evaluation.

What are the keys to changing this state of affairs? I should like to suggest a number of priorities, only some of which are addressed in the papers under review. The level of achievement and sophistication in evaluation varies among agencies, so my points are not equally pertinent to every situation. Still, in a great number of cases, the priorities, I think, are to work toward raising quality at entry and the evaluability of projects and programs, to improve performance monitoring and post-completion evaluation (also of projects and programs), and to deepen the reflection about the authorizing environment, the incentives, and the issues at stake in evaluation.

On quality at entry, World Bank data (from the Operations Evaluation Department and the Quality Assurance Group) indicate that both quality at entry and the number of projects rated as satisfactory *ex post* have improved in recent years. Does this translate into an improvement in development indicators on the ground, particularly in countries where the role played by the institution is large? OED's 2002 *Annual Review of Development Effectiveness* is silent on this question.

On *ex ante* evaluability (a dimension of quality at entry), published and unpublished works including the Leeuw-Cooksy and Kruse papers suggest that many activities in development assistance cannot be evaluated: their goals and objectives are not well defined; their problem diagnosis is partial or faulty; the indicators they provide (if any) do not respond to the objectives in meaningful ways and fail to come with baselines, milestones, and targets; and they lack analysis and mechanisms to cope with and mitigate risk.

The improvement of evaluability (primarily a task for the agencies' operational departments, but one where evaluators can help) is in the first place justified because it is likely to improve the project. At the same time, tautologically, it has the benefit of making the project more evaluable on its own terms.

Performance monitoring—that is, the collection and analysis of data on the rate of implementation and on the achievement of objectives—is another area deserving of attention. If this information is not being collected, or is not being collected for meaningful indicators (the apparent situation of many donor-funded and NGO-sponsored projects today), results cannot be demonstrated, even if they are achieved.

On post-completion evaluation, I would distinguish between project completion reports, sustainability assessments, and impact evaluation. The bulk of the effort in many development agencies at this time should be to produce professional project completion reports with systematic analyses of results and a reflection on the lessons that can be derived.

Beyond the project completion report, there may be a case for carrying out sustainability assessments: Is the project still there and do the benefits continue to flow? Actual impact evaluation, on the other hand, should probably be reserved for rare occasions, because of its complexity and cost. Experimental projects designed to facilitate learning are the obvious candidates for impact evaluation.

Country program evaluation (taking the country, rather than the project, as the unit of account) can add important insight about the role of development agencies in a strategic sense. Are the agencies' instruments deployed coherently? Is the program "relevant" to the country's development problematique? Is the country's investment program being improved as a result of the partnership with the agency? These are questions that elude project-level evaluation, but can be addressed when the focus shifts to program assessments.

Finally, on the deeper meaning and the demand for evaluation, how does the evaluator know whether he or she has produced a good report? The answer, in my view, is not so much linked to the level of "noise" and the controversy that may reign after the presentation of the report, but to whether or not the work provokes thought—a subtle, but more appropriate signal of "success" than the number of the evaluator's recommendations that are being taken up in (for example) the agency's next country strategy. Let us note, however, that evaluation doing and saying the right thing, and thereby provoking thought, inevitably requires a measured disposition to take risks.

Floor Discussion

Participant: I am from a developed country, but having heard your presentations, I strongly feel the need to add the viewpoint of developing countries that are actually implementing development assistance and trying to make it more effective. On the one hand, for accountability purposes, international organizations and donor countries must focus on evaluation. But on the other hand, evaluation is for future policy improvement, and if evaluation findings are actually to be implemented by aid-recipient governments, recipient countries should be heavily involved in evaluation. I would like to hear your opinions about the effect of incorporating the perspectives of developing, aid-recipient countries.

Participant: I would like to get some comments about how to strengthen evaluation capacity in government. Within some governments there are risks to people who promote rigor and transparency. In such circumstances, what can be done to set up good monitoring and evaluation units and to protect the independence of evaluators?

Participant: Management within governments needs to promote transparency and promote the good use of monitoring and evaluation data while making it clear that individual staff are not going to be penalized for producing that information. Armed with good monitoring and evaluation data, policymakers can take corrective actions; can adapt a program so that it works better, or maybe phase it out and introduce other programs. But individual staff should not be punished for bringing results to light.

Participant: To illustrate a point that Frances Stewart made, a kind of postmodernist plea for pluralism in thinking about evaluation, I want to highlight that several other studies of the effectiveness of DFID have been done in addition to the evaluation analyzed in Leeuw and Cooksy's paper. All come to slightly different conclusions. So my question is, To what degree should we begin to think more seriously about the differences between audit evaluation and policy research? And also, how should we begin to think about bringing them together in a more useful and productive way?

Participant: I offer you a little joke. A man got stuck about 500 feet above the ground, in the middle of a field, and another man was passing through the field. And the man who was stuck above the ground asked him, "Hey, where am I? Can you help me?" And the man who was passing through the field said, "Well, you are about 500 feet above the ground, and you are in the middle of a field 500 by 2,000 feet." So the man who was stuck asked him, "Are you an evaluator?" He said, "Yes, how do you know?" He answered, "Because whatever you told me is right, but it doesn't help me in any way." Then the man at the bottom asked, "Are you an academic?" He said, "Yes, how do you know?" He answered, "Look: you don't know where you are going. You got stuck. I'm trying to help you, and you are now blaming me for what I am doing." Anyway, the good thing is at least both the evaluator and the academic are talking!

Participant: I want to offer two questions combined with comments. One regards the perspective of the nongovernmental organizations, given by Stein-Erik Kruse. While I agree a lot with what he said, I did not find the perspective of the Southern NGOs in his presentation. Also, I don't know whether the NGO perspective equals that of civil society as a whole. Coming from a developing country, I see that a lot of changes have happened because of the pressure that civil society has put on governments; it is important that we recognize that particular role.

Second, evaluators often complain that they have to produce reports with limited budgets under severe time pressure. We do need to respond to managers' demands, but if we are serious about evaluation being important and also helping to change the development business, should we be claiming more of a share of the pie than we are at present?

Participant: To evaluate the impact of NGO intervention, is there a need for specific tools to apply to this category of development agents? Do their actions need a particular kind of attention?

Kruse: Most of the donor evaluations described in my paper were carried out by experienced evaluators, but Southern evaluators were in the minority. Most of the team leaders were external—and some were consultants who might have worried about their next job. I have been involved now for a number of years in evaluations in Eastern and Southern Africa, and the difficulty of finding experienced local evaluators is an extremely sore point. I would say the Southern perspective is weak in most of these reports. I know of examples where Northern NGOs have invited Southern evaluators to carry out evaluations in the North, but these are relatively rare.

Let me also say that most of the evaluation projects that we looked at are NGO projects. In the last few years, the civil society perspective has become much more pronounced. In practical terms, most of the funds from bilateral and multilateral organizations still go to the NGOs, but an increasing amount is going to a broader range of organizations.

Just one comment about the logical framework analysis. Most of the Scandinavian NGOs that I know about are using the logical framework approach now in their presentations or when they submit project proposals to funding agencies. To what extent this improves quality is a hard question. If you follow the logical framework also for evaluation, you may miss out certain dimensions of the work of NGOs. I think the work of NGOs should be evaluated on the same terms as other programs and other organizations, but that it may have some unique features that need to be addressed using other types of evaluation models.

Leeuw: Let me respond on two topics. The first deals with the observation that different studies of DFID's effectiveness have come up with different conclusions. Believing that different viewpoints might all be equally relevant is risky; it may lead you to add together the conclusions of studies whose implicit theories are quite different. As an alternative, in a number of social science disciplines there are now repositories of CMOs—contexts, mechanisms, and outcomes—that allow us to say we know, from research and from the evaluation literature, that under such and such conditions and such and such contexts, a certain kind of program probably has more impact than other types of programs under similar conditions. We should accept these findings, at least as starting points, because they are based on a lot of experience.

My second point is that we need to understand better the differences between auditing, evaluation research, and policy research. Some policymakers appear to see all these things as the same, and unfortunately, in many evaluation studies the distinction is a bit unclear. But there is a big difference between the type of knowledge that auditors produce (whether they are performance auditors or compliance auditors), and the type of knowledge that evaluators should produce.

6

What Causes Aid Dependency? Evaluating Thirty Years of Swedish Bilateral Aid to Tanzania[1]

Claes Lindahl and Julie Catterson

Some years ago we were asked by the Expert Group on Development Issues, set up by the Swedish Ministry of Foreign Affairs, to undertake a study of issues related to aid dependency and the problems of phasing out of aid. Tanzania was suggested as a case for the study. The reasons for choosing Tanzania are not difficult to understand. As we pointed out in the study, few countries can compete with Tanzania in terms of its high profile in the aid debate. For the critics of aid, Tanzania is the proof that aid does not work; for the defenders, Tanzania is a case of soul searching and of finding the weaknesses in the aid management systems to improve effectiveness.

This paper describes the study and its findings, draws conclusions for the allocation and management of aid, and offers lessons for evaluators.

1. The Study and Its Findings

Our approach to the study had three major elements:

- A review of what at the time was written on the issues of aid-dependency, sustainability, and phase-out.

Director, Management Perspectives International, a consultancy firm specializing in international development. Claes Lindahl has led and participated in numerous evaluations for bilateral and multilateral development organizations, including the World Bank.

Julie Catterson has participated in extensive evaluations for SIDA and other organizations. She has also worked in project management for various consultancy firms.

- A macro approach tracing the history of official development assistance and of Tanzania's development since the early 1960s.
- A micro approach based on an assessment of twelve major Swedish-funded development projects during 1970-97.

Macro Analysis

Tanzania has been Sweden's most important partner country in bilateral development assistance. It is also one of the leading recipients of official development assistance internationally. Yet Tanzania at the time of the study had a reputation as a basket case, one of the black holes of development assistance. The country was poorer in the mid-1990s than at Independence in 1961, in spite of billions of dollars of aid over the years. Tanzania had become heavily aid-dependent despite an overall peaceful history, plenty of natural resources, the leadership of one of the most enlightened African leaders, strong local ownership over the development agenda, and, as far as can be judged, an overall non-corrupt regime.

Bad policies. In the current paradigm of development, Tanzania's failure began when the country abandoned the open market and private sector-oriented policies it had pursued since Independence, because their expected benefits had not materialized. It adopted the policies promulgated in the Arusha declaration of 1967: socialism (meaning abandoning the private sector and short-circuiting the market principle) and self-reliance (meaning a closed and import-substituting economy). Arusha was followed by other policies that added insult to injury: the Basic Industry Strategy in 1974, a twenty-year Soviet-style plan for rapid industrialization based on state ownership and import substitution, that led to the establishment of government-owned industries in everything from cement, steel, textiles, paper, and pulp to school books. Parallel to this, the infamous Ujamaa policy resulted in forced movement of people to new villages in order to provide a more "rational" agriculture and better social services to the population. Donors were not silent on these policies, but it took two decades until the "bad" policies began to be changed back, largely to those of the early 1960s, essentially as the result of pressure from the donor community led by the IMF and the World Bank. It also took the resignation of the architect of the Arusha declaration, Julius Nyerere, for things to begin to move in the direction of "good" policies.

It is difficult to criticize a newly independent country for its choice of "bad" policies, especially at a time when such policies were popular and seemed to be paying off at least in some countries. But why did the donor community so willingly support Nyerere's Tanzania for two decades? Not only the Scandinavians with their social democratic traditions and some socialist "brothers" in the Third and Second World, such as Bulgaria and China, but the World Bank and the rest of the donor community also stood behind

Tanzania, financially underwriting Nyerere's experiments. Tanzania was truly a darling among donors. One answer might be that knowledge of what were "good" and "bad" policies was not discovered by the donor community until the 1980s, when development began to go sour in places such Tanzania while development success stories elsewhere, such as in the Asian miracle economies, provided ideas of what good policies in fact were. Meanwhile, in some socialist developing countries such as China and Vietnam, Communist leaders themselves began embracing the open-market concept, disillusioned by the results of the import-substituting, planned type of economy. A related explanation is that at this time there was a shift from largely micro-oriented aid, and its concern for "successful" projects, to more macro-focused support designed to create "successful" countries. This might be called learning in development and also learning in the donor community.

Swedish aid. Sweden was the largest bilateral contributor to Tanzania in 1970-96, with a total aid volume in terms of grants (US$ 2 billion) that was almost as much as the World Bank's soft loan disbursements to Tanzania over the same period. Swedish development assistance to Tanzania in the earlier years was strongly shaped by a belief in Nyerere's vision. Sweden saw its assistance in the late 1960s and 1970s as a partnership based on mutual trust and optimism about development, in which the Tanzanians decided on their policies and strategies and what they wanted, and the Swedes provided technical and financial resources towards that end.

Sweden was unlucky to some extent in this partnership, as the Tanzanian government wanted Sweden to focus on industries in its support. Thus, Swedish aid had the misfortune of being associated with many of the industrial failures of the 1970s and 1980s, which exemplified a type of industrialization process that Sweden itself had not pursued. The concentration on state-owned industrial development led to complementary support in related sectors, such as industrial vocational training and various industrial service functions such as standardization. Many of these activities also failed, as their basis—rapid industrialization—never materialized. Swedish development assistance was probably no worse than other development assistance during these years; those who traveled in Tanzania in the 1980s found the ruins of ill-fated industrial projects financed by Sweden, other Scandinavians, the World Bank, and many others, side by side.

Sweden, like the other Scandinavians, was more reluctant than many other donors to give up its support for Nyerere's policies, and never reduced its support during the disagreements that took place over macroeconomic policies in the mid-1980s. But eventually Sweden and the other Scandinavians sided with the International Monetary Fund and the World Bank, apparently providing a decisive reason for Nyerere to step down in 1985.

Sweden maintained a high and increasing flow of aid to Tanzania to the end of the 1980s, but thereafter a sharp drop took place. By 2001, Swedish bilateral aid to Tanzania was about US$ 50 million, or less than 5 percent of total net official development assistance to Tanzania, making Sweden only the seventh largest contributor, far beneath today's major donors, Japan, United Kingdom, and the World Bank. With Nyerere gone and the failures of the 1970s and 1980s accepted, Tanzania has certainly lost much of its glory as a favored recipient country in Swedish aid.

How bad were the "bad" policies? Tanzania's failure economically in the 1970s and 1980s is difficult to dismiss. By the mid-1990s, Tanzania had fallen to the bottom of the league of nations in terms of income per capita (whether measured conventionally or in purchasing power parity terms), where it found itself in company with countries such as Mozambique and Ethiopia that had been devastated by wars. Looking at social indicators such as literacy, school enrolment, longevity, infant mortality, access to basic services such as safe water, however, Tanzania had better standards than Sub-Saharan Africa on average. Also, Tanzania had a smaller percentage of its population living in extreme poverty (on less than US$ 1 per day in purchasing power parity terms), than the rest of Sub-Saharan Africa (Table 6.1).

Table 6.1
Tanzania: Basic Indicators 1993 and 2000

Indicator	Tanzania		Sub-Saharan Africa		Rank from bottom in the world	
	1993	2000	1993	2000	1993	2000
GNP/capita* (US$)	630	523	1385	1690	3	2
Life expectancy at birth (years)	52	51	51	49	33	27
Adult literacy (%)	66	75	56	62	47	52
Combined school enrollment (%)	34	32	42		20	15
Infant mortality rate (%)	85	104	97	107	39	18
Prevalence of malnutrition among children under 5 (%)	25	29	31		30	20
Access to safe water (%)	50	54	45	54	27	15
UNDP Human Development Index	0.365	0.440	0.379	0.471	30	23

* At purchasing power parity.

Source: UNDP, *Human Development Report* 1996 and 2002 (some figures under 2000 are for 1999).

Thus, it appeared that during the late 1960s to 1980s, Tanzania with the help of donors had pursued bad policies in the economic sphere, especially in its industrialization drive, but fairly good policies in the social sphere. And as new economic theory argued that human capital is critical for long-term economic growth, it could be hoped that donor support had been paving the way for a healthy long-term development process.

Tanzania had also been quite successful in building a national identity and basic institutions, besides a human resource base. In a continent plagued by collapsing nations, ethnic conflicts, and tribal warfare and civil wars leading to genocide, Tanzania has been comparatively stable, including during its current shift to democracy. In terms of nation building, Tanzania must be considered one of the most successful cases in Sub-Saharan Africa. A bold hypothesis is that, while it is difficult to prove a causal relationship, development assistance played a significant role in this process. If Julius Nyerere and his vision were instrumental for the nation and institution building in the 1970s, he gained at least a part of his legitimacy and most of the resources from his relationship with the donor community.

What happened in Tanzania after the "bad" policies were replaced by better policies? We undertook our study mainly in 1997, about a decade after the reform process had begun in earnest. While a dramatic change in Tanzania's economic development had yet to emerge, there was considerable optimism at that time. Tanzania was heralded as one of the most promising cases of the new partnership between donors and recipients. Development assistance, frozen during the years of conflict over macroeconomic policies, had resumed an increasing trend at a level of about US$ 1 billion a year.

We have not revisited Tanzania since 1997 and cannot provide a detailed update of our report. However, comparing some of the key development indicators from the study (mainly for 1993) with most recent data (mainly for 2000) provides a pessimistic picture. In 1993, Tanzania's per capita income in purchasing power parity terms was about half the average for Sub-Saharan Africa, while in 2000 it had fallen to less than a third.[2] And while the trends in social indicators give a mixed picture, in the sphere of human development overall, the world is leaving Tanzania behind (Table 6.1).

What is the explanation for Tanzania's poor performance in the 1990s, in spite of the persistent work to introduce "good" policies by the donor community, supported with ever- more generous flows of development assistance for a decade? While bad policies were at the forefront of explaining poor economic performance in the 1980s and 1990s, today the focus in the donor community is on bad institutions, that is, a broader set of explanatory factors. But how do we know that this is the magic bullet for development, and that five or ten years from now the donor community will not have shifted its attention to yet other set of factors, while Tanzania, perhaps, still is struggling at the bottom of the poverty league? We have no answer to this question, except, perhaps, that donors need to be less sure of their time-bound blueprints for development.

The Micro Study

The main thrust of our study was at the project and program level. Our approach to this was a review of twelve Swedish-supported development projects in different sectors, selected to fit the pre-selected typology in Figure 6.1. Criteria for their selection are given in Table 6.2.

The projects selected are shown in Table 6.3.

These projects represent about 10 percent of Swedish aid to Tanzania during the thirty years covered by the study, and most of the sectors in which Sweden has been active: industrial development, infrastructure, education, natural resources, water and sanitation, and public administration. Most of them were Swedish bilateral projects with no other donors involved, but two, Pangani and TAZARA, were multi-donor projects in which Sweden participated. The latter were of the blueprint type, while the others were process-

Figure 6.1
Typology of Projects Studied

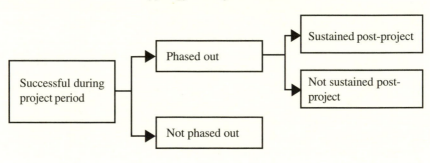

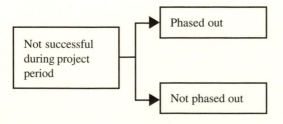

Table 6.2
Criteria Used for Project Selection

Success during the project period	• Defined activities were delivered during the project. • The project objectives were achieved. • Unplanned results were achieved during the project, significant enough to justify the project.
Sustainability	• The planned activities continued after the cessation of SIDA funding and other external funding. • The intended or unintended positive results and/or planned development objective fulfilled during the project were maintained after the cessation of SIDA funding.

Table 6.3
Projects Featured in the Evaluation

Type of project/program	Name	Started	Phased out	Cost (*million Swedish Kroner*)
Soil conservation	HADO	1973	1996	20
Food and nutrition institute	TNFC	1973	Planned 1999	70
Adult education (folk development colleges)	FDC	1975	1996	120
Industrial vocational training	MVTC	1976	Planned 1998	200
Small industries development organization	SIDO	1976	1992	400
Bureau of standards	TBS	1977	1992	80
Public auditing organization	TAC	1978	1993	60
Statistics bureau	TAKWIMU	1983	Planned 1999	90
Government-owned cement factory	TPCC	1984	1991	??
Rural water and sanitation program	HESAWA	1985	Planned 2002	600
Tanzania-Zambia railways	TAZARA	1986	1995	280
Government hydro-electric power plant	Pangani	1991	1996	210

style.[3] In all cases but one (HADO), the projects had a strong organizational/institutional focus in the sense that they aimed at developing effective Tanzanian organizations in the public sphere.

The time the selected projects had been supported until the support was phased out (or was planned to be phased out at the time of the study) varied from five years (Pangani hydroelectric power plant), to twenty-five years (Tanzanian Food and Nutrition Center). Overall, the duration of Swedish assistance was surprisingly long: in a third of the cases, it was two decades or more, and in only two cases was it less than ten years. Except in the multi-donor investment programs, the Swedish International Development Agency (SIDA) and the designers had clearly not foreseen such extended support at the time the projects were conceived. While Swedish development assistance sometimes is based on an implicit long-term commitment, aid is generally provided only a few years at a time; hence all projects had involved a series of decisions to extend the support.

The selected projects were assessed through research of SIDA archival information and published information such as research reports and evaluations. They were also assessed through our field interviews with Tanzanian and other stakeholders, and through interviews with stakeholders on the Swedish side. For most of the projects, one or several independent evaluations had been carried out during their course, and these provided critical information for our assessment.

Our assessments of the selected projects were broadly based. We tried to understand not only what the projects had or had not achieved, but also their historical context in Tanzania's development process and in the history and politics of Swedish development assistance. We were particularly interested in the decision making processes in SIDA and in Tanzania prior to the projects, during their course, and—given the objective of the study—in the phasing out of the assistance. We tried to identify the key stakeholders in the projects, and their roles in decisions on phasing out.[4]

Each of the projects was described following the same format and the drafts were provided to key stakeholders for review. While the reviewers did not challenge their factual accuracy, our conclusions were in one case (MVTC) contested by the SIDA officer who had been directly responsible for the project for most of its duration.[5]

Several problems common in the evaluation of development assistance made it difficult to assess what projects had achieved and to reach objective judgments about them:

- Project objectives had been stated in broad, qualitative terms.
- Baselines were not established in any of the projects we reviewed.
- The monitoring of key indicators related to the objectives of the projects tended to be poor or lacking. Assessments of change had to rely largely

on the views of Swedish and Tanzanians with a long record in the projects.

These deficiencies also affected the independent project evaluations on which we based many of our judgments. However, we believe that the case materials overall were as accurate as can be achieved. Our general conclusion is that the many efforts to establish elaborate and quantitative objectives, baselines, and even monitoring of indicators tend to yield much less in accuracy than expected. Development projects, and development, are complex processes, not easily captured in data systems.

Findings of the Case Studies. A similar pattern of aid dependency seems to occur both at the micro/project level and at the macro/country level. Plotting the degree of success during the project period in our estimation on a time scale of how long the projects had been supported by Swedish aid gave the results shown in Figure 6.2.

The conclusion from this is that the degree of success during implementation seems to have no direct relationship to the length of the Swedish support for the project. If anything, the case material suggests a reverse relationship, that is, a link between longer support and a lower degree of success.

Looking at the performance of the projects during their implementation we found to our surprise that some of the longest-supported projects never had shown much success, yet had been supported for two decades or more. To us this represented a clearly dysfunctional form of aid, posing the question of why SIDA had not phased out earlier. We could conclude that in these cases certain stakeholders had been able to maintain the Swedish support despite the projects' lackluster performance. These stakeholders were non-Tanzani-

Figure 6.2
Correlation between Success and Project Support Time for the 12 Projects

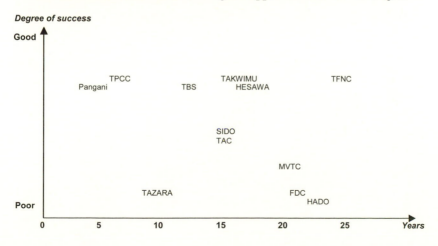

ans, either desk-officers at SIDA with a very strong personal, even emotional, commitment to "their" projects, or representatives of institutions to which SIDA had delegated implementation. The views of the Tanzanian stakeholders in these projects appeared to have been less important in the decision making. Only one of the projects rated poor in success had been phased out within a (relatively) short time. This project, TAZARA, was a fixed-term multi-donor investment program over ten years, and the timing of the Swedish phase-out was not really an issue.

Plotting the degree of post-project sustainability, in our estimation, against the support time (Figure 6.3) indicates a fairly clear inverse relationship between the length of the Swedish support and the assessed post-project sustainability.

The case material gives an explanation for this: Swedish support for individual projects was often renewed on the basis that without such support, the project or institution might collapse, that is, the investment risked being wasted. In practice, however, only rarely would such extended support enhance the project's sustainability, and eventually the Swedish assistance was phased out anyway, often in a mood of what might be characterized as donor fatigue. A separate analysis of the six projects that we had rated as successful during implementation showed that those with shorter support times were overall sustained, and those with longer support times were overall unsustainable.

A conclusion from the above is that the length of time a project is supported has little to do with its probability of being successful, or its sustainability post-project. The project period, especially for the process-oriented projects, appeared to be determined first and foremost by the donor's opportunities to

Figure 6.3

Correlation between Sustainability and Project Support Time for the 12 Projects

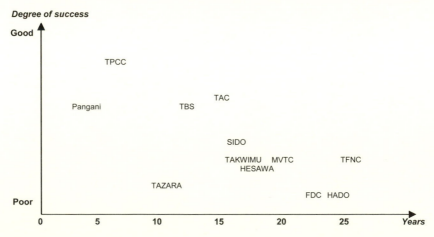

phase out its funding. Poor performance and lack of sustainability triggered more protracted, rather than shorter, support.

Technical and Financial Sustainability. In trying to understand why successful projects did not achieve sustainability in spite of the extended years of support, it is important to distinguish what we called technical (or professional) sustainability from financial sustainability. We found in the case material that the projects and the supported organizations generally established a technical/professional capacity rather quickly, often after only a few years of support, but at this time these organizations were not financially viable, so that there were problems of phasing out the support even if the know-how had been successfully transferred. Such lack of financial viability generally had to do with the government's unwillingness or inability to provide public service organizations with the funds required for their operations, and/or the poor capacity of the supported projects and organizations to generate their own resources. Linked to this, of course, was the fact that project success generally was not defined in terms of financial sustainability.

We also found that once this lack of financial sustainability emerged, there was a tendency to prolong the Swedish support along the same lines as previously, i.e. to continue the development of professional skills, but with no direct attention to how the project/organization could develop its capacity to better generate resources. A contributing reason for this was that the implementing agencies used by Swedish assistance often had limited skills in this respect. As a result, the project/institution tended over time to be seen as a Swedish organization, both by the supported organization itself and by the Tanzanian government. Hence, the government's motivation to provide funding declined, and its position in the bargaining over who would finance strengthened, as the "psychological" Swedish ownership escalated. This trend was usually not changed until there was a clear threat by the donor to phase out, changing the bargaining positions.

Schematically, the cycle might look as in Figure 6.4:

Figure 6.4
Sustainability in the 12 Projects

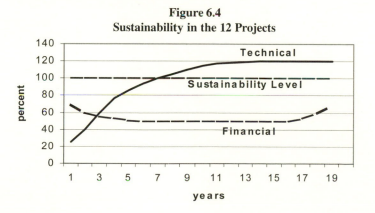

Today it is quite easy to see why technical and financial sustainability took different courses. Many of the projects were initiated during the 1970s, when it was assumed that the Tanzanian government would pick up the bill for operating and maintaining these public sector undertakings, once the transfer of know-how or the investments were completed by donor support. This proved to be an unrealistic assumption, given the combination of poor economic growth, poor public management, and an increasingly overextended government budget. At the micro/project level, it created a dilemma: project officers in SIDA had little ability to influence the macro-environment that the projects took place in, and hence to secure local funding for these operations. By the time the project had achieved its objectives (generally expressed in technical/professional terms), the officers either had to face the fact that ending the donor support would lead to a high risk that the project/supported organization would collapse, or continue the support in the hope that conditions would improve. With the changed policy environment in the latter 1980s and the 1990s, the plethora of public sector service organizations had an even smaller chance of government funding. In addition, the industrial projects that had been conceived in the era of the Basic Industry Strategy turned out generally to be very poorly adapted to a new commercial environment. It was a long, psychological process for Swedish development assistance to accept that many of the long-supported projects would not be the flagship of development they were expected to be. As a result, a lot of good money was thrown in after bad.

Other factors contributed to poor financial sustainability. Most of the projects incorporated in their design certain assumptions of how they would be financed post-project, in addition to funding through the government budget. A common feature for such non-commercial projects as folk development colleges, vocational training, water supply and sewerage, was the assumption that they would generate part of their own resources. However, in reality this happened to a very small extent, and as a result, there was an increasing overall dependency on public funding (including Swedish aid) for their operations.

Figure 6.5 plots the projects in terms of their assumed degree of dependency on government funding for their operations, and the actual trend in funding (the arrow). It shows that most of the projects became more dependent on budget support than had been anticipated.

The explanation for this was a combination of unrealistic expectations of revenues (partly because of the decline in the overall economy, which limited, for example, the fees that a vocational school, a development college, a rural water supply system, or a small industry organization could charge their clients), and of much worse than expected commercial performance by a railway and small industries, which in turn were affected by the poor economy. Only in one case did the reality take a different direction: the Tanzanian Bureau of Standards. This was to a great extent due to a concerted effort by Swedish development assistance to commercialize the operations of the organization

Figure 6.5
Assumed and Actual Government Funding of 12 Studied Projects

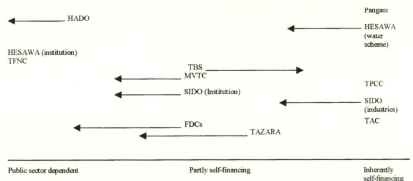

through a special project. It is noteworthy that such an effort was unique among the non-industrial projects.

2. Conclusions from the Study

The study of Swedish development assistance to Tanzania over the thirty-year period leaves an impression of how little economics really mattered, in the sense of using scarce resources as efficiently as possible to fulfill society's demands for goods and services. The incentive structure built into the development assistance was in many ways the reverse, for several reasons:

- The Swedish government established yearly country budgets based on political considerations. These budgets meant in many cases that the available financial resources for aid were greater than what could be disbursed in a prudent manner in worthwhile projects. Under such circumstances there were hardly any incentives for the desk officer or the project manager to use resources efficiently. Likewise, the recipient organization had no incentive to argue for prudent use of resources, such as an early phase-out of Swedish assistance, as this would mean using scarce government funds instead of free donor funds. Neither had the implementing organizations and consultants any incentives to function in a particularly cost-effective manner, as they were not judged against such criteria.
- Swedish development assistance was almost entirely micro-focused. It was projects and programs that mattered, not the fate of the overall economy. Projects were often justified as demonstrations—ways of showing modern systems in developed countries to the developing. Performance was judged at the project level, not in terms of what this project did for the country or economy as a whole, and even less in terms of how the same Swedish and Tanzanian resources could be used elsewhere. Projects could, at least for a considerable time, be rescued by throwing good money after bad.

- Projects tended to be high in technical ambition, and not adapted to the resources of a poor, non-industrialized country. In many ways, they emulated Swedish models, with little regard for their financial implications for reasons given above. The Swedes wanted to show what they could deliver, and the Tanzanians did not want second best. Many such projects became islands of modernity and excellence, increasingly isolated from an otherwise highly traditional and resource starved economy. Bypassing existing procedures and budgets was more a rule than an exception.
- Donors, including Sweden, favored the support of investments and building up organizations and structures, rather than support for operations and maintenance. Thus, from the recipient organization side, the investment phase was "'free,'" while the operation and maintenance phase was costly. From the recipient side it made more sense to let a road, a power plant, a school, deteriorate and get support for a new one, than to maintain the existing one with domestic resources.
- There was a considerable herd instinct in the donor community. Donors tended to be drawn to certain issues in development in vogue at a particular time, with little concern for the cumulative effect of such support. Donors competed for projects and attention in such fields, often disregarding the required needs or the capacity to absorb resources. As a result, the concern for overall cost-effective use of the resources declined, waste increased, and local management became very relaxed.

Learning in Development Assistance

Our study in Tanzania concerned decision making in the 1970s to the mid-1990s. Over the last three decades, considerable learning has taken place in the development assistance industry. There has been a shift from an almost exclusive focus on projects to more macro-oriented approaches. Bilateral projects are increasingly being replaced by multi-donor, sectorwide approaches. General budget support is common. Development research has taught the importance of good policies and good governance, and development economists are increasingly discovering the factors behind economic growth. Like so many other donor countries and international development agencies, Sweden has introduced country strategies for its aid. Thus, a country analysis and an analysis of experience of past involvement form the basis of three- to five-year strategies for Swedish assistance. The project cycle has improved: for example, logical framework analysis is today mandatory in Swedish development assistance, providing a better basis for assessments of achievements and fulfilling objectives. Over the years, the methodology for evaluations has also improved, and considerable resources are spent on the learning from past and from ongoing projects and programs.

Perhaps the problems discussed in our study in Tanzania could be considered teething problems in an industry that, after all, is fairly young. However, while many of the reforms of development assistance are weeding out problems and dysfunctional aspects of aid, our general belief is that the root problems remain. This is based on continuous work in development (although not in Tanzania). These remaining root problems are essentially that (1) development assistance is largely a supply-driven process; and (2) there is a low degree of responsibility in the donor industry for what it accomplishes and for the results it creates.

Our Vision for a New Style of Development Assistance

In our study we outlined a vision of a Swedish aid system in many ways radically different from the one in place. The key in this was to get away from the disbursement pressure embedded in country budgets (or loan volumes in international organizations). Development assistance should never be driven by even the remotest hint of a need to get rid of money or to expand loan volumes. We saw many of the current problems in Swedish development assistance to be the result of Sweden allocating a certain amount of money annually as a percentage of national income, and then dividing up this sum to favored developing countries in "country frames."[6] These country frames were then distributed to projects and programs, almost exclusively for public sector undertakings, and largely without consideration of the country's capacity to absorb resources, nor of its past efficiency in using these resources. "Needs" and "problems" determined allocations and governments were assumed to deal with them. As a result, there was to a large extent a premium for bad behavior, and a high tax on "good" behavior by governments.

Our vision of a different Swedish development assistance was based on two approaches.

The first approach would be a development assistance that provides strong incentives for efficient use of resources and effective performance, based on healthy competition among nations, projects, commercial, public, and non-governmental organizations; and even individuals. We suggested a development fund, open to project requests and proposals from a wide variety of countries and a wide variety of players. These proposals would be scrutinized for their development merits, taking into account the credibility of the owner as a major factor. In our vision it was a fund operating similarly to a good research or scientific foundation, trying to maximize the overall effect of its scarce resources. The criteria for the use of resources would be based on the overall objectives of Swedish development assistance, such as reduction of poverty, economic growth, gender equality, promotion of democracy, or human rights. If not enough worthy proposals were presented, the fund could accumulate resources. Countries, governments, organizations, and people that used the aid resources well would have a greater chance of receiving additional resources. In such a system, corrupt practices and sloppy management, whether in government, public, or private organizations, would be heavily punished, however imperative the "needs" were.

This idea was based on the belief that: (1) the key constraints in development generally are not financial resources, but leadership, management, and systems, and (2) the resources provided by Swedish development assistance are marginal given the needs of developing countries and the poor; hence only investments with very high leverage make any sense. The fund should seek out change agents, that is, projects, persons, and/or organizations with a potential to create change, for example in central government, local administrations, organizations, or NGOs.

The second approach is more radical. In certain countries, and in some key sectors of critical importance for long-term development and poverty eradication, Swedish development assistance would take joint responsibility with the government or the responsible authority to manage and finance the sector over a period of time. The funding would be joint and the management joint, but with a gradually declining input of Swedish assistance. For example, Swedish development assistance would commit itself to decent universal primary schooling in Tanzania for a twenty-year period with the objective that after this period, Tanzania would run the system technically and financially. The joint management would allow the donor agency to pursue required reforms and pursue systems for local financing. It would be judged on sector performance, not as an isolated project, and the gradual take-over by the local authority would be a significant criterion. The system would have to be tailored to the resources eventually available and could not be made a luxury project.

This would be an approach to use only in exceptional cases, for sectors that are absolutely vital for the poor and for poor countries to establish a foundation to get out of poverty. Primary schooling and primary health are the obvious cases; their provision is a necessary condition for human development and development in general, and also a fundamental human right. They are too important to allow certain countries and governments to make a mess of them.

3. Lessons in Evaluation

Was the evaluation methodology chosen for the study valid for drawing far-reaching conclusions, as we have? There are a number of caveats: First, the studied projects were not selected randomly, but chosen to fit certain criteria related to aid dependency and phase-out. Second, data limitations meant that the assessments of the projects were not based on quantitative data. Third, the project evaluation methodology was simple and might even be called impressionistic. As noted above, it relied on piecing together pictures from written and oral sources and, based on this, making judgments on aspects such as degrees of success, sustainability, and so forth. These judgments were largely based on the views of different stakeholders. Fourth, some of our judgments about success and sustainability had to be made before projects closed, and hence they were based on our predictions.

When the study was presented in various forums, the validity of the approach was not questioned (which of course is not proof that it was valid). The stakeholders were willing to accept the results, even when these results implied considerable criticism and the findings could have been contested on methodological grounds.

We believe that the merit of the study for these stakeholders was that it provided an unusual insight into the process of development assistance, and was of value for its broader reflections on development assistance. This was due to a combination of factors: (1) it covered an unusually long period; (2) it reviewed some projects that had ended long ago and hence could be revisited with sometimes surprising results; (3) it used a micro approach towards a fairly large number of projects, combined with a macro assessment, and thus shed some light on the often discussed micro-macro paradox in Tanzanian development assistance; and (4) it touched on decision-making processes and related psychological rationales behind development assistance.

Nevertheless, the Tanzanian study reflected the common difficulties in evaluation of development assistance that are due to the lack of hard facts—something that has frustrated evaluators as long as the profession has existed. Since at least the 1970s, concerted efforts have been made to establish more quantitative and objective methods, both at the design stage and during implementation, reflected in systems such as logframe analysis; identification of verifiable indicators; baseline surveys; establishment of monitoring and evaluation (M&E) units in projects and organizations; and built-in systems to provide continuous M&E data to management and donors. While much has been accomplished, and still much more can be done to develop more accurate and scientific evaluations, we would like to raise the question whether more soundly based evaluation is the real answer to the dilemma of effectiveness of development assistance. If not, a different approach is required at least as a complement.

Development of Market-like Feedback Systems

Official development assistance is essentially a relationship between a supplier and a consumer. On the one hand, taxpayers in rich countries, through their political decisions, agree to use a share of their income for development assistance. On the other hand, the intended recipients—poor people in poor countries—through such assistance will improve their lives and get out of poverty. In between, a number of intermediaries act on behalf of the suppliers and consumers: parliaments, which decide on taxes and budgets and broad objectives for the ODA; governments, which, inter alia, allocate funds to countries and to implementing organizations; specialized bilateral and multilateral organizations, which translate these resources into programs and projects; consultants, who assist at different levels in this process; and governments in "partner" countries, which propose programs, projects, and strategies to ODA funding organizations, and translate the assistance received into projects, programs or services, which are expected to assist the ultimate beneficiaries.

The point is not to make this a simple one-way process, which it is not. Rather it is that the process is almost exclusively controlled and managed by the intermediaries, including the assessment of whether taxpayers' money is used effectively to help the poor get out of poverty. A feedback loop between the ultimate supplier and the ultimate consumer hardly exists. The taxpayer usually knows very little about what happens to his and her taxes used for development assistance, and poor people in poor countries generally have no idea of the origin of the funding of the services they receive or don't receive. And even in cases when the latter happen to know, they generally have no way of expressing satisfaction or dissatisfaction with this to the "supplier." Furthermore, as the relationship between a donor and a recipient is highly asymmetrical, it is unlikely that the ultimate recipient would express strong demands about the effective use of the resources donated.

It is difficult to imagine a system in which the intermediaries do not play a strong role in determining the effectiveness of development assistance. Hence, the effectiveness of development assistance depends on their professionalism, honesty, and readiness to learn from past efforts, including processes of objective evaluations. However, in our view much more could be done to promote more direct feedback loops in the system and stimulate independent flows of information for correctives. Examples of this are:

- Independent evaluators accountable to parliaments, preferably in both donor and recipient countries (at least if the latter are democracies). Such evaluators would be at arms length from the organizations more directly involved, and hence operate under conditions that at least in principle would allow greater objectivity.
- Participatory evaluations, that is, instruments designed by the donor community to provide more direct feedback. These have been tried mostly in rural development projects and programs, but could be extended to many different forms of assistance.
- The media, both in donor and recipient countries, can demystify complex development processes and short-circuit lengthy information flows which otherwise never reach the supplier or the consumer. While the media have a tendency to look for negative news and scandals, they often, nevertheless, are effective correctives. Furthermore, they tend to be a key instrument for mobilizing the suppliers of development assistance through providing direct pictures of poverty and human suffering.

- Civil society organizations, such as issue-driven national or international NGOs, are usually very effective in communicating directly with the ultimate suppliers. While the civil society groupings have their own agendas, they add a voice that often provides insight to suppliers and they often are also close to the ultimate consumers.
- Last, but not least: in our view pluralism and market-like systems in development assistance encourage effective feedback. Many independent channels for development assistance lead to competing organizations, which require direct means both to communicate with taxpayers and the poor and to establish feedback systems. Using the market analogue, such competitiveness will, in our view, contribute to more effective development assistance.

Notes

1. This paper is based on a study carried out by Julie Catterson and Claes Lindahl, with contributions by William Lyakurwa, Samuel Wangwe, and Petra Stark. That study was commissioned by the Expert Group on Development Issues (EGDI), which was established by the Swedish Government in 1995 under the Ministry of Foreign Affairs. The study was published by EGDI in 1999 under the title: *The Sustainability Enigma. Aid Dependency and the Phasing out of Projects. The Case of Swedish Aid to Tanzania.* When the present paper was presented at the OED Conference in July 2003, several participants independently approached us afterwards with viewpoints similar to this: "There was only one fault in your presentation. Instead of Swedish assistance, you should have used our country, our organization.... We all made the same mistakes in Tanzania. It is to the credit of the Swedes that they are willing to discuss those problems openly."
2. UNDP, *Human Development Report 2002.* Tanzania is still the world's second poorest country (in purchasing power parity terms) after Sierra Leone, and among the very poorest, it is the only non-war-torn country.
3. Aid dependency and the phase-out problem at the project or program level might to some extent be a special problem for bilateral development agencies, which have commonly provided assistance "process-style," rather than as "blueprint" investments with a clearly articulated endpoint for the support. As the process style entails fairly open-ended support, often with an implicit long-term commitment and without a detailed investment plan, phasing out is a built-in problem. The dilemma with phase-out does not imply that the process-style approach should be considered inferior to the old blueprint; rather, it means that different styles of development assistance have their own generic problems, which donors need to be aware of and counter as best they can.
4. The assessment gave a fairly rare opportunity for an aid organization to determine what happened "afterwards." Most evaluations of development assistance tend to be carried out during the project, or shortly after it ends, but in this study we revisited some projects and institutions to which the Swedish support had ended quite a few years earlier.
5. The case material is included in the study report.
6. SIDA uses the concept of "country frame" to indicate its aid budget for a particular partner country.

7

An Approach for Country Assistance Evaluations

John Johnson and Ruben Lamdany

Over the past seven years, the World Bank's Operations Evaluation Department (OED) has completed evaluations of assistance programs in nearly sixty countries. With growing experience and feedback from stakeholders, the methodology behind these evaluations has gradually improved.[1] This short paper discusses the key concepts and caveats underlying OED's methodology and introduces the basic rating template used in these evaluations. The focus of OED's country assistance evaluations (CAEs) is to assess and rate the outcome of the World Bank's assistance programs. CAEs assess the World Bank's past performance, distill lessons, and provide recommendations. Ratings are thought of as accountability tools as well as a framework to organize the analysis.

1. Assistance Program Outcome: The Main Focus of the Evaluation

To avoid confusion about what is being evaluated,[2] it is necessary to be clear about the difference between:

- The country's overall development progress, as measured by indicators such as changes in poverty measures, per capita GDP, and consumption growth, and other measures of well-being in the country.
- The outcome of the assistance program (the main focus of the evaluation). In general, to assess the outcome, OED would consider the objectives of the assistance as stated in the World Bank's country assistance strategy for the relevant period.
- The performance of the donor or lender (in this case, the World Bank) in designing and implementing the assistance program.

Senior adviser, Operations Evaluation Department, World Bank.
Director, World Bank Institute.

On occasion, stakeholders and readers of OED's country assistance evaluations have challenged the outcome ratings by asking questions such as:

- How could the outcome of an assistance program be judged unsatisfactory, when the country's *overall* development situation improved so much—or vice versa?
- If the assistance to the corresponding country had a satisfactory outcome, does that not mean that Bank performance must also have been satisfactory—or vice versa?

The reality is that the outcome of a donor's assistance can, and often does, diverge from the overall development outcome of a country and—more surprisingly—from the quality of the design and implementation of the program. Key factors contributing to this divergence are the scale of the program relative to the country, the fact that the objectives of assistance programs are often only a subset of a client's overall development goals, and the materialization of unexpected exogenous shocks.

For example, in countries that have large populations, complex development requirements, many agents involved in development, and ample access to alternative sources of finance, an individual donor or lender's assistance program may have no more than a modest impact on the overall development situation. In these circumstances, the assistance program (as specified in the donor's corresponding country assistance strategy) is likely to aim from the start at more modest objectives. Competing domestic and exogenous influences, such as events of nature, political instability, and abrupt changes in the country's international terms of trade, will be equally or more important, and the program's total resources will not constitute more than a small fraction of the total development resources available to the client. In such circumstances, the assessment of an assistance program often diverges from an assessment of the client's overall development progress, and there would be no logical imperative why they should be the same.

At the opposite end of the spectrum, the outcome of World Bank (or any other agency's) assistance is much more likely to be closely aligned with the country's overall development outcome in a small country where the assistance sets out to influence the country's high-level objectives and where this assistance represents a significant share of all the development resources available to the client.

OED's country assistance evaluations have found many different combinations of country developments and outcomes of World Bank assistance. For example, in El Salvador, Ghana, and Poland the Bank's assistance programs achieved a satisfactory development impact in client countries that displayed a corresponding advance in their overall development. In several cases, such as in Ethiopia, assistance programs delivered significant benefits to a client country that made little or no development progress. And in a few other cases, OED found that the client country made better overall progress in addressing its development constraints without external assistance.

The paragraphs above explain the difference between country outcomes and the outcomes of the World Bank's country assistance. Similarly, OED distinguishes between these two concepts and the Bank's performance, which is defined as the quality of the design and implementation of the Bank's assistance program. Clearly, a well-designed and implemented program could fail as a result of unforeseen natural disasters, or of other factors not under the Bank's control, for example, unexpected changes in government. Also in this case, OED has found that at times the design and implementation of the Bank's assistance program is better/worse than the outcome of such assistance, for example as the result of worse/better performance of a borrower's performance or of a positive/negative natural shock. For example, OED found that the Bank's assistance to Honduras for developing infrastructure was well designed and was being implemented in a successful manner until it was wiped out by a large hurricane.

Country assistance evaluations focus on the outcome of the World Bank's assistance. However, they also look at the overall country performance and at Bank performance, in part to assess this outcome. Overall country performance is assessed to understand the background to the implementation of the Bank's assistance and to construct the appropriate counterfactuals. Bank performance is assessed as part of the process of triangulation that is used to rate the Bank's assistance. These concepts are explained below.

2. Judging Program Outcome

In assessing and rating outcome, or the expected development impact of a program, OED gauges the extent to which major strategic objectives were relevant and achieved, without shortcomings. Programs typically set as their central aims higher-order goals such as poverty reduction. However, such higher-order goals can rarely be achieved directly. Instead, programs will typically identify intermediate interventions through which to pursue these higher-order goals, such as targeted delivery of social services, accelerated economic growth, and integrated rural development. Ideally, the World Bank's country assistance strategy will have clearly identified the causal links between intermediate and higher-order outcomes, but, if it has not, it is the task of the evaluator to scrutinize the relationship and validate the links, if any. Work can then proceed toward assessing and rating the implementation and outcome.

Other factors go into assessing program design and relevance. For example, not every client will respond in the same way to the development priorities that are embodied in the Millennium Development Goals, nor to the mandates of the World Bank's corporate advocacy priorities such as safeguards. Normally, any disagreements between the client and the Bank on these issues would be identified and resolved in the country assistance strategy, enabling the evaluator to focus on whether the tradeoffs adopted were appropriate. However, in some instances, the strategy may be found to have glossed over certain disagreements, or to have avoided addressing some of a client's key development constraints. In either case, the consequences could include a diminution of program relevance, a loss of client ownership, and/or unwelcome side-effects, such as safeguard violations, all of which must be taken into account in judging program outcome.

3. Attribution of Outcome is Complex

Attribution is one of the most difficult challenges of any evaluation, and particularly when evaluating the impact of World Bank assistance when this forms part of a much larger government program that is supported by many other donors. This is a key reason why program outcome will often be assessed differently than overall development outcomes and/or Bank performance. The Bank's contribution to an assistance program, no matter how positive, is unlikely to be sufficient to ensure a satisfactory program outcome. That is because outcome will usually be the joint product of four agents: the client; the Bank; aid partners and other stakeholders; and exogenous factors (events of nature, international economic shocks, and so forth). A negative contribution from any one of these agents could overwhelm the positive contributions of the other actors and produce an unsatisfactory outcome.

Hence OED assesses the World Bank's performance on the basis of actions that the Bank could directly control, notably (1) the professional quality of the Bank's services; (2) the prudence and probity of its interventions; (3) its exercise of participation and partnership; (4) its application of selectivity, operating only in areas where the Bank had a comparative advantage; and (5) its creativity, initiative, and efficiency. In keeping with its mandate, OED does not rate client country performance or that of aid partners and stakeholders. However, it needs to develop a clear view of what those contributions were, as well as the effect of exogenous events, so as to provide a full context for the assessment and rating of Bank performance.

4. Evaluation by Triangulation

The best analytical solution for the problem of attribution would be to build a rich and widely accepted "counterfactual model" specifying alternative actions and all their possible consequences. A good counterfactual would also enable the development of a good metric for ratings. In fact, this is not practical and in general it is not even theoretically possible. Thus, OED generally only compares outcomes with historical trends and with developments in similar countries. One of the ways in which OED mitigates the inherent subjectivity of judgments and ratings, in view of these limitations, is by testing the consistency of its judgments across three distinct dimensions of the assistance program:

- A products and services dimension, involving a "bottom-up" analysis of major program inputs—loans, analytical and advisory services, aid coordination, and resource mobilization. Most of these inputs are separately assessed and rated in isolation, thus providing an independent source of information.
- A development impact dimension, involving a "top-down" analysis of the principal program objectives for their relevance, efficacy, satisfactory outcome, sustainability, and high institutional impact.
- An attribution or contribution dimension, where the evaluator looks at the outcome as the result of the contributions of the four categories of actors alluded to above.

5. Building a Metric

Each of these three dimensions is assessed and rated independently, using a rating template referred to as the country information form or CIF (reproduced in Appendix 2 to this chapter). In order to mitigate the impact of each individual judgment, the CIF subdivides the ratings of each of these dimensions into judgments on a much larger number of contributory elements. For example, to reach an assessment of the overall impact of Bank products (the first dimension) OED aggregates the ratings and assessments on individual loans and advisory products (which are evaluated independently). Similarly, for the second dimension, OED subdivides ratings on higher-order objectives such as contribution to poverty alleviation, into judgments on a large number of components of such an objective, for example, the impact on specific relevant, sectoral indicators. Appropriate weights are needed in order to aggregate the assessments on these lower-order objectives. Using the size or number of loans is a relatively easy choice of weights when looking at lending. Agreeing on appropriate weights for other aspects of the assistance is much more difficult, and this is certainly the case when trying to aggregate across the achievement of different objectives of the assistance program.[3]

To rate the outcome of country assistance programs, OED uses the same six categories that it uses to rate the outcome of investment projects. The definitions of each rating category in this scale, which ranges from highly satisfactory to highly unsatisfactory, are presented in Table 7.1.

After identifying the main objectives of the assistance program and studying the program inputs and outputs, OED evaluators complete the country information form using these outcome-rating categories. To further validate their judgments, evaluators consult on individual assessments with relevant stakeholders, including officials of client countries, beneficiaries, partners, and World Bank managers. Ratings are then aggregated using pre-established weights, and a single rating for outcome is be calculated from each of the three

Table 7.1
Categories for Rating the Outcome of Country Assistance Programs

Highly satisfactory	The assistance program achieved significant progress toward all major relevant objectives, possibly with minor shortcomings. Best practice development impact was achieved in one or more areas.
Satisfactory	The assistance program achieved acceptable progress toward all major relevant objectives, possibly with minor shortcomings.
Partially or moderately satisfactory	The assistance program achieved acceptable progress toward most major relevant objectives, possibly with a major shortcoming, such as a safeguard violation, and/or failure to address a key development constraint.
Partially or moderately unsatisfactory	The assistance program did not make acceptable progress toward most of its major relevant objectives, possibly with a major shortcoming, such as a safeguard violation, and/or failure to address a key development constraint.
Unsatisfactory	The country assistance program did not make acceptable progress toward any of its major relevant objectives, or failed to address multiple key development constraints, or had multiple major shortcomings, such as safeguard violations.
Highly unsatisfactory	The country assistance program did not make acceptable progress toward any of its major relevant objectives, and either failed to address multiple key development constraints, or exhibited multiple major shortcomings, such as safeguard violations.

components of the CIF, corresponding to the three aspects or dimensions of the assistance program.

The overall ratings for each of these three dimensions should be equal, or nearly so, because they are measuring different facets of the same assistance result. When large scoring disparities arise, this is treated as a signal that the detailed supporting judgments contain inconsistencies, and must be reconsidered in whole or in part. For example, if the scoring of the top-down analysis suggested the program outcome was unsatisfactory, but the products and services of that program scored significantly higher, OED would reexamine whether, say, product objectives were sufficiently relevant to the achievement of the program's strategic priorities, or whether some gaps or incompatibilities existed among the services provided. Of course, it might also be the case that the original "top-down" judgment of outcome in the development impact dimension was exceedingly pessimistic, in which case this too would be rechecked.

6. The Way Forward

Country assistance evaluations prepared using this methodology have served to improve many of the World Bank's country assistance strategies. The methodology has also enabled OED to create a large database on the outcomes of Bank assistance at the country level. This will make it possible to track how these outcomes change over time. Thus far, indicators on investment project performance have served as the only indicator of the Bank's effectiveness.

The methodology still has several obvious shortcomings, some of which are inherent in an evaluation of this type and therefore have no solution. The evolving development agenda may change the nature of these problems, mitigating some but augmenting others. The drive towards partnership and harmonization among donors will mitigate the need to deal with the attribution problem, but it will also complicate the assessment of performance by individual donors and thus dilute accountability. The Results Agenda that the World Bank is now adopting and incorporating into its country assistance strategies will align the goals of these assistance programs more closely with the development goals of client countries. This will facilitate the choice of objective outcome indicators, but it is likely to make more difficult for a country assistance evaluation to identify areas where the Bank could improve its performance (since these indicators would be less correlated with this performance).

Appendix 1

Frequently Asked Questions about Country Assistance Evaluation

Would a program's poverty reduction impact always be taken into account in applying this approach? Yes, poverty reduction impact is always factored in, either because it is an explicit objective of the country assistance strategy (as in the vast majority of cases), or because OED viewed poverty reduction as a key relevance criterion in judging program outcomes from the perspective of the Bank's own priorities.

How can deliveries of country assistance evaluations be timed so as to ensure maximum impact on the design of the next assistance strategy? It has been OED's preferred practice to deliver a draft of the country assistance evaluation several months before the consideration of the next country assistance strategy by the World Bank's Board of Directors, so that the operational country team can benefit from the evaluation findings early in the course of strategy preparations.

What is OED doing to ensure a participatory role for borrowers in country assistance evaluation deliberations? OED has taken a number of steps to include the borrower in the country assistance evaluation process. Consultation begins when the approach paper for the evaluation is discussed by the Committee on Development Effectiveness (CODE) of the World Bank's Executive Board. In selected cases, approach papers have been discussed with country authorities even before they were conveyed to CODE. Additionally, the draft and final versions of the country assistance evaluation are shared with the borrower. Governmental authorities are provided ample time to submit written comments for inclusion, verbatim, in the final version of the country assistance evaluation before it is submitted to CODE and the Board. An OED mission and/or a videoconference to discuss the key findings frequently reinforce these consultations.

Do country assistance evaluations incorporate the results only of closed projects? No, OED reviews ongoing projects as well, drawing from project supervision reports, assessments by the Bank's Quality Assurance Group, Network and OED studies, and external sources, where relevant.

How do the ratings of project performance relate to the overall outcome rating in the country assistance evaluation? Lending services are just one of the products and services OED takes into account in its bottom-up assessment of program impact. The impact of non-lending services, notably analytical and advisory activities, resource mobilization, and aid coordination, is also assessed as part of arriving at an overall rating of program outcome. Additionally, to validate this bottom-up perspective, OED undertakes a top-down review, investigating whether the program achieved acceptable progress toward the objectives laid out in the Bank's country assistance strategy and toward any other key development priorities that were identified during the course of the evaluation.

How do these evaluations assess the capacity building component as well as the long-term sustainability of the Bank's assistance? OED borrowed, from its project evaluation methodology, the concepts and rating scale used to assess the sustainability of outcome and institutional development impact of the assistance program. The *institutional development impact* can be rated as high, substantial, modest, or negligible. Ratings are based on an assessment of the extent to which the Bank's assistance has strengthened the client country's ability to draw on its physical, financial, and human capital to advance development results in the following areas:

- economic management;
- the structure of the public sector, and, in particular, the civil service;
- the institutional soundness of the financial sector;
- legal, regulatory, and judicial systems;
- monitoring and evaluation systems;
- aid coordination;
- financial accountability;
- building NGO capacity; and
- social and environmental capital.

Sustainability measures the likelihood that the development benefits of the country assistance program will be resilient to risk. Sustainability can be rated as highly likely (4), likely (3), unlikely (2), highly unlikely (1), or non-evaluable.

Appendix 2

Country Information Form: A Rating Algorithm for Country Assistance Evaluations

Client Country:
Assistance program implementation period under review:
Dates of country assistance strategy covering implementation period:
Date of most recent poverty reduction strategy discussed by World Bank Board:
Date of client survey:
This country information form is being completed by:
Title:
Date:

On a scale of 1-6, where 1 indicates highly unsatisfactory, and 6 indicates highly satisfactory,* please provide your assessment of the following components of the World Bank assistance program for _____, during the period ____-__:

I. World Bank Products and Services
   A. Lending Services (Weight: 50%)
      1. Taking into account evaluations you regard as pertinent, how well did projects closed during this period perform?
         Rating: __
      2. How did the portfolio of on-going projects perform, taking into account those assessments of project quality you regard as pertinent?
         Rating: __
   B. Analytical and Advisory Services (Weight: 30%)
      1. Were analytical and advisory services initiated during this period:
         (a) timely?
            Rating: __
         (b) of high analytical quality?
            Rating: __
         (c) appropriately disseminated?
            Rating: __
         (d) of high impact on their intended audiences?
            Rating: __
   C. Aid Coordination and Resource Mobilization (Weight: 20%)

---

* Highly Satisfactory = 6; Satisfactory = 5; Moderately Satisfactory = 4; Moderately Unsatisfactory = 3; Unsatisfactory = 2; Highly Unsatisfactory = 1.

    1. Did aid coordination and resource mobilization effectively
        support the goals of the assistance program?
           Rating: __

II. Development Impact of the Assistance Program
    A. Please list the three or four most important development goals of
       the assistance program:
          (1)
          (2)
          (3)
          (4)
    B. How would you rate the relevance of these objectives individually to
       the client's key development constraints and priorities?
          (1) Rating: ___ (Sub-weight: ?)
          (2) Rating: ___ (Sub-weight: ?)
          (3) Rating: ___ (Sub-weight: ?)
          (4) Rating: ___ (Sub-weight: ?)
    C. Were there any important objectives that, in hindsight, should have
       been pursued, but, in the end, were not?
       If so, please specify these omitted objectives:
          (5)
          (6)
          (7)
    D. Did the assistance strategy maintain its relevance to the client's
       development constraints and priorities over time?
       Rating: ___
    E. Overall, how would you assess the relevance of the objectives of the
       assistance program, taking into account what was included and what
       was omitted? (Weight in Overall Program Impact: 30%)
       Rating: __
    F. Now, in your judgment, how effectively did the assistance program
       achieve progress toward each of its stated objectives?
          (1) Rating: __
          (2) Rating: __
          (3) Rating: __
          (4) Rating: __
    G. In achieving those objectives, were there any major shortcomings, such
       as unintended social costs, environmental damage, etc.?
       If so, please list those shortcomings:
          (1)
          (2)
          (3)

H. Overall, how would you rate the efficacy of the assistance program in achieving its major objectives, taking into account the sub-weights you listed in II.A.2 above, as well as any listed shortcomings?

　　　Rating: __   (Weight in Overall Program Impact: 40%)

I. To what extent did the assistance program achieve a satisfactory institutional development impact by:

(1) strengthening the capacity of public institutions to ensure stable, transparent, enforceable, and predictable execution of their mandates?

　　　Rating: ___   (Sub-weight: ?)

(2) improving the rules of the game for efficient, broad-based private sector development?

　　　Rating: ___   (Sub-weight: ?)

(3) improving the stability, diversity, and growth potential of financial sector services?

　　　Rating: ___   (Sub-weight: ?)

J. Overall, how would you rate the institutional development impact of the assistance program, weighting (1), (2), and (3) as you have specified above?

　　　Rating: ___ (Weight in Overall Program Impact: 15%)

K. How would you assess the likelihood that the development benefits associated with each objective of the assistance program will be maintained (Sustainability)?

　　　(1) Rating: ____   (Sub-weight: ?)
　　　(2) Rating: ____   (Sub-weight: ?)
　　　(3) Rating: ____   (Sub-weight: ?)
　　　(4) Rating: ____   (Sub-weight: ?)

L. How do you rate the overall sustainability of the assistance program benefits?

　　　Rating: ___   (Weight in Overall Program Result: (15%)

M. Weighting your responses to Questions E, H, J, and L as indicated, how would you rate the overall development impact of the assistance program?

　　　Rating: ___

N. What do you see as the key lessons emerging from this program?

　　　1.
　　　2.
　　　3.
　　　4.

III. Contributions to the Results of the Assistance Program by Source (Attribution)

A. According to best practices in force at the time when the program was designed, prepared, and implemented, did the Bank uphold corporate mandates to:

1. build client ownership of the assistance program?
    Rating: __
2. build a strong monitoring and evaluation framework within the CAS?
    Rating: __
3. maintain throughout the CAS implementation period an assistance strategy relevant to the client's long-term development constraints and priorities?
    Rating: __
4. build strong linkages between the CAS strategy and:
    (a) AAA?
        Rating: __
    (b) the lending program?
        Rating: __
5. provide high quality AAA?
    Rating: ___
6. maintain a high quality dialogue with the client Government?
    Rating: ___
7. initiate or deepen a direct dialogue with civil society?
    Rating: ___
8. aid the client to develop a holistic, long-term vision of its potential, constraints, linkages, and synergies?
    Rating: ___
9. incorporate the lessons learned from previous evaluations?
    Rating: ___
10. maintain a high quality at entry for new projects?
    Rating: ___
11. detail staff with the appropriate skill mix to the program?
    Rating: ___
12. explain and train in Bank policies and procedures?
    Rating: ___
13. adopt a results-oriented focus on development impact?
    Rating: ___
14. undertake comprehensive risk assessment?
    Rating: ___
15. provide adequate institutional capacity analysis?
    Rating: ___
16. provide adequate social and stakeholder analysis?
    Rating: ___
17. provide adequate environmental analysis?
    Rating: ___
18. provide adequate gender analysis?
    Rating: ___

19. incorporate performance indicators and monitoring and evaluation systems?
    Rating: ___
20. report on progress and problems in implementing the country assistance program?
    Rating: ___
21. build client evaluation capacity?
    Rating: ___
22. assess client funding requirements realistically?
    Rating: ___
23. strengthen the client's capacity for financial management and accountability?
    Rating: ___
24. enforce compliance with project procurement guidelines, audit requirements, and other project cost controls?
    Rating: ___
25. enforce loan covenants and exercising remedies?
    Rating: ___
26. manage the country portfolio effectively?
    Rating: ___
27. provide timely notice to the Board of fundamental changes in Bank assistance strategy?
    Rating: ___
28. foster client leadership of aid coordination?
    Rating: ___
29. coordinate adequately within the Bank Group (IBRD, IDA, IFC, MIGA, WBI)?
    Rating: ___
30. fulfill a catalytic role in resource mobilization?
    Rating: ___
31. partner with aid providers effectively?
    Rating: ___
32. foster participation?
    Rating: ___
33. coordinate and mobilize aid resources effectively?
    Rating: ___
34. focus on areas of Bank comparative advantage?
    Rating: ___
35. contain overhead costs through burden sharing?
    Rating: ___
36. employ an appropriate mix of assistance instruments?
    Rating: ___
37. ensure readiness for implementation of all products and services?

Rating: ___

38. provide new products and innovative solutions adapted to the client's circumstances?
    Rating: ___
39. exhibit appropriate flexibility in dealing with unforeseen problems?
    Rating: ___
40. keep costs in line with Bank norms (average cost and elapsed time per report, etc.)?
    Rating: ___
41. monitor and enforce compliance with safeguard policies?
    Rating: ___
42. provide timely delivery of products and services?
    Rating: ___
43. *Overall rating of Bank* performance, taking into account responses 1-40: ___ (Weight of 40 Percent in attribution)

B. How do you assess client's performance, *taking into account the country's initial endowments and capabilities,* in:
    1. shaping and assuming ownership of the CAS strategy?
       Rating: __
    2. maintaining a high-level dialog with Bank staff and management?
       Rating: __
    3. consulting with civil society and stakeholders on the CAS strategy and implementation?
       Rating: __
    4. preparing Bank-supported projects?
       Rating: __
    5. providing counterpart funds in timely fashion?
       Rating: __
    6. following procurement guidelines?
       Rating: __
    7. collaborating earnestly with supervision missions?
       Rating: __
    8. preparing ICRs and providing other feedback on Bank operations?
       Rating: __
    9. discussing the findings of ESW at a high governmental level?
       Rating: __
    10. embracing Bank advocacy priorities?
        Rating: __
    11. *Overall rating of client* performance, taking into account the responses 1-10: ___ (Weight of 40 Percent in Attribution)

C. How do you assess aid partner performance in terms of:
    1. shared vision?
            Rating: ___
    2. agreement on strategic selectivity?
            Rating: ___
    3. collaboration in implementing external assistance?
            Rating: ___
    4. collaboration in implementing Bank projects?
            Rating: ___
    5. *Overall rating of aid* partner *performance,* taking into account responses 1-4: ___
            (Weight of 20 percent in attribution)
D. How, if at all, did the following exogenous factors affect achievement of the assistance program objectives (here, you may rate by high, substantial, modest, or negligible):
    1. world economic shocks/trends/terms of trade?
    2. events of nature (floods, hurricanes, drought, etc.)?
    3. events of man (civil conflict, war, etc.)
    4. other (specify)? _____
    5. *Overall* rating *of exogenous factors,* taking into account responses 1-4:___
            (Variable weight of 0-100 percent)**

** Please indicate how weightings of other actors should be adjusted.

Notes

1. OED is currently undertaking a review of country assistance evaluations.
2. Some terms frequently used below include:
    Assistance program: a package of loans, advisory and analytical services and aid mobilization and coordination provided by an outside source, in this case the World Bank.
    Client: the country receiving the benefits of the assistance program.
    Triangulation: the use of three or more theories, sources, or types of information, or types of analysis to verify and substantiate an assessment.
    Counterfactual: an estimate of what would have occurred in the absence of the assistance program.
    World Bank performance: measures whether, according to best practices in force at the time an assistance program was designed, prepared, and implemented, the Bank provided a professional quality of services with prudence, probity, innovation, and efficiency.
3. OED tends to use uniform weights when no other objective criterion seems to apply.

Comments on the Papers by Lindahl-Catterson and Johnson-Lamdany

Colin Kirk

On the face of it, the papers by Lindahl and Catterson (chapter 6) and by Johnson and Lamdany (chapter 7) seem quite different: one takes a long-term view of the aid relationship between Sweden and Tanzania, and the other presents methodological proposals for evaluation of the World Bank's country assistance strategies. But the two have a number of themes in common. In particular, I would like to discuss the way in which they address questions of the scope of the evaluation effort.

I mean scope in four senses: first, the time frame covered by evaluations; second, the content of the program being evaluated; third, the context within which programs are set; and fourth—linking program content and program context—I want to address the difficult issues of attribution and influence that the papers raise. This last issue brings us back to the overall question, Does what the development agencies do make sense?

1. A Tale of Two Cities?

The paper by Lindahl and Catterson raises questions about the quality and effectiveness of Sweden's aid to Tanzania in the thirty years up to the mid-1990s. This was something of a passionate relationship—a Swedish love affair. But did it make any difference to Tanzania, or indeed to Sweden?

The paper presents rather the depressing evidence of Tanzania's failure to develop economically over the thirty-year period, and documents the mixed results of Swedish-funded projects. What does make the paper particularly interesting is the long historical view it takes; very few evaluations cover such a long period. And this long historical view has prompted Lindahl and his team to come up with a "bold hypothesis" that challenges the conventional view that progress in those decades was so limited. The bold hypothesis claims that, although these decades of Swedish support were on the face of it a failure in economic terms, they nonetheless laid the institutional foundations on which Tanzania has subsequently begun to make progress and, in particular, they built secure foundations for democracy and sound governance. This is a big claim to make, and an important one to validate.

Unfortunately, the way in which the evaluation was designed meant that these claims were not explored or tested. The study focused mainly on project-level activities on the one hand, and macro-level economic indicators on the other, and seems to have had little to say about institutional development or

Head, Evaluation Department, United Kingdom Department for International Development.

governance. But their bold hypothesis is just the kind of challenging proposition that evaluators should address. It raises very significant questions about the nature of aid and the long-term sequencing of assistance required for sustained development. It is not a claim that can be readily assessed through the usual kind of program monitoring. Nor can we make sense of an issue of this scope through the limited time frame adopted by the country assistance evaluations undertaken by most agencies, which typically look at strategies and programs covering less than five years.

So the question of time frame can be seen to be very important if we wish to make sense of longer-run development processes. A longer historical view—not for every evaluation but for selected strategic evaluations—could help to answer some of the very big questions of the sort raised by the bold hypothesis.

Another reason why the Swedish study cannot answer the important question raised by Lindahl and Catterson also has to do with scope, but scope in another sense: in this case, the limited treatment of links between program *content* and program *context*. The study focused on national economic indicators and on local project-level activities funded by Sweden. We see little analysis linking the two, except the observation that Swedish aid policy for many years also failed to make a connection between poor economic performance at the national level and the rather mixed success at the project level. Questions about the impact of Swedish aid on Tanzania's development could not be satisfactorily addressed without a fuller analysis of the links between the Swedish aid program and the changing national social, political, institutional, and economic context over the period covered by the evaluation.

There is another dimension in which the Swedish study falls short. It is—with apologies to Charles Dickens—very much "A Tale of Two Cities": a story of Stockholm and Dar-es-Salaam. Were there not other parties with an interest? One wonders how far the Swedes, both in Tanzania and internationally, were engaged in dialogue with other agencies, especially the multilaterals that were setting the pace on macroeconomic policy. Once again, in order to make sense of Sweden's contribution to Tanzania's development, one would need to look more widely and link the program to its wider setting.

Finally, Lindahl and Catterson propose some radical solutions to the problems they diagnose. They focus on the question of incentives, and propose that a performance fund should be set up to encourage performance by rewarding and financing those who can deliver good results. Good performers would appeal to the fund and receive funding for further activities. Solutions of this kind are currently fashionable, and I recognize echoes of this approach in the UK public sector at present, where there is a plethora of funds of this kind. Indeed, the Department for International Development (DFID) itself has set up a variety of performance funds and challenge funds, aimed at creating incentives for good performance and at funding work towards what DFID believes to be good policies. While such funds may not be inappropriate, it would be interesting to review the evaluation literature for evidence on whether they are an efficient use of public funds, given their potentially high administration costs.

Lindahl and Catterson's other suggestion is that a form of direct management might lead to better aid results. Again, there is an echo here of current approaches to public sector management: for example, in the state-funded part of the UK's education system, where schools are the responsibility of local government, we see so-called "failing schools" being taken into direct management by special teams appointed by central government. But while such measures may be appropriate for a government to take with regard to its own public sector (and we should be looking for evaluation evidence on this point, too) it is doubtful whether it would be appropriate for donors to adopt a management model of this sort with respect to a sovereign state such as Tanzania. Tanzania should be run by Tanzanians.

A much more constructive suggestion can be found in Killick's paper (chapter 3). This noted that an independent monitoring group, of the kind already established in Tanzania, could review and evaluate issues around policy, operations, performance, and funding. Opening up space for informed dialogue helps to build trust, so that positive experiences can be shared and ways forward found even where progress seems to have stalled. At the level of sovereign states, establishing more formal, deliberative space and solving problems through partnership promises a better way forward than attempting to impose tight management by external players.

Lindahl and Catterson's paper deals with a very large and complex topic, and it is perhaps not surprising that they find few useful answers. But the real value of this paper lies in the ambitious questions it raises, and the challenge it poses to all of us trying to make sense of what development agencies do.

2. Around the World Bank in 80 Ratings

Johnson and Lamdany's paper has a more modest focus; it presents proposals being considered in the World Bank's Operations Evaluation Department to conduct future country assistance evaluations in a more systematic way. This is a very welcome gesture of transparency. The paper provides a look "behind the scenes" and will help those reading future country assistance evaluations to understand the approach taken.

Johnson presents the results of some hard thinking about how to render more systematically measurable something as contentious and difficult to measure as the quality of a country program. That said, the long appendix on ratings puts one in mind of the global sweep of Jules Verne's novel *Around the World in 80 Days*—although perhaps this should read, in relation to the OED paper, Around the World Bank in 80 Ratings!

The paper outlines how the ratings set out in that appendix are derived. They represent an attempt to move away from subjective views about program achievements or problems or shortcomings towards lesser, basic elements on which all can agree, and thereby to establish bedrock on which to build the evaluation's findings and conclusions. But while the ratings seem to provide solid numbers, and help to defuse debate, it is important to remember that they are based on subjective judgments, and should not be used in a mechanistic way.

This issue is picked up in an illuminating way in the paper by Roche and Kelly (chapter 8), which describes the Australian government's efforts to develop a system of ratings with which to assess the performance of NGOs it funds. The NGO community was uncomfortable with some of the ratings devised by the government, and this led to a dialogue between the government and NGOs about the system of ratings. The ratings were neither objective nor, initially, uncontroversial. But the system was opened up to discussion and debate, leading to eventual agreement on a system that made sense to all parties and could be used as a basis for understanding and dialogue about agency performance—in this case, the performance of Australian NGOs.

Ratings are, as Johnson and Lamdany note, inherently subjective. This does not make them useless but it does mean that we need to know their limitations and that we need to be sure there is common understanding about how they are being used. Nor should ratings be the end of analysis: they are a jumping off point, to be used with other information, from which to develop lines of inquiry. It may necessary, in the light of analysis, to revisit and revise specific ratings and indeed the entire system of ratings. From this point of view, transparency about a system of ratings and its use is not only welcome but contributes significantly to the proper and responsible use of ratings.

Johnson and Lamdany's paper is also helpful in its clarity about the difficult attribution issues that we all face in evaluating the effectiveness of development agencies. The paper distinguishes among, first, progress made by the partner country "on the ground," that is, the partner country's own development; second, the results of particular programs and development interventions; and, third, the specific contributions made by the World Bank and by other development agencies. This brings us back to questions of program content and context.

Two sets of attribution problems arise here. First, looking at the World Bank's own program of assistance to a particular country, Johnson and Lamdany themselves note that the results chain is not always clearly specified in the Bank's country assistance strategies. The alignment between activities and programs and sectoral or national goals may not always be clear and there may be discontinuities between the various levels. Linking the Bank's efforts and national development outcomes is inherently difficult, given the range of external contextual factors in play. There are strong echoes here of the failure to connect project activities and national results, described by Lindahl and Catterson.

The second set of problems relates specifically to context, at least from the standpoint of understanding Bank performance. Johnson and Lamdany themselves note how difficult it is to get an accurate picture of what other donors are doing or of the results of their activities. But if you do not know what other donors are contributing, or what the partner government itself is achieving, it becomes difficult to reach any sound assessment of what the Bank itself is contributing. Who is generating which result? No matter how substantial the program, what seems solid melts into air: to make robust, defensible claims for the Bank's effectiveness, one must be able to identify and assess the contribution of other actors. Again, there is an echo here of Lindahl and Catterson's paper, where the narrow focus on Swedish assistance raises, by default, important but unanswered questions about the role of other agencies.

This tangled web of attribution issues clearly calls out for resolution. And to me it seems clear that resolution must come through collective action, rather than through the action of individual agencies. Collective action is linked to the issue of collective responsibility—an issue that has been highlighted for us all by the shared Millennium Development Goals, which, as Johnson and Lamdany themselves note once again, change the focus and locus of accountability.

Country partners must be key players in any collective effort. Accordingly, mobilizing national capacity and building evaluation capacity are part of the answer. But the critical step is to establish effective evaluation systems, built into national finance and planning institutions, and keyed into national planning processes such as poverty reduction strategies.

Another part of the answer lies in joint or parallel evaluations. This returns us to a question posed in Stewart's proposition favoring a pluralistic approach to evaluation (chapter 1). Should evaluation partners move in lockstep, doing a limited number of tightly coordinated joint evaluation studies, no doubt limited in scope and number? Or should we take a more pluralistic approach, perhaps using a looser framework within which to address a wider variety of questions in different ways? This would allow us to bring the picture together in the form of a jigsaw puzzle with many pieces, rather than as unitary, monolithic studies. And a more pluralistic approach would allow space for the occasional long-term study of the sort undertaken by Lindahl and his colleagues.

While the Millennium Development Goals provide us with a common purpose and an overarching framework, the strategic focus of development operations lies at the country level. As frequently mentioned in the papers in this volume, the country level is increasingly seen as a crucial area for analysis and for evaluation. The national level is where many questions of accountability make the clearest sense, particularly where poverty reduction strategies are the pivot for development action. Further, as Killick points out (chapter 3), the operation of new aid instruments such as general budget support can only be understood at the national level. This means that evaluation at the country level is of key significance. And it is at this level that we can perhaps begin to untangle the knotty web of attribution issues.

To conclude: the theme of this conference session concerns evaluating the effectiveness of development agencies. As agencies increasingly recognize, the country level is the key level for strategic planning, and thus an increasingly appropriate level for making sense of agencies' performance. In this light it is extremely useful to have Johnson and Lamdany's clear exposition of the way the World Bank is tackling evaluation at this level. That said, country assistance strategies are very much a moving target. The Bank is beginning to develop results-based country assistance strategies, and bilateral agencies including DFID are increasingly orienting their assistance towards the goals set in country partners' poverty reduction strategies. As such poverty reduction strategies evolve, and as the design of country assistance strategies adapts, so will the methodology for evaluation of country strategies need to evolve and adapt to changes in development policy and practice.

Comments on the papers by Lindahl-Catterson and Johnson-Lamdany

Uma Lele

As to Johnson and Lamdany's interesting paper, I fully support and have practiced the analytical distinction they make between country performance, World Bank performance, and country outcomes.

In the 1980s, I led a systematic cross-country comparative study of six African countries in the period 1970-86. We carried out a comparative analysis of aid to agriculture by eight donors in these countries, and measured the impacts of historical endowments, six African countries' agricultural and macroeconomic policies, donor aid policies and investments, and external shocks as they affected outcomes in the rural sector—outcomes considered in terms of agricultural and social sector indicators.[1] Respected analysts who were nationals of the donor countries carried out the studies.

We found that in Tanzania, thirty-two donors contributed a total of US$8.1 billion in official development assistance during 1970-87. By comparison, in Kenya, with a population of comparable size, thirty-one donors provided $5.5 billion. Malawi received only $2.1 billion during the same period. For Tanzania, aid receipts were supplying up to 70 percent of government expenditures

Senior adviser, Operations Evaluation Department, World Bank.

by the end of the 1980s. Real transfers were substantially smaller than the nominal figures, however, because a significant share of aid was in the form of technical assistance, often of an inappropriate nature. The remaining aid was often tied either to source or end use in the form of projects, substantially reducing its real value.

Yet concessionality also matters. Compared with the other countries studied, Tanzania received the largest share of resource transfers in concessional terms. We also showed, for instance, that while Tanzania's performance had been poor, so had that of the donors. By the end of the 1970s, Tanzania's import-substituting industrialization policies and excessive emphasis on the social sectors, in the absence of growth-oriented policies, had resulted in a severe overvaluation of the exchange rate, had implicitly taxed the agricultural sector heavily, and had reduced agricultural production and export performance. External shocks affected Tanzania's economic performance further. Donor-assisted programs reinforced Tanzania's import-substituting industrialization, contributing to the poor performance through excessively high aid levels and poor allocation of aid. Tanzania was then the darling of the international community and this was not a popular message. The World Bank had its share of the bad portfolio of agricultural and industrial projects in Tanzania.

Despite severe external shocks, Tanzania's neighbor Kenya capitalized on its favorable initial conditions (a thriving European agriculture and strong cash-crop-based smallholder agriculture) and pursued a combination of favorable macroeconomic and sector policies that supported its export-led smallholder agriculture. This caused broadly based agricultural growth and because agriculture was important in GNP overall economic growth, Kenya did well despite the fact that many aid projects performed poorly.

In response to Catterson and Lindahl's thoughtful paper, I want to assure them that Sweden was not alone in its poor aid record. The comparative study of aid donors and lenders including the World Bank showed that they all performed poorly! I was not popular for having demonstrated that donors were partly to blame for Tanzania's poor performance. I was even less so for demonstrating that even though donor aid to Kenyan agriculture had not performed well (with a few notable exceptions of smallholder tea and coffee), Kenya had performed well as the result of its own policies. Unlike Tanzania, Kenya was able to weather adverse external shocks because of its resilient domestic performance which, in contrast to Tanzania's, substantially increased export volumes, for example in tea and coffee. Smallholders' share in the growth of Kenya's export volumes was significant and their products received a quality premium in export markets. In Tanzania, by contrast, despite a far more diversified export base, export volumes of cotton, tea, cashews, and coffee plummeted and the quality of output deteriorated.

In a study of aid and capital flows that I also directed in the 1980s, the developing-country authors who prepared case studies of their countries argued that donors were willing to support their policies with large investments until things began to sour, particularly with adverse external shocks.[2] Then the donors left countries to carry the burden of the expansionary policies they had so mightily supported. India had had a similar experience in the 1960s.[3]

In short, historical endowments, external shocks, macroeconomic and sector policies, and aid policies all interact in a complex way to explain country performance, donor performance, and country outcomes. These factors need to be understood through systematic quantitative analysis. By the same token, comparative studies provide considerable insights into why some countries and some donors do better than others, and why they do better at some times than at others.

Notes

1. The donors/lenders covered were Denmark, the European Union, France, Germany, Sweden, United Kingdom, United States, and the World Bank. The countries studied were Cameroon, Kenya, Malawi, Nigeria, Senegal, and Tanzania. Lele, ed. (1991).
2. Lele and Nabi (1990).
3. Aid to India was much smaller in per capita terms, however. At its peak it amounted to 30 percent of government expenditures. But the aid was of higher quality in India than in the African countries studied, and with tremendously greater investment in its human capital India made better use of aid than they did. The most successful example was the help to generate the Green Revolution, which had huge impacts on poverty reduction and food security.

References

Lele, Uma, and Ijaz Nabi. (1990). *Transitions in Development: The Role of Aid and Commercial Flows*. San Francisco, CA: ICS Press.

Lele, Uma, ed. (1991). *Aid to African Agriculture, Lessons from Two Decades of Donors' Experience*. Baltimore: John Hopkins University Press.

8

Evaluating the Performance of Development Agencies: Perspectives from NGO Experience

Chris Roche and Linda Kelly

Evaluating the performance of development agencies is a subset of the overall dilemma of how to measure the effectiveness of aid. Like the wider aid effectiveness debate, the task of measuring the effectiveness of development organizations has moved from counting activities and costs to asking what results are achieved and why. As with aid evaluation more generally, there appears to be agreement that the focus should be on outcomes and impact, that is, on the ultimate aims and goals of organizations. There is also an acknowledgment that the evaluation of organizational performance differs from, yet relates to, the assessment of specific projects or programs, and an assumption that an organization, as a whole, should be able to credibly demonstrate its achievements.[1]

The key difficulty is how. Running through the attempts at organizational performance measurement is a major tension related to method and approach. On the one hand, methods are sought that allow the ready identification of organizational achievement—usually based on simple comparisons with targets and indicators—in ways that can be easily communicated to wider audiences. On the other hand, it is increasingly seen that methods that provide valid and reliable evidence about organizational performance are not necessarily simple; at a minimum they require input from multiple stakeholders and

Program director, Oxfam Community Aid Abroad.

Linda Kelly is an independent consultant with experience in social research and evaluation both for community and government organizations in Australia and internationally.

approaches, they need appropriate conceptualization, and they require ongoing learning and engagement in key issues.[2]

This tension is sometimes caricatured as a choice between quantitative and qualitative methods, but that characterization does a disservice to such methods, both of which have much to offer organizational performance measurement. Behind the stereotype lie a number of key issues. These include:

- The choice between simple and relatively cheap methods that will satisfy the appearance of accountability, and those more difficult and challenging methods that will uncover more about the reality of how organizations are (or are not) helping to change the lives of poor people. To date, few if any large-scale attempts to measure organizational performance can be said to be firmly based on valid, reliable, and replicable methods.
- Different views about what constitutes appropriate rigor and validity. This debate is sometimes understood to be about differences between quantitative and qualitative approaches, or about objectivity versus subjectivity. But in many cases the issue is much more one of ensuring an appropriate and achievable reduction in bias.[3]
- An ongoing debate about the degree to which results-based management, or at least the current ways in which this is practiced, actually improves organizational performance and/or accountability.[4]

These methodological and practical dilemmas leave us with few easy clear directions. To date, many effectiveness studies in the official aid sector have tended to use some form of project or program scoring system, whose results are then aggregated into overall performance measures against a number of benchmarks and indicators (such as the proportions of projects meeting objectives, having satisfactory quality at launch, or likely to be sustainable). The degree to which these data are produced internally rather than through independent evaluations varies across agencies. What is perhaps most striking is that despite the claims of rigor, objectivity, and best practice for some of these studies, the potential for disagreement among observers about the performance of the same organization does not seem to have diminished.

Even some of the most well resourced organizations are struggling with this challenge. The United Kingdom Department for International Development (DFID) recently commissioned an independent desk-based review of its effectiveness.[5] That review concludes that only very tentative conclusions can be drawn about DFID's policy, processes, and resources, for lack of adequate performance assessment systems; that the material available to assess DFID's bilateral and multilateral performance is of limited reliability; and that the evidence is too patchy to make an overall judgment on whether DFID has contributed to development effectiveness over the last decade.

Certainly, as DFID states, the way it conducted this exercise indicates "DFID's maturity, and its commitment to the professional, self-critical, evidence-based approach appreciated by the National Audit Office and Treasury..."[6] But the agency has concluded, based on this experience, as well as a National Audit Office review of its performance management systems, that it needs to improve the quality and quantity of its performance information.

DFID's experience and that of others suggests that collectively we are only in the foothills of effective performance measurement. This in turn begs two important questions. First, how far should multilateral and bilateral agencies uncritically promote results-based management and processes of performance assessment in countries with very limited resources? Second, how firm are the policy and practice conclusions drawn from these processes?

Nongovernmental organizations have experienced the same pressure to prove and justify their worth as organizations and they are struggling in similar ways to generate evidence-based assessments of their organizational performance. The rest of this paper draws from the experiences of NGOs in Australia and Britain and suggests that some of their lessons learned might well have relevance to bilateral and multilateral aid organizations.

1. The Australian Experience

In Australia, international NGOs have found themselves increasingly under scrutiny and their relationship with the Australian government has been characterized by a regular focus on proof of their effectiveness and relevance.[7]

There is nothing new in suggesting that it is difficult to assess NGO effectiveness,[8] or that few NGOs have been able to demonstrate effectively their long-term impact.[9] And a number of authors agree that NGOs enjoy a mixed if not fraught relationship with official donors, one often characterized by misunderstanding and simplistic interpretations each of the other.[10] The funding component of the relationship is usually seen to dominate and often distort the role of the NGOs.[11] In recent years in Australia, a conservative political climate has only heightened the scrutiny, with NGOs spending more and more time and resources responding to requests related to their accountability, especially from the Australian government, and dealing with attacks from right-wing think tanks such as the Institute of Public Affairs.[12]

Early in 2002, the NGOs in Australia decided to take more control of the situation. They set out first to define what makes for effective NGO practice, in their own terms, and then to assemble evidence about the extent to which Australian NGOs are demonstrating this effective practice. Now they are looking for ways to develop their findings into effective organizational performance assessment.

The stimulus for this decision began with a new attempt by the Australian government to assess NGOs as development organizations. The review process of Australian NGOs undertaken by AusAID[13] was the Quality Assurance Group assessment of International NGOs.[14] A framework that AusAID had developed for assessing the quality of bilateral projects and programs[15] was adapted for NGO assessment, after consultation with NGOs in Australia, and applied to a random selection of twenty organizations.[16] The results of this assessment were mixed, suggesting that NGOs were reasonable at implementing projects and programs but poor in project design and in some other areas, such as their understanding of the contexts they work in and their planning for long-term sustainability. These findings are not dissimilar to those of other studies of NGOs.[17]

The Australian NGOs were dissatisfied with both the outcomes and process of this review because they believed it presented a limited picture of their role. It appeared to capture important elements and critical areas for improvement, but from the NGO perspective it did not address the totality of what they were trying to achieve and the critical processes that underpinned their approaches. From their perspective, this process was one in a long line of assessments using inappropriate instruments. Perhaps most importantly, they felt that because the review did not match their experience and intentions it gave them little basis for real learning and further improvement.

Critically, however, the momentum generated by the subsequent debates became the stimulus for the Australian NGO community to take more control over defining and demonstrating good development practice and then developing a model that would serve as a basis for organizational assessment and improvement in the NGO sector.

The Australian Council for Overseas Aid (ACFOA), the umbrella organization for the NGO industry in Australia, managed this research process on behalf of its member organizations. The first step was to develop a clear understanding of what made for effective NGO work. Organizations were strongly committed to developing theory from practice, so a research process was developed using a methodology of appreciative inquiry.[18] The research began in 2002 and all ACFOA members from across Australia were invited to participate.[19] The research focused initially on defining the link between what organizations do and good outcomes for people.[20] The purpose of this first stage was to develop an agreed model of organizational performance for Australian NGOs.

The critical finding of the research suggested that Australian NGO effectiveness needs to be assessed not just in relation to what happens in the field, or other areas of program engagement, but also at other levels. Results are a product of organizational principles and values, as well as the approaches to intervention and the standards and quality of work on the ground. For example, one of the key elements of NGO practice was identified as the ability to develop long-term and effective relationships with partner groups and beneficiary communities.[21] The research suggested that effective partnership, when combined with good preparation, implementation, and management of activities, was more likely to lead to effective and sustained change for people. Equally good program design and management, in the absence of effective partnership, was at least implicitly found to be a less critical variable.

The AusAID approach to measuring the performance of NGOs, and by extension other aid delivery mechanisms, relied on the assumption that organizations are simply what they do, that is, that an aggregation of project assessments was a good enough proxy for judging organizational performance. In fact, NGOs and other organizations achieve results both directly, through their projects or formal interventions, and also indirectly, though their relationships and the influence they have on others and through the values they represent and spread. Organizational assessment frameworks need to be able to capture more of this multi-dimensional engagement in the development process.[22]

The first stage of the research began to capture accurately (at least from the perspective of the NGOs) this systemic nature of the organizations and therefore provide a more comprehensive basis for assessment. Importantly, because the NGOs were involved in the process and "owned" the results, it constituted the first step in their active engagement in ongoing performance assessment that would lead to organizational change and improvement.

A further important difference that emerged between the AusAID and NGO approach lay in the use of indicators. There is already a strong critique of the simplistic and uncritical use of indicators as measures of aid effectiveness in general,[23] yet indicators continue to dominate the organizational performance discussion. In the case of the Australian NGOs, AusAID assumed that it could assign top-level and uniform indicators and targets related to the design, implementation, and management of field interventions that would allow comparisons from one context and type of agency to another.[24] Organizations could be assessed against specific indicators and the resulting information aggregated to judge organizational effectiveness.

There were two major problems with this approach. First, the nature of the indicators and "quality standards" themselves often did not allow for conclusive or objectively verifiable measurement.[25] Many if not most of the measures called for a qualitative judgment, which was then translated by the various groups of assessors into a standard measure. This was the classic mistake of trying to convert poorly defined, de-contextualized and un-triangulated qualitative judgments into quantitative measures—a process that does a major injustice to good quantitative and qualitative methods and one that immediately undermines the validity of the resulting analysis. As is often the case in such processes,[26] the resultant numbers or scores gained a spurious credibility, despite their provenance. Conclusions were drawn on the basis of careful calculation of averages, totals, and variances that the underlying data simply did not justify.

The second mistake was to assume that the indicators had meaning across contexts and types of interventions. While the NGO framework actually identified many elements of activity design and implementation similar to those developed by AusAID, the NGO research suggested that trying to assign context-free and universal indicators against these areas made little sense. Indeed, further research suggested that change accomplished by any intervention needs to be understood within its context,[27] and that simple and globalized/uniform targets and indicators are inadequate to capture the interaction between interventions and the development process in any given situation.

The broader process for NGOs in Australia now includes various types of field research designed to test the validity of the effectiveness framework against the experience of poor people and communities, so as to find out whether the NGO definition of what makes for effective practice actually leads to more sustained and positive change for people.[28] Notably, the Australian NGOs have been prepared to support and participate in this research, with agencies volunteering to have their programs examined for the purpose of wider learning across the sector.

A further phase, currently underway, is the development of an organizational tool, based on the areas and themes identified in the effectiveness framework, that the various NGOs can use to assess their fit with the key areas of effectiveness. The intention is to use this tool as a starting point for agency learning and improvement.

2. The British Experience

In Britain, NGOs are addressing a key challenge in their attempts to develop systems of organizational performance assessment. Recent work from this group has identified the issue of the relevance of measurement and assessment processes to their own organizations (in similar fashion to the Australian experience) but also to the men, women, and communities that they are trying to serve.[29]

This challenge is mirrored in the wider discussions on aid effectiveness. For example, the recent World Bank progress report on the Comprehensive Development Framework notes:

> The discourse has shifted from aid expenditures as a measure of achievement to increasing acceptance that stakeholders should be held accountable for achieving development outcomes. The poverty reduction strategy papers and the high visibility of the Millennium Development Goals have contributed to this shift. Sectorwide assistance programs have helped to institutionalize a results focus and medium-term expenditure frameworks have emerged as a viable vehicle for introducing a results orientation into the budgetary process. Still, many recipient countries appear to have adopted a results-oriented approach primarily to satisfy donors, at least initially. Application of the results approach is primarily limited to specific aid-funded projects and has rarely been embedded in the normal operations of government. And donors continue to encourage the development of measurement systems that meet their own institutional needs first and foremost.[30]

In light of this concern, some British NGOs have been experimenting with various approaches to performance measurement. These include developing dimensions or domains of change, instead of (or as well as) systems of indicators; using monitoring and evaluation systems that increase learning, downward accountability, and transparency; and using methods that increase stakeholder involvement and external scrutiny. Each of these is discussed briefly below.

Domains of Change

Both Oxfam Great Britain (Oxfam GB) and Save the Children United Kingdom (SCF UK) have defined, at an organizational level, the major domains of change that they seek to promote (changes in the lives of men, women, and children, changes in the policies and practices that perpetuate poverty in the first place, changes in equity, and changes in the capacities or empowerment of men, women, or children). Both agencies are using these domains to provide a conceptual framework and common language for learning and discussion across very different contexts, and with partners and allies. These domains also provide a means of determining core questions for internal and external evaluation and review processes, so that these may crosscheck each other. Finally, they contribute to a framework for more specific indicators or processes of validation to occur at local levels, and in consultation with local partners and people.

This approach has the great advantage of helping organizations to explain and communicate their objectives and underlying values while allowing flexibility about how the objectives might be achieved.[31] Oxfam GB and SCF UK have found that participatory assessments around the domains with stakeholders have produced critical and rich information, debate, and analysis. Staff, partners, and allies seem to be able to understand and relate to the fundamental concepts of change and improvement that necessarily arise from the correct application of this approach. However, the agencies have also noted that it takes time for new systems to become embedded and to evolve in large organizations, and for consistency of understanding to develop around core concepts.

Participatory Monitoring and Evaluation Systems

ActionAid's Accountability, Learning, and Planning System, as well as other participatory monitoring and evaluation systems developed by British NGOs, have indicated that more transparent and accountable processes can emerge, with appropriate drive from senior management, in these organizations. With imagination, these processes can be made to include activities like participatory budget analysis that have often been seen as difficult, if not impossible. These processes force agencies to make their values explicit if they are to really develop the mutual accountability and trust that are the foundation of effective partnerships.[32]

The findings, from the experience of ActionAid and others, are that if people participate in measuring the changes in their situation, their country, or their work then they are much more likely to participate in the required improvement. This sits in some contrast to processes that focus on upward accountability alone and appear to work against learning and change within organizations.[33]

Increasing Stakeholder Involvement and External Scrutiny

While it is recognized that participatory processes of assessment and developing downward accountability are critical, it is also acknowledged that complementary methods are needed to crosscheck findings and add other perspectives. Many agencies use independent reviews and evaluations to validate internal self-assessments and judgments.

Over and above this, both Oxfam GB and Action Aid have instituted deliberate processes of stakeholder surveys and reviews, which aim to assess how not only how well they are achieving their objectives, but also how well they are adhering to their underlying values and principles. For example, Oxfam GB undertakes a regular stakeholder survey and an assembly, including accountability workshops that are designed to allow stakeholders to ask questions of senior managers responsible for key areas of strategy. It is felt that these processes provide key insights into areas that a simple aggregation of project or program achievement would not provide.

3. Assessment of Advocacy and Campaigning

Recent work in Britain and Australia on the assessment of advocacy provides interesting insights into organizational assessment more generally. For various reasons, the outcomes of advocacy work are traditionally seen as even more difficult to capture than other aspects of development work;[34] the policy process is rarely linear or predictable, the contexts are dynamic and open to multiple influence from many actors, and the process of advocacy itself is complex, ranging from lobbying and campaigning, through networking and alliance building, to developing the capacity of people to act on their own behalf. However, recent discussions suggest that non-linearity, multiple actors, dynamic contexts, and unpredictability are not exclusive to advocacy contexts. Thus, it may well be that the findings of assessments related to advocacy are of much wider relevance.[35]

Research suggests that performance assessment of organizations undertaking advocacy work might best start by looking at the organizations themselves and their match with known elements of effective advocacy work—a key element being the organization's ability to work effectively with others.[36]

The consensus in the literature appears to be that few organizations are big enough or multi-skilled enough to cover all the change processes required for successful advocacy. NGOs and others need to work together in coalitions or alliances to achieve sustainable policy change[37] and the most successful advocacy is built upon the strength of many different organizations undertaking different roles and often approaching the key issue from different perspectives. The tension that arises for these advocacy organizations is to be able to identify their individual effectiveness in order to meet performance requirements, while still effectively cooperating with others:

> Because outcomes are more likely to be achieved with others (individuals or organizations) this actually makes attribution to single actors more difficult. This leads to the managerial tendency to focus more on intermediate and SMART objectives and targets as measures of performance, because these are more easily attributable to specific actions. This in turn therefore provides incentives a) to downplay or ignore the contribution of others, b) to stick to intermediate objectives and targets, or proxy indicators, even when they may not be the most effective means of achieving broader or more long-term objectives and c) to downplay professional judgment particularly on qualitative and difficult-to-measure variables. (Roche, 2001)

The way forward may be to assess the contribution that NGOs and others make to the coalitions or groups of organizations working for change—that is, to assess the quality of the working relationships.[38] Another strategy is to have NGOs and other organizations more publicly expose their assumed outcomes and their paths of influence, for review and testing by peers and others.[39]

As the principles developed in the Comprehensive Development Framework suggest, partnership and ownership are critical elements of any successful development approach. The key point is that if effective development is more likely to be achieved through organizations working together—not just in advocacy work, but also in development work more generally—then perhaps the performance assessment of individual organizations has limited relevance.

4. Ways Forward

The NGO experience does not provide a neat and comprehensive picture of what effective organizational performance assessment might look like. It may be too early to expect this, but it may also be that a nice neat model will never be achieved. What the NGO experience does suggest is that the following elements are key for effective organizational performance assessment:

- An ability to assess organizational attributes that are more than an aggregation of project achievements;
- Methods that embrace but are not limited to indicators and one-dimensional measurement tools;
- An ability to assess how well an organization contributes to broader processes by working with others and developing effective partnerships, as well as change that it achieves through its own actions.[40]

- An ability to listen to, and cross-check, a range of stakeholder opinions, and ensure that the least powerful stakeholders get at least an equal say;
- An ability to develop and promote learning and accountability processes that, at the least, do not work at cross-purposes.

The findings of the recent multi-stakeholder Comprehensive Development Framework evaluation[41] confirm the importance of ownership, participation, and results orientation and the difficulty of bringing all three together for effective organizational development. Some of the critical issues raised are how far developing countries will be supported to assess these issues. Achieving effective organizational performance will not necessarily be simple or inexpensive:

> All the evidence suggests that successful evaluation and measurement strategies depend on significant investment of funds. The transaction costs of such frameworks are high, and if they are to be implemented successfully, donors need cover the direct and indirect management costs and associated overheads. If this is not done, such processes will be poorly implemented, generate little information of operational value and suffer from limited credibility. If donors are not prepared to cover the full cost of effective and appropriate measurement processes, they must question whether they should continue to impose them. The minimalist approach to project funding with its emphasis on trust and low transaction costs is a viable and cost-effective alternative that should be considered. One can only conclude that unless performance measurement systems are reliable, credible, and trusted, they have little role in measuring success. (Hailey and Sorgenfrei, 2003, p. 19)

If increased investment is made, a final question remains. Will the resources and responsibility for assessing the effectiveness of aid remain only in the hands of researchers and institutions concentrating on ever more esoteric levels of aggregation, or will they be shared with the practitioners and governments on the front line? NGO experience suggests that people engaged in practice and in the outcomes of development have much to contribute to the measurement and improvement of the same.

Notes

1. It is also recognized, however, that in order to assess impacts or results, one also needs to be able to track the link between budgets and what people actually do, and broader results. Indeed, a recent study on the process of attempts to monitor poverty reduction strategy papers concludes that the focus on ultimate results has tended to downplay intermediate outcomes, which have become the "missing middle" in the process. See Booth and Lucas (2002).
2. Charlish et al. (2003); Marsden (2003).
3. Roche (1999).
4. Perrin (1998); O'Neill (2002); World Bank (2003).
5. Flint et al. (2002).
6. *Development Effectiveness:* Covering Note from Colin Kirk to the June 2002 Development Committee, http://62.189.42.51/DFIDstage/FOI/dc/20jun02_der_cover.pdf

7. AusAID (1995); Australian National Audit Office (1996); AusAID (2002).
8. ODI (1996).
9. Oakley (1999); Roche (1999); Madon (2000).
10. Kilalo and Johnson (1999).
11. Edwards and Hulme (1996); Davies (1997); White (1999).
12. The Institute of Public Affairs is a privately managed and funded policy and research organization. It includes, among its other activities, a regular "NGO watch" that claims to keep a check on the activities and accountability of NGOs.
13. AusAID is the Australian government department responsible for management of the Australian official aid program.
14. AusAID (2002).
15. Based upon a similar process developed at the World Bank, the framework used by AusAID has a set of ten key indicators of quality, under four overall attributes. A further forty specific quality standards break down each of the indicators into smaller elements of quality. Activities implemented by NGOs are assessed against the framework, with assessment made on a rating scale from 1 to 5 for the applicable quality standards, then the ten indicators, and then the four attributes. Finally the overall activity is rated based upon the scores received across the whole framework.
16. About 150 organizations in Australia undertake overseas aid and development work. Of these ninety are members of the Australian Council for Overseas Aid (ACFOA), the official umbrella body for the industry; 120 are signatories to the ACFOA Code of Conduct, and fifty-two are accredited to receive funds from AusAID.
17. ODI (1996).
18. The intention of the first step in this research was to develop a model of effective NGO work that matched the NGO experience, in so far as that experience could be uncovered. The appreciative inquiry approach allows the researcher to look to what are considered good practice examples—in this case, those already considered by both the NGOs and external groups such as AusAID and external evaluations—and from a wide sample draw out the consistent and key elements. This allows for the development of a hypothesis about effective practice, which then needs to be tested with the sample group and then verified by wider research and field examination. Hammond (1996).
19. Forty-seven percent of members were engaged in this first stage of the research. The NGOs participating included a spread of large (all but one of the largest eleven agencies participated in the research) and small; those based in Sydney, Melbourne, and Canberra; and also faith-based and non-faith-based agencies. Significantly, 72 percent of agencies accredited with AusAID participated in the research.
20. An independent researcher was employed to review the material submitted by the organizations. The initial research was undertaken as a desk study. It involved a systematic examination of a wide range of case examples of what were considered to be effective development practice supported by Australian NGOs. A discussion paper was developed and circulated confidentially to the NGOs for comment. The findings of this first stage were tested through focus group discussions and then further examined through a nationwide conference held in mid-2002, both processes enabling a wider group of NGOs to participate. At the conclusion of the conference, the findings were circulated among all ACFOA members for comment and a report was developed, outlining what has come to be known as the NGO Effectiveness Framework. Finally the ACFOA Annual Council reviewed the framework in August 2002, endorsing the findings and supporting the ongoing process of further research.
21. ACFOA (2002).

22. Gasper (1999); Smillie and Hailey (2001).
23. Perrin (1998); Roche (2001).
24. NGOs did contribute to the wording and inclusion of some indicators. However, theirs was a limited contribution that never allowed for debate about the overall worth of trying to have simple indicators against many of the fields of performance under review.
25. Indicators included statements such as "NGO and partner have appropriate implementation process." Quality standards included statements such as "Design sits conformably within broader development program and is likely to provide and benefit from synergy with other development agencies," or "Project takes steps to ensure that poorest and most marginalized groups of the community actively participate and derive benefits from the project."
26. Boyle (2000)
27. The Australian NGOs, through ACFOA, sponsored follow-up research to test the effectiveness framework in the field. Field research was undertaken focusing on the outcomes of the work of three organizations located in different parts of Papua New Guinea (PNG). The research focused on the effectiveness or otherwise of the work of those agencies but was designed to test the validity of the NGO effectiveness framework. The research tended overall to support the key elements of the framework, but also strongly suggested that the outcomes of NGO work could only be understood with reference to the context of that work, and that in a very difficult context such as PNG, there would inevitably be significant limitations upon what NGOs could achieve by themselves.
28. At the time of writing, field research in PNG had been completed and is currently being prepared for public dissemination. Research is under way to examine a major advocacy program and a humanitarian relief program to assess the fit of the effectiveness framework with these program outcomes. Further research is planned.
29. Charlish et al. (2003).
30. World Bank (2003).
31. Dart and Davies (forthcoming).
32. Hailey and Sorgenfrei (2003).
33. Ibid.
34. Fowler (1997); Roche (1999); Sutton (1999); IIED (2000); Davies (2001).
35. Charlish et al. (2003).
36. Davies (2001); Kelly (2002).
37. For example, in Australia 90 percent of the nongovernment organizations that had undertaken advocacy work had done so in cooperation with other organizations Ollif (2001).
38. Davies (2001); Earl et al. (2001).
39. Mayne (1999); Davies (2001).
40. See Mayne (1999) for more on this.
41. World Bank (2003).

References

Australian Agency for International Development (AusAID). (1995). *Review of the Effectiveness of NGO Programs*. Canberra: Goanna Print.
_____. (2002). *Rapid Review of NGO Project Quality: Work in Progress Report No. 5*. Quality Assurance Group Program Evaluation Section, Office of Review and Evaluation, AusAID. Canberra: Goanna Print.
Australian Council for Overseas Aid (ACFOA). (2002). *Report on Australian NGO Effectiveness*. Canberra: ACFOA.

Australian National Audit Office. (1996). *Accounting for Aid: the Management of Funding to Nongovernmental Organizations*. Australian Agency for International Development Audit Report. Canberra: Australian National Audit Office.

Booth, D., and H. Lucas. (2002). "Good Practice in the Development of Poverty Reduction Strategy and Monitoring Systems." London: Overseas Development Institute

Boyle, David. (2000). *The Tyranny of Numbers: Why Counting Can't Make Us Happy*. London: New Economic Foundation.

Chapman, J., and T. Fisher. (2000). "The Effectiveness of NGO Campaigning: Lessons from Practice." *Development in Practice* 10 (2), pp.151-165.

Charlish, D., R. David, M. Foresti, L. Knight, and M. Newens. (2003). "Towards Organizational Performance Assessment: Experiences of Strengthening Learning, Accountability and Understanding Social Change." Paper for Development Assistance Committee Conference, France, March.

Crooke, M. (1996). "NGOs and Official Development Assistance." In P. Kilby (ed.), *Australia's Aid Program: Mixed Messages and Conflicting Agendas*. Melbourne: Monash Asia Institute and Community Aid Abroad.

Dart, J., and R. Davies. (forthcoming). "A Dialogical Story-Based Evaluation Tool: The Most Significant Change Approach." *American Journal of Evaluation*.

Davies, R. (1997). "Donor Information Demands and NGO Institutional Development." *Journal of International Development* 9 (4), pp. 613-620.

_____. (2001). "Evaluating the Effectiveness of DFID's Influence with Multilaterals. Part A: A Review of NGO Approaches to the Evaluation of Advocacy Work." Mimeo. Cambridge, UK.

_____. (2002). "Improved Representations of Change Processes: Improved Theories of Change." Paper presented at the Seville 2002 5th Biennial Conference of the European Evaluation Society: Three Movements in Contemporary Evaluation, Learning, Theory, and Evaluation.

Earl, S., F. Carden, and T. Smutylo. (2001). *Outcome Mapping: Building Learning and Reflection into Development Programs*. Ottawa: International Development Research Center. http://www.idrc.ca/evaluation/ombrochure_e.html.

Edwards, M., and D. Hulme. (1996). "Too Close for Comfort? The Impact of Official Aid on Nongovernmental Organizations." *World Development* 24 (6), pp. 961-973.

Flint, M., C. Cameron, S. Henderson, S. Jones, and D. Ticehurst. (2002). "How Effective is DFID? Development Effectiveness Report." London: United Kingdom Department for International Development.

Fowler, A. (1997). "Assessing Development Impact and Organizational Performance." Chapter 7 in A. Fowler, *Striking a Balance*. London: Earthscan.

Gasper, D. (1999). "Problems in the Logical Framework Approach and the Challenges for Project Cycle Management." *The Courier* No.173, January/February.

Hailey, J. and M. Sorgenfrei. (2003). "Measuring Success? Issues in Performance Management." Keynote Paper, Intrac's 5th International Evaluation Conference, The Netherlands. March/April.

Hammond, S. (1996). *The Thin Book of Appreciative Inquiry*. Plano, TX: Thin Book Publishing Co.

International Financial Institution Advisory Commission (IFIAC). (2000). *Final Report of the International Financial Institution Advisory Commission to the US Congress and Department of Treasury*. Washington, DC: IFIAC.

International Institute for Environment and Development. (2000). "The Policy Influence of NGOs in Sub-Saharan Africa: Assessing Effectiveness and Impact." http://www.iied.org/agri/proj-ngopolicyinfluence.html.

Kelly, L. (2002)."Performance Measurement: A Model for FDC." Brisbane: Foundation for Development Cooperation.

Kilalo, C., and D. Johnson. (1999). "Missions Impossible? Creating Partnerships among NGOs, Governments, and Donors." *Development in Practice* 9 (4).

Madon, S. (2000). "International NGO: Networking, Information Flows, and Learning." Development Information Working Paper Series, Working Paper No. 8. London School of Economic and Political Science.

Marsden, D. (2003). "Rights, Culture and Contested Modernities." Keynote paper, Intrac's 5th International Evaluation Conference, The Netherlands. March/April.

Mayne, P. (1999). "Addressing Attribution through Contribution Analysis: Using Performance Measures Sensibly." Discussion paper. Ottawa, Canada: Office of the Auditor General of Canada http://www.oag-bvg.gc.ca/domino/other.nsf/html/99dp1_e.html

Oakley, P. (1999). *Danish NGO Impact Study: A Review of Danish NGO Activities in Developing Countries: Synthesis Report.* Oxford and Copenhagen: INTRAC/BECH Distribution.

Ollif, C. E. (2001). "Australian NGOs and Advocacy. Summary of Responses." Unpublished research. University of New England School of Human and Environmental Studies.

O'Neill, O. (2002). "A Question of Trust." British Broadcasting Corporation Reith Lectures 2002. http://www.bbc.co.uk/radio4/reith2002.

Overseas Development Institute (ODI). (1996). "The Impact of NGO Development Projects." Briefing Paper 2. London: Overseas Development Institute.

Perrin, B. (1998). "Effective Use and Misuse of Performance Measurement." *American Journal of Evaluation* 19 (3), pp.367-379.

Pretty, J. (1994). "Alternative Systems of Inquiry for a Sustainable Agriculture." *Institute of Development Studies Bulletin* 25 (2).

Roche, C. (1999). *Impact Assessment for Development Agencies.* Oxford: Oxfam.

_____. (2001). "Partnering for Development Results—An NGO Perspective." Paper for DFID-UNDP Conference, Oxford. September.

Smillie, I., and John Hailey. (2001). *Managing for Change.* London: Earthscan.

Sutton, R. (1999). "The Policy Process: An Overview." Working Paper No.118, Overseas Development Institute, London.

Wallace, Tina, S. Crowther, and A. Shepherd. (1997). *Standardizing Development: Influences on UK NGOs' Policies and Procedures.* Oxford: Worldview Press.

White, S. C. (1999). "NGOs, Civil Society and the State in Bangladesh." *Development and Change* 30 (2), pp. 307-326.

World Bank. (2003). "Multi-partner Evaluation of the Comprehensive Development Framework." Report 25882, May 16.

Part 3

Improving the Evaluation Evidence

9

Operational Reflections on Evaluating Development Programs

Laura Rawlings[1]

The growing emphasis of the development community on results-based management, including the adoption of the Millennium Development Goals, calls for setting explicit objectives and measuring progress toward achieving those objectives. Impact evaluations that examine causality are also required where policymakers are interested in knowing whether particular programs are directly responsible for the achievement of specific outcomes.

Impact evaluations assess the effectiveness of specific outcomes attributable to a particular intervention using a counterfactual that represents the hypothetical state the beneficiaries would have experienced without the intervention.

There are two basic approaches to constructing the counterfactual. Experimental designs (also known as randomized control designs) construct the counterfactual through the random selection of treatment and control groups. Given appropriate sample sizes, the process of random selection ensures equivalence between treatment and control groups in both observable and unobservable characteristics. By contrast, quasi-experimental designs (also called non-experimental designs) rely on statistical models or design features to construct a counterfactual, and include approaches such as regression discontinuity design, propensity score matching, differences-indifferences, and instrumental variables. Quasi-experimental methods are much more common than randomized control designs.[2]

This paper briefly summarizes the debate between experimental and quasi-experimental methods in Section 1, reviews selected experiences with ran-

Senior monitoring and evaluation specialist, Human Development Department, Latin America and Caribbean Region, World Bank.

domized control designs of social programs in developing countries in Section 2, offers recommendations for strengthening impact evaluations in Section 3, and concludes with reflections on and recommendations for conducting evaluations in the World Bank and international development institutions more broadly.

1. The Debate on Experimental versus Quasi-Experimental Methods

The lively debate on experimental versus quasi-experimental methods encompasses a vast literature that has been particularly prolific over the past fifteen years and is reflected in experience with the evaluation of training programs in the United States.[3]

Phases of the Debate

The experimental versus quasi-experimental debate can be viewed in three phases, roughly corresponding to the past three decades.

In the 1980s, the debate gained momentum when Fraker and Maynard (1984) found the results of the quasi-experimental evaluation of the United States Comprehensive Employment Training Act (CETA) to be unsound. They reached this conclusion by replicating CETA's quasi-experimental methods using data from a experimental design of a randomly assigned training program (the National Supported Work program), and comparing those results to the experimental design results. Lalonde (1986) further criticized the quasi-experimental results, pointing to large biases resulting from a number of quasi-experimental econometric methods. Summarizing these results, Lalonde and Maynard (1987) concluded that the quasi-experimental methodology was often incorrect and that "the current skepticism surrounding the results of non-experimental evaluations is justified."

Largely as a result of this criticism, the U.S. Congress issued a mandate calling for a randomized control design as the basis for the evaluation of the Job Training Partnership Act, the program that replaced CETA. Research was commissioned to accompany this experience, which generated the next wave in the debate, characterized by strong advocacy of experimental designs in the 1990s. During this phase, the evaluation community largely endorsed the experimental design approach, which became the "new orthodoxy" in impact evaluation work, as characterized by Manski and Garfinkel (1992).

Today, the debate is more nuanced. It is recognized that the growing robustness and sophistication of quasi-experimental methods strengthens their validity. First, many of the advances in this area—particularly those associated with James Heckman, including sample selectivity correction and specification tests—can be used to shape the use of quasi-experimental designs and are seen as viable approaches to evaluation. Second, growing data availability makes the application of good prospective quasi-experimental designs more achievable. Third, there is growing skepticism about experimental designs, which has arisen mainly because of a recognition of implementation problems that can introduce a worrisome divergence between the designed and implemented evaluation.

Most evaluators today recognize the debate as narrow, and instead call for an examination of the specific evaluation needs of the case at hand and, often, for the use of more than one approach.

A Closer Look at the Pros and Cons of Randomization

Where does the debate leave development practitioners interested in pursuing robust evaluations? There is little dispute over many of the benefits of randomization. First, while quasi-experimental designs may contain large and unknown biases stemming from specification errors, experimental designs can address selection issues through the mere process of random assignment that (with adequate sample sizes) ensures equivalency between the treatment and control groups. Second, experimental designs provide very clear results that are easy to interpret.

However, these benefits can only be realized if the experimental designs are properly implemented—and social experiments are almost never implemented as designed. The divergence between designed experiments and actual implementation has given rise to a series of criticisms of experimental designs that can be grouped into three categories:

Behavioral responses of subjects. In several ways, the behavioral responses of the subjects of the experiment can undermine a randomized social experiment. First, initial selection bias can be introduced whereby ambitious individuals may not apply for a program if they know they might not be selected. Second, there is the well-known and recognized Hawthorne effect, whereby the treatment group modifies its behavior in some way in response to the evaluation itself, as opposed to the program. Third, there is the John Henry effect, whereby the control group modifies its behavior in response to the evaluation. There is also substitution bias, when subjects who were not selected through randomization are able to find good substitutes for the program that they were initially denied. Finally, there can be nonrandom attrition in treatment and control groups.

Program implementation changes. Changes in the nature of the program intervention can result in a divergence between the evaluation as designed and the evaluation as implemented. These changes compromise the integrity of the evaluation design. For example, changes in the content of the intervention may invalidate the outcome variables chosen for the evaluation. Or changes in the implementation strategy (such as a modification of the targeting criteria) may induce a departure from the selected treatment and control groups. Or the program may not be implemented on the planned schedule, leaving some in the treatment group untreated and inducing a divergence between the intention to treat and the treatment. Finally, experimental designs can fall prey to control group contamination whereby some in the control group actually receive the intervention being evaluated. These changes are common and are particularly damaging after baseline data have been collected.

Political economy. Experimental designs are criticized because their costs can be high and results can take a long time to emerge, given the need for both baseline and follow-up data. Ethical considerations are often also raised regarding the appropriateness of denying benefits to eligible beneficiaries. One of the more cogent criticisms of experimental designs is that unlike multivariate analysis and other quasi-experimental approaches that provide parameters for the relative importance of the variables that affect outcomes, experimental design methodologies provide no insight into why the observed outcomes were produced. The determinants of success or lack thereof are left relatively unclear. Hence experimental designs may not be as useful to policymakers who need information in order to adjust a particular policy or a program.

Most of these criticisms would, in fact, pertain to any prospective evaluation that contemplates the collection of baseline and follow-up data, with the use of treatment and control groups. For example, the ethical considerations often raised in the use of experimental evaluation designs apply to any program that is unable to reach the entire population of eligible beneficiaries. In addition, while there is always a cost associated with the collection of data, particularly baseline and follow-up from treatment and comparison groups, the costs of experimental designs may actually be lower given the greater statistical efficiency of the design which allows for smaller sample sizes. In sum, many of the challenges present in implementing both experimental and quasi-experimental designs stem from the basic challenge of attempting to apply the scientific method to the social sciences, where the replication of clinical trials poses ethical, scientific, and operational difficulties inherent in the study of human behavior.

Most evaluators today have concluded that experimental designs remain the most reliable and efficient approach to impact evaluation. These designs provide the only recognized way to ensure equivalence between treatment and control groups in all characteristics, observed and unobserved. The evaluation literature continues to point to sources of bias in quasi-experimental methods, despite the advances to date; and experimental designs still serve as the benchmark in the evaluation literature against which quasi-experimental evaluations are assessed. For example, Glazerman, Levy, and Myers (2003) review twelve "within-study comparisons" (design replication studies that estimate an impact using an experimental approach and re-estimate it using quasi-experimental methods) that all pertain to estimating the earnings impact of job training and employment services programs.

They find that whereas some factors may reduce bias in quasi-experimental estimates, there is no reliable strategy for eliminating bias, and that in many cases the bias is quite large. They conclude that "those who wish to evaluate the impacts of training programs on participants' earnings can use this empirical evidence to improve upon quasi-experimental designs, but not to justify their use." These findings confirm some doubts raised by Lipsey and Wilson (1993) in their review of seventy-four meta-analyses conducted in applied psychology, comparing experiments and quasi-experiments. They found that whereas the average treatment effect sizes were similar, the standard errors for the quasi-experiments were much larger. This suggests not only that experimental designs are more efficient, but that many quasi-experiments are needed to produce, on average, a result approximating the experimental result.

2. Experience in Applying Impact Evaluations in Developing Countries

Development practitioners should be aware of the feasibility of conducting experimental design-based impact evaluations of social programs in developing countries. As described below, randomized control designs have been applied to test program effectiveness against the counterfactual; to test the effectiveness of alternative interventions; and, through a meta-analysis, to test how a particular program performs in a variety of settings.[4]

Testing Program Effectiveness

Bolivia Social Investment Fund. Bolivia's social fund used an experimental design to test whether investments in education were achieving their desired impacts, including enrollment, attendance, and achievement. The offer to participate in the fund was randomly allocated to a group of poor communities in the Chaco region, since the very nature of the community-driven process for applying for the social fund did not allow for randomizing on the intervention. Nonetheless, randomizing on the offer created the basis for a valid experimental design.

Early childhood education in Turkey. Mothers of preschoolers were randomly selected to receive training in early childhood development as part of a longitudinal study of the longer-term benefits of educating mothers on their children's cognitive development. The experiment consisted of the collection of baseline data and two rounds of follow-up data, one year after the training and nine years after the training, from both treatment and control groups.

Testing Alternative Interventions

Treating malnutrition in Colombia. An experimental design was used to test alternative interventions in Cali, Colombia, where different combinations of interventions were randomly allocated to malnourished children. Four different approaches were tested, combining food supplements with various education, nutrition, and health services. A noteworthy element of the evaluation is that once the at-risk group of malnourished children had been identified, no control group was selected; the experiment consisted of testing the best combination of interventions.

Family planning in Taiwan. Evaluators tested a variety of approaches to family planning, combining mailings and house visits—each of which was randomly allocated—to men and women separately as well as to both genders together. The evaluation also varied the intensity of treatment introduced, so as to determine to what extent the beneficiary population could be used as agents for spreading information to their neighbors. A matching approach was used in constructing three equivalent "density" sectors in the city where the experiment was carried out. As such, the evaluation effectively combined both experimental and quasi-experimental methods.

Combining supply and demand incentives in Honduras. An ongoing program uses randomization to test different combinations of demand-side subsidies (in the form of cash transfers to households) with supply-side subsidies to schools and health clinics, to test which alternative or combination is most effective in encouraging low-income households to send their children to school and bring them to health clinics.[5]

Testing Programs in a Variety of Settings

Conditional cash transfers in Latin America. Programs can also be tested in a variety of settings using experimental designs, as illustrated by recent experience with conditional cash transfer programs in Latin America. These programs give cash transfers to poor families contingent upon investments in human capital—usually sending children to school or bringing them to health clinics. Experimental designs of these programs have been applied in Mexico in the PROGRESA program,[6] in Honduras in the case listed above, and in Nicaragua. The use of robust methodologies in a variety of country settings provides a solid foundation for both individual program evaluations and cross-country comparisons. The comparative examination of outcomes across settings can be useful to understanding the role of context in influencing outcomes (Rawlings and Rubio, 2003).

3. Moving the Debate Forward

Both experimental and quasi-experimental designs can be used to conduct rigorous evaluations of social programs in developing countries. However, there is a need to improve both types of approaches as well as to broaden the focus beyond impact evaluations.

Improving on Quasi-Experimental Methods

A particularly promising approach to ensuring technical excellence is within-study comparisons that estimate a program's impact using randomization and then re-estimate it using one or more quasi-experimental methods. The United States-based CETA job training program study (Fraker and Maynard, 1984) and the recent review of training programs by Glazerman, Levy, and Meyers (2003) mentioned earlier both use within-study comparisons. This approach has also recently been applied to data from Mexico's PROGRESA program to examine the robustness of a regression discontinuity design approach to evaluation (Buddelmeyer and Skoufias, 2003).

The collection of detailed background baseline data on both participants and non-participants allows for the construction of credible comparison groups, particularly when applied with specification tests to examine the validity of quasi-experimental estimators, as suggested by Heckman and Hotz (1989).

A new approach that has been used in the World Bank is to use projects in the pipeline (that have been approved but not yet implemented) as a comparison group, thereby addressing many of the initial selection factors associated with both managers' decisions and participants' actions. The approach provides the added advantage of generating baseline data against which future results can be compared (Rawlings, Sherburne-Benz, and van Domelen 2002).

Pursuing and Strengthening Experimental Methods

Experimental designs can be introduced and strengthened by taking advantage of opportunities for randomization, pursuing these opportunities creatively, and applying mixed-method approaches in situations where the experiment is not carried out as planned.

Pursuing opportunistic randomization. Often budgets, information constraints, or limited operational capacity prevent programs from reaching all eligible people, particularly at the same time. In these cases, randomization can be used to select from among equally eligible participants. Indeed, randomization can be promoted as an equitable way to allocate a scarce good or service, since it is often a more transparent and less politicized method than the alternatives.

There is room for creativity in applying randomization. One approach is to apply randomization to the middle of the distribution of a group of eligible beneficiaries. For example, program administrators might want to include the very poorest and exclude the richest and to randomize among those in the middle of the poverty distribution.

Randomization can also be built into a program's expansion path, with the first to receive the program serving as the treatment group and the last as the control group. Under this implementation strategy, once the program reaches full capacity no people who were originally considered eligible for the program are denied the program. Since it is often logistically difficult to reach all eligible participants at the same time, this can be an effective approach to both implementation and evaluation challenges.

Finally, evaluators should be creative concerning the unit of randomization, which does not have to be the individual or the household. Cluster randomization has been successfully applied to municipalities, school districts, and neighborhoods. Cluster randomization can make the process of setting up an experimental design much more operationally feasible.

Strengthening experimental methods. To the extent possible, evaluators and program administrators should collaborate to ensure that experimental designs and the corresponding interventions are carried out as planned. Second, approaches combining experimental methods with quasi-experimental methods can be applied to address imperfect implementation. For example, bounds estimates can be applied, or instrumental variable approaches introduced, taking advantage of random assignment as the instrument. Additionally, to the extent permitted by the data, the exogenous variation often created by randomization can be used to develop structural models to peer inside the "black box" mentioned above, as has been done by Attanasio, Meghir, and Santiago (2001) using the Mexican PROGRESA data. Finally, qualitative methods can be applied to complement the analysis of survey-based data.

Complementing Impact Evaluations

Perhaps most importantly, as the next section explores, the development community must look beyond the narrow debate of experimental versus quasi-experimental methods and pursue impact evaluations as a strategic activity within a balanced program of evaluation.

4. Impact Evaluation in the World Bank

Impact evaluations remain quite rare in the World Bank, as in other multilateral and bilateral development institutions. A review of the World Bank's project appraisal documents found that from 1998 to 2000 the share of projects with planned impact evaluations rose from 5 to 10 percent. However, the share of completed evaluations is likely to be smaller than the share of designed evaluations.

Why is so little attention paid to impact evaluations? The World Bank has no dedicated teams or resources for doing strategic impact evaluation work. The Operations Evaluation Department (OED) has a mandate to provide an independent assessment of World Bank operations to the Bank's Board of Directors. In applying this mandate, OED has avoided getting involved in the Bank's operational work except to provide ex post assessments of projects. This rules out the possibility of getting involved in strategic prospective impact evaluations, which remain largely ad hoc. When applied, impact evaluations are a result of initiatives taken by particular task managers or staff in the research department, not the result of a strategic choice made by management and backed by financing earmarked for evaluation research.

A Needs Assessment

Good impact evaluations, especially experimental ones, are central to the World Bank's need to know whether it is doing an effective job in fighting poverty. An understanding of the causal relationship between the investments that the World Bank finances and the outcomes they produce is critical to building an empirically based knowledge bank on development strategies and to enhancing development effectiveness. And the ability to point to robust results can enhance the World Bank's and other development institutions' credibility in the fight against poverty.

However, the development community must look beyond impact evaluations and the experimental versus quasi-experimental debate and recognize that there is a pressing need for new monitoring and evaluation approaches, in order to:

- *Understand the role of context.* Knowledge about why certain outcomes are or are not achieved, and a focus on the external validity of evaluation findings, are key to the ability to replicate successful experiences.
- *Expand strategic evaluations beyond the project level, to program, sector, and country-level assessments.* Many of the interventions that the development community is interested in evaluating are carried out on a national scale and are of a general equilibrium nature, and consequently do not lend themselves to traditional methods of impact evaluation. This is particularly important as the role of policy-based lending grows in the World Bank portfolio. It is also relevant given the importance of the sector-wide strategies that are promoted in health, education, and other critical areas of social development.
- *Improve forecasts of the impact of policy design options.* With proper data, simulations can be used to estimate the effect of various policy options on outcomes.[7] Although not a substitute for prospective evaluation using baseline and follow-up data, these simulations can be a useful policy tool, especially at the program design stage when managers seek to understand the implications of alternative options.
- *Improve monitoring.* A good monitoring system depends on good data, stemming from administrative systems and household surveys, and on the governmental and nongovernment institutions that collect, analyze, and use those data. Building the technical capacity for good monitoring is probably more important, and easier, than ensuring good evaluation.

- *Move from measurement to management.* Performance-based management is arguably the key evaluation challenge for the World Bank and its client countries today. It calls upon institutions to use monitoring and evaluation data to improve the effectiveness of programs and to enhance performance by linking measurement to management and by looking at systems as opposed to single interventions. Results-based management is key to the effectiveness, efficiency, transparency, and accountability of public institutions, and only by taking a more strategic and holistic approach to monitoring and evaluation will it be possible to achieve some of the key challenges and specific targets set by the Millennium Development Goals and by poverty reduction support programs.

Recommendations

The World Bank and the international community need to support more impact evaluations, especially where robust randomization control designs can be implemented. These designs should be applied selectively and strategically in projects and policies that are innovative, replicable, have well-defined interventions, and are likely to involve substantial resource allocations.

How could this be achieved?

First, since good evaluations are a public good that will be undersupplied without subsidization, incentives are needed to undertake them. The World Bank and the development community should more broadly provide financial resources and technical support to evaluation and not expect clients to meet the full costs of evaluations from project loans.

Second, there is a need to strive for high technical quality. Regardless of the type of methodology applied, evaluations should be considered at the beginning of the project, when a range of evaluation options are available, including the opportunities to collect baseline data and introduce randomized control designs. There is also a need to focus on the basics, including sound initial evaluation designs, power calculations for sample sizes, and pilot testing for data collection instruments. Cost-effectiveness studies should be included as a standard part of project monitoring and evaluation.

Third, the World Bank needs to ensure that the evaluations carried out are objective, and recognized as such. Perhaps the best way to ensure this is to assign respected research organizations and academics to carry out evaluation while the World Bank, its development partners, and clients remain involved in developing the terms of reference, applying the results of the evaluations, and thoroughly reviewing the evaluation results in order to ensure that the evaluation results are used to inform policy decisions.

Moving beyond impact evaluations, high-quality monitoring and evaluation systems need to be developed as a key component of results-based management. This is probably the preeminent evaluation challenge facing the development community today. Impact evaluations are one tool in the overall monitoring and evaluation toolkit. They should be used selectively and strategically, recognizing their importance within the broader context of a well-developed monitoring and evaluation system based on streams of data tailored to informing different decisions, at different points in time, with various degrees of precision. Adopting this holistic approach will be of more use to clients than focusing on the narrow debate on experimental versus quasi-experimental methods.

Notes

1. I would like to thank Dan Levy, Osvaldo Feinstein, and George Keith Pitman for comments.
2. For an overview of impact evaluation methodologies, see Rossi, Freeman, and Lipsey (1999).
3. For a good summary of the experience evaluating U.S. training programs, see Grossman (1994).
4. Many of these cases are reviewed in greater detail in Newman, Rawlings, and Gertler (1994).
5. IFPRI (2000a, 2000b).
6. PROGRESA, now called *Oportunidades*, is Mexico's flagship conditional cash transfer program. Introduced in 1997, by 2002 it had reached more than four million families, or close to 20 percent of the Mexican population.
7. Bourguignon and Ferreira (2003) have carried out some recent ex ante simulations examining the *Bolsa Escola* program in Brazil.

References

Attanasio, Orazio, Costas Meghir, and Ana Santiago. (2001). "Education Choices in Mexico: Using a Structural Model and a Randomized Experiment to Evaluate PROGRESA." Processed. Washington, DC: Inter-American Development Bank.

Bourguignon, Francois, and Francisco Fereira. (2003). "Conditional Cash Transfers, Schooling and Child Labor: A Micro-Simulation of Bolsa Escola." Processed, Washington, DC: World Bank.

Buddelmeyer, Hielke, and Emmanuel Skoufias. (2003). "An Evaluation on the Performance of Regression Discontinuity Design on PROGRESA." Discussion Paper No. 827, Institute for Study of Labor.

Feinstein, Osvaldo, and Robert Picciotto (eds.). (2001). *Evaluation and Poverty Reduction*. Washington, DC: World Bank.

Fraker, Thomas, and Rebecca Maynard. (1984). *An Assessment of Alternative Comparison Group Methodologies for Evaluating Employment and Training Programs*. Princeton, NJ: Mathematica Policy Research, Inc.

Glazerman, Steve, Dan Levy, and David Myers. (2003). "Nonexperimental versus Experimental Estimates of Earnings Impacts." Processed. Princeton, NJ: Mathematica Policy Research, Inc.

Grossman, Jean Baldwin. (1994). "Evaluating Social Policies: Principles and US Experience." *World Bank Research Observer* 9 (2) (July).

Heckman, James. (1979). "Sample Selection Bias as a Specification Error." *Econometrica* 47 (1), pp. 153-162.

Heckman, James, and Joseph Hotz. (1989). "Choosing among Alternative Non-experimental Methods for Estimating the Statistical Impact of Social Programs: The Case of

Manpower Training." *Journal for the American Statistical Association* 84 (408), pp. 862-874.

International Food Policy Research Institute (IFPRI). (2000a). "Second Report: Implementation Proposal for the PRAF/IDB Project—Phase II." Washington, DC: International Food Policy Research Institute.

_____. (2000b). "Third Report: Monitoring and Evaluation System for PRAF." Washington, DC: International Food Policy Research Institute.

Lalonde, Robert, (1986), "Evaluating the Econometric Evaluations of Training Programs with Experimental Data," *American Economic Review* 76 (4), pp. 604-20.

Lalonde, Robert, and Rebecca Maynard, (1987), "How Precise are Evaluations of Employment and Training Programs? Evidence from a Field Experiment," *Evaluation Review* 11 (4), pp. 212-217.

Lipsey, Mark W., and David B. Wilson. (1993). *"The Efficacy of Psychological, Educational, and Behavioral Treatment: Confirmation from Meta-analysis." American Psychologist* 48 (12), pp. 1181-1209.

Manski, Charles, and Irwin Garfinkel (eds.), (1992). *Evaluating Welfare and Training Programs.* Cambridge, MA: Harvard University Press.

Newman, John, Laura Rawlings, and Paul Gertler. (1994). "Using Randomized Control Designs in Evaluating Social Sector Programs in Developing Countries." *World Bank Research Observer* 9 (2) (July).

Rawlings, Laura, and Gloria Rubio. (2003). "Evaluating the Impact of Conditional Cash Transfer Programs: Lessons from Latin America." Processed. Washington, DC: World Bank.

Rawlings, Laura, Lynne Sherburne-Benz, and Julie van Domelen. (2002). "Evaluating Social Fund Performance: A Cross-country Analysis of Community Investments." Processed. Social Protection Network, World Bank.

Rossi, Peter, Howard E. Freeman, and Mark W. Lipsey. (1999). *Evaluation: A Systematic Approach.* Thousand Oaks, CA: Sage Publications.

10

Use of Randomization in the Evaluation of Development Effectiveness[1]

Esther Duflo and Michael Kremer

Historically, prospective randomized evaluations of development programs have constituted a tiny fraction of all development evaluations. In this paper we argue that there is scope for considerably expanding their use, although they must necessarily remain a small fraction of all evaluations.

The benefits of knowing which programs work, and which do not, extend far beyond any program or agency, and credible impact evaluations are global public goods in the sense that they can offer reliable guidance to international organizations, governments, donors, and NGOs beyond national borders. Traditional methods of measuring program impact may be subject to serious bias due to omitted variables.

For a broad class of development programs, randomized evaluations can be used to address these problems. Of course, not all programs can be evaluated with randomized evaluations; for example, examinations of issues such as central bank independence must rely on other methods of evaluation. Programs targeted to individuals or local communities (such as sanitation, local government reforms, education, and health) are likely to be strong candidates for randomized evaluations; this paper uses the case of educational programs in developing countries as an example.

We do not propose that all projects be subject to randomized evaluations. But we argue that there is currently a tremendous imbalance in evaluation

Department of Economics, Massachusetts Institute of Technology, BREAD, and National Bureau of Economic Research.

Department of Economics, Harvard University, BREAD, The Brookings Institution, Center for Global Development, and National Bureau of Economic Research.

methodology, and that increasing the share of projects subject to randomized evaluation from near-zero to even a small fraction could have a tremendous impact on knowledge about what works in development. All too often development policy is based on fads, and randomized evaluations could allow it to be based on evidence.

The paper proceeds as follows: Section 1 discusses the methodology of randomized evaluations: we present the impact evaluation problem, review why other current evaluation methods may often be unable to control adequately for selection bias, and discuss why randomized evaluations can be useful in addressing the problems encountered by other evaluation practices. Section 2 reviews recent randomized evaluations of educational programs in developing countries, including programs to increase school participation, provide educational inputs, and reform education. Section 3 extracts lessons from the evaluations described in Section 2, and Section 4 reviews an example of current practice, offers political economy explanations for why randomized evaluations are so rare, and discusses the role that international agencies can play in promoting and financing rigorous evaluations, including randomized evaluations. Section 5 discusses the value of credible impact evaluations as international public goods.

1. The Methodology of Randomized Evaluations

The paragraphs below discuss the selection bias problem that can arise when conducting impact evaluations, and the subsection that follows discusses non-randomized evaluation methods that are used in attempting to control for this bias.

The Evaluation Problem

Any impact evaluation attempts to answer an essentially counterfactual question: how would individuals who participated in the program have fared in the absence of the program? How would those who were not exposed to the program have fared in the presence of the program? The difficulty with these questions is immediate: at a given point in time, an individual is observed to be either exposed or not exposed to the program. Comparing the same individual over time will not, in most cases, give a reliable estimate of the impact the program had on him or her, since many other things may have changed at the same time as the program was introduced. We cannot therefore seek to obtain an estimate of the impact of the program on each individual. All we can hope for is to be able to obtain the average impact of the program on a group of individuals by comparing them to a similar group of individuals who were not exposed to the program.

The critical objective of impact evaluation is therefore to establish a credible comparison group, a group of individuals who *in the absence of the program* would have had outcomes similar to those who were exposed to the program. This group should give us an idea of what would have happened to the members of the program group if they had not been exposed, and thus allow us to obtain an estimate of the average impact on the group in question.

In reality, however, the individuals who participated in a program generally differ from those who did not: programs are placed in specific areas (for example, poorer or richer areas), individuals are screened for participation in the program (for example, on the basis of their poverty or their motivation), and, in addition, the decision to participate is often voluntary. For all of these reasons, those who were not exposed to a program are often a poor comparison group for those who were, and any differences between the groups can be attributed to two factors: preexisting differences (the so-called "selection bias") and the impact of the program. Since we have no reliable way to estimate the size of the selection bias, we typically cannot decompose the overall difference into a treatment effect and a bias term.

To solve this problem, program evaluations typically need to be carefully planned in advance in order to determine which group is a likely control group. One situation where the selection bias disappears is when the treatment and comparison groups are selected randomly from a potential population of participants (such as individuals, communities, schools, or classrooms). In this case, on average, we can be assured that those who are exposed to the program are no different from those who are not, and thus that a statistically significant difference between the groups in the outcomes the program was planning to affect can be confidently attributed to the program.

As we will see later in this paper, the random selection of treatment and comparison groups can occur in several circumstances. Using the example of PROGRESA, a program designed to increase school participation in Mexico, we discuss how prospective randomized evaluations can be used and how their results can help in scaling successful programs; using examples of school-based health programs in Kenya and India we illustrate how prospective randomized evaluations can be used when implementing adapted replications of programs; and using the example of a school voucher program in Colombia we illustrate how program-induced randomization can occur.

It is worth briefly outlining a few clarifications regarding the use of randomized evaluations to estimate program effects. First, a distinction can be made about what exactly the evaluation is attempting to estimate. Randomized evaluations can be used to estimate the effect of a treatment on either the entire population that was subject to the randomization or on a subset of the population defined by predetermined characteristics, whereas instrumental variable techniques estimate local average treatment effects.[2] Second, randomized evaluations estimate partial equilibrium treatment effects, which may differ from general equilibrium treatment effects.[3] It is possible that if some educational programs were implemented on a large scale, the programs could affect the functioning of the school system and thus have a different impact.

Other Techniques to Control for Selection and Other Omitted Variable Bias

Natural or organized randomized evaluations are not the only methodologies that can be used to obtain credible impact evaluations of program effects. Researchers have developed alternative techniques to control for bias as well as possible, and progress has been made, most notably by labor economists.[4] Below we briefly review some of the techniques that are most popular with researchers: propensity score matching, difference-in-difference estimates, and regression discontinuity design.

One strategy to control for bias is to attempt to find a control group that is as comparable as possible to the treatment group, at least along observable dimensions. This can be done by collecting as many covariates as possible and then adjusting the computed differences through a regression, or by "matching" the program and the comparison group through forming a comparison group that is as similar as possible to the program group. One possibility is to predict the probability that a given individual is in the comparison or the treatment group on the basis of all available observable characteristics, and to then form a comparison group by picking people who have the same probability of being treated as those who were actually treated ("propensity score matching"). The challenge with this method, as with regression controls, is that it hinges on having identified all the potentially relevant differences between the treatment and control groups. In cases where the treatment is assigned on the basis of a variable that is not observed by the researcher (demand for the service, for example), this technique can lead to misleading inferences.

A second strategy is what is often called the "difference-in-difference" technique. When a good argument can be made that the outcome would not have had differential trends in regions that received the program if the program had not been put in place, it is possible to compare the *growth* in the variables of interest between program and non-program regions. However, it is important not to take this assumption for granted. This identification assumption cannot be tested, and even to ascertain its plausibility one needs to have long time series of data from before the program was implemented in order to be able to compare trends over long enough periods. One also needs to make sure that no other program was implemented at the same time—which is often not the case. Finally, when drawing inferences one must take into account that regions are often affected by time-persistent shocks that may look like "program effects." Bertrand, Duflo, and Mullainathan (2002) found that difference-in-difference estimations (as commonly performed) can severely bias standard errors: the researchers randomly generated placebo laws and found that with about twenty years of data, difference-in-difference estimates found an "effect" significant at the 5 percent level of up to 45 percent of the placebo laws.

As an example of where difference-in-difference estimates can be used, Duflo (2001) took advantage of a rapid school expansion program that occurred in Indonesia in the 1970s to estimate the impact of building schools on schooling and subsequent wages. Identification was made possible by the fact that the allocation rule for the schools was known (more schools were built in places with low initial enrollment rates), and by the fact that the cohorts participating in the program are easily identified (children twelve years and older when the program started did not participate in the program). The increased growth of education across cohorts in regions that received more schools suggests that access to schools contributed to increased education. The trends were quite parallel before the program and shifted clearly for the first cohort that was exposed to the program, thus reinforcing confidence in the identification assumption. However, this identification strategy is not usually valid; often when policy changes are used to identify the effect of a particular policy, the policy change is itself endogenous to the outcomes it was meant to affect, thus making identification impossible (Besley and Case, 2000).

Finally, a third strategy, called "regression discontinuity design" (Campbell, 1969), takes advantage of the fact that program rules sometimes generate discontinuities that can be used to identify the effect of the program by comparing those above a certain threshold to those just below it. If resources are allocated on the basis of a certain number of points, it is possible to compare those just above to those just below the threshold. Angrist and Lavy (1999) use this technique to evaluate the impact of class size in Israel, where a second teacher is allocated every time the class size grows above 40. This policy generates discontinuities in class size when the enrollment in a grade grows from 40 to 41 (as class size changes from one class of 40 students to one class each of 20 and 21 students). Angrist and Lavy compared test scores in classes just above and just below this threshold, and found that those just above the threshold have significantly higher test scores than those just below—which can confidently be attributed to the class size, since it is very unlikely that schools on both sides of the threshold have any other systematic differences.[5] Such discontinuities in program rules, when enforced, are thus sources of identification.

In developing countries, however, it is often likely to be the case that rules are not enforced strictly enough to generate discontinuities that can be used for identification purposes. For example, researchers attempted to use as a source of identification the discontinuity in the policy of the Grameen Bank (the flagship microcredit organization in Bangladesh), which is to lend only to people who own less than one acre of land (Pitt and Khandker, 1998). It turns out that in practice, the Grameen Bank lends to many people who own more than one acre of land, and that there is no discontinuity in the probability of borrowing at the threshold (Morduch, 1998).

These three techniques are subject to large biases that can lead to either overestimation or underestimation of program impact. Lalonde (1986) found that many of the econometric procedures and comparison groups used in program evaluations did not yield accurate or precise estimates, and that such econometric estimates often differ significantly from experimental results.

Identification issues with non-randomized evaluation methods must be tackled with extreme care because they are less transparent and more subject to divergence of opinion than are issues with randomized evaluations. Moreover, the differences between good and bad non-randomized evaluations are difficult to communicate, especially to policymakers, because of all the caveats that must accompany the results. In practice these caveats may never be provided to policymakers, and even if they are provided they may be ignored; in either case, policymakers are likely to be drastically misled. This suggests that while non-randomized evaluations will continue to be needed, there should be a commitment to conduct randomized evaluations where possible.

2. Examples of Randomized Evaluations of Educational Programs

In this section, we present recent randomized evaluations of three types of educational programs in developing countries: programs designed to increase school participation, programs providing educational inputs, and educational reform programs.

Increasing School Participation

Education is widely considered to be critical for development: the internationally agreed-upon Millennium Development Goals call for universal primary school enrollment by 2015. However, there is considerable controversy over how best to achieve this goal and how much it would cost. For example, some argue that it will be difficult to attract additional children to school since most children who are not in school are earning income their families need, while others argue that children of primary-school age are not very productive and that modest incentives or improvements in school quality would be sufficient. Some see school fees as essential for ensuring accountability in schools and as a minor barrier to participation, while others argue that eliminating fees would greatly increase school participation.

Because one obvious means of increasing school participation is to decrease or remove financial barriers, we review recent randomized evaluations of programs designed to increase school participation through reducing the cost of school, or even paying for school attendance.[6]

PROGRESA

Because positive results can help to build a consensus for a project, carefully constructed program evaluations form a sound basis for decisions on whether or not to scale up existing projects. The PROGRESA program in Mexico, designed to increase school participation, is a striking example of this phenomenon. PROGRESA provides cash grants to women that are conditional on children's school attendance and on preventative health measures (nutrition supplementation, healthcare visits, and participation in health education programs). When the program was launched in 1998, officials in the Mexican government decided to take advantage of the fact that budgetary constraints made it impossible to reach the 50,000 potential participant communities of PROGRESA immediately, and instead began with a program in 506 communities. Half of those communities were randomly selected to receive the program, and baseline and subsequent data were collected in the remaining communities (Gertler and Boyce, 2001). Part of the rationale for this decision was to increase the probability that the program would be continued if there were a change in the party in power, because the proponents of the program understood that the program would require continuous political support in order to be scaled up successfully. The task of evaluating the program was given to academic researchers through the International Food Policy Research Institute (IFPRI); the data were made accessible to numerous researchers, and a number of papers have been written on PROGRESA's impact.[7]

The evaluations show that the program was effective in improving both health and education: comparing PROGRESA participants and non-participants, Gertler and Boyce (2001) show that children on average had a 23 percent reduction in the incidence of illness, a 1-4 percent increase in height, and an 18 percent reduction in anemia. Adults experienced a reduction of 19 percent in the number of days lost due to illness. Schultz (2001) finds an average 3.4 percent increase in enrollment for all students in grades 1 through 8; the increase was largest among girls who had completed grade 6, at 14.8 percent.

In part because the randomized phase-in of the program allowed such clear documentation of the program's positive effects, PROGRESA was indeed maintained when the Mexican government changed hands: by 2000, PROGRESA was reaching 2.6 million families (10 percent of the families in Mexico) and had a budget of US $800 million, or 0.2 percent of GDP (Gertler and Boyce, 2001). The program was subsequently expanded to urban communities and now, with support from the World Bank, similar programs are being implemented in several neighboring Latin American countries. Mexican officials transformed a budgetary constraint into an opportunity, and made evaluation the cornerstone of subsequent scaling up. They were rewarded both by the expansion of the program and by the tremendous visibility that the program acquired.

School Meals, Cost of Education, and School Health in Kenya: Comparing the Cost-Effectiveness of Different Interventions

A central policy concern for developing countries is the relative cost-effectiveness of various interventions intended to increase school participation. This section discusses research on several programs to decrease the costs of education and compares the cost-effectiveness of these different interventions.

Evaluations of cost-effectiveness require knowledge of a program's costs as well as its impact, and comparability across studies requires some common environment. It is difficult to compare the impact of PROGRESA's cash transfers with that of, say, school meals in Kenya, since it is unclear whether the resulting differences are associated with the type of program or the larger environment. In general, analysts and policymakers are left with a choice between retrospective studies, which allow comparison of different factors affecting school participation, and randomized evaluations, which yield very credible estimates of the effect of single programs. One exception to our general inability to compare cost-effectiveness estimates is a recent set of studies conducted in Kenya of programs seeking to improve school participation. By evaluating a number of programs in a similar setting (a specific district in Western Kenya), it is possible to compare explicitly the cost-effectiveness of different approaches to increasing school participation. Looking at the effect of school meals on school participation, Vermeersch found that school participation was 30 percent greater in twenty-five Kenyan pre-schools where a free breakfast was introduced than it was in twenty-five comparison schools. However, the provision of meals cut into instruction time. Overall, test scores were .4 standard deviations greater in the program schools, but only if the teacher was well trained prior to the program (Vermeersch, 2002).

Kremer and others (2002) evaluate a program in which a nongovernmental organization, Internationaal Christelijk Steunfonds Africa (ICS), provided uniforms, textbooks, and classroom construction to seven schools that were selected randomly from a pool of fourteen poorly performing candidate schools in Kenya. As in many other countries, parents face significant private costs of education, either for school fees or for other inputs such as uniforms. In particular, they are normally required to purchase uniforms costing about $6—a substantial expense in a country with per capita income of $340. Dropout rates fell considerably in treatment schools and after five years pupils in treatment schools had completed about 15 percent more schooling. In addition, many students from nearby schools transferred into program schools, raising class size by 50 percent. This suggests that students and parents were willing to trade off substantially larger class sizes for the benefit of free uniforms, textbooks, and improved classrooms. Given that the combination of these extra inputs and a 50 percent increase in class size led to no measurable impact on test scores, but that the cost savings from a much smaller increase in class size would have allowed the Kenyan government to pay for the uniforms, textbooks, and other inputs provided under the program, these results suggest that existing budgets could be productively reallocated to decrease parental payments and substantially increase school participation.

Poor health may also limit school participation. For example, intestinal helminthes (such as hookworm) affect a quarter of the world's population, and are particularly prevalent among school-age children. Miguel and Kremer (2004) evaluate a program of twice-yearly school-based mass treatment with inexpensive de-worming drugs in Kenya, where the prevalence of intestinal worms among children is very high. Seventy-five schools were phased into the program in random order. Health and school participation improved not only at program schools but also at nearby schools, due to reduced disease transmission. Absenteeism in treatment schools was 25 percent (or 7 percentage points) lower than in comparison schools. Including the spillover effect, the program increased schooling by 0.15 years per person treated.

Because these programs were conducted in similar environments, cost-effectiveness estimates from numerous randomized evaluations can be readily compared. De-worming was found to be extraordinarily cost-effective at only $3.50 per additional year of schooling (Miguel and Kremer, 2003, forthcoming). In contrast, even under optimistic assumptions the provision of free uniforms would cost $99 per additional year of school participation induced (Kremer et al., 2002). The school meals program, which targeted preschoolers rather than primary school age children, cost $36 per additional year of schooling induced (Vermeersch, 2003). This suggests that school health programs may be one of the most cost-effective ways of increasing school participation.

School Inputs

This subsection reviews recent randomized evaluations of programs that provide various inputs to schools in Kenya and India.

Retrospective and prospective studies of inputs in Kenyan primary schools. Based on existing retrospective evaluations, many authors are skeptical about the effects of educational inputs on learning (Hanushek, 1995). One potential weakness of such evaluations is that observed inputs may be correlated with omitted variables that affect educational outcomes. The evaluation could be biased upward, for example, if observed inputs are correlated with unobserved parental or community support for education, or downward if compensatory programs provide assistance to poorly performing schools.

Although retrospective studies provide at best mixed evidence on the effect of many types of school inputs, they typically suggest that the provision of additional textbooks in schools with low initial stocks can improve learning. Indeed, cross-sectional and difference-in-difference analyses of Kenyan data would suggest that textbooks have dramatic effects on test scores. Results from a randomized evaluation, however, point to a subtler picture. Provision of textbooks increased test scores by about 0.2 standard deviations, but only among students who had scored in the top one or two quintiles on pre-tests prior to the program. Textbook provision did not affect the scores of the bottom 60 percent of students (Glewwe et al., 2002). Many students may have failed to benefit from textbooks because they had difficulty understanding them: Kenyan textbooks are in English, the official language of instruction, but English is most pupils' third language, after their mother tongue and Swahili. More generally, the Kenyan curriculum is set at a level that, while perhaps appropriate for elite families in Nairobi, is far ahead of that typically attained by rural students, given the high rates of student and teacher absence from school.

Given the results of the textbook study, researchers tried providing flipcharts, an alternative input that presumably was more accessible to weak pupils. Glewwe and others (forthcoming) compared retrospective and prospective analyses of the effect of flip charts on test scores. Retrospective estimates using straightforward ordinary-least-squares regressions suggest that flip charts raise test scores by up to 20 percent of a standard deviation, robust to the inclusion of control variables. Difference-in-difference estimates suggest a smaller effect, of about 5 percent of a standard deviation—an effect that is still significant though sometimes only at the 10 percent level. In contrast, prospective estimates based on randomized evaluations provide no evidence that flip charts increase test scores. These results suggest that using retrospective data to compare test scores seriously overestimates the charts' effectiveness. A difference-in-difference approach reduced but did not eliminate this problem. Moreover, it is not clear that such a difference-in-difference approach has general applicability.

These examples suggest that the ordinary-least-squares estimates are biased upward rather than downward. This is plausible, since in a poor country with a substantial local role in education, inputs are likely to be correlated with favorable unobserved community characteristics. If the direction of omitted variable bias were similar in other retrospective analyses of educational inputs in developing countries, the effects of inputs may be even more modest than retrospective studies suggest.

Placing additional teachers in non-formal education centers. Banerjee et al. (2003) evaluated a program in which Seva Mandir, an Indian NGO, placed second teachers in non-formal education centers that the NGO runs in Indian villages. These non-formal schools seek to provide basic numeracy and literacy skills to children who do not attend formal school, and, in the medium term, to help "mainstream" these children into the regular school system. The centers are plagued by high teacher and child absenteeism. A second teacher (when possible, a woman) was randomly assigned to twenty-one out of forty-two of these centers, and the hope was to increase the number of days the centers were open, increase children's participation, and increase performance by providing more individualized attention to the children. By providing a female teacher, the NGO also hoped to make school more attractive for girls. Teacher attendance and child attendance were regularly monitored throughout the duration of the project.

The project reduced the number of days a center was closed: one-teacher centers were closed 44 percent of the time, whereas two-teacher centers were closed only 39 percent of the time. Girls' attendance had increased by 50 percent. However, there were no differences in test scores. It is worth noting that careful evaluations form a sound basis for decisions of whether or not to scale up existing projects. In the example just discussed, the two-teacher program was *not* implemented on a full scale by the NGO, on the grounds that the benefits were not sufficient to outweigh the cost, and the savings were then used to expand other programs.

Remedial education programs. In 1994, Pratham, an Indian NGO, implemented a remedial education program that now reaches more than 161,000 children in twenty cities. The program hires young women from the communities to provide remedial education in government schools to children who have reached grades 2, 3, or 4 without having mastered the basic grade 1 competencies. Children who are identified as lagging are pulled out of the regular classroom for two hours a day to receive this instruction. Pratham wanted to evaluate the impact of this program, one of the NGO's flagship interventions, at the same time as they were looking to expand it; the expansion into a new city, Vadodara, provided an opportunity to conduct a randomized evaluation (Banerjee et al., 2003). In the first year (1999-2000), the program was expanded to forty-nine (randomly selected) of the 123 Vadodara government schools. In 2000-01, the program was expanded to all the schools, but half the schools received a remedial teacher for grade 3, and half received one for grade 4. Grade 3 students in schools that were exposed to the program in grade 4 serve as the comparison group for grade 3 students who were directly exposed to the program. Simultaneously, a similar intervention was conducted in a district of Mumbai, where half the schools received the remedial teachers in grade 2, and half received the teachers in grade 3. The program was continued for an additional year, with the school switching groups.

The program was thus conducted in several grades, in two cities, and with all schools participating in the program. On average, after two years the program increased student test scores by 0.39 standard deviations. Moreover, the gains were largest for children at the bottom of the distribution: children in the bottom third gained 0.6 standard deviations after two years. The impact of the program is rising over time, and is very similar across cities and child gender. Hiring remedial education teachers from the community appears to be ten times more cost-effective than hiring new teachers. One can be relatively confident in recommending the scaling up of this program, at least in India, on the basis of these estimates, since the program was continued for a period of time, was evaluated in two very different contexts, and has shown its ability to be rolled out on a large scale.

School Reform

There is reason to believe that many school systems could benefit from considerable reform. For example, evidence from the Kenyan evaluations discussed previously suggests that budgets are misallocated and that the curriculum focuses excessively on the strongest students. Teacher incentives in Kenya, as in much of the developing world, are quite weak, and absence among teachers is quite high, at around 20 percent. Proposed school reforms range from decentralization of budget authority to strengthening links between teacher pay and performance to vouchers and school choice. As an example, a decentralization program in Kenya that provided small grants to parent-run school committees induced them to purchase textbooks, with educational consequences similar to those of the textbook program mentioned above (Glewwe et al., 2003). Providing larger grants led school committees to shift their spending toward construction—and no educational impact could be observed from this, at least in the short run.

Teacher incentives. Some parent-run school committees in Kenya provide gifts to teachers whose students perform well. Glewwe et al. (2003) evaluate a program that provided prizes to teachers in schools that performed well on exams and had low dropout rates. In theory, this type of incentive could lead teachers to either increase effort or, alternatively, to teach to the test. Empirically, teachers responded to the program by teaching to the test: they did not increase their attendance but provided more sessions to prepare students for the exams. Consistent with a model in which teachers respond by increasing their effort to manipulate test scores rather than to stimulate long-term learning, the test scores of students who had been part of the program initially increased but by the end of the program had fallen back to levels similar to those of the comparison group.

School vouchers. Angrist et al. (2002) evaluate a Colombian program in which vouchers for private schools were allocated by lottery because of limitations in the program's budget. Vouchers were renewable, conditional on satisfactory academic performance. The researchers found that lottery winners were 15-20 percent more likely to attend private school, 10 percent more likely to complete 8th grade, and scored 0.2 standard deviations higher on standardized tests, equivalent to a full grade level. The effects of the program were greater for girls than for boys. Winners were substantially more likely to graduate from high school and they scored higher on high school completion/

college entrance exams. The benefits of the program to participants clearly exceeded the additional cost, relative to the alternative of providing places in public schools.

3. Lessons

The evaluations described in Section 2 offer both substantive and method-ological lessons. School participation can be substantially increased through implementing inexpensive health programs, reducing the costs of school to households, or providing school meals. Given the features of the education system in Kenya—which like many developing countries has a curriculum focused on the strongest students, limited teacher incentives, and sub-optimal budget allocation—simply providing more resources may have a limited im-pact on school quality. A remedial education program in India suggests that it is possible to improve student test scores substantially at a very low cost. Decentralizing budgets to school committees or providing teacher incentives based on test scores had little impact in Kenya, but a school choice program in Colombia yielded dramatic benefits for participants.

Below we review some of the methodological lessons that can be drawn from the examples discussed in Section 2.

Results from Randomized Evaluations Can be Quite Different from Those Drawn from Retrospective Evaluations

As seen in the studies of textbooks and flip charts in Kenya, estimates from prospective randomized evaluations can often be quite different from the ef-fects estimated in a retrospective framework, suggesting that omitted-variable bias is a serious concern (Glewwe et al., 2003). Similar disparities between retrospective and prospective randomized estimates arise in studies of the impact of de-worming in Kenya (Miguel and Kremer, 2003, forthcoming) and of the impact of social networks on the take-up of de-worming drugs (Miguel and Kremer, 2003b).

Comparative studies that estimate a program's impact using experimental methods and then re-estimate impact using one or several different non-ex-perimental methods suggest that omitted-variable bias is a significant prob-lem beyond just the examples mentioned here. Although we are not aware of any systematic review of studies in developing countries, one recent study in developed countries suggests that omitted-variable bias is a major problem when non-experimental methods are used (Glazerman et al., 2002). This study assessed both experimental and non-experimental methods in the context of welfare, job training, and employment service programs and found that non-experimental estimators often produce results dramatically different from those of randomized evaluations, that the estimated bias is often large, and that no strategy seems to perform consistently well.[8]

One recent study not included in the analysis of Glazerman, Levy, and Meyers (2002) is that of Buddelmeyer and Skoufias (2003). Buddelmeyer and Skoufias use randomized evaluation results as a benchmark to examine the performance of regression discontinuity design for evaluating the impact of the PROGRESA program on child health and school attendance and find the performance of regression discontinuity design in this case to be good.

Future research along these lines would be valuable, as such comparative studies can help to show how significant are the biases of retrospective estimates. However, when the comparison group for the non-experimental portions of these comparative studies is decided *ex post*, the evaluator may be able to pick from a variety of plausible comparison groups, some of which may have results that match experimental estimates and some of which may not. (As discussed below, this is also an issue for retrospective studies in regard to problems with publication bias). Possible ways of addressing these concerns in the future include conducting non-experimental evaluations first, before the results of randomized evaluations are released, or having researchers conduct blind non-experimental evaluations without knowledge of the results of randomized evaluations or other non-experimental studies.

Randomized Evaluations are Often Feasible

As is clear from the examples discussed in this paper, randomized evaluations are feasible and have been conducted successfully. They are labor-intensive and costly, but no more so than other data collection activities. Political economy concerns may sometimes make it difficult to not implement a program in the entire population: for example, "Oportunidades," the urban version of PROGRESA, will not start with a randomized evaluation because of the strong opposition to delaying the access of some people to the program. Such concerns can be tackled at several levels. For example, when financial or administrative constraints necessitate phasing-in programs over time, randomization may be the fairest way of determining the order of phase-in.

NGOs are Well-Suited to Conduct Randomized Evaluations, but Will Require Technical Assistance (for example, from academics) and Outside Financing

Governments are not the only vehicles through which randomized evaluations can be organized. Indeed, the evidence presented in this paper suggests that one possible model is that of evaluation of NGO projects. Unlike governments, NGOs are not expected to serve entire populations. Even small NGOs can substantially affect budgets in developing countries. Given that many NGOs exist and that they frequently seek out new projects, it is often relatively straightforward to find NGOs willing to conduct randomized evaluations: hitches are more often logistical than philosophical.

For example, the set of recent studies conducted in Kenya has been carried out through a collaboration with the Kenyan NGO Internationaal Christelijk Steunfonds (ICS) Africa: ICS was keenly interested in using randomized evaluations to see the impact its programs are having, as well in sharing credible evaluation results with other stakeholders and policy makers. A second example is the collaboration between the Indian NGO Pratham and researchers from the Massachusetts Institute of Technology, which led to the evaluations of the remedial education and computer-assisted learning programs (Banerjee et al., 2003). This collaboration was initiated when Pratham was seeking partners to evaluate their programs; Pratham understood the value of randomization and was able to convey the importance of such evaluations to the schoolteachers involved in the project.

However, while NGOs are well placed to conduct randomized evaluations, it is less reasonable to expect them to finance these evaluations. The evaluations of the ICS de-worming programs were made possible by financial support from the World Bank, the Partnership for Child Development, and U.S. National Institutes of Health (NIH), and the MacArthur Foundation. In the case of the Indian educational programs, Pratham was able to find a corporate sponsor; India's second-largest bank, ICICI Bank, was keenly interested in evaluating the impact of the program and helped to finance part of the evaluation. In general, given that accurate estimates of program effects are international public goods, randomized evaluations should be financed internationally.

Costs Can be Reduced and Comparability Enhanced by Conducting a Series of Evaluations in the Same Area

Once staff are trained, they can work on multiple projects. Since data collection is the most costly element of these evaluations, crosscutting the sample can also dramatically reduce costs. For example, many of the programs seeking to increase school participation were implemented in the same area and by the same organization. The teacher incentives (Glewwe et al., 2003) and textbook (Kremer et al., 2002) programs were evaluated in the same 100 schools: one group had textbooks only, one had textbooks and incentives, one had incentives only, and one had neither. The effect of the incentive program should thus be interpreted as the effect of an incentive program conditional on half the schools having extra textbooks. Likewise, in India, a computer-assisted learning program was implemented in Vadodara in the same set of schools as the remedial education study.

This tactic must take into account potential interactions between programs (which can be estimated if the sample is large enough), and may not be appropriate if one program makes the schools atypical.

Randomized Evaluations Have a Number of Limitations, but Many of These Limitations also Apply to Other Techniques

Many of the limitations of randomized evaluations also apply to other techniques. In this subsection we review four issues that affect both randomized and non-randomized evaluations (sample selection bias, attrition bias, spillover effects, and behavioral responses), and argue that randomized methods often allow for easier correction for these limitations than do non-randomized methods.

First, sample selection problems could arise if factors other than random assignment influence program allocation. For example, parents may move their children out of a school that is outside the program into a school that is within the program. Conversely, individuals allocated to a treatment group may not receive the treatment (for example, because they decide not to take up the program). Even if randomized methods have been used and the intended allocation of the program was random, the actual allocation may not be. This problem can be addressed through "intention to treat (ITT)" methods or by using random assignment as an instrument of variables for actual assignment. Although the initial assignment does not guarantee in this case that someone is actually either in the program or in the comparison group, in most cases it is at least more likely that someone is in the program group if he or she was initially allocated to it. The researcher can thus compare outcomes in the initially assigned group and scale up the difference, by dividing it by the difference in the probability of receiving the treatment in those two groups, to obtain the local average treatment effect estimate (Imbens and Angrist, 1994). Methods such as ITT estimates allow selection problems to be addressed fairly easily in the context of randomized evaluations, but it is often much more difficult to make these corrections in the case of a retrospective analysis.

A second issue affecting both randomized and non-randomized evaluations is differential attrition in the treatment and the comparison groups: those who participate in the program may be less likely to move or otherwise drop out of the sample than those who do not. For example, the two-teacher program analyzed by Banerjee and others (2001) increased school attendance and reduced dropout rates. This means that when a test was administered in the schools, more children were present in the program schools than in the comparison schools. If children who are prevented from dropping out by the program are the weakest in the class, the comparison between the test scores of children in treatment and control schools may be biased downwards. Statistical techniques can be used to bound the potential bias, but the ideal is to try to limit attrition as much as possible. For example, in the evaluation of the remedial education program in India (Banerjee et al., 2003), an attempt was made to track down *all* children and administer the test to them, even if they had dropped out of school. Only children who had left for their home village were not tested. As a result, the attrition rate remained relatively high but did not differ between the treatment and comparison schools—increasing confidence in the estimates.

Third, programs may create spillover effects on people who have themselves not been treated. These spillovers may be physical, as found for the Kenyan de-worming program by Miguel and Kremer (2003, forthcoming) when de-worming interferes with disease transmission and thus reduces worm infection both among children in the program schools that did not receive the medicine and among children in neighboring schools. Such spillovers might also operate through prices, as when the provision of school meals leads competing local schools to reduce their fees (Vermeersch, 2002).

Finally, there might also be learning and imitation effects (Duflo and Saez, forthcoming; Miguel and Kremer, 2003b).

If such spillovers are global (for example, due to changes in world prices), total program impacts will be difficult to identify with any methodology. However, if such spillovers are local then randomization at the level of groups can allow estimation of the total program effect within groups and can generate sufficient variation in local treatment density to measure spillovers across groups. For example, the solution in the case of the de-worming study was to choose the *school* (rather than the pupils within a school) as the unit of randomization (Miguel and Kremer, 2003, forthcoming), and to look at the number of treatment and comparison schools within neighborhoods. Of course, this requires a larger sample size.

One issue that may be harder to address is that the provision of inputs might temporarily increase morale among students and teachers, and hence improve performance. While this would bias randomized evaluations, it would also bias fixed-effect or difference-in-difference estimates. However, it is unclear how serious an issue this is in practice, whereas we know that selection is a serious concern.

In summary, while randomized evaluation is not a bulletproof strategy, the potential for biases is well known and can often be corrected. This stands in contrast to most other types of studies, where the bias due to the non-random treatment assignments often cannot be signed nor estimated.

Publication Bias Appears to be Substantial with Retrospective Studies; Randomized Evaluations Can Help Address Publication Bias Problems, but Institutions are Also Needed

Publication bias is a particularly important issue that must be addressed. Positive results naturally tend to receive a large amount of publicity: agencies that implement programs seek publicity for their successful projects, and academics are much more interested in and able to publish positive results than modest or insignificant results. However, clearly many programs fail, and publication bias will be substantial if positive results are much more likely to be published. Available evidence suggests the publication bias problem is severe (DeLong and Lang, 1992) and especially significant with studies that employ non-experimental methods.

Publication bias is likely to be a particular problem with retrospective studies. *Ex post,* the researchers or evaluators define their own comparison group, and thus may be able to pick a variety of plausible comparison groups; in particular, researchers obtaining negative results with retrospective techniques are likely to try different approaches, or not to publish. In the case of "natural experiments" and instrumental variable estimates, publication bias may actually more than compensate for the reduction in bias caused by the use of an instrumental variable, because these estimates tend to have larger standard errors, and because researchers looking for significant results will only select large estimates. For example, Ashenfelter et al. (2000) show that the there is strong evidence of publication bias in instrumental variables-based estimates of the returns to education: on average, the estimates with larger standard errors also tend to be larger. This accounts for most of the oft-cited result that instrumental estimates of the returns to education are higher than ordinary-least-squares estimates.

In contrast, randomized evaluations commit in advance to a particular comparison group: once the work is done to conduct a prospective randomized evaluation the results are usually documented and published even if the results suggest quite modest effects or even no effects at all.

As we will discuss in Section 4, it is important to put institutions in place to ensure that negative results are disseminated. Such a system is already in place for medical trial results, and creating a similar system for documenting evaluations of social programs would help to alleviate the problem of publication bias. Beyond allowing for a clearer picture of which interventions have worked and which have not, this type of institution would provide the level of transparency necessary for systematic literature reviews to be less biased in their conclusions about the efficacy of particular policies and programs.

Although Any Given Randomized Evaluation is Conducted within a Specific Framework with Unique Circumstances, Randomized Evaluations Can Shed Light on General Issues

Without a theory of why a program has the effect it has, generalizing from one well executed randomized evaluation may be unwarranted. But similar issues of generalizability arise no matter what evaluation technique is being used. One way to learn about generalizability is to encourage adapted replications of randomized evaluations in key domains of interest in several different settings. It will always be possible that a program that failed in one context would have succeeded in another, but adapted replications, guided by a theory of why the program was effective, will go a long way towards alleviating this concern. This is one area where international organizations, which are already present in most countries, can play a key role. Such an opportunity was seized in implementing adapted replications of PROGRESA in other Latin American countries. Encouraged by the success of PROGRESA in Mexico, the World Bank encouraged (and financed) Mexico's neighbors to adopt similar programs. Some of these programs, for example, the Programa de Asignación Familiar program in Honduras, have included randomized evaluations and are currently being evaluated.

Often the results of the first phase of a project may be difficult to interpret because of circumstances that are unique to the first phase: a project may have failed as the result of implementation problems that could be avoided in later phases of the project; or a project may have succeeded because it received more resources than a project in a more realistic situation or less favorable context. Even if the choice of the comparison and treatment groups ensures the internal validity of estimates, any method of evaluation is subject to problems with external validity due to the specific circumstances of implementation. That is, the results may not be able to be generalized to other contexts.

One problem that is specific to randomized evaluations is that members of either the treatment or comparison group could potentially change their behavior, not because of the intervention, but simply because they would know that they are a part of a randomized evaluation. Of course, to the extent that both groups change their behavior in the same way, this will not lead to bias. It is also perhaps less likely that this will occur over a long period and that it will occur immediately after the introduction of the intervention.

One way to address questions about the external validity of any particular study, whether it is a randomized evaluation or not, is to implement adapted replications of successful (and potentially unsuccessful) programs in different contexts. Such adapted replications have two advantages: first, in the process of "transplanting" a program, circumstances will change and robust programs will show their effectiveness by surviving these changes; second, obtaining several estimates in different contexts will provide some guidance about whether the program has notably different impacts on different groups. Replication of the initial phase of a study in a new context does not imply delaying full-scale implementation of the program if that is justified on the basis of existing knowledge. More often than not, however, the introduction of the program can only proceed in stages, and the evaluation only requires that participants be phased into the program in random order. In addition, such adapted replications can be used to check whether program effects within samples vary with covariance. For example, suppose that the effect of a given program is smaller in schools with good teachers; one might consider whether in a different setting with much better teachers the effect would be smaller.

One example is the work in India of Bobonis, Miguel, and Sharma (2002), who conducted an adapted replication of the de-worming study in Kenya. The baseline revealed that, although worm infection was present, the levels of infection were substantially lower than in Kenya (in the India case, "only" 27 percent of children suffered from some form of worm infection). However, 70 percent of children had moderate to severe anemia, and thus the program was modified to include iron supplementation. The program was administered through a network of preschools in urban India. After a year of treatment, the researchers found a nearly 50 percent reduction in moderate to severe anemia, large weight gains, and a 7 percent reduction in absenteeism among 4-6 year olds (though not for younger children). Their findings support the conclusion of the de-worming research in Kenya (Miguel and Kremer, 2003, forthcoming) that school health programs may be one of the most cost-effective ways to increase school participation and, importantly, suggest that this conclusion may be relevant in low-income countries outside Africa.

It is worth noting that the exogenous variation created by randomization can be used to help identify a structural model. Attanasio et al. (2001) and Behrman et al. (2002) are two examples of using this exercise in combination with the PROGRESA data to predict possible effects of varying the schedule of transfers. For example, Attanasio and others (2001) found that the randomized component of the PROGRESA data induced extremely useful exogenous variation that helped in the identification of a richer and more flexible structural model. These studies rest on assumptions that one is free to believe or not, but at least they are freed of *some* assumptions by the presence of this exogenous variation.

The more general point is that randomized evaluations do not preclude the use of theory or assumptions: in fact, they generate data and variation that can be useful in identifying some aspects of these theories. For example, evaluations suggest that the Kenyan educational system is heavily geared towards top students and that reallocating budgets within primary education could lead to considerably better outcomes; they point to perverse incentives created by Kenya's mix of local and national school finance (Kremer et al., 2002; Glewwe et al., 2002).

4. The Role International Agencies Can Play

In this section we review an example of current practice that failed to provide opportunities for rigorous evaluations due to a lack of planning, then present some political economy arguments for why randomized evaluations are so rare, and lastly discuss how international agencies can support the use of credible evaluation methods, including randomized evaluations.

The District Primary Education Program: An Example of Lost Opportunity

The District Primary Education Program (DPEP) in India, the largest World Bank-sponsored education program, is an example of a large program with potentially very interesting evaluations that have been jeopardized by lack of planning.[9] DPEP was meant to be a showcase example of the ability to "go to scale" with education reform (Pandey, 2000). It is a comprehensive program involving teacher training, inputs, and classrooms that seeks to improve the performance of public education. Districts are generally given a high level of discretion in how to spend the additional resources.

Despite the apparent commitment to a careful evaluation of the program, several features make a convincing impact evaluation of DPEP impossible. First, the districts were selected according to two criteria: low level of achievement (as measured by low female literacy rates), but high *potential for improvement*. In particular, the first districts chosen to receive the program were selected "on the basis of their ability to show success in a reasonable timeframe" (Pandey 2000, quoted in Case, 2001). The combination of these two elements in the selection process makes clear that any comparison between the level of achievement of DPEP districts and non-DPEP districts would probably be biased downwards, while any comparison between improvement of achievement between DPEP and non-DPEP districts (difference-in-difference) would probably be biased upwards. This has not prevented the DPEP from putting enormous emphasis on monitoring and evaluation: large amounts of data were collected, and numerous reports were commissioned. However, the data collection process was conducted *only in DPEP districts*. These data will only be useful for before/after comparisons, which clearly do not make sense in an economy undergoing rapid growth and transformation. If a researcher ever found a credible identification strategy, he or she would need to use existing data, such as census or National Sample Survey (NSS) data.

Why are Randomized Evaluations So Rare? Some Political Economy Arguments

We have argued that the problems of omitted-variable bias that randomized evaluations are designed to address are real and that randomized evaluations are feasible. They are no more costly than other types of surveys, and are far cheaper than pursuing ineffective policies. So why are they so rare? Cook (2001) attributes their rarity in education to the postmodern culture in American education, which is hostile to the traditional conception of causation that underlies statistical implementation. Pritchett (2002) argues that program advocates systematically mislead swing voters into believing exaggerated estimates of program impacts. Advocates block randomized evaluations since they would reveal programs' true impacts to voters.

A complementary explanation is that policymakers are not systematically fooled, but rather have difficulty gauging the quality of evidence in part because advocates can suppress unfavorable evaluation results. Suppose retrospective regressions yield estimated program effects equal to the true effect plus measurement error plus a bias term, possibly with a mean of zero. Program advocates then select the highest estimates to present to policymakers, while any opponents select the most negative estimates. Knowing this, policymakers rationally discount these estimates: for example, if advocates present a study showing a 100 percent rate of return, the policymaker might assume the true return is 10 percent. In this environment there is little incentive to conduct randomized evaluations: since the resulting estimates include no bias term, they are unlikely to be high enough or low enough for advocates to present them to policymakers. Even if results are presented to policymakers, those policymakers unable to gauge the quality of particular studies will discount them. Why fund a project that a randomized evaluation suggests has a 25 percent rate of return when advocates of competing projects claim a 100 percent rate of return?

Evaluation in International Organizations

International organizations could play several roles in promoting and financing rigorous evaluations.

It is almost certainly counterproductive to demand that *all projects* be subject to impact evaluations. Clearly, all projects need to be monitored to make sure that they actually happen and to avoid misuse of funds. However, some programs simply cannot be evaluated with the methods discussed in this paper. And even among projects that could potentially be evaluated, not all need impact evaluations. In fact, the value of a poorly identified impact evaluation is very low and its cost, in terms of credibility, is high, especially if international organizations take a leading role in promoting quality evaluation. A first objective is thus to cut down on the number of wasteful evaluations; any proposed impact evaluation should be reviewed by a committee before any money is spent on data collection. The committee's responsibility would be to assess the ability of the evaluation to deliver reliable causal estimates of the project's impact. A second objective would be to conduct credible evaluations in key areas. In consultation with a body of researchers and practitioners, each organization should determine key areas where it will promote impact evaluations. Randomized evaluations could also be set up in other areas when the opportunity occurs.

Credible impact evaluations require a great deal of work and, in addition, the benefits of credible impact evaluations (as we discuss in Section 5) extend far beyond the organization conducting the evaluation; these factors mean that incentives to conduct rigorous evaluations are less than socially optimal. One promising remedy is to embed within the institutional framework of international agencies structures that will provide sufficient incentives for evaluators. Given the current scarcity of randomized evaluations within the institutional environment of international organizations, there may be scope for setting up a specialized unit to encourage, conduct, and finance rigorous impact evaluations, and to disseminate the results. As we will briefly discuss below, the potential for such a unit is tremendous: there exists a ready-made potential supply of evaluators both within the international agencies them-selves as well as within academia, and collaborations with NGOs offer many opportunities for evaluating policies of wide relevance.

Such an evaluation unit would encourage data collection and the study of true "natural randomized evaluations" with program-induced randomization. As we mentioned in Section 2 above, randomized evaluations are not the only method of conducting good impact evaluations. However, such other evalua-tions are conducted much more routinely, while randomized evaluations are conducted much too rarely in light of their value and the opportunities to conduct them. Part of the problem is that no one considers conducting such evaluations to be their job, and hence no one invests sufficiently to conduct them. In addition, all evaluations have common features, and thus would benefit from a specialized unit with specific expertise. Since impact evalua-tions generate international public goods, the unit should have a budget that would be used to finance and conduct rigorous evaluations of internal and external projects. The unit should conduct its own evaluation projects in the key areas identified by the organization.

As previously discussed, the unit should also work with partners, espe-cially NGOs and academics. For projects submitted from outside the unit, a committee within the unit (potentially assisted by external reviewers) could receive proposals from within the organization or from outsiders, and from there choose projects to support. The unit could also encourage replication of important evaluations by sending out calls for specific proposals. The project could then be conducted in partnership with people from the unit or other researchers (academics, in particular). The unit could provide both financial and technical support for the project, with dedicated staff and researchers. Over time, on the basis of the acquired experience, the unit could also serve as a more general resource center by developing and diffusing training modules, tools, and guidelines (survey and testing instruments, as well as software that could be used for data entry and to facilitate randomization—similar in spirit to tools produced by other units in the World Bank) for randomized evalua-tion. The unit could also sponsor training sessions for practitioners.

Another role the unit could serve, after establishing a reputation for quality, is that of a dissemination agency (a "clearing house" of some sort). To be useful, evaluation results must be accessible to practitioners both within and outside development agencies. A key role of the unit could be to conduct systematic searches for all impact evaluations, assess their reliability, and publish the results in the form of policy briefs and in a readily accessible searchable database. The database would ideally include all information that could be useful in interpreting the results (estimates, sample size, region and time, type of project, cost, cost-benefit analysis, caveats, and so forth), as well as references to related studies. The database could include both randomized and non-randomized impact evaluations satisfying some criteria, provided that the different types of evaluation are clearly labeled. Evaluations would need to satisfy minimum reporting requirements to be included in the database, and all projects supported by the unit would have to be included in the database, whatever their results.

As previously discussed, such a database would help alleviate publication bias, which may be substantial if positive results are more likely to be published. Academic journals may not be interested in publishing the results of failed programs, but from the policymakers' point of view knowledge about negative results is just as useful as knowledge about successful projects. Comparable requirements are placed on all federally funded medical projects in the United States. Ideally, over time, the database would become a basic reference for organizations and governments, especially as they seek funding for their projects. This database could kick-start a virtuous circle, with donors demanding credible evaluations before funding or continuing projects, more evaluations being conducted, and the general quality of evaluation work rising.

5. Conclusion

Rigorous and systemic evaluations have the potential to leverage the impact of international organizations well beyond simply their ability to finance programs. Credible impact evaluations are international public goods: the benefits of knowing that a program works or does not work extend well beyond the organization or the country implementing the program.[10] Programs that have been shown to be successful can be adapted for use in other countries and scaled up within countries, while unsuccessful programs can be abandoned. Through promoting, encouraging, and financing rigorous evaluations (such as credible randomized evaluations) of the programs they support, as well as of programs supported by others, the international organizations can provide guidance to the international organizations themselves, as well as other donors, governments, and NGOs in the ongoing search for successful programs. Moreover, by credibly establishing which programs work and which do not, the international agencies can counteract skepticism about the possibility of spending aid effectively and build long-term support for development. Just as randomized trials revolutionized medicine in the twentieth century, they have the potential to revolutionize social policy during the twenty-first.

Notes

1.   This paper draws on work that each of us has done in the field with numerous co-authors, primarily in India and Kenya, respectively, and on pieces we have written synthesizing this work and discussing issues related to randomized evaluations (Duflo, forthcoming; Kremer, 2003). Among other collaborators, we would like to

thank Josh Angrist, Abhijit Banerjee, Eric Bettinger, Erik Bloom, Raghabendra Chattopadhyay, Shawn Cole, Paul Glewwe, Nauman Ilias, Suraj Jacob, Elizabeth King, Leigh Linden, Ted Miguel, Sylvie Moulin, Robert Namunyu, Christel Vermeersch, and Eric Zitzewitz. We thank Ted Miguel for extremely detailed and useful comments. We are particularly grateful to Heidi Williams for outstanding research assistance. We are also very grateful to Francois Bourguignon, Anne Case, Angus Deaton, Rachel Glennerster, Emily Oster, and Paul Schultz.

2. Imbens and Angrist (1994); Heckman et al. (1997, 1998, 1999).

3. Heckman, Lochner, and Taber (1998).

4. There are numerous excellent technical and non-technical surveys of these techniques as well as their value and limitations. See Angrist and Krueger (1999 and 2001); Card (1999); and Meyer (1995).

5. Angrist and Lavy note that parents who discover they received a bad draw in the "enrollment lottery" (e.g., an enrollment of 38) might then move their children out of the public school system and into private schools. However, as Angrist and Lavy discuss, private elementary schooling is rare in Israel outside of the ultra-orthodox community.

6. By school participation, we denote a comprehensive measure of school participation: a pupil is considered a participant if she or he is present in school on a given day, and a non-participant if she or he is not in school on that day.

7. Most of these papers are accessible on the IFPRI web site.

8. One recent study not included in the analysis of Glazerman, Levy, and Meyers (2002) is that of Buddelmeyer and Skoufias (2003). Buddelmeyer and Skoufias use randomized evaluation results as a benchmark to examine the performance of regression discontinuity design for evaluating the impact of the PROGRESA program on child health and school attendance and find the performance of regression discontinuity design in this case to be good.

9. Case (2001) gives an illuminating discussion of the program and the features that makes its evaluation impossible.

10. In fact, the benefits of a credible evaluation are often negative for the person or organization promoting the program.

References

Angrist, Joshua, Eric Bettinger, Erik Bloom, Elizabeth King, and Michael Kremer. (2002). "Vouchers for Private Schooling in Colombia: Evidence from a Randomized Natural Experiment." *American Economic Review* 92 (5), pp. 1535-58.

Angrist, Joshua, and Alan Krueger. (1999). "Empirical Strategies in Labor Economics." In Orley Ashenfelter and David Card (eds.), *Handbook of Labor Economics*, Vol. 3A, pp. 277-1366. Amsterdam: North Holland.

_____. (2001). "Instrumental Variables and the Search for Identification: From Supply and Demand to Natural Experiments." *Journal of Economic Perspectives* 15 (4), pp. 69-85.

Angrist, Joshua, and Victor Lavy. (1999). "Using Maimonides' Rule to Estimate the Effect of Class Size on Scholastic Achievement." *Quarterly Journal of Economics* 114 (2), pp. 533-575.

Ashenfelter, Orley, Colm Harmon, and Hessel Oosterbeek. (2000). "A Review of Estimates of Schooling/Earnings Relationship, with Tests for Publication Bias." NBER Working Paper 7457.

Attanasio, Orazio, Costas Meghir, and Ana Santiago. (2001). "Education Choices in Mexico: Using a Structural Model and a Randomized Experiment to Evaluate PROGRESA." Processed. Inter-American Development Bank.

Banerjee, Abhijit, and Ruimin He. (2003). "The World Bank of the Future." *American Economic Review*, Papers and Proceedings 93 (2), pp. 39-44.

Banerjee, Abhijit, Shawn Cole, Esther Duflo, and Leigh Linden. (2003). "Improving the Quality of Education in India: Evidence from Three Randomized Experiments." Processed. Massachusetts Institute of Technology.

Banerjee, Abhijit, and Michael Kremer with Jenny Lanjouw and Peter Lanjouw. (2002). "Teacher-student Ratios and School Performance in Udaipur, India: A Prospective Evaluation." Mimeo. Harvard University.

Banerjee, Abhijit, Suraj Jacob, and Michael Kremer with Jenny Lanjouw and Peter Lanjouw. (2001). "Promoting School Participation in Rural Rajasthan: Results from Some Prospective Trials." Mimeo. Massachusetts Institute of Technology.

Behrman, Jere, Piyali Sengupta, and Petra Todd. (2002). "Progressing through PROGRESA: An Impact Assessment of a School Subsidy Experiment in Mexico." Mimeo. University of Pennsylvania.

Bertrand, Marianne, Esther Duflo, and Sendhil Mullainathan. (2002). "How Much Should We Trust Difference in Differences Estimates?" NBER Working Paper 8841. Washington DC: National Bureau of Economic Research.

Besley, Timothy, and Anne Case. (2000). "Unnatural Experiments? Estimating the Incidence of Endogenous Policies." *Economic Journal* 110 (467), pp. F672-F694.

Bobonis, Gustavo, Edward Miguel, and Charu Sharma. (2002). "Iron Supplementation and Early Childhood Development: A Randomized Evaluation in India." Processed. University of California, Berkeley.

Buddelmeyer, Hielke, and Emmanuel Skoufias. (2003). "An Evaluation on the Performance of Regression Discontinuity Design on PROGRESA," Discussion Paper No. 827. Institute for Study of Labor.

Campbell, Donald T. (1969). "Reforms as Experiments." *American Psychologist* 24, pp. 407-429.

Card, David. (1999). "The Causal Effect of Education on Earnings." In Orley Ashenfelter and David Card (eds.), *Handbook of Labor Economics*, Vol. 3A, pp. 1801-63. Amsterdam: North Holland.

Case, Anne. (2001). "The Primacy of Education." Mimeo. Princeton University.

Chattopadhyay, Raghabendra and Esther Duflo. (2001). "Women as Policy Makers: Evidence from an India-wide Randomized Policy Experiment," NBER Working Paper 8615.

Cook, Thomas D. (2001). "Reappraising the Arguments against Randomized Experiments in Education: An Analysis of the Culture of Evaluation in American Schools of Education." Mimeo. Northwestern University.

Cronbach, L. (1982). *Designing Evaluations of Educational and Social Programs*. San Francisco: Jossey-Bass.

Cronbach, L., S. Ambron, S. Dornbusch, R. Hess, R. Hornik, C. Phillips, D. Walker, and S. Weiner. (1980). *Toward Reform of Program Evaluation*. San Francisco: Jossey-Bass.

Cullen, Julie Berry, Brian Jacob, and Steven Levitt. (2002). "Does School Choice Attract Students to Urban Public Schools? Evidence from over 1,000 Randomized Lotteries." Mimeo. University of Michigan.

DeLong, J. Bradford, and Kevin Lang. (1992). "Are All Economic Hypotheses False? " *Journal of Political Economy* 100 (6) (December), pp.1257-72.

Duflo, Esther. (forthcoming). "Scaling Up and Evaluation." Annual World Bank Conference in Development Economics Conference Proceedings. Washington, DC: World Bank.

_____. (2001). "Schooling and Labor Market Consequences of School Construction in Indonesia: Evidence from an Unusual Policy Experiment." *American Economic Review* 91 (4), pp. 795-814.

Duflo, Esther, and Emmanuel Saez. (forthcoming). "The Role of Information and Social Interactions in Retirement Plan Decisions: Evidence from a Randomized Experiment." *Quarterly Journal of Economics*.

Gertler, Paul J., and Simone Boyce. (2001). "An Experiment in Incentive-based Welfare: The Impact of PROGRESA on Health in Mexico." Mimeo. University of California, Berkeley.

Glazerman, Steven, Dan Levy, and David Myers. (2002). "Nonexperimental Replications of Social Experiments: A Systematic Review." Washington, DC: Mathematica Policy Research, Inc.

Glewwe, Paul, Nauman Ilias, and Michael Kremer. (2003). "Teacher Incentives." NBER Working Paper 9671. National Bureau of Economic Research.

Glewwe, Paul, Michael Kremer, Sylvie Moulin, and Eric Zitzewitz (forthcoming). "Retrospective vs. Prospective Analyses of School Inputs: The Case of Flip Charts in Kenya." *Journal of Development Economics*.

Glewwe, Paul, Michael Kremer, and Sylvie Moulin. (2002). "Textbooks and Test Scores: Evidence from a Prospective Evaluation in Kenya." Mimeo. Harvard University.

Hanushek, Eric A. (1995). "Interpreting Recent Research on Schooling in Developing Countries." *World Bank Research Observer* 10 (August), pp. 227-246.

Heckman, James, Robert Lalonde, and Jeffrey Smith. (1999). "The Economics and Econometrics of Active Labor Market Programs." In Orley Ashenfelter and David Card (eds.), *Handbook of Labor Economics*, Vol. 3.O. Amsterdam: North Holland.

Heckman, James, Lance Lochner, and Christopher Taber. (1998). "General Equilibrium Treatment Effects: A Study of Tuition Policy." NBER Working Paper 6426. Washington, DC: National Bureau of Economic Research.

Heckman, James, Hidehiko Ichimura, Jeffrey Smith, and Petra Todd. (1998). "Characterizing Selection Bias Using Experimental Data." *Econometrica* 66 (5), pp.1017-98.

Heckman, James, Hidehiko Ichimura, and Petra Todd. (1997). "Matching as an Econometric Evaluation Estimator: Evidence from Evaluating a Job Training Program." *Review of Economic Studies* 64 (4), pp. 605-54.

Imbens, Guido, and Joshua Angrist. (1994). "Identification and Estimation of Local Average Treatment Effects." *Econometrica* 62 (2), pp. 467-475.

Kremer, Michael. (2003). "Randomized Evaluations of Educational Programs in Developing Countries: Some Lessons." *American Economic Review Papers and Proceedings* 93 (2), pp.102-115.

Kremer, Michael, Sylvie Moulin, and Robert Namunyu. (2002). "Decentralization: A Cautionary Tale." Mimeo. Harvard University.

Krueger, Alan. (1999). "Experimental Estimates of Education Production Functions." *Quarterly Journal of Economics* 114 (2), pp. 497-532.

Lalonde, Robert (1986). "Evaluating the Econometric Evaluations of Training with Experimental Data." *American Economic Review* 76 (4), pp. 604-620.

Meyer, Bruce D. (1995). "Natural and Quasi-experiments in Economics." *Journal of Business and Economic Statistics* 13 (2), pp.151-161.

Miguel, Edward, and Michael Kremer. (2004). "Worms: Identifying Impacts on Education and Health in the Presence of Treatment Externalities." *Econometrica* 72 (1) (May).

Miguel, Edward, and Michael Kremer. (2003b). "Social Networks and Learning about Health in Kenya." Processed. Harvard University.

Morduch, Jonathan. (1998). "Does Microfinance Really Help the Poor? New Evidence from Flagship Programs in Bangladesh." Mimeo. Princeton University.

Narayanan, Deepa (ed.). (2000). *Empowerment and Poverty Reduction: A Sourcebook.* Washington, DC: World Bank.

Pandey, Raghaw Sharan. (2000). *Going to Scale with Education Reform: India's District Primary Education Program, 1995-99.* Education Reform and Management Publication Series, Vol. I, No. 4. Washington, DC: World Bank.

Pitt, Mark, and Shahidur Khandker. (1998). "The Impact of Group-based Credit Programs on Poor Households in Bangladesh: Does the Gender of Participants Matter?" *Journal of Political Economy* 106 (5), pp. 958-996.

Pritchett, Lant. (2002). "It Pays to be Ignorant: A Simple Political Economy of Rigorous Program Evaluation." *Journal of Policy Reform* 5 (4), pp. 251-269.

Rosenbaum, Paul R. (1995). "Observational Studies." In *Series in Statistics*. New York, Heidelberg, and London: Springer.

Sen, Amartya. (2002). "The Pratichi Report." Pratichi India Trust.

Schultz, T. Paul. (2001). "School Subsidies for the Poor: Evaluating the Mexican PROGRESA Poverty Program." Yale Growth Center Discussion Paper No. 834 (August). Yale University. (Forthcoming in *Journal of Development Economics*, June 2004.)

Vermeersch, Christel. (2003). "School Meals, Educational Achievement, and School Competition: Evidence from a Randomized Experiment." Mimeo. Harvard University.

Comments on the papers by Rawlings and Duflo-Kremer

Robert Boruch

The papers by Laura Rawlings (chapter 9) and by Duflo and Kremer (chapter 10) are very informative. They recognize that randomized trials are a scientifically important approach to producing statistically unbiased estimates of the relative effects of social and educational interventions, as indeed such trials are crucial in the health sector. They provide excellent examples, which help us to understand the feasibility of randomized trials.

For Rawlings, these examples include Mexico's PROGRESA, Nicaragua's Red de Proteccion Social, and Honduras' Programa de Asignacion Familiar. These tests of conditional cash transfer programs, and their effect on education and health-related outcomes, are ably described by Rawlings (2003), Rawlings and Rubio (2003), and Newman et al. (2002).

From Duflo and Kremer, we learn about randomized trials in Kenya to understand the effect of school meals on preschool children's achievement, trials on the effects of textbooks, uniforms, and construction, studies on flip chart effects and on other potentially important ways to enhance children's educational achievement. We also learn about Indian trials on using second teachers in informal classrooms and on forms of remedial education, and about Colombian trials on vouchers.

University Trustee Chair Professor, University of Pennsylvania.

To their examples, we might add the Nicaraguan trials on radio-based mathematics education and the Colombian trials on educational and health programs during the 1970s.[1] I was privileged to be an advisor on both. In the more speculative vein that workshops invite, participants in the Operations Evaluation Department's International Program for Evaluation Development Training seminars in July 2003 in Ottawa produced interesting ideas about how randomized trials might be mounted so as to inform understanding of whether new tourist programs work in eastern Europe, what drilling programs might work in parts of Africa, and how one might configure trials on other loan-based programs.

Most important, Rawlings and Duflo–Kremer reiterate the World Bank's announced interest in less equivocal evidence about what interventions work, or what works better. But the authors of both papers also recognize that, in recent years, the World Bank has made little investment in randomized trials to generate better evidence on the effects of Bank-supported interventions. Bravo for their candor and courage in this.

I have no substantive disagreements with what these authors have said about randomized trials. So let me build on their research and on their ideas. Further, let me take seriously the World Bank's theme for this Fifth Biennial Operations Evaluation Department Conference on evaluation: "Challenges and the way forward." Because some challenges are obvious, I stress the way forward here.

1. Fair Comparisons of Interventions: Unbiased and Biased Estimates of the Effect of Social Interventions

Randomized trials, when conducted well, produce statistically unbiased estimates of the relative effects of economic, medical, behavioral, and other social interventions. That is, the random allocation of entities or people to different interventions ensures that there is no systematic difference, at the outset, among the entities or people that were assigned to the different interventions.

Analyses of data from passive surveys or from administrative records or quasi-experiments cannot similarly ensure unbiased estimates of the interventions' relative effect. We cannot ensure unbiased estimates, in the narrow sense of fair comparison, even when the surveys are conducted well, the administrative records are accurate, and analyses of resultant data are based on thoughtful economic models. The risk of mis-specified models, including unobserved differences among groups, is arguably high.

Do estimates of the effects of interventions based on nonrandomized trials (quasi-experiments) really differ from estimates that are based on randomized trials? In this regard, the empirical methodological studies to which both Rawlings and Duflo–Kremer refer are critical. The Glazerman, Levy, and Myers (2002) study is a case in point. It is a test bed project mounted by the

Campbell Collaboration (http://campbellcollaboration.org) and supported by the Smith Richardson Foundation.

Its results should worry, if not terrify, those of us who build models based on observational studies and quasi-experimental designs rather than on randomized trials. In the employment, training, and welfare sectors, the biases in estimates of effect that are based on nonrandomized trials are often substantial and usually cannot be predicted. As a consequence, for example, we can make useless programs look harmful, using some statistical and econometric methods. At other times, using different models, we can make useless programs appear to have a positive effect.

The Glazerman et al. (2002) results are new in some respects, but not in others. The Salk vaccine trials of the 1950s, for instance, involved both randomized trials and a parallel set of uniform nonrandomized trials. Estimates of the effect of the vaccine on the incidence of poliomyelitis differed appreciably depending on whether one relied on the results from the randomized trials or from the quasi-experiments (Meier, 1972). The medical community depended on the randomized trials to make a decision about the effects of the vaccine.

Recent contributions to this topic in the healthcare field convey the same dismal news.[2] Estimates of the effects of interventions based on nonrandomized trials cannot be trusted unless there is some other evidence that the comparison is fair, or one is willing to make assumptions that are often not testable.

Lest one think that the physical sciences and engineering are free of such concerns, recall that one of the reasons for the Columbia space shuttle failure has been attributed to the "Crater Equation" used to estimate a projectile's damage to the shuttle's wing. The equation, or its application, was wrong, to judge from experiments carried out as part of the research on Columbia's failure (Chang, 2003).

An implication is this. One way forward for OED and the World Bank Group and many other organizations, including the Campbell and Cochrane Collaborations, lies in encouraging such methodological reviews. People who value scientific evidence as a basis for decisions need to know about potential biases in estimates of the effects of interventions, and about the domains in which bias can be substantial, using randomized trials as a standard.

The way forward lies partly in using such methodological studies to build capacity and incentives. People ought to understand plainly that some useless programs can be made to appear harmful, in some statistical and economic analyses, when those analyses are not based on randomized trials. They ought to understand the idea of fair comparison. They ought to understand this based on randomized trials, as opposed to model-based analyses of passive administrative records or surveys.

Of course, an important challenge lies in mounting randomized trials so as to ensure unbiased estimates. The trials are important in themselves to learning what works better. They also help us to learn whether alternatives to randomized trials perform acceptably.

2. Learning about Randomized Trials

From Rawlings and Duflo–Kremer, we learn about interesting contemporary examples of trials in different countries in which the World Bank works. Well done! But ask yourself this. Where can the World Bank, and we, learn generally about randomized trials in the social sector, in education, housing, crime prevention, health risk reduction, and welfare? Why did we learn about the illustrations at this excellent Fifth Biennial World Bank Operations Evaluation Department meeting, rather than easily through the World Wide Web?

Until recently, there has been no reliable and readily accessible resource for locating randomized trials. The situation changed in 1993, when the international Cochrane Collaboration was created to prepare, maintain, and make accessible systematic reviews of studies of effects of health interventions. Randomized trials have been the main ingredients for these systematic reviews. The Cochrane electronic library on trials contains more than 350,000 entries. Cochrane set a remarkable precedent for accumulating and building a knowledge base of this sort.[3]

In 2000, the international Campbell Collaboration was created as the younger sibling to Cochrane to prepare, maintain, and make accessible systematic reviews of studies of the effects of interventions in education, crime and justice, welfare, and other social arenas. Like Cochrane, the Campbell Collaboration depends heavily, but not exclusively, on randomized trials. The Campbell Collaboration's web-accessible library, the C2 Social, Psychological, Educational, and Criminological Trials Register (C2-SPECTR) contains nearly 12,000 entries on randomized and possibly randomized trials in its ambit. It grows as reports on more trials are located.[4]

C2-SPECTR includes some of the randomized trials that Rawlings and Kerman identified, such as PROGRESA in Mexico. Rawlings and Kerman have also educated us about other trials. Rest assured that the Campbell Collaboration and Cochrane Collaboration will register those trials also.

For the World Bank Group and OED, the way forward lies partly in fostering and using electronic registers of randomized trials. Building reliable, continuously improved, and comprehensive registers of this sort is a non-trivial challenge, however. Duflo–Kremer identify the publication bias problem, one that both Campbell and Cochrane have confronted. Both those organizations recognize, for instance, that the results of trials are not always made public (especially if the news runs contrary to a particular political view), and that keeping abreast of new trials is important to ensure that we can then recognize the suppression of reports as well as keep track of the new studies. For this reason, Campbell is creating a prospective register of trials as part of C2-SPECTR. That is, grants and contracts for new trials are put into a register.[5]

The further and arguably more serious problem is the coverage bias in electronic search engines. That is, the search engines on which the World Wide Web depends do not pick out many of the trials. Hand searching academic journals, for instance, typically yields three times the number of trials that can be identified in a web-based search (Turner et al., 2003). Surveys of organizations that sponsor or conduct such trials are also essential, partly because many of these do not produce reports in refereed academic journals.

3. Learning How Trials are Done: Place-Randomized Trials

Many of the trials identified by Rawlings and Duflo–Kremer were place-randomized trials. These are also known as "cluster-randomized" or "group-randomized trials," "macro-experiments," and "saturation trials" in various research literatures. They involve the random allocation of entities, geopolitical jurisdictions, villages, and so on to alternative interventions and perhaps to control conditions. Ask yourself the question, How did these trials get off the ground? What political institutional problems were confronted and how were they resolved? How was the thing managed?

Part of the answer and part of the way forward for the World Bank and OED lies in identifying such trials and learning the answers to questions about how they are run. How can OED exploit the opportunity to identify such trials? One answer is easy. Synopses of more than 260 reports on them are given in C2-SPECTR at http://campbellcollaboration.org.[6] But this register needs to be continuously improved and updated. Perhaps OED or the Bank can take re-sponsibility to meet some of this challenge.

Part of the more important future lies in bringing people together to share understanding of how place-randomized trials, and other kinds of trials have been mounted. The Rockefeller Foundation, for example, has sponsored a set of commissioned papers and meetings on this topic. Convened by the Campbell Collaboration's Secretariat, the aim is to build the knowledge base across disciplines—education, crime and justice, welfare, health and welfare. It is also to build the knowledge base across country, inasmuch it covers trials in Mexico, China, the UK, U.S., Canada, and elsewhere. The World Bank Group and OED can do much more than a private foundation can.

4. Economic Prediction, Astronomy, and Fair Trials

A member of the audience at this conference offered the advice that econo-mists ought to behave like astronomers, that is, improve on their ability to predict, instead of doing randomized trials. No one can disagree with an aspi-ration to predict better. But asking economists, or medical people for that matter, to predict what happens in the absence of a new and untested interven-tion is akin to asking them to levitate.

More to the point, we need to recognize that our ability to forecast is domain-specific. For instance, during the early 1970s, the effectiveness of bulletproof cloth was under debate. To test the effectiveness of the intervention, police researchers draped the cloth over a pig, fired a large caliber weapon at the pig, and then determined whether there was any bloodshed. The "intervention worked" in that the cloth prevented the bullet's penetrating the pig, that is, no bloodshed. How many control pigs do you think were needed to ensure that this estimate was fair? That is, how many naked pigs had to face possible extinction?

The answer then, as now, is none. This is because the consequences of firing a high caliber weapon at a pig are predictable, if the aim is right, the weapon functions properly, and the pig is not equipped with body armor.

This ability to predict, however, is specific to the domain of ballistic equations whose origins date from the seventeenth century if we use Galileo and Newton as benchmarks. In any case, Galileo, as a good scientist, learned how to develop prediction models as well as how to experiment under controlled conditions (Coyne, Heller, and Zycinski, 1985). The World Bank Group and OED cannot wait 400 years for answers to the question: "What is the relative effect of a Bank-supported intervention?" Randomized trials provide brisker answers.

5. Conditions for Randomized Trials

Of course, the larger question is when the World Bank or anyone else ought to consider supporting a randomized trial to understand the relative effects of an intervention that the Bank supports. For OED and the Bank, a challenge and a way forward lies in making the necessary conditions explicit. Let me suggest that the decision whether to do a trial should be based on affirmative answers to the following simple questions. This interrogatory approach is based on Boruch (1997) and the references therein:

1. *Is the social or economic problem serious?* If the answer is yes, then consider a randomized trial. Otherwise, a trial is not worth the effort. Nor is it ethical.
2. *Are purported solutions to the problem debatable?* If yes, then consider doing a randomized trial. If the answer is no, then adopt the purported solution if the evidence is sufficient to do so.
3. *Will randomized trials yield more defensible (less equivocal and unbiased results) than alternative approaches to estimating effects?* If the answer is yes, consider mounting a randomized trial. If the answer is no, then rely on the alternative approach. Of course, one must have evidence that the alternatives produce unbiased estimates. The methodological studies identified in Rawlings' and Duflo–Kremer's papers are important here, as is the domain-specific ability to forecast.
4. *Will the results be used?* If the answer is yes, then consider mounting a randomized trial. If the answer is no, be wary. Of course, one cannot be certain that any given study result will be used, nor can we ensure agreement on what "use" means. Nonetheless, this standard is important.

5. *Will human rights be protected?* If yes, then consider a randomized trial. If not, forget about the trial. Or, redesign the randomized trial so that rights are indeed protected. The lottery-based "rollout" of interventions across regions of a country, and the lottery-based allocation of interventions to different grades in different schools, that Rawlings and Kremer described, constitute a trial design that satisfies a social standard of ethics at times.

For example, the problem of keeping children in school and out of the fields has been important to Mexico. The purported solutions to the problem, including conditional income transfer programs, have been debatable partly because of equivocal evidence and our inability to make confident predictions at the local and regional levels. The PROGRESA trial that Rawlings and Kremer, and Parker and Teruel (2002) describe is a case in point. Families and villages that clearly do not need conditional income transfers do not receive them—an ethical and political judgment. Families and villages at the margin and beyond are identified as eligible based on census and other data. Because the resources for conditional income transfers are scarce, a lottery allocation meets a reasonable standard for protecting one kind of right: equitable distribution of resources at a certain level to families/villages when the total resources are scarce *and* the level is important.[7]

These questions are plain. But they are sensible in delimiting the conditions under which we may consider mounting randomized trials to estimate the relative effects of different interventions that are purported to reduce poverty, enhance well-being, and advance societies in various ways. They can be used by the World Bank to decide when a randomized trial can be justified. They may have to be tailored, of course, to the Bank's ethical, social, and evidential standards, and will need to take into account the interests and values of the countries that serve and are served by the World Bank Group. But they are a beginning.

6. Concluding Remarks

The aims of the Fifth Biennial World Bank Group OED Conference on evaluation are admirable: to understand fair comparisons, and how to produce scientifically defensible estimates of the effects of loan-supported interventions in exceedingly complex environments. This is not easy. Societal values that differ from scientific ones, or differ from human rights values, may have to take precedence. Fair comparison depends partly on the idea of randomized trials.

To close this discussion, let me borrow from Walter Lippman who, in the 1930s, distrusted Franklin D. Roosevelt in the United States, for what Lippman regarded as Roosevelt's misleading claims that the country had to try out different approaches to reducing social problems. Lippman said: "Unless we are honestly experimental, we will leave the great questions of society and its improvement to the ignorant opponents of change on the one hand, and to the ignorant advocates of change on the other." The OED and the World Bank could build productively on this theme.

Notes

1. See the abstracts in Riecken et al. (1974).
2. See, for instance, the October 31, 1998 issue of the *British Medical Journal* on results from examining eighteen meta-analyses.
3. See http://cochrane.org
4. See http://campbellcollaboration.org
5. Personal contacts and networks count heavily in this effort to build registers, of course. See Turner et al. (2003).
6. Use the non-indexed field designation "CRT" to download these.
7. See Parker and Teruel (2003).

References

Boruch, Robert F. (1997). *Randomized Experiments: A Practical Guide*. Thousand Oaks, CA: Sage Publications.

Chang, K. (2003). "Questions Raised on Equation NASA Used on Shuttle Peril." *New York Times,* 9 June. Section 1, p. 38.

Coyne, G. V., M. Heller, and J. Zycinski. (1985). "The Galileo Affair: A Meeting of Faith and Science." Proceedings of the Cracow Conference, May 24- 27, 1984. Citta Del Vaticana: Specola Vaticana.

Glazerman, Steven, Dan Levy, and David Myers. (2002). "Nonexperimental Replications of Social Experiments: A Systematic Review." Washington, DC: Mathematica Policy Research, Inc.

Meier, Paul. (1972). "The Biggest Public Health Experiment Ever: The 1954 Field Trial of the Salk Poliomyelitis Vaccine." In Judith Tanur, Frederick Mosteller, and William Kruskal (eds.), *Statistics: A Guide to the Unknown*, pp. 2-13. San Francisco: Holden Day.

Newman, John, Menno Pradham, Laura Rawlings, Geert Ridder, Ramiro Coa, and Jose Eviva. (2002). "An Impact Evaluation of Education, Health, and Water Supply Investments of the Bolivian Social Investment Fund." Revised *World Bank Economic Review* submission (March 2002). Authors: World Bank and other organizations.

Parker, Susan, and Gabriela Teruel. (2003). "The PROGRESA Trials in Mexico." Paper presented at the Campbell Collaboration Conference on Place-Randomized Trials. Rockefeller Foundation Center, Bellagio, Italy (November 21-25, 2002).

Rawlings, Laura, and Gloria Rubio. (2003). "Evaluating the Impact of Conditional Cash Transfer Programs: Lessons from Latin America." Draft Manuscript (May 14). Latin American and Caribbean Human Development Department, World Bank.

Riecken, H. W., R. F. Boruch, N. Caplan, D. T. Campbell, T. K. Glennan, A. Rees, J. Pratt, W. Williams. (1974). *Social Experimentation: A Method for Planning and Evaluating Social Programs*. New York: Academic Press.

Turner, H., R. Boruch, A. Petrosino, D. de Moya, J. Lavenberg, and H. Rothstein. (2003). "Populating an International Register of Randomized Trials." *Annals of the American Academy of Political and Social Sciences* 589, pp. 203-225.

Comments on the paper by Duflo and Kremer

Martin Ravallion[1]

Randomization is the theoretical ideal for assessing programs that are assigned more or less exclusively to certain observational units (such as people, households, villages, or larger geographic areas). When a program is randomly assigned across units, every one has the same chance *ex ante* of receiving it. Attributes prior to the intervention are thus independent of whether or not a unit actually receives the program. Then the observed *ex post* differences in the outcome indicators are attributable causally to the program. A truly randomized evaluation is also the natural benchmark for assessing non-experimental methods.[2]

There are sometimes opportunities in practice for randomizing the assignment of an anti-poverty program on a pilot basis. These are often called "randomized field trials." Much has been learnt about welfare policy reform in the United States from such randomized trials (Moffitt, 2003). The Duflo and Kremer paper (chapter 10 in this volume) discusses a number of interesting examples of randomized trials from developing-country settings, drawing mainly on the authors' work, often in collaboration with nongovernmental organizations. Duflo and Kremer argue forcefully for greater use of randomized trials by the World Bank.

Though the Bank has relied more on non-experimental methods, in which assumptions must be made about how unobserved factors jointly influence program placement and outcomes, there are exceptions. A recent example of a randomized field trial by the World Bank is the Proempleo Experiment done in collaboration with the Government of Argentina and documented in Galasso et al. (2003). This was a randomized evaluation of a pilot wage subsidy and training program for assisting workfare participants in Argentina to find regular, private-sector jobs. For expositional purposes I will use this example to illustrate a number of more general points. In doing so I will try to put the case for randomized trials—as argued with force by the Duflo and Kremer paper—into a broader context, recognizing both the strengths and weaknesses of randomization as an evaluation tool.[3] I will also try to draw some lessons for evaluation work in development, and in the World Bank in particular.

I will argue that, while these authors are right that randomization can be a powerful tool for assessing impact, it is neither necessary nor sufficient for a good evaluation. Randomization deserves to be the first option to consider when designing an evaluation. But it should not be the last.

Research manager, Development Research Group, World Bank.

1. Limitations of Randomized Trials

As is recognized in the evaluation literature, randomized designs confront two main practical concerns. The first is a problem of *internal validity*; this arises from behavioral effects (selection bias, spillovers) that often do not go away in randomized evaluations. The second is about *external validity*; this stems from the fact that the context of a specific intervention often matters to its outcomes, thus confounding inferences for "scaling up" from randomized trials. Let me explain these problems in turn.

Internal Validity Concerns

Internal validity concerns can arise from selective compliance with the theoretical randomized assignment. People are (typically) free agents. They do not have to comply with the evaluator's randomized assignment. Then non-experimental methods will still be needed. For example, matching methods may be needed to check that the "randomized in" and "randomized out" groups are in fact balanced in terms of the distributions of observables. Partially randomized designs can also create great instrumental variables for non-experimental methods.

In the Proempleo Experiment, welfare recipients were given a wage subsidy and a training program. One-third received the voucher; one-third received both the voucher and training; while one-third received nothing beyond existing programs, and thus formed the control group.

Given that access to the training component was assigned randomly, if everyone who was offered the training automatically took it up then an unbiased estimate of mean impact for those given training could be obtained, by taking the mean difference in the outcome measure between the treatment and control groups. Under the assumption of perfect take-up, neither the employment nor the incomes of those receiving the training differed significantly from those of the control group 18 months after the experiment began.[4]

However, it is often the case in randomized evaluations such as this that some of those selected for the program do not want to participate. Then actual treatment ceases to be exogenous, even when this is true of the assignment to treatment. There may well be some latent correlate of the outcome measure that influenced the choice to take up the training among those who were assigned it. On a priori grounds, one might argue that workers with intrinsically lower employment prospects (at given program placement) would tend to be more likely to take up the training to try to compensate. If so, then correcting for endogenous compliance would give higher estimates of the impact of training.

In addressing this problem, one can interpret selective take-up as a classic endogeneity problem, for which the now-standard non-experimental solution is to find an instrumental variable (IV) that is correlated with actual treatment but uncorrelated with outcomes given treatment. While finding a valid IV is often difficult in practice, the randomized assignment is a natural choice in this context. The impact estimator is then the two-stage least squares (2SLS) regression coefficient of the outcome measure on a treatment dummy variable, using a dummy variable for assignment as the IV.[5] As with all IV estimators, this requires an exclusion restriction, namely that being randomly assigned to the program only affects outcomes via actual participation. However, there is no obvious reason to question this exclusion restriction.

The Proempleo Experiment revealed a clear selection bias resulting from endogenous compliance with the randomized training component. Some of those randomly assigned the training component did not want it, and this selection process was correlated with the outcomes from training. An impact of training was revealed for those with secondary schooling—but only after correcting for compliance bias using assignment as the instrumental variable for treatment (Galasso et al., 2003).

Keeping the experiment a secret is often hard in social experiments, and failure to do so can be another source of bias, notably if it induces a change in behavior. An effort was made to keep the Proempleo experiment a secret locally; local Ministry of Labor staff were not told how people had been assigned to the three groups, and people from different groups were not given appointments at the local labor office on the same day. But even then, some people in the control group found out that there were voucher and training programs available to others and applied for this assistance. They were refused. Whether this would affect the results is unclear on a priori grounds; tests done excluding those among the control group who had applied for the program did not suggest this was a problem in this case.

The main lesson in all this is that randomization is only one item on the evaluation menu. Non-experimental methods such as propensity score matching and instrumental variables estimators will often be needed even when randomization is feasible. Qualitative methods can also help, such as in finding defensible instrumental variables. The art of good evaluation is to draw eclectically from the whole menu of methods to find the most cost-effective combination appropriate to each setting.

Spillover effects are a further source of internal validity concerns about evaluations in practice. Assigning a program to some units but not to others can induce behavioral responses from third parties that cloud impact identification. For example, a higher level of government may adjust its own spending, counteracting the experimental assignment. Indeed, this may well be a bigger problem for randomized evaluations. Randomization can induce spillovers that do not happen with selection on observables; the higher level of government may not feel the need to compensate units that did not get the program when this was based on credible and observable factors, but it may feel obliged to compensate for the "bad luck" of being assigned randomly to the control group.

External Validity Concerns

I turn now to the external validity concerns about randomized trials. Many of these concerns also pertain to non-experimental trials, but they are still relevant in this context. The essential problem is that if you allow properly for contextual factors it can be hard to make meaningful generalizations for scaling up and replication from trials. The same program works well in one village but fails hopelessly in another, not far away. This was illustrated by the results of Galasso and Ravallion (2003), studying Bangladesh's Food for Education Program. The program worked well in reaching the poor in some villages but not in others. The revealed differences in program performance are attributable in part to observable village characteristics, such as the extent of intravillage inequality, with more unequal villages being less effective in reaching their poor through the program.

When randomized trials are tied to the activities of specific NGOs as the facilitators (as in the Duflo-Kremer examples), there is a concern that the same intervention on a national scale may have a very different impact in places where the NGO is not the facilitator. Making sure that the control group areas also have the NGO can help, but even then we cannot rule out interaction effects between the NGO's activities and the intervention. In other words, the effect of the NGO may not be "additive" but "multiplicative," such that the difference between measured outcomes for the treatment and control groups does not indicate the impact in the absence of the NGO.

A further concern is that while partial equilibrium assumptions may be fine for a pilot project, they cease to be so when the program is scaled up nationally, and general equilibrium effects (sometimes called "feedback" or "macro" effects in the evaluation literature) become important. Active labor market interventions such as those studied by the Proempleo Experiment are a classic example. A small pilot wage subsidy program is unlikely to have much impact on the market wage rate, but when the program is scaled up the impact may be much bigger. Here again the external validity concern stems from the context-specificity of randomized trials; outcomes in the small-scale context of the trial may differ appreciably (in either direction) once the intervention is scaled up and prices and wages respond.

Impacts on scaling up can also differ from the trial results (whether randomized or not) because the socioeconomic composition of program participation varies with scale. Ravallion (2003) discusses how this can happen in theory, and presents results from a series of three country case studies, all of which suggest that the incidence of program benefits improves with scaling up. Trial results may well underestimate how pro-poor a program is likely to be after scaling up, because the initial benefits tend to be captured more by the non-poor.

Returning to the example of the Proempleo Experiment, the results showed that the wage-subsidy voucher had a significant impact on employment but that very few firms took up the wage subsidy. The scheme was highly cost effective; the government saved 5 percent of its workfare wage bill for an outlay on subsidies that represented only 10 percent of that saving.

However, this was because of supply side effects; the voucher had credential value to workers, acting like a "letter of introduction" that few people had (and how it was allocated was a secret). This would be unlikely to happen if the program went national: the voucher would lose credibility and have possibly little impact. This illustrates how an impact of the pilot may vanish when the pilot is scaled up.

Repeating randomized trials across different settings and different scales would clearly help to address these concerns, as Duflo and Kremer note. The practical feasibility of being able to do enough trials (to span the relevant domain of variation found in reality) remains a moot point. The scale of a randomized trial needed to test a large national program could well be prohibitive. Nonetheless, varying the contexts for trials is a good idea, subject to feasibility.

The key point here is that the institutional context of an intervention can be hugely important to its impact, and this clearly matters for scaling up. At the risk of overstating the point, in certain contexts anything will work, and in others everything will fail. Often a crucial factor in program success is adapting properly to the institutional and socioeconomic context in which you have to work. That is what good project staff do all the time. They might draw on the body of knowledge from past evaluations, but these can almost never be conclusive and may even be highly deceptive if used mechanically.

2. Lessons for the Role of Evaluation in Development

While randomization is a powerful tool for impact assessment, non-experimental methods will often be needed to deal with selective compliance with the randomized assignment. So randomization alone is unlikely to be sufficient for reliably assessing impacts. Nor is randomization even essential for a good evaluation; while economists have sometimes been too uncritical of their identification strategies, credible means can sometimes be found to isolate the exogenous variation in an endogenously placed program, for example by exploiting the details of program design. External validity is also a potential concern: randomization is not always feasible beyond pilot projects, but it can be difficult to draw valid lessons for scaling up. Extrapolation to a national context is often problematic.

Evaluation for Knowledge vs. Evaluation for Monitoring

There are other lessons from the debate on randomized trials. A distinction is sometimes made between "evaluation for knowledge" and "evaluation for monitoring," with randomized evaluations of pilot projects playing a key role in the former. (This also raises issues of the public-good nature of evaluation, with implications for funding, as discussed by Duflo and Kremer.) One can readily agree on the importance of building knowledge, while recognizing the importance of context in drawing conclusions for other settings. However, I would also point to the seemingly under-exploited opportunities for using evaluation tools to make existing projects work better. Even a well conceived project (*ex ante*) needs adjustment along the way. We see this all the time in practice. Evaluations done across different contexts can help. It is great to see good "evaluations for knowledge" that contribute to better projects and policies in the longer term, and across contexts. But this is just one aspect of the whole story about the role of evaluation and monitoring in development. I believe that evaluation for monitoring should be a core activity in development projects.

Evaluative Monitoring Tools

This points to another important implication for evaluation in a development context, namely the need for more rapid evaluative monitoring tools. Too often the project monitoring data and the information system have negligible evaluative content. This is not inevitably the case. For example, the idea of combining spending maps with poverty maps for rapid assessments of the targeting performance of a decentralized anti-poverty program is a promising illustration of how, at modest cost, standard monitoring data can be made more useful for providing sufficiently rapid feedback to a project to allow corrections along the way (Ravallion, 2000).

I believe that there is also an important need for the World Bank to provide technical support for establishing the capacity for evaluation *within* government, as Rawlings (chapter 9 in this volume) emphasizes. While I expect that Duflo and Kremer are right that there are unexploited opportunities for involving NGOs, external technical support on evaluation must retain a primary focus on governments if it is to have a major impact.

There is also a pressing need for developing better tools for large, "economy wide" programs. The evaluation tools discussed by these papers are ideal for assigned programs, but have little obvious role in economy-wide programs in which no explicit assignment process is evident, or if it is, the spillover effects are pervasive. Of course (as Duflo and Kremer acknowledge), such programs will almost certainly be unsuitable for randomized experiments. When some countries get the economy-wide program but some do not, cross-country comparative work (such as growth regressions) can reveal impacts. That identification task is often difficult, notably because there are typically latent factors at the country level that simultaneously influence outcomes *and* whether a country adopts the policy in question. And even when the identification strategy is accepted, using the generalized lessons from cross-country regressions to shape policymaking in any one country can be highly problematic.

There are also a number of promising examples of how simulation tools for economy-wide policies, such as computable general equilibrium models, can be combined with household-level survey data to assess impacts on welfare distribution.[6] These simulation methods make it much easier to attribute impacts to the policy change, though this advantage comes at the cost of the need to make many more assumptions about how the economy works. Nonetheless, I see this route as the most promising one currently available for studying economy-wide policies.

In drawing lessons for evaluations at the World Bank, I would also emphasize the need to better address the coordination problems within the Bank, and with and within governments. Good evaluations typically require inputs from diverse sources, spanning existing departmental divisions within the Bank and within the governments that the Bank works with. Failure to properly coordinate these inputs can severely impede prospects for good evaluations in practice.

Notes

1. These are the views of the author, and should not be attributed to the World Bank or any affiliated organization. I have had useful comments from Emanuela Galasso, Ritva Reinikka, Dominique van de Walle, Michael Woolcock, and participants at the session on randomized evaluations at the OED conference, 2003.
2. See for example the discussions in Rosenbaum and Rubin (1983) and Heckman et al. (1998).
3. On the arguments for and against social experiments see, inter alia, Heckman (1992); Heckman and Smith (1995); Burtless (1995); and Moffitt (2003). For introductory overviews of the range of evaluation methods found in practice see Mofitt (1991); Meyer (1995); Blundell and Costa Dias (2000); and Ravallion (2001).
4. The wage subsidy did have a significant impact on employment, but not on current incomes, though it is plausible that expected future incomes were higher; see Galasso et al. (2003) for further discussion.
5. Angrist et al. (1996) provide a precise statement of the exclusion restriction and other conditions under which this 2SLS estimator gives a consistent estimate of the impact of treatment on the treated. This is equivalent to deflating the "intention to treat" effect (given by the difference in mean outcomes between those assigned to the program and those not assigned) by the "compliance rate," given by the proportion of those assigned the program who in fact take it up (Galasso et al., 2003).
6. See, for example, Bourguignon et al. (2003) and Chen and Ravallion (2003).

References

Angrist, Joshua, Guido Imbens, and Donald Rubin. (1996). "Identification of Causal Effects Using Instrumental Variables." *Journal of the American Statistical Association* XCI, pp. 444-455.

Blundell, Richard, and Monica Costa Dias. (2000). "Evaluation Methods for Non-experimental Data." *Fiscal Studies* 21 (4), pp. 427-468.

Bourguignon, Francois, Anne-Sophie Robilliard, and Sherman Robinson. (2003). "Representative versus Real Households in the Macroeconomic Modeling of Inequality." Working Paper 2003-05. Paris: DELTA.

Burtless, G. (1995). "The Case for Randomized Field Trials in Economics and Policy Research." *Journal of Economic Perspectives* 9 (2), pp. 63-84.

Chen, Shaohua, and Martin Ravallion. (2003). "Welfare Impacts of China's Accession to the WTO." *World Bank Economic Review*.

Galasso, Emanuela, and Martin Ravallion. (2003, in press). "Decentralized Targeting of an Anti-poverty Program." *Journal of Public Economics.*

Galasso, Emanuela, Martin Ravallion, and Agustin Salvia. (2003). "Assisting the Transition from Workfare to Work: A Randomized Experiment." Policy Research Working Paper. Washington, DC: World Bank.

Heckman, J. (1992). "Randomization and Social Policy Evaluation." In C. Manski and I. Garfinkel (eds.), *Evaluating Welfare and Training Programs.* Cambridge, MA: Harvard University Press.

Heckman, J., and J. Smith. (1995). "Assessing the Case for Social Experiments." *Journal of Economic Perspectives* 9 (2), pp. 85-110.

Heckman, J., H. Ichimura, J. Smith, and P. Todd .(1998). "Characterizing Selection Bias Using Experimental Data." *Econometrica* 66, pp.1017-1099.

Meyer, Bruce D. (1995). "Natural and Quasi-Experiments in Economics." *Journal of Business and Economic Statistics*, April.

Moffitt, Robert. (1991). "Program Evaluation with Nonexperimental Data." *Evaluation Review* 15 (3), pp. 291-314.

_____. (2003). "The Role of Randomized Field Trials in Social Science Research: A Perspective from Evaluations of Reforms of Social Welfare Programs." Cemmap Working Paper, CWP23/02. Department of Economics, University College London.

Ravallion, Martin. (2000). "Monitoring Targeting Performance when Decentralized Allocations to the Poor are Unobserved." *World Bank Economic Review* 14 (2), pp. 331-45.

_____. (2001). "The Mystery of the Vanishing Benefits: An Introduction to Impact Evaluation." *World Bank Economic Review* 15 (1), pp. 115-140.

_____. (2003). "Who is Protected? On the Incidence of Fiscal Adjustment." Policy Research Working Paper. Washington, DC: World Bank.

Rosenbaum, Paul, and Donald Rubin. (1983). "The Central Role of the Propensity Score in Observational Studies for Causal Effects." *Biometrika* 70, pp. 41-55.

11

A System Dynamics Approach to Monitoring and Evaluation at the Country Level: An Application to the Evaluation of Malaria Control Programs in Bolivia

John Newman, Maria Alejandra Velasco, Leslie Martin,
and Alvino-Mario Fantini

This paper considers the monitoring of progress towards targets within a results-based management (RBM) framework. We argue that progress is more likely to be rapid if an underlying structural model that explicitly links policy actions to results is developed and if the planning, monitoring, and evaluation activities are integrated. The focus on structural models is similar in spirit to a theory-based evaluation approach[1] or the approach of logic models.[2] Using the example of malaria control in Bolivia, the paper shows how modeling tools adapted from the discipline of system dynamics (SD) can be used in a practical way to develop underlying structural models that link policy actions to results.

A results-based management framework (RBM) has been promoted by Canada, the UK, the United States, and the Netherlands over the past five years. According to the Canadian International Development Agency, RBM can be understood to mean a process by which realistic, expected results are defined and progress towards these results is monitored with the use of appropriate indicators. In fact, a "results framework" is now widely used by USAID as a planning and evaluation tool that sets in motion a process for the identification of strategic objectives with corresponding results arranged around these in a descending hierarchy.[3]

The authors are, respectively, resident representative, junior professional associate, and consultants at the World Bank Bolivia Country Office.

The RBM approach has also been incorporated into broader international initiatives. The UN Millennium Summit in September 2000, followed by the International Conference on Financing for Development in Monterrey in March 2002, resulted in a broad consensus around the Millennium Development Goals (MDGs) as a framework for working towards specific targets and results. Increasingly since Monterrey, more bilateral and multilateral agencies and developing country governments have adopted the focus on results—although not always in the context of the MDGs.

The RBM agenda emphasizes the need to clarify the underlying cause and effect relations between actions and results. However, many agencies appear to be stuck at the conceptual level of fixing results, without putting into place practical, operational systems to monitor intermediate indicators. The system dynamics approach described in this paper provides a way of developing rather complex, graphic, structural models of these dynamic relations in a given system easily and intuitively. A system dynamics approach is particularly useful since a result is rarely due to a single action.[4] Even in simple cases, results depend on a multitude of policy actions—each with its own dynamic path—that affect outcomes within that system. The approach also allows for the representation of the dynamic aspects of feedback effects and time lags in a system and helps to avoid the difficulty of keeping multiple dynamic relationships in one's head. It also offers important benefits for planning and for monitoring and evaluation activities.

1. System Dynamics in Evaluation

Virtually all strategic planning today involves the identification of indicators that will be used to monitor progress, and most involves the use of quantitative targets. As part of a results-based management approach, some reward or penalty can be attached to achieving the targets. However, attempts are rarely made to link explicitly the policy actions to the results, tracing through exactly how a given set of policy actions is expected to lead to the final outcome. The ideas regarding what needs to be done and how to proceed are usually implicit, buried within the minds of policymakers.

Developing explicit links between policy actions and results is akin to developing a structural model and can be contrasted with those monitoring approaches that, in essence, take a reduced-form approach. In a reduced-form approach, one applies a program designed to generate a particular outcome or result and then tries either to (1) obtain point estimates of the total expected impact; or (2) define a performance standard—subsequently determining whether that performance standard has been met or not.[5] If the relation between a set of policy actions and the results is well known, then working with the reduced form may be sufficient. But if the causal relations are not well known, it may be possible to reach the proposed targets faster by specifying an initial structural model and then updating it as new information becomes available.

The lack of an underlying structural model can become a problem if one wants to go beyond the task of simply analyzing whether progress has been achieved and, instead, wishes to assess rewards or penalties on the basis of the outcomes. If targets are achieved, there is less of a problem (although one could wonder whether the targets had been sufficiently ambitious).

The problem is more serious if targets are not met and one has to consider imposing a penalty. If no explicit structural model was developed, it is difficult to know whether the targets set were, in fact, achievable. Should one choose to waive the penalty? If so, this could cause those involved in carrying out the program not to take the focus on results seriously. Or should one impose the penalty even if the target may not have been achievable? Program staff might resent being held accountable for something that was not achievable, and could lower their productivity or leave the program in response.

Or should one try to understand what led to the outcome before applying penalties? If so, then one must squarely face the problem of having to specify a structural model that links policy actions to results. This is particularly important if a results agreement is viewed as a form of a contract. Using this analogy, it is best to define the terms of the contract up front. If there is substantial uncertainty among policymakers as to how to reach desired targets, and if an agreement is made without explicit hypotheses about what determines the results, then unrealistic expectations may be imposed on both the program and program staff. The system dynamics approach forces policymakers to acknowledge up front if there is uncertainty and to identify where the uncertainty lies. This acknowledgment may make it easier to get people to buy in to the more systematic approach to results that is considered in this paper.

It is important to note that the SD approach to monitoring and evaluation does not consist merely of the modeling of a complex problem. Rather, it should be conceived more as a *process* in which various things occur. First, at the policymaking level, one must specify how a particular target will be reached. That is, one specifies a structural model underlying the achievement of the target. System dynamics tools can help develop such structural models. Second, one must identify exactly what information is needed to ensure that one is on track to achieve the desired results. Third, there should be an ongoing review of a program's outcomes, comparing what happened to what was expected and, if actual outcomes fell short of expected outcomes, why this occurred. The expected outcomes may not have been achieved because the planned policy actions were not carried out, or, if they were carried out, because certain key parameter values were misestimated. If the actions were carried out and the key parameter values were, indeed, correct, it may be that the underlying structural model was incorrect and needs be reconsidered. With the SD approach, the model is constantly being reconsidered and appropriate modifications and adjustments are expected in the course of one's work.

As one can imagine, taking a more structural approach through systems thinking is much more intensive in the use of information and requires more work than with a reduced-form approach. Although collecting information and allocating the necessary human resources all involve significant burdens, there are certainly ways to reduce these information costs. For example, by identifying the key drivers of desired outcomes within a given system, one can focus efforts on generating the data needed only for those particular areas. This also helps to reduce the (potentially considerable) financial costs of collecting information. In doing this, one can thus develop a work program that concentrates work efforts only in certain areas.

Our hypothesis is that, in many cases, the benefits of the SD approach outweigh the costs. To give a clearer idea of what is involved, we consider the example below.

2. Bolivia's Malaria Control Program

The case of malaria in Bolivia was chosen for several reasons. First, the underlying links between proposed policy actions to control malaria and their expected results are relatively well known. Second, malaria prevalence has dramatically declined in Bolivia over the past five years, suggesting that we do know which policy actions lead to the desired outcomes.

(There are, however, some problems that could be attributed to deficiencies in the monitoring and evaluation of malaria control activities in Bolivia. In the past, the principal problem was that malaria prevalence would decrease but re-emerge later. Currently, even with the strong improvement, the latest data suggest that malaria prevalence no longer receives adequate attention from the relevant authorities, so that the problem may re-emerge once again.) Third, there is global interest in making advances in malaria, exemplified by the Roll Back Malaria program.[6] Considerable effort has been extended in developing a monitoring and evaluation system for the Roll Back Malaria effort, yet that system appears to have some deficiencies.[7]

By using the system dynamics approach to make explicit the links between the policy actions pursued and the results obtained, the fact that the behavior of malaria prevalence is largely predictable over time—and a direct consequence of action (or inaction)—could be highlighted for everyone. A strong monitoring and evaluation system could bring the right information to the attention of the proper authorities, particularly the Minister of Health and the Minister of Finance, in time for them to allocate the resources necessary to keep the problem under permanent control.

The Malaria Problem

Bolivia was at high risk of malaria transmission in the late 1990s, with 40 percent of the population living in endemic areas. After a decade of only modest increase, the number of malaria cases rose dramatically, from 19,000 in 1991 to more than 74,000 in 1998. The jump can be traced to the low level of political and financial commitment to the anti-malaria program (financing dropped from US$ 257,936 in 1996 to just US$ 57,471 in 1997) and to the inappropriateness of the interventions—an excessive dependence on vector control by massive insecticide spraying.

In the late 1990s, the authorities took the first steps to reverse the poor outcomes by establishing the National Program of Malaria Control, which was strongly supported by the government and external donors. As in many other countries, the approach to tackling the problem changed, with the introduction of a comprehensive set of strategies not only for vector control but also for diagnosis and treatment of infected people; strengthening of research capacities (to provide feedback to better direct the activities under the program); and an initiative aimed at involving the community in the control of the disease, by educating populations in endemic areas about the risk of communicable diseases.

The program largely succeeded in controlling malaria and improving health outcomes. After the increase observed until 1998, the number of malaria cases fell again to 5,000 in 2002—only one-fourth of the number a decade earlier. The corresponding Annual Parasitic Index (API) dropped substantially, from 24.8 per 1,000 inhabitants living in endemic areas in 1998 to 1.6 in 2002.[8]

Despite the remarkable reductions in malaria, the potential risk of transmission still affects 136 out of Bolivia's 314 municipalities. In 2001, it was estimated that 38 percent of the population lived in malaria-endemic areas, covering 75 percent of the country's area. And despite the overall reduction in the API, highly risky endemic areas still exist. For instance, 27 out of every 1,000 inhabitants living in the Amazonian region were infected in 2001, accounting for more than half the malaria cases in the country. Eco-epidemiological and geographic conditions make it costly to keep reducing malaria incidence. But unless the disease is controlled in that region, malaria will remain a primary health concern.

3. The Application of System Dynamics Tools

In conjunction with Bolivia's Ministry of Health and PROCOSI, the major NGO network in health, the World Bank has started using a commercial software package[9]—*ithink*—to model the complex and dynamic system represented by the malaria problem in Bolivia.[10] The software has allowed the authorities to take into account the explicit links among the different subprocesses that make up the problem. Through its intuitive, dynamic, graphical modeling capabilities, the software has provided users with a functional organizational framework for integrating a range of sub-models and sub-processes in the context of the problem of malaria. This range of sub-models is, in turn, linked to a high-level map that allows the user to zoom up (or down) between different levels of detail.

The model developed in Bolivia analyzes the relations between health sector policies and underlying epidemiological risks that together determine the prevalence of malaria in the country. The model takes into account the feedback between infected individuals and the rate of transmission of the disease, as well as the actions undertaken and the government's planned 2001-05 strategic sector plan, and also tracks the costs and financing needs contemplated by the plan. Socioeconomic factors that affect, say, the responses by different groups to a diagnosis and treatment program can be factored into the model. Similarly, exogenous factors that may affect the outcome, but may not be amenable to public policy, can be incorporated.

Figure 11.1 shows a high-level map of the principal variables (or sub-models) that make up this health system.

Figure 11.1
High-Level Map of Variables in the Malaria-Control Program

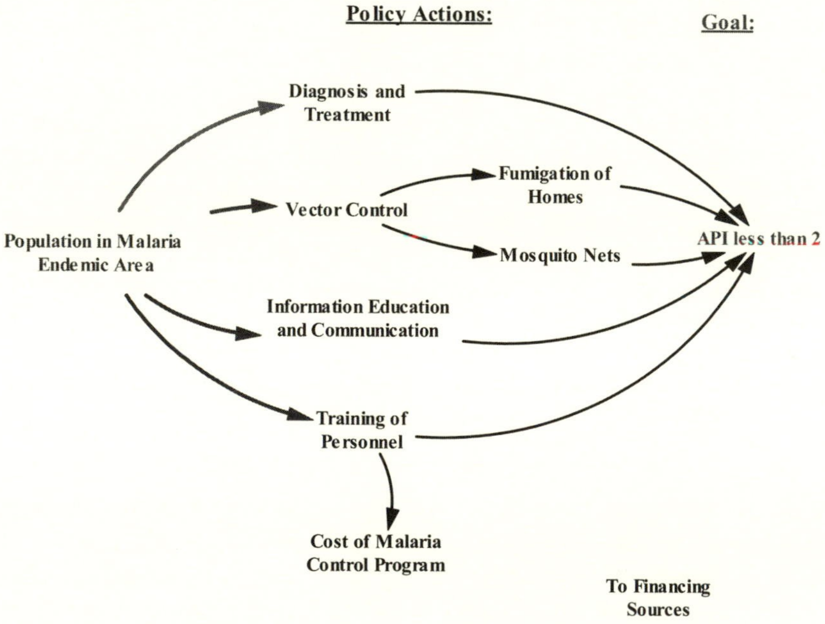

Note: API is Annual Parasite Index.

In this high-level map, each of the variables (such as Diagnosis and Treatment or Fumigation of Homes) is a sub-model by itself. For example, if one were to click on the variable "Malaria by *plasmodium falciparum*" one would be taken to the structure of that particular sub-model, which is a visual description of the structure determining the transmission of the disease by *plasmodium falciparum* and the manner in which the interventions of diagnosis and treatment, vector control, and Information, Education, and Communication (IEC) reduce the likelihood of transmission (Figure 11.2).

The sub-model in Figure 11.2 is created using icons representing stocks and flows, the basic language of the SD approach. In the figure, squares represent stocks, pipes represent flows, circles represent variables that can affect either stocks or flows, and arrows represent the connections between and among variables. The relationships between and among these different elements can be made as mathematically complex as one would like—which helps to better represent the actual system that one is modeling and facilitates the analysis of the stocks and flows within it.

Figure 11.2 also illustrates a classic feedback loop within a systems model. Specifically, one can see the reinforcing dynamic of the malaria epidemic by *plasmodium falciparum*: the greater the number of people sick due to

Figure 11.2
Example of Sub-Model in the Malaria-Control Program

Malaria by Plasmodium Falciparum

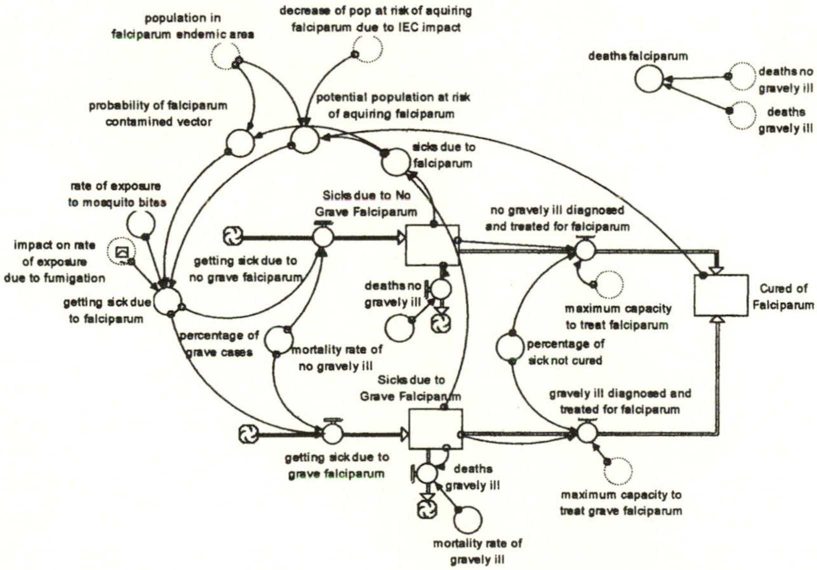

falciparum, the greater the probability of a *falciparum*-contaminated vector (mosquito). This, together with the rate of exposure to mosquito bites, determines the overall number of people infected with malaria.

In fact, with additional information and values that can be incorporated for each of the different variables, a simulation of the entire model (comprising all of the various sub-models) of the system can be run. If particular values are not known, the user can specify ranges—and determine sensitivity—to different values. The results can then be used to develop a work program for identifying information needs and for proposing ways of collecting and gathering the needed data.[11]

After the modeling, the software itself writes a system of nonlinear difference equations based on the system of stocks and flows modeled graphically. Modeling these complex relationships within the system mathematically and without the software would otherwise be very difficult and time-consuming.

Data Sources

This approach is intensive in its use of data, as mentioned above. To develop and use the malaria model, for example, required several sets of data:

- *Data from information systems.* These are data regarding population, birth and mortality rates, population living in endemic areas, number of health facilities in endemic areas.
- *Productivity measures.* These cover, for example, treatment effectiveness,[12] useful life of laboratory equipment, liters of insecticide needed per fumigated house, and productivity of fumigation technicians.
- *Impact parameters.* This refers to the impact of information, education, and communication on the population at risk of acquiring malaria,[13] the impact of fumigation on the rate of exposure, and the impact of mosquito nets on the rate of exposure (assumption, also a graphical function).
- *Cost parameters.* These include the cost per microscope, the unit cost per *vivax* treatment, the unit cost per *falciparum* treatment, fumigation equipment cost, the unit cost of impregnated mosquito bed-nets, training costs for laboratory and fumigation technicians, and annual salaries for personnel.

4. Some Initial Findings

While international health organizations provide general guidelines for the control and treatment of communicable diseases such as malaria, the effective treatment of such diseases at the country level relies on the development of strategies adjusted to meet local conditions. For example, vector-control activities in Bolivia should be designed based on local entomological studies. In the same way, the treatment of people infected should be the result of evidence regarding the effectiveness of drugs and possible drug-resistance in specific endemic areas of the country.

But the control and treatment of malaria can also benefit from incorporating findings from the results of the modeling and simulation of the malaria problem using *ithink*.

The main findings of the system dynamics modeling and simulation process for malaria in Bolivia indicate that it would cost roughly US$ 7.5 million and roughly 3.3 years to bring the key malaria index (the Annual Parasitic Index) below the target of 2. It would also cost roughly US$ 580,000 a year to maintain this index below 2 once it has been reached—a large sum for a country with limited financial resources.

Unfortunately, donor financing declined dramatically in 2002 as previous programs came to an end. Actual expenditure fell substantially below $ 580,000. As a result, the number of cases in the first three months of 2003 jumped up to 3,700 (74 percent of the number of cases registered in all of 2002). This increase in the number of cases was predictable, given the shortfall in the financing provided.

The simulations suggest the costs and benefits associated with different courses of action. For example, some reductions could be made in malaria prevalence if spending were reallocated away from vector control towards diagnosis and treatment, but the reductions would not be dramatic. But significant results could be achieved if resources were reallocated to strengthen the capacity of epidemiological surveillance systems, which help to measure the number of deaths due to malaria, as well as the number of asymptomatic people, population migration rates to malaria-endemic areas, and the rate of exposure to mosquito bites. Additionally, allocating resources to scientific research on mosquito infestation rates and drug resistance, for example, could produce some positive and encouraging results. On the other hand, reallocating funds away from diagnosis and treatment towards greater vector control would significantly raise the costs of reaching the target to US $9.3 million.

The modeling of the malaria problem at the national level can also be extended to different municipalities, each of which faces different decisions than those faced at the national level. Attempting to understand why some municipalities achieve better results than others given their characteristics is important, both to improve the design and implementation of malaria-control programs at the municipal level as well as to analyze extreme cases at the municipal level.

Additional Considerations

Bolivia's achievements in controlling malaria can be seen as a great success story in improving health outcomes. To a large extent, they can be attributed to the implementation of a comprehensive strategy to address the problem and a clear focus on results, coupled with the knowledge of the link between proposed policy actions and their expected results. But with the use and application of system dynamics tools to the problem, much more can be achieved in the near future, especially by refocusing government efforts on the monitoring and evaluation of malaria control efforts.

Within the context of development programs, *ithink* takes the spirit of the traditional Logframe and extends it by using graphical tools that allow the user to build up a system of different elements and components, making explicit the links between a proposed action, its expected result, and its cost. Once data and other information are introduced for the different variables, one can simulate what would happen to the final outcomes over time if one or more actions were to take place. Users can modify assumptions and simulate the impacts of policies in real time and generate visual projections of the impact of proposed actions on a given set of indicators.

A well-designed model, then, can generate graphical projections of the impact of proposed policy actions on key indicators and target results, permit an estimate of financing requirements in order to achieve those results, and serve as a useful tool for a constructive dialogue on prioritizing policy interventions. By enforcing this kind of systematic approach to the analysis of the problem of malaria in Bolivia, it is hoped that more rapid progress may be made in reaching targets than with the current rather *ad hoc* approach.

Despite the positive aspects of the SD approach that we have highlighted, there are some caveats:

First, it is important to recognize that there are always multiple ways of achieving a target. This leads to the question: why model anything at all? The example used to illustrate the SD approach in this paper focuses on the particular path chosen by decision makers and policymakers for tackling a social sector problem. There may be many possible paths, but with a public policy focus, what is important is modeling and analyzing the path actually chosen by public agencies and authorities.

Second, the simulations that can be run based on the model developed are only valid for analyzing small changes around a local optimum. The changes suggested by the malaria model and its simulation were simply marginal shifts in spending from one activity to another but did not represent a radical change in approach. To reflect major changes—such as the identification of a completely different path to achieving the outcome—might require a completely different model.

Some additional thoughts regarding the use of the SD approach in general for the analysis, planning, and evaluation of public policy programs are worth mentioning here:

Be realistic about expectations. We are not saying that a single modeling process generates the results. Our hypothesis is that by following a SD approach, one may reach a target faster than by following a more *ad hoc* approach (maybe in 7 years rather than 12 years). However, in using such an approach, one must constantly compare what one thinks is going to happen with what actually happened, so that the approach can be constantly modified.

Recognize that there are significant costs. One has to decide individually—and according to particular circumstances—whether pursuing the SD approach is worth the costs. To test the hypothesis that the SD approach is worth the effort, one could, for example, conceivably design a random experiment over different municipalities where they are all given the same amount of financial resources; but in one case, there would be the added requirement that they must spend a small percentage on the SD approach. Then, after three years, one could see how much closer the "treatment" municipality is to the target compared to "control" municipalities. Municipalities would need to be randomly assigned to the different groups.

It may be difficult to model what policy actions lead to results. That may be true; but people still make decisions based on certain mental constructs. As one expert in SD has put it: "All models are wrong. But some models are useful." Before proceeding, people must have a mental model of what they think is needed to achieve results. All one is trying to do with systems thinking is force that model into the open so it can be debated, discussed, and analyzed. Just as the act of writing forces one to be clear about the thinking process, the use of systems thinking forces one to be explicit about the problem being considered. Especially for the purposes of achieving quantitative targets, modeling forces one to be clear about presumed relationships and hypotheses about cause and effect.

Other Applications of the SD Approach in Bolivia

The initial models completed for malaria control efforts have allowed for the identification of constituent parts of the problem and show considerable promise. Several other important modeling efforts undertaken in Bolivia are noteworthy. For example, modeling has been completed in collaboration with public agencies of the health problems represented by tuberculosis and the *chagas* disease. The challenge faced now is how to make the results from these models operational. Like those for malaria, the tuberculosis and *chagas* models developed at the national level need to be adapted to reflect the way municipalities actually work as important links in the achieving-results-chain. A model has also been developed of the dynamic processes involved in reaching universal primary education in Bolivia. Developed in collaboration with the Ministry of Education, this model makes explicit the links between policy actions and results, generating graphical projections of the impact of proposed actions on key education indicators, and provides estimates of financing requirements. The core sub-model is a cohort model of the flow of students through different primary school grades.

5. Conclusions

Based on experience with the models described above, whenever a target is specified for a public policy program, it may be useful both for public agencies and international agencies supporting the program to consider making explicit the links between the specified target and the actions required to achieve it. As indicated, the SD approach allows one to break systems down into their constituent parts and work with very complex systems in a manageable way, allowing users to think systematically of inputs, outputs, and the relationships between them. Taking this kind of structural approach can be conceived more as an ongoing process that not only helps specify how a particular target will be reached but also helps identify the kind of information that will be needed in order to track the achievement of desired results.

In the context of monitoring and evaluation activities, the SD approach helps to provide an ongoing review of a program's outcomes by allowing the user to compare a program's expected outcomes to the observed outcomes. Thus, a given model can be constantly reevaluated and reconsidered in the course of program implementation with the necessary modifications and adjustments carried out as needed. The kind of understanding that the SD approach provides regarding a problem, the identification of a desired approach, and the tracking of desired results are quite valuable in the context of the growing emphasis on result—and as an innovative approach to ongoing monitoring and evaluation efforts in the field of development.

Notes

1. Weiss (1972; 1977) or Chen (1990).
2. Gill et al. (1998); Malbry and Baik (1998).
2. Bertrand et al. (1999).
4. Hummelbrunner (2000) also takes a system dynamics approach to evaluation, but with a different emphasis than the approach taken in this paper. Senge (1990) and Sterman (2000) provide useful descriptions of System Dynamics.
5. Manski et al. (2002).
6. For details see www.rbm.who.int
7. Macintyre et al. (2002) state, "...the conceptual framework spells out the major elements of a malaria control program. However, it does not further clarify the processes, outputs and outcomes within each element. Such definitions are critical in helping to develop national-level monitoring and evaluation plans, particularly in the selection of indicators and the timing of data collection."
8. Specifically, the program has succeeded in the struggle against malaria transmitted by *plasmodium falciparum*, the lethal type of the disease. The number of cases caused by *plasmodium falciparum* dropped from 11,400 in 1998 to 250 in 2002; in relation to the total number of malaria cases, the proportion dropped from 15.4 percent to 5.1 percent between 1998 and 2001, revealing a change in the epidemiological distribution of malaria in Bolivia and a relative reduction re-

garding the seriousness of the situation. At the same time, the incidence of malaria by *plasmodium vivax*—the other type of malaria that prevails in Bolivia—also decreased. When compared to the Annual Blood Test Index (ABTI), it can be clearly seen that the number of positive cases due to *plasmodium vivax* is decreasing with the number of examined blood samples, reflecting a complete coverage of *vivax* reservoirs.

9. There are various software tools, each with different strengths and weaknesses. More information on the *ithink* package can be found on their website, www.hps-inc.com

10. Guido Monasterios and Rene Mollinedo were the people most involved in this activity within the Ministry of Health. Ramiro Bernal, a consultant for PROCOSI, also worked on the models.

11. Briggs (chapter 14 in this volume) discusses Bayesian approaches to assessing sensitivity and to deciding whether to invest in additional information to reduce the uncertainty associated with taking decisions.

12. The number of pills an infected person has to take is determined by malaria protocols, which are designed taking into account general guidelines provided by international health organizations, but are adapted for local conditions on the basis of local research.

13. There have been some pilot experiences, but uncertainty remains. In our model, IEC impact is a range between 10 percent and 20 percent.

References

Bertrand, J., M. Toffolon-Weiss, and S. Terrell. (1999). "The Results Framework: An Innovative Tool for Program Planning and Evaluation." *Evaluation Review* 23, pp. 336-359.

Chen, H. T. (1990). *Theory-driven Evaluations*. Newbury Park, CA: Sage Publications.

Gill, S. J., R. A. Millett, et al. (1998). "Program Logic: A Tool for Evaluating Social Change." American Evaluation Association Annual Meeting, Chicago, Illinois.

Hummelbrunner, R. (2000). "A Systems Approach to Evaluation: Application of Systems Theory and Systems Thinking in Evaluation." Paper prepared for the 4th EEC Conference, Lausanne, Switzerland. October 12-14.

Macintyre, K., E. Eckert, and A. Robinson. (2002). *Assessment of the Roll Back Malaria Monitoring and Evaluation System*. Measure Evaluation Working Papers, WP-02-55. February.

Malbry, L., and S. Baik. (1998). "Ideological and Structural Logic Models." American Evaluation Association Annual Meeting, Chicago, Illinois.

Manski, C., J. Newman, and J. Pepper. (2002). "Using Performance Standards to Evaluate Social Programs with Incomplete Outcome Data: General Issues and Application to a Higher Education Block Grant Program." *Evaluation Review* 26, pp. 355-381.

Senge, P. M. (1990). *The Fifth Discipline: The Art and Practice of the Learning Organization*. New York: Doubleday/Currency.

Sterman, J. (2000). *Business Dynamics: Systems Thinking and Modeling for a Complex World*. New York: McGraw-Hill.

Weiss, C. H. (1972). *Evaluation Research: Methods for Assessing Program Effectiveness*. Englewood Cliffs, NJ: Prentice Hall.

_____. (1997). "How Can Theory-based Evaluation Make Greater Headway?" *Evaluation Review* 21, pp. 501-524.

12

Some Remarks on Randomization, Econometrics, and Data

Angus Deaton

There is a long tradition of economic evaluation in academia, and a long and impressive relationship between the academic side of evaluation and the World Bank and other development organizations. Perhaps the heyday of this interactive relationship was in the 1960s, when the UNIDO and the OECD guidelines were produced.[1] Among the authors of those two reports were two people who are now Nobel laureates (Amartya Sen and James Mirrlees) and those guidelines were turned into manuals and guides for action within the World Bank. A version of them produced by Squire and Van der Tak was used around the World Bank for many years and used for teaching in many places around the world.[2] There is a magisterial survey of project evaluation by Lyn Squire in the *Handbook of Development Economics*, and there is a somewhat later and equally fine survey by Nick Stern and Jean Drèze in the *Handbook of Public Economics*.[3]

That interaction has come alive again over the last ten or fifteen years, to address two big problems that characterized the earlier literature. The first of these was that the guidelines and manuals were set within a theoretical framework of optimal public finance and optimal growth, which assumed the existence of a social welfare function that was being maximized by the government that was running the country. We have since come to realize that this is a very naive and, in many ways, an extremely unhelpful way of thinking about the development process, and I think it is an important reason why that literature

Dwight E. Eisenhower Professor of International Affairs and professor of economics, Princeton University. These remarks are an edited version of an informal lunchtime talk to conference participants.

seems much less relevant today than it once did. The second problem was that these guidelines and manuals assumed from the start that we knew what the project's outcomes would be, so that the challenge was to attach prices to the outcomes. Thus, these books essentially deal with deriving shadow prices, thinking about shadow prices within an optimal growth and a public policy framework, and then working out cost/benefit ratios using the proper prices.

Most of these authors acknowledged that in practice you might not know what the project's outcomes would be—but they nonetheless ignored this problem and left it for the evaluators to handle. Over the last fifteen years, however, academic economists and statisticians have spent a lot of time thinking about methods by which we can convincingly find out what a project or a policy actually does. There is now a large and growing literature on this, both on methodology and on practical project evaluation.

Meanwhile, important changes have taken place in the World Bank. In particular, the Bank now supplies a much smaller share of lending in the world than it once did. In the old days, the primary role of the Bank's Operations Evaluation Department was to make sure that the large share of development lending that the Bank supplied was actually evaluated ex post, and to find out whether the lending had been done properly. Now, in a world in which the Bank has a much smaller role, a key task for OED is to produce the international public good of knowledge about what works and what does not work. That is not the only function of project evaluation by any means, but it is an increasingly important one. And that means that project evaluation needs to be refocused towards generating knowledge. The other factor influencing the role of project evaluation is the increased pressure that the Bank is facing from donors, whose citizens and policymakers are demanding to see concrete results and convincing evidence that the Bank's programs and projects actually do what they are supposed to do, and help reduce poverty in the world.

Against this background, I want to discuss briefly three topics: randomized experiments, econometrics, and data.

1. Randomized Experiments

In a randomized experiment, controls and experimentals are chosen at random. That is, of course, why it is called randomization. This does not guarantee that the control group and the experimental group are the same, because, after all, we only have finite groups, and by chance, these groups will always differ from one another in some respect. But what it allows you to do—as R. A. Fisher, the father of randomized trials, emphasized—is to find out how significant are the differences between the control and the experimental group. Basically, it allows you to calculate a standard error.

Randomization also allows you to establish causality. There is no doubt about the direction of causality in a randomized trial, because you are manipulating one variable, and the other variable either responds or it does not. In other methods of project evaluation, by contrast, causality is almost always an issue.

Randomization also controls not just for observables but also for "unobservables"—other things that might affect the outcome but that cannot be observed. If we knew exactly how people in the control group differed from those in the treatment group, we could adjust for the differences in some way. But we do not in fact know what those differences are, and randomization is the only way that anyone has discovered of controlling for what we do not know about people. We can adjust for observables, but randomization is the only known way to adjust for unobservables.

Now there are lots of objections to randomization. People will tell you that it is unfair; it is costly; it wastes time; it wastes resources; it delays getting on with the job. They will say, "We know what works. Let us go and do it. Let us not mess around doing these academic exercises to find out things that we already know."

Some of these objections result from a misunderstanding. A randomized experiment is a tool for learning. Certainly, if you think you already know what works, then a randomized experiment is at best a nuisance, and, worse, it can lead you to withhold treatment from people who you think ought to get the treatment. Once you have learned, you do not randomize anymore. Once a drug is established to be safe and effective, we do not expect doctors to prescribe it on a random basis.

Equally, randomization is not a panacea. It obviously does not apply to a very large and important part of what the World Bank does—advising on macroeconomic policies, for example. But it is illegitimate to say just because randomization is not important for, say, macroeconomic policy decisions, randomization is not important, and we should not do it at all. That would be to throw the baby out with the bath water.

Another common argument is that the World Bank funds projects that are often cherry-picked by governments, so that the evaluation of these projects really tells you nothing about the money that the Bank is putting in, because money is fungible. That argument has much to be said for it, and it leads in the direction that the Bank has been moving, towards much more policy-based and budgetary support type lending. But the argument about fungibility doesn't actually affect the argument about randomized control trials, because randomized control trials are not about evaluating projects—they are about finding out what works. The important feature of randomization is that it generates knowledge that is an international public good; much less important is its ability to deliver a cost/benefit analysis for a particular project.

Let me talk about what does seem to me one of the major limitations of randomization: what I think of as the "averages" problem. This has been a battleground in the medical literature for probably about 300 years, but it is not always well appreciated. Here it is useful to use a medical analogy, because there are similarities between what is going on in our community and what goes on in the medical community. In a randomized control trial in medicine, you take a treatment group and a control group; you administer the drug; you count how many people die, how many get better, and you have the net effect of the drug. That net effect is an average, and an average is what any controlled trial will give you. There may be different sorts of averages, for example the average among those actually treated, or among those designed for treatment, but including those who, for some reason or other, did not receive it. But the essence of the matter is that the answer from the trial is an average that does nothing to recognize the heterogeneity among individuals. People are commonly assumed to have a biological, deterministic reaction to a drug that is the same for everyone. But in fact the reaction depends on the hospital, it depends on the physician, on the patient, and on a lot of individual characteristics. And the randomized control trial gives you an average of those things.

Many people would argue that as a consequence of the "averages" problem, randomized control trials have had limited effect on clinical practice. Doctors, when they are treating a patient, use a tremendous amount of contextual information that is not taken into account in a clinical trial. So when a doctor sees a particular patient in a particular clinical setting, he/she may know that a drug performed poorly in a randomized control trial, but still may judge that this drug will be good for this particular patient. And that is why it is not possible, when you do a randomized trial and get a clear result, to decide on that basis alone. The FDA, for example, will take drugs off the market if they are positively harmful, but it does not prohibit doctors from prescribing certain drugs; it just labels drugs in terms of their known effects.[4] In the development field, we must recognize the importance of these contextual factors. For example, when we consider school administrators in India setting up schools with Indian schoolteachers and specific Indian children in a specific area, there will be an enormous amount of heterogeneity in the outcomes, that we must explicitly recognize when using the results from randomized controlled trials.

By analogy with the FDA, a lot of what the World Bank should be doing is to provide international public goods in terms of labeling and then letting individual development practitioners use that information in the best way they can, given what is there, and avoid reinventing the wheel. Within the development community, for people who know the answer, the randomized control trial is a waste of time. But there is a really serious underproduction of this sort of information, and the World Bank needs to set incentives for producing it, and require its production wherever possible.

So to sum up, randomization is a terrible way of working, but to paraphrase what Winston Churchill said about democracy—it is a terrible system of government, until you consider the alternatives.

2. Econometrics

One of the great advantages of econometrics over the randomized control trial is that it is much more widely applicable. In principle, at least, you can study the effect of policies as well as projects. You can study the effects of structural adjustment. You can study the effects of economic openness and other things that are really hard to evaluate, by looking at data across, say, countries or regions. Econometrics is quite cheap; it only takes a person with a computer who can run some regressions, and you have your answer. And whereas big experiments are expensive, econometric studies can quite readily be replicated with the same data to see whether they were done properly.

The disadvantage of econometrics, of course, is that it is not an experiment. All the time, within econometrics, we hear terms like natural experiments or quasi-experiments, which reflect the view that the experiment is the ideal. But in econometrics, the ideal is not really attainable.

Since I am an econometrician, I will take the liberty of criticizing my own tribe. A tremendous amount of the econometrics published and cited within the development literature is really quite appallingly bad. An old joke used to be told about someone in a railway carriage in England: a chap is standing at the window with a newspaper, tearing it up and throwing it out of the window. And his fellow passengers say, "What on earth are you doing?" And he says, "I am tearing up paper to make sure we keep elephants out of England." And the fellow passengers say, "But there are no elephants in England," and the chap says, "So, it is working." The elephants example is just like when someone regresses poverty or incomes on the left-hand side and infra-structure on the right-hand side. It is well known that "the reason" why London is such a rich city is that it has a lot of train stations! And two or three large airports. Another favorite, being done on an everyday basis, is to regress mortality, infant mortality, or adult mortality on the number of doctors, as if doctors and clinics were dropped from the skies in a randomized experiment. But, sadly, editors apparently do not see the joke when they get presented with papers like these.

Fundamental problems of causality and selection cannot be solved by tech-nical fixes. They require new information or new insights: what in the lan-guage of the tribe is called an identification strategy. There needs to be some way to persuade people that the outcome they are seeing here is a genuine effect on the dependent variable of the explanatory variable that you are examining. Over and over again, someone has run a regression where the causality is doubtful, to say the least, and you ask, "But is it not possible that the causality works the other way around?" And they say, "But we used instru-mental variables," sometimes without even telling us what the instruments are—as if a computer, or a research assistant, can mechanically solve the prob-lems of causation and selection that have defied researchers for decades.

More generally, my point is that there are a range of econometric techniques—such as instrumental variables, or matching propensity score estimation—all of which are useful and all of which have their place. But they are often much more successful in intimidating policymakers and development practitioners who question econometric results, than they are in actually resolving fundamental problems of causality and selection that stand in the way of our learning what works.

Now, of course, some of the best econometric work gets very close to experimentation: quasi-experiments or natural experiments, as they are sometimes called. There is a long tradition of that in health, most famously perhaps in John Snow's experiments with cholera in London in the 1850s, and in the modern economics literature there are some very fine examples.[5]

A problem with natural experiments is that they are hard to design. You cannot always rely on nature doing an experiment for you in place of the one that you omitted to do when you were starting the project. Yet there are many cases where, if you pay enough attention to the way the program is administered, you will find some arbitrariness in there—by which different groups of people who are affected the same were treated in different ways—which allows you to identify the effect of the program. (Of course, if you can do this, it also shows that there is some way in which you could have randomized when you were doing the program in the first place.)

There is an unfortunate history of many natural experiments coming apart, in the sense that though at first sight they are persuasive, flaws become apparent over time. After all, natural experiments are exercises in persuasion, and basically what you are trying to do is to persuade your audience that the two groups that were separated by some sort of accident are actually the same. And often, evidence comes out later to suggest that they are actually not the same. Again, a good example of this comes from the epidemiological literature, where there is a whole catalog of cases where substances or drugs or procedures were incriminated on the basis of widely agreed, apparently enormously robust, statistical evidence and which, when the randomized control trials were done, were found to have been completely wrongly judged.

There is a saying in the epidemiological literature that observational studies propose, and randomized control trials dispose. In practice what they dispose of is often the observational results!

3. Data

Finally, let me say something about data. Econometrics cannot work without data; project evaluation cannot work without data. Even if you cannot randomize—and now, I am talking about some of the bigger projects and programs where there is no reasonable possibility of randomizing—project and program managers can do much to ensure that there is an adequate baseline survey before work is done. For example, sometimes there exists a household survey in the country that will do the job for you; a much larger fraction of the world is now covered by adequate poverty household surveys than was the case twenty years ago. More than 90 percent of the population in the Third World is covered on a regular basis by large-scale household surveys, which are used, among other things, for monitoring poverty. Sometimes, one can use the relevance to poverty monitoring as a reason to establish special-purpose surveys. Surveys are often not very expensive relative to the amount that is being spent on investment projects, and they obviously yield externalities beyond the project. And sometimes it is possible to add a module to an existing survey to get the baseline information you need.

In South Africa in 1994, a group from the South African Labor and Development Research Unit in Capetown, led by Francis Wilson, and funded by various European donors and with technical assistance from the World Bank, ran the first nationally representative household survey in South Africa very shortly before the transition. This was an imperfect survey in many ways, but it was nationally representative and covered everybody in South Africa in a way that had never been done by the apartheid regime. Those data are still being used today. They have been used very heavily in all of the internal debates on policy in South Africa, both prospectively and to evaluate things that have happened. And in India, the debate on the nature of reforms and their effect over the last ten years has centered around the National Sample Survey data on poverty.

Even if some big issues, like the effects of openness on poverty, or the ultimate effects of structural adjustment, can never be conclusively evaluated, for reasons that Frances Stewart and others have talked about, the World Bank should fuel the internal and external debate by making the necessary data available.

4. Recommendations

First, there currently is no appropriate balance in the Bank between randomization and other approaches. There ought to be more randomization. Econometric methods are useful in many cases, but standards need to be upgraded; the development literature is still a good deal weaker in this respect than frontier literatures—those in labor or public economics, for instance. Improvements are a matter of training, and of applying skepticism to econometricians and demanding verbal explanations of what they are doing, as well as coherent nontechnical answers to the question of exactly how they have overcome the causality and selection issues that bedevil all attempts at evaluation. The answers, "instrumental variables," or "two-stage least squares," get an automatic fail!

Second, it is really important to think about data needs prior to implementation. Some mechanism, whether randomized experiments or data collection or whatever, must be built in from the beginning. Given the structure of the World Bank, that is not something the Operations Evaluation Department alone can do, even though OED can give bad grades to projects that did not set up an appropriate framework for evaluation.

This leads to my third positive point, that in a knowledge Bank, OED ought to be evaluating projects according to the contribution they make to knowledge, as well as according to what they do in their own terms. This implies that projects that are not designed so as to allow decent evaluations ought to be downgraded on that criterion, and that staff ought to be held responsible for not having incorporated an evaluation mechanism, which should be a standard part of the package.

Lastly, a point on what not to do. The $850 million District Primary Education Program (DPEP) in India is one of the largest educational programs that the World Bank has ever been involved in. You would think that the evaluation methodology had been set up to yield only a positive outcome. Data were only collected on the experimental groups, not on the controls. This is not really the fault of the Indians; they presumably knew what they wanted and asked the Bank and others to fund it. But if they are not prepared to have serious evaluation, they should fund it from their own resources. One of the primary reasons to use other countries' resources for such projects is because the other countries learn something that can be applied somewhere else. The Indians get their school system; the rest of the world gets the knowledge. The Bank should not be funding projects in which the evaluation structure prevents that knowledge being obtained. And when critics come along and say you are not doing a decent job, and you cannot tell us what is going on, then the DPEP is Exhibit A.[6]

Notes

1. Dasgupta, Sen, and Marglin (1972); Little and Mirrlees (1974).
2. Squire and van der Tak (1975).
3. Squire (1989); Stern and Drèze (1990).
4. Of course, there is a tremendous amount of less well-based opposition by physicians to randomized control trials. Physicians have fought very hard to maintain their autonomy against invasion by statisticians and others who want to lay down rules for what they ought to do. We are in the difficult situation here of not knowing how much law to lay down. And, in fact, there are many examples in the medical literature where two sides were at loggerheads over the appropriate treatment for a condition, and almost the only thing they could agree on was the undesirability of doing a randomized control trial!
5. On John Snow, see David Freedman's splendid 1991 essay on statistical models and shoe leather.
6. See chapter 10 in this book by Duflo and Kremer, where it is shown that the District Primary Education Program is an example of a large program with potentially very interesting evaluations that have been jeopardized by lack of planning.

References

Dasgupta, Partha, Amartya Sen, and Stephen Marglin. (1972). *Guidelines for Project Evaluation*. New York: United Nations Industrial Development Organization.
Freedman, David A. (1991). "Statistical Models and Shoe Leather." *Sociological Methodology* 21, pp. 291-313.

Little, Ian M. D., and James Mirrlees. (1974). *Project Appraisal and Planning for Developing Countries*. London: Heinemann.

Squire, Lyn. (1989). "Project Evaluation in Theory and Practice." In H. Chenery and T. N. Srinivasan, eds., *Handbook of Development Economics* Vol. II. Amsterdam: Elsevier Science Publishers.

Squire, Lyn, and Herman van der Tak. (1975). *Economic Analysis of Projects*. A World Bank Research Publication. Washington, DC: World Bank.

Stern, Nicholas, and J. Drèze. (1990). "Theory of Cost-benefit Analysis." In A. J. Auerbach and Martin Feldstein, eds., *Handbook of Public Economics* Vol. II. Amsterdam: North-Holland/Elsevier.

Floor Discussion

Participant: How can randomization be made meaningful to citizens? Do you have any perspectives on how to combine randomization with more qualitative citizen-based participatory approaches to evaluation?

Deaton: A very good place to look is the debate between AIDS activists and the U.S. Federal Drug Administration over the development of treatment for HIV/AIDS. A group who originally was enormously hostile to randomized control trials finished up being a very strong supporter of them.[1] People who would pay the highest possible price if answers were not found quickly came in saying, "This is a complete waste of time; you are withholding treatment from us; you are doing randomization when people are dying." They finished up realizing that many more people would die if you did not do the randomization. That was a process of active engagement, and perhaps it only happened because the FDA had legal authority to say it could not approve a drug without a randomized control trial. There is a Federal act that basically prohibits FDA approving drugs that have not gone through randomized control trials. The FDA changed the way trials were done, and I think provided a model for activist groups all around the world: which is to engage with evaluators on the discussion concerning the use of random trials, and challenge them to come and explain the benefits and the disadvantages of not doing it.

Participant: Frequently in the World Bank, people pick the low-hanging fruit in undertaking new projects or new initiatives. The incentives are set so that staff choose projects that they know will work. Could you give us your views on that sort of approach?

Deaton: The rule of cost/benefit analysis is to pick the low-hanging fruit first, go for the things that have the highest rate of return. But, in some sense, these low-hanging fruits may not be as good as they look. That is an argument, then, for appropriate evaluation, because if evaluation is done right, you find out how good they really are.

Note

1.   This simplifies the story to some extent, because in response to the AIDS critics the FDA made changes in the ways the randomized control trials and evaluations were done.

Part 4

Evaluating Sustainability

13

Institutional and Distributional Aspects of Sustainability in Community-Driven Development

Jean-Philippe Platteau

In recent decades, development economists have stressed the pervasive incidence of market imperfections in poor countries as well as the adverse welfare consequences of these imperfections, especially when they are not mitigated by the operation of non-market mechanisms. The microeconomic analysis of development thus suggests that the critical difference between poor and rich countries lies in the extent to which market imperfections uncorrected by appropriate institutions are present in their economies. At the same time, disappointment with the performance of many states in the developing world has led economists to conclude that in varied circumstances public authorities cannot be relied upon to overcome market failures effectively. It has even been suggested that state failures can actually be more serious than market failures.

Would that imply that it is better to leave the market alone even though it performs poorly in many situations, with potentially tragic consequences for vulnerable people? Fortunately, the discovery of a third actor enables us to get out of the deadlock created by the simultaneous presence of market and state imperfections. This third actor is comprised of the groups, communities, or networks that form the social fabric of most developing areas.

The great hopes placed in communities, in fact, mirror the immense problems left unsolved by both the market and the state. But such hopes are likely to prove disproportionate to what communities can really achieve. It is as

Professor and director of the Center for Research on the Economics of Development, Faculty of Economics, University of Namur, Belgium.

though miscalculated optimism regarding the possible accomplishments of the state, itself following upon excessive confidence in the virtues of the market, was bound to lead to a third phase characterized by exaggerated enthusiasm for development approaches based on communities.

Social scientists have led the way in this significant evolution. Development practitioners have been involved too. Largely as a response to critiques of top-down development, most bilateral donors and big international organizations have started to include participatory elements in the design of their large-scale development assistance programs (for example, the World Bank's social investment funds, or the participatory development programs sponsored by the International Fund for Agricultural Development), or to channel substantial amounts of aid money through nongovernmental organizations.[1] The move to put participation and empowerment of the poor squarely on the agenda is especially noticeable in the case of the World Bank, which has made so-called community-driven development (CDD) one of the cornerstones of its Comprehensive Development Framework.[2]

But so far as we can judge from recent surveys,[3] the evidence does not unambiguously confirm that CDD projects are more effective than conventional approaches in terms of efficiency, equity (reaching the poor), or sustainability. NGOs themselves, contrary to a widespread belief, have not produced impressive results, even with respect to alleviation of poverty and promotion of participation.[4] The same agnostic conclusion emerges from a recent review of empirical studies of the decentralized delivery of public services: although the studies suggest generally positive effects of decentralization, "it is hard to draw conclusive lessons."[5] Caution is required because most studies are essentially descriptive and point to correlations rather than to carefully tested causal relationships.

Sustainability is usually deemed to be a key criterion to be satisfied by the CDD approach. This implies that communities cannot be considered simply as channels through which grant funds are disbursed, but must be seen as genuine agents of their own development. "Ownership" of projects is a criterion that would automatically follow from the requirement of sustainability; indeed, how could communities perpetuate projects or activities that they have not sufficiently identified with? Now, for communities to "own" their projects, they must be sufficiently empowered to express their preferences and to make their own perceptions of the world prevail over those of donor agencies.

In the World Bank literature dealing with CDD, the above chain of requirements seems to be accepted as the logical consequence of the need for participatory projects to be sustainable. For example, we read that the idea underlying CDD is that "putting communities in charge or actively engaging them in their own development will harness the social capital of the community to improve livelihoods." And, "because a CDD operation promotes local consultation and participation" it is likely "to ensure that the current investments made in the natural resource system in the community are maintained and future development needs are also locally handled (albeit often with technical and financial support from outside the community)." "Hence a CDD operation is expected to put in place elements of sustainability."[6]

What tends to be underestimated, however, is the complexity of the task involved as well as the tradeoffs that unavoidably emerge when these principles must be put into practice. The goal of this paper is to highlight these difficulties and tradeoffs by raising conceptual questions and bringing into focus some key characteristics of rural communities in poor countries. Section 1 emphasizes the need to distinguish between two different approaches to participatory development and the consequences for the definition of a sustainability criterion. Section 2 discusses key principles for the effective support of participatory development by donor agencies, while Section 3 draws attention to the poverty-reduction dimension of CDD and its implications for sustainable efforts to mobilize targeted communities. Section 4 addresses the issue of potential incompatibility between the objectives of sustainability and poverty reduction. Section 5 concludes and emphasizes the implications of the analysis for sustainability assessment.

1. Two Different Approaches to Participatory Development and Sustainability

The concept of sustainability is often poorly defined and confusion about the donor's strategy easily follows from this lack of precise definition. The adjective "sustainable" refers to something that can be maintained over a long period, but the crucial issue is to define *what* should be so maintained. It seems natural to think that the criterion of sustainability requires that the activities covered by a given CDD project should be able to continue and produce their benefits after donor funding has been withdrawn.

Such a way of looking at sustainability has the advantage of leading to rather straightforward measures with a view to assessing the extent to which the criterion has been satisfied. In this approach, henceforth dubbed the instrumental approach, the participation of targeted communities is seen as instrumental to achieving better performance and sustainability in a set of well-defined activities. This is because of their better knowledge of local conditions and constraints (environmental, social, and economic), and their better ability to enforce rules, monitor behavior, and verify actions, as well as because of the dense network of continuous inter-individual interactions on which they can rely.

Alternatively, however, we can think of sustainability as the continuing ability of the targeted group or community to undertake, adjust, discontinue, restart, and redefine objectives and activities according to changes in the surrounding circumstances, to the lessons drawn from previous experiences, and to the possible evolution of the preferences of its members. In this second conception, henceforth called the comprehensive approach, sustainability is defined in terms of collective action. Clearly, it implies that the aim pursued by CDD does not consist of carrying out particular actions valued for themselves, but of promoting local capacities to devise and implement collective ways of improving the community's livelihoods. The underlying conception of participation also differs from that in the first approach. Participation is now viewed as an end in itself: a situation in which people can behave as "citizens" by being genuinely involved in discussions and decisions that bear upon their lives is deemed superior to a situation where they cannot.

The literature typically eschews the question of whether greater participation should be sought at the price of poorer performance. It is indeed easier to assume that "all good things go together" so that no difficult choices need to be confronted. This trade-off is discussed further in Section 3.

It must be emphasized that a genuine participatory approach intended to make communities responsible for their own development should, as a matter of principle, allow them to make mistakes and learn from them. In other words, it must recognize their right to fail and to correct their own actions. The fact that very few aid agencies are willing to accept such consequences testifies that truly playing the game of participation with targeted beneficiaries is extremely demanding. Unfortunately, the development rhetoric used by aid agencies is often misleading, because everyone employs the vocabulary of participation indiscriminately.

Measuring performance is, of course, much harder when a comprehensive approach to participation is adopted. This is because particular, predetermined project outcomes are not the main objectives pursued. Moreover, a failure should be counted as a positive achievement if it is born of genuine experimentation and then exploited to redefine programs and actions in a more realistic manner. But there is a paradox here, which can be stated thus: while performance is much more difficult to measure under the comprehensive than the instrumental approach, sustainability may be easier to measure under the comprehensive approach. Indeed, the instrumental approach appears to be in difficulty when a judgment must be made about whether an activity supported by an external donor is viable or not. On the one hand, it seems evident that sustainability can only be assessed by revisiting the project site several years after the final disbursement of funds, "when an operational history is available."[7] But, on the other hand, given the high costs and constraints implied by this solution, donor agencies tend to look for an alternative formula that would not involve repeated post-project evaluations.

For example, the World Bank's Operations Evaluation Department has adopted an evaluation approach that assesses sustainability at the time of project completion by identifying the potential conditions for it to prevail. Aimed at testing the robustness of a project with respect to economic, financial, institutional, and environmental risks, OED's approach establishes a strong link between sustainability analysis and risk analysis at appraisal. The core methodology used for that purpose is traditional sensitivity analysis, which consists of varying the values of key variables according to different assumptions about the environment, and then noting the impact of these variations on the project's return. An important problem with this method is that not all the variables that impinge upon projects' results can be reliably quantified and varied. For example, a crucial factor in success may lie in the availability of some expertise in the group. If the persons with the specialized skills leave the area without being replaced, they will seriously disrupt the activities concerned. To assess such a risk, it is therefore necessary to estimate not only the probability that key professionals will depart but also the time that will elapse before suitable replacements are found (assuming that they can be found). Such estimates may be just guesswork.

If the departing person is a good leader rather than a person possessing a special technical skill, the sustainability of CDD will be jeopardized whether the approach is instrumental or comprehensive. But the comprehensive approach is less vulnerable than the institutional approach to the loss of skills. Under the comprehensive approach, the collective action potential of the group might ensure that an activity intensive in the lost skill will be succeeded by another activity that uses other skills still present in the group. Given the unavoidably high risks that rural communities confront, a comprehensive approach to participatory development appears to be advisable insofar as it aims to enhance the adaptability of local collective structures.

Another problem with sustainability assessments that are undertaken at the time of project completion is that some reported facts on which they are based have been strategically manipulated by beneficiaries and are therefore incorrect. For example, the participants in an irrigation scheme may all declare that they have regularly paid their contributions to the maintenance of the infrastructure, whereas, in fact, some large farmers have made the payments on behalf of poorer farmers. The "big men" have done so because, although they know quite well that poor farmers' long-term participation is jeopardized by poverty constraints, they are keen to give the donor agency the impression that the project is sustainable and that the whole target group can benefit from it. In this way, they ensure that the donor agency will not want to redefine its strategy and modify the project. Or, to take another example, an executive board may conceal the real uses of the funds at the disposal of the group because such uses are illegitimate and, if known, would raise embarrassing questions.

It must be stressed that assessing the sustainability of a comprehensive CDD program comes down to appreciating whether the ground has been laid for continuing, solid, collective action in the locality concerned. This obviously requires much more than data measuring the outputs of various activities. Complementary insights are needed that can be gained both from measurements of attributes of the group—such as the stability of its member-ship, regularity of meetings, extent of attendance, and relative number of members speaking in the course of meetings, nature of the questions raised (are they constructive or do they reflect personal antagonisms; do they arouse genuine debates or do they reflect a passive acceptance of the board's deci-sions?)—and from more qualitative assessments pointing at its internal dy-namics—such as descriptions of its formative stages, internal rules and decision-making procedures, formal or informal relationships with surround-ing institutions, and, more importantly, how it has responded to various kinds of challenges (for example, how did the group react when it discovered irregu-larities in the board's management, or when factional divisions threatened to disrupt it?). The latter, dynamic aspects are clearly the most critical to grasp in order to assess sustainability. Unfortunately, they are also the most difficult to unearth and to quantify.

From the above, it follows that sustainability assessment cannot be effec-tively made in one shot upon completion of a CDD project. What is needed is a series of evaluative steps taking place at intervals over the project's life cycle, as well as after the withdrawal of the donor agency. To rely on impact assessment methods using treatment and control groups (whether selected randomly or purposively) or propensity score matching is not an easy alterna-tive route. It is quite difficult in practice to detect initial differences in collec-tive action potential within a community and, hence, to construct valid counterfactuals. Moreover, CDD interventions using the comprehensive ap-proach are bound to violate the randomization principle. As a matter of fact, such interventions are typically initiated through personal contacts that gradu-ally build into trust relations. As a result, communities cannot be targeted on a random basis.

This said, it must be stressed that, when a genuinely participatory outlook is adopted, the outcomes of collective action may not be easily predicted even after project completion. To illustrate, it is useful to mention the story of an informal women's self-help group in Kibera slum (Nairobi), which received grant money from an international organization for a specific purpose. The money was almost immediately embezzled by the leader, who ran away, never to be seen again. But the other members continued to participate in the group and redefined its objectives and activities on the basis of their limited self-generated resources. Though modest, their results proved to be quite sustain-able, as we could observe after several years of the group's existence. Clearly, the outcomes differed from those expected by the donor agency that triggered the birth of the group. But they were appropriate to the members' most urgent needs and reflected their organizational capacity.[8]

To take another example, in the South Indian state of Tamil Nadu, an NGO rural development project contained a subproject devoted to developing women's self-employment activities. The most significant result of this subproject was that women started riding bicycles in a society where such behavior was previously unthinkable. This women's empowerment effect was deemed more important than the economic results achieved, partly because of its long-term significance and partly because of the spillover effects that were generated throughout the local society.

2. Key Principles for the Effective Support of Participatory Development by Donor Agencies

After the above clarification about two different ways of looking at participation, we are ready to discuss the conditions for sustainable development, especially when considered in the perspective of the comprehensive approach. This section outlines two key principles for intervention on the part of donor agencies.

Accept the Need for Protracted Institutional Support

A first key principle to be followed by donor agencies is to accept the need for protracted support of organizing efforts by targeted communities. Even when local associations exist, they often need to be buttressed institutionally, so they can acquire efficient rules and procedures and clarify their preferences and choices. Regarding the latter objective, the informational advantage rightly ascribed to communities should not blind us to the fact that their members may not clearly perceive the stakes or the feasibility of various development projects or programs; that they do not necessarily agree on what to do, in which order of priority and in which manner; and that their views may differ in crucial respects from those held by donor agencies.

Thus, members of a community may not have reached a consensus on some critical dimensions of an aid program. In particular, they may not agree on who is poor and who is not, or on the nature of the more important problems to be addressed and how best to address them. For example, Bergeron, Morris, and Banegas (1998) have shown that in Honduras when different randomly selected subgroups of community members were asked to establish wealth and food security ratings, the correspondence between the rankings obtained was quite weak. The author's own experiment with wealth and power rankings in fishing villages in South India (Kerala state) led him to a similar conclusion. And his experience with NGOs' work in participatory development in West Africa has shown that villagers are not always clear or well informed about the causes of their problems, what their priorities should be, and what strategies ought to be followed to meet those priorities. Confusion or ignorance is especially likely when the matter concerned is rather technical or complex.[9] These are the kind of circumstances that make people very prone to influence by external agencies, in the sense that they tend to demand the sort of things that they know will appeal to these agencies, especially if they are simply asked to answer an invitation to submit subproject proposals.[10]

If participation is to mean anything in such a context, outside facilitators are needed. Their role should consist of initiating and supervising a process whereby a community can form an opinion about a list of valid objectives and a suitable sequencing of their realization over time, as well as a coherent and feasible action program to achieve them through appropriate methods. This process will necessarily be slow. It is essential that the facilitators do not impose their own ideas on people. Instead, they must carefully listen and then make suggestions to stimulate discussions within the community that will drive the members to reflect on critical issues and eventually agree on some way to address them.

This very delicate work calls for facilitators with the right kind of motivations and combination of qualities, as well as patient donor agencies ready to wait before disbursing funds. These two conditions are rarely met. For one thing, facilitators are too often young, poorly paid, and inexperienced individuals who are driven by incentives that are poorly aligned with the needs of CDD projects; indeed, the availability of facilitators with the required qualities is the most constraining factor for CDD programs. For another thing, project implementers typically want to show rapid results, while increased participation does not necessarily improve project performance, at least in the short and medium term.[11] Too often, participatory planning is an ideal that exists in speeches rather than in reality. Aid agents initiate a process of analysis within the target community that finishes as soon as posters reporting the "agreed upon" objectives and methods have been taken to the agency to form the basis of its project interventions.[12]

In some cases, community members may, in fact, have a clear and consensual perception about who needs to be helped, what is the cause of their predicament, what is to be done, and how, yet their views and preferences may differ substantially from those of the donor agency. Thus, it is often observed that the intended beneficiaries pay much less attention to long-term, strategic considerations (including the building of autonomous organizational capacities), and attach much greater weight to immediate improvements in living conditions, than do external aid agencies. Also, they tend to place too much hope in externally provided resources and to demand that the scale of development activities be increased beyond the limit of their own absorptive capacity. More fundamentally, meaning systems may differ so widely between donors and target groups that the latter may not understand the very concept of development at the heart of the donors' approach.[13]

Further, community members' idea of eligibility may not match that held by the donor agency. A recent study of Southern Sudan found that local views about who should benefit from famine relief efforts were very much at variance with those of the aid workers, resulting in a host of problems in the implementation of the project.[14]

Unfortunately, it may often be the poorest members of a community who are deemed undeserving because they are known to be lazy, frequently drunk, or undisciplined, or because they have broken some local social norm (a son who has not shown respect to his father, or a daughter who has separated from her husband and returned to her native village against the wishes of her parental family). When such is the situation, discussions are required in the hope that the stances of the two parties will converge without the donor imposing its will. But this is a time-consuming process,[15] and the danger always looms that the intended beneficiaries will again strategically adapt to the demands of the donors and pursue their own agenda while using the aid resources. In the words of an anthropologist with a long field experience in Mossi villages of Burkina Faso:

> Local people, confronted with the hegemonic "project" of the donor, prefer to remain silent about their practices and aspirations, for fear of losing the aid offer. This is because these practices and aspirations are perceived to be so far away from those of the donor that they are better not disclosed. Such is the vicious circle of development cooperation: the fear of avowing the discrepancy between the two views because it could lead to the discontinuation of the aid relationship, has the effect of strengthening the donor's confidence in the validity of its approach. (Laurent, 1998, p. 212—my translation.)

Institutional support also ought to be directed at the mode of functioning of local associations. Some of these bodies are indigenous institutions that need to be adapted to modern exigencies; many of them lack clear rules and procedures, keep no written records of decisions made, deal ad hoc with novel situations, and give predominance to status considerations over competence criteria. Other local associations are endowed with ill-understood formal rules and by-laws, imitated from without or suggested and possibly imposed by official or donor agencies. In these associations it is worth emphasizing that the participatory approach to development—insofar as it promotes the values of equality and democracy—runs into major obstacles born of traditional patterns of authority. For example, that the chairman of an association can be freely chosen among its members, that the most competent person should be the most liable to be elected, and that an incompetent, ineffective, or corrupt leader should be removed from a position of responsibility, are all ideas that many rural societies still find it difficult to accept. Also difficult to accept is the idea that the same rules and the same sanctions should apply to all members irrespective of their personal identity and their place in the local sociopolitical hierarchy. In the minds of both the elite and the common people, the logic of ascriptively fixed status and power positions, combined with particularistic ethics and unequal treatment of different people, still holds sway. Competence criteria are not allowed to guide the choice of leaders and office-holders, whereas privileges and rights, duties and obligations, sanctions and awards are neatly differentiated in accordance with the positions people occupy in the social matrix.

By imposing rules and institutions that embody modern values of democratic governance and protection of the poor, as well as the transparency of decisions and accounts, the participatory approach to development drives a wedge between the patterns of behavior that people have always experienced in most aspects of their lives, and the patterns they are expected to follow within the ambit of a CDD program. In CDD, formal rules and general principles are adopted that reflect the objectives pursued by the participatory approach (for example, democratic election and voting mechanisms, division of labor between chairman and treasurer, accountability of the executive committee before the general assembly of members, predefined accounting procedures and reports, use of competence-based criteria for the selection of office-holders, uniform treatment of members) yet, in practice, these rules and principles are ignored, circumvented, or subverted. For example, in a lineage-based society, how can a youngster talk on an equal footing with an elder in a meeting of a participation-minded village association when he knows he must address him respectfully and humbly as soon as he steps out of the meeting? And could the elder, who has always been accustomed to deference, accept such a shift in behavior? The same question arises for a client vis-à-vis his patron in socially and economically differentiated societies, or for a low-caste villager vis-à-vis high-caste persons in caste-based societies.

To the extent that subversion of the above rules and principles is the result of a sheer failure to grasp their meaning and requirements, it cannot be considered as a deliberate attempt to undermine the new approach. But the fact is that, rather than the general society being influenced by the institutional experience of a decentralized program, people tend to behave in the new institutional set-up according to the norms and patterns that prevail in the general society: primacy of personal relationships and loyalty to kith and kin, particularistic ethics, and respect of traditional authority and its status symbols.

As should be evident by now, the claim that CDD has the advantage of harnessing the social capital of communities is profoundly misleading. Indeed, it bypasses the fact that the social capital available within communities does not necessarily have desirable characteristics in regard to the objectives pursued by the CDD approach.

To be genuinely participatory, CDD interventions should rely on the patient work of catalysts or facilitators who aim at gaining the confidence of the intended beneficiaries. Ignoring this critical condition for success can only lead to post-program impressions that people have "returned to their old ways" as soon as donor agencies have withdrawn—whereas in reality they have never given them up; they just behaved strategically by putting up a false appearance of compliance in order not to miss the aid money that was on offer.

A major lesson from the preceding discussion is that CDD endeavors will yield sustainable benefits only if beneficiaries have appropriated not only the infrastructure and the technical advances involved, but also the thinking and acting processes that have accompanied the creation of these material achievements, and the responsibilities (maintenance efforts, financing of recurrent costs, and so forth) that they entail.

Allow Flexibility in Planning and Budgeting

A second important principle for aid agencies truly committed to CDD logically follows from the above. Maximum flexibility should be allowed for the planning and budgeting of development activities. In this respect, it is interesting to quote the conclusion reached by a Belgian NGO after evaluating its long experience with participatory development in West Africa:

> The intervention is flexible as regards the time framework. Rather than being predetermined, its content is gradually constructed as time elapses, according to a dynamic that relies on experience, learning by doing, action-oriented research, iteration, self-evaluation, etc. Local actors are involved at each and every step of the process. As a consequence, the interventions of Islands of Peace need not have a strict operational and budgetary programming... Islands of Peace agree to wait the time required so that the intended beneficiaries can bear their responsibilities in the activities concerned. The implication of this principle is that the speed with which an activity is carried out, and the respect of strict deadlines, are not considered to be valid criteria for the assessment of the quality of interventions. Moreover, the range of activities (and their recurrent costs) must be in tune with the global financial strategy of the local partner association so that the latter does not become overburdened with financial commitments that exceed its capacity once Islands of Peace has withdrawn its support. For this reason, it is reckoned that activities are slow to start. (Islands of Peace, 2003—my translation)

If a community is coaxed to work within a time frame that suits the donor's constraints rather than its own rhythm of organizational development, it will unavoidably skip the various steps through which it must pass if it is to grasp the main stakes of the decisions made and their long-term implications. In particular, it will not have time to acquire enough experience to devise its own solutions to the problems encountered, including the organizational forms that are most appropriate to the community's particular situation and cultural background. A direct implication is that the reward systems in use within donor agencies should not be based—as they often are when the agency is a large bureaucracy—on the volume of activities carried out or the amount of funds disbursed within a given period of time. Such incentive systems risk undermining the sustainability of CDD programs, which is the main criterion on which success or failure ought to be decided.[16]

3. Efficiency and Sustainability of Collective Action in the Context of Heterogeneous Communities

This section explores the consequences for CDD of the heterogeneous nature of most rural communities—a central concern given that poverty reduction is the main objective of CDD programs. It focuses on three key reasons why wealth inequality can hinder collective action.

Cooption or Sabotage by the Elite

First, the economic elite may decide to participate in collective endeavors so as to influence decisions to suit their private interests, as the following examples show.

From a case study on the Jamaica Social Investment Fund (funded by the World Bank), Rao and Ibanez (2001) concluded that the overall match between local preferences and project achievements was poor. Only in two of the five communities studied did the project reflect the preferences of a majority in that community. Furthermore, better educated and better networked people were more likely to obtain projects that matched their preferences.

In their analysis of sugar cooperatives in the Indian state of Maharashtra, Banerjee et al. (forthcoming) have shown how the weight of wealthy and influential users in collective decision making tends to distort collective regulation towards their interest, at the cost of efficiency. Their empirical estimates show that distortions (and inefficiency) in collective regulation tend to be highest when inequality is large among users.

When irrigated rice cultivation was introduced by a Western NGO to Yalogo, Burkina Faso, villagers were asked to organize themselves into village-level peasant associations in order to manage the irrigation schemes. In doing so, they were required to elect an executive committee comprised of a chairman, a secretary, and a treasurer. As the NGO discovered, the local chief was systematically chosen to act as the chairman of each association. Moreover, in the only village for which detailed information is available regarding the internal functioning of the local association, it appears that the chief makes all important decisions without consulting the members and the other persons in charge. The secret character of some of his dealings—in particular, his refusal to disclose the names of the persons to whom he claims to have granted loans as well as the amounts and repayment terms involved—aroused serious misgivings about his honesty. Such an attitude is all the more unacceptable to the association members as the loans have never been repaid. Another serious problem arose from the fact that the chief decided to sell the rice produced in the irrigation scheme to a trader who turned out to be his brother and who cheated the farmers by underpaying them (setting purchase prices at levels much below the current market prices). The chief was unable or unwilling to compel his brother to pay the farmers their due. When asked why they do not remove their mischievous chairman, the members' typical answer is that such a step is inconceivable precisely because he is their chief.[17]

Not only benefit sharing but cost sharing may be distorted in favor of village elites. Thus, in their study of irrigation schemes in Mexico and India,

Bardhan (2000) and Dayton-Johnson (2000) find that higher inequality is strongly associated with proportional water allocation in combination with equal division of costs—an arrangement that directly favors large landowners. In the same study, they also find that, in South Indian irrigation schemes, maintenance is poorer where many farmers believe that the rules have been crafted by the local elite.

Sharing of costs is extremely asymmetrical when a group of low social status, which hardly benefits from the village commons, is required to bear costs in the same manner as those who draw sizeable gains from the use of the resource. For example, in the irrigation system of the Ziz Valley in Morocco, there prevails the rule that the Haratine, a group of people of dark complexion and subservient status, must help to operate and maintain the irrigation infrastructure of the village even though they do not own any land. Moreover, "they are barred from the right to cut and collect grass on the banks of the river and the canals as well as on field boundaries." As for others, the rule provides that in normal times the labor provided by each holder is a function of his holdings, except for religious authorities who are exempt from manual work on grounds of their divine power (Ilahiane, 2001, p. 106).

In highly differentiated or stratified societies, decisions involving an unequal sharing of benefits and costs are often arrived at through unanimous voting.[18] In fact, mechanisms whereby a consensus is forged among contending parties are almost always a tool used by the elite to impose its own views behind a screen of democratic discussions. If these tactics do not work, the elite can resort to intimidation or other forms of coercion over poorer members, especially if the latter are their clients.

In Yalogo, Burkina Faso, a rice mill provided to a women's group by a Western NGO was soon confiscated by the local chief. That he saw the mill as a status symbol rather than a productive asset is evident from the fact that it lay unused in his backyard. All the efforts undertaken to get the mill back and return it to the intended beneficiaries proved unavailing. In Canhabaque in the Bijagos islands (Guinea Bissau), to take another example, the same NGO targeted dynamic young people to receive training and assets so they could better exploit the surrounding fish resources. The elderly local traditional king could not accept that young members of his community received boats, nets, and engines whereas he himself did not. All the attempts to enlist young people into the project and transform them into independent professional fishermen met with passive resistance. The only individual who dared challenge the king's authority by keeping his equipment and operating it productively had to leave the island and resettle on the Continent.[19]

The following story of the Rajasthan Canal (India) also shows that the elite may not hesitate to block components of a project that entail costs but no direct benefits for them. The central government of India built up the main headworks and a central canal with a view to bringing a large swathe of land under irrigation in the semi-arid state of Rajasthan. This was on the understanding that the beneficiary communities would build at their own expense the field channels needed to carry the water from the main canal to the parcels situated at some distance from it. In practice, however, these complementary works were rarely undertaken because the rich farmers, strategically located along the main canal, had no interest in allowing channels to be built that would cross their lands in order to reach the remote fields of the disadvantaged farmers.[20]

What all these stories show is that village elites may go a long way to protect their status and power whenever they fear that an external intervention, by calling into question their priority claim to new resources, will eventually disrupt the traditional economic and social hierarchy. If they fail to capture a significant share of the bounties of a CDD program, whether by guile or by force, they may not hesitate to sabotage the donor's intervention. One way of doing this is to manipulate community members so that they boycott the aid program.

Tagging may seem an obvious way for an external agency to surmount diverging preferences or interests between the elite and the poor. Tagging involves categorical targeting that offers eligibility to all members of a group defined by an easily identifiable characteristic or trait.[21] Things may not be so simple, however. For one thing, there are many ways for community members to subvert a program if they think that it runs against some local social norm. These ways may not be easy for the external observer to detect, especially if the benefits received by, say, nomads or migrants, are not withdrawn openly but cancelled out through the withdrawal of some other benefit that they previously enjoyed. For another thing, by imposing eligibility or other criteria that are not compatible with the local culture, the external agency may cause tensions within the community that may hamper its ability to act collectively in other circumstances. Again, time is needed to overcome such differences.

Because disadvantaged people can be easily manipulated by powerful and experienced elites, granting them reserved seats on a village council along the lines of an affirmative action strategy is likely to prove insufficient. Where social structures are asymmetrical, there is no alternative to empowering underprivileged groups—that is, mobilizing and organizing them in such a way that they can assert their rights to participate in decision making, even if that implies challenging existing social structures and antagonizing the elite. This is quite an arduous task, and one that goes much beyond the usual understanding behind CDD. As aptly noted by Brett (1999, pp. 12-13): "...participatory systems are rarely a response to demands from local people who may well be locked into hierarchical and deferential structures, but rather promoted in response to western values imported by donors. This obliges local communities to develop different kinds of organization from those they have used in the past, thus demanding new skills and the ability to overcome local opposition if they are to succeed." Participatory development, therefore, "cannot be treated as a process in which facilitators merely 'enable' local people to do what they would have wanted to do anyway."[22]

This poses a big constraint on participatory development. In fact, project facilitators tend easily to fall prey to the local elite, either because they are in a rush to show results and therefore gloss over local power relations[23] or because they are too weak to resist the pressure and the donor agency is unwilling or unable (often because of long distances between headquarters and the field) to support them effectively.

A last remark is in order before turning to another type of impact of economic inequality. Because the elite can draw a disproportionate share of the benefits of collective action, they are often ready to bear most of the costs involved in initiating processes of organization as well as in setting up and enforcing regulatory structures, if needed.[24] Since the poor have a smaller stake, they tend to follow the elite's lead rather than take any initiative. If they stand to lose from the collective endeavor initiated by the rich, they should be expected to oppose it, yet they may not wield enough power to do so, at least in highly inegalitarian societies. By virtue of their power position, only the rich can block an undertaking that is contrary to their interests. They may do so even if the undertaking promises not to lower their incomes but merely to worsen their position relative to the poor.[25]

Requirements for Cash Contributions May Disadvantage the Poor

A requirement for cash contributions, rather than labor contributions, to a local public good can bar the poor from access to that good. Many village-level collective projects for which external donors provide funds for a limited period prove unsustainable for the poor when, after the donor's withdrawal, they are required to contribute to the recurrent costs involved.

In such circumstances, a CDD project may collapse. In the Philippines, for example, the efforts of the National Irrigation Administration to decentralize have failed more often than they have succeeded; state agencies have reduced their operation and maintenance activities but irrigators' associations have not filled the gap—causing alarming consequences for agricultural production.[26]

In projects that continue, but require cash to fund recurrent costs, the poor will tend to be excluded. There are well-documented cases of health, education, and irrigation projects that eventually fail to benefit the poor. This is because, when the community confronts the task of ensuring the proper functioning and regular maintenance of the social infrastructure (including paying decent salaries to teachers or health staff in order to keep them motivated), it has to require from the beneficiaries the payment of appropriate fees and contributions. Since the poor cannot afford such payments, they gradually drop out of these projects that were initially intended to benefit the whole community.[27] In this case, the poor are deprived of the benefits of participatory development owing to a process of self-selection that operates to their disadvantage.

There is a way out of the above dilemma if local governments can be called upon to finance recurrent expenditures. It is the expected duty of all governments to provide financial support for basic services such as education, health, and water. Consequently, a sustainable CDD intervention ought to help empower community members—especially the most needy among them, to persuade local governments or administrations to bear responsibility for maintaining village-level public goods and providing essential services to the poor. Unless this is done, a CDD program will not be sustainable.[28] Note that it is inappropriate for an external donor agency itself to lobby local governments or administrations. (After the donor's withdrawal, indeed, these official local bodies could well renege on their previous commitments.) Pressure has to come from the rural dwellers themselves if it is to bear long-term fruits. Empowerment is therefore an unmistakable dimension of the participatory approach to development, and all the more so if donors cannot rely on a dedicated and committed local elite.[29]

The More Unequal a Community the Less Efficient the Regulation of Resource Use

A third manner in which economic inequality can undermine CDD pertains to collective regulation, and especially the management of village-level natural resources such as forests, pastures, or inland fisheries. Regulatory instruments are often imposed in the form of uniform quotas or constant tax rates that are calibrated for average characteristics. If we require the collectively regulated management of the village resources to result in greater efficiency, it is more likely to hurt the interests of some users, and therefore to be opposed by them, if inequality among users is large. Or, conversely, if we require the regulated solution to Pareto-dominate the *ex ante* unregulated situation (so that everybody supports the change from the latter to the former), the greater the inequality, the smaller the efficiency gains to be expected from the adoption of regulation.[30]

There is thus a distinct possibility that, in a community where wealth (or skill) disparities are very wide, no agreement will be reached about how to manage a local resource, that is, how to set the (optimal) level and mode of its exploitation and, more problematically, how to share among the heterogeneous members the reduction of harvesting efforts that is required for higher efficiency. This conclusion is evidently based on the implicit assumption that all members of the community enjoy equal voting power. If such power is asymmetrically distributed, on the other hand, we are back to the kind of situations referred to at the beginning of this section.

4. Are sustainability and poverty reduction mutually compatible objectives?

It is often assumed in the literature that sustainability and poverty reduction are two mutually reinforcing objectives: when pursuing one, the other is necessarily met. Unfortunately, as should be clear from the preceding discussion, things may not be so simple. Strong leadership in the hands of a well-entrenched village elite can ensure the sustainability of particular projects or activities while the local poor just get a paltry share of the benefits thus generated. For example, an irrigation scheme whose construction has been funded by an external donor may continue to be properly maintained because rich landowners have succeeded in making it profitable. Meanwhile, owing to severe liquidity constraints and other market imperfections, poorer participants may be unable to keep their plots in the irrigation service area; their lands are transferred to richer farmers or members of the non-farmer elite through distress sales or through seizure following debt defaults. As pointed out earlier, transactions that effectively concentrate the improved lands in the hands of a narrow elite may well be kept secret from the donor agency.

Conversely, an external intervention that succeeds in improving the livelihood of the poor within a rather short time span may well prove unsustainable if the disadvantaged sections of the population lack cohesion and the ability for collective action. This is especially likely in rural societies pervaded by patron-client relationships, which have the effect of fragmenting the society according to patronage ties, thereby preventing the poor from organizing themselves in order to solve their common problems.

Moreover, a selection bias can exclude the poorest communities from access to CDD funds precisely because they lack the ability to organize themselves sustainably—for example because of deficient leadership, general apathy, low levels of literacy, deep-rooted internal divisions, or family feuds that breed suspicion and distrust.

There is no way out of this deadlock unless donor agencies agree that CDD programs must include considerable efforts to mobilize the poor, and to teach them to become active citizens who are aware of their rights and willing to take their destiny in their own hands, as Paulo Freire emphasized a long time ago. The whole question remains as to how such a complex objective can be promoted from outside.

5. Conclusion

Decentralized development implies that communities are called to take on more responsibility for the activities and services on which their well-being depends. External donor interventions are typically meant to help them assume these new responsibilities, and to create or rehabilitate the infrastructure required for the proper functioning of the activities involved (school buildings, water control works, and so forth). For such interventions to yield sustainable outcomes and hence lead to long-term improvements in people's levels of living, it is of course essential that their recurrent expenditures (on operation and maintenance) be effectively financed.

In the case of basic social services, such as health, education, and water delivery, financing through a user fee system is likely to lead to one of two results: a collapse of the community-based project, or a self-selection process that ends in the exclusion of the village poor. It is difficult to see how essential social services can be provided on a widespread basis at village level if central, state, or municipal governments do not supply regular resources to make them run. A donor agency must therefore ensure that local people can obtain these needed resources from their public authorities, yet the key roles and front position in negotiations with officials must be played and occupied by the villagers themselves. This implies that the latter should be sufficiently empowered in the course of the project.

When the external intervention aims at financing and supporting a directly productive investment, the problem of sustainability may be simpler, to the extent that the recurrent expenditures can be financed from the additional incomes created by the investment. However, many market imperfections (and power relations) effectively deprive the poor of the benefits intended. There are many stories of externally supported productive projects that did not eventually help the poor improve their livelihoods. This regrettable outcome tends to be strategically concealed from the donor by the richer participants, who rightly fear that the donor would change the project's strategy if it discovered that the poverty reduction goal was not being reached. Note that the better-off elite may well have anticipated the exclusion of the poor if they hold most of the important cards in their hands and if the poor depend too much on them to use the project's opportunities to challenge their power. We must again conclude that empowerment should be an essential component of any CDD program.

In rural societies, strong links exist among the various aspects of people's lives and, as a result, the power game is played all across village life. For this reason, and also because of the serious risks that affect many rural activities, a comprehensive approach to rural development and participation has many advantages over a more instrumental or sector-based approach. In other words, the most sustainable way to support local development and to remove or reduce poverty probably consists of promoting collective action capacities across the board, so that people learn how to adjust to varying circumstances and to modify their plans and strategies. To reach that goal, a donor agency must agree both to devote a lot of attention to institutional support of the targeted community and to adopt a highly flexible approach to programming and budgeting. On both counts, donor agencies must show a good deal of patience, and they must be aware that increased reliance on people's participation does not necessarily improve performance in the short or medium term. In particular, failures on the part of community organizations must be seen as healthy signs of a dynamic process of institution building.

This said, the limited availability of suitable facilitators constrains the scale on which a genuinely participatory approach can be applied. But, if good facilitators are at work, their inside knowledge of local decision-making mechanisms and power relationships should play a critical role in any assessment regarding the sustainability of the external intervention. A potentially problematic situation arises if new activities or projects that differ from initial expectations turn out to be quite effectively managed with the local elite at the helm. The question is then to know whether the elite draw disproportionate benefits from the externally funded activities, in which case the poverty reduction objective of CDD is missed, or achieved less effectively than planned.

Concerning the evaluation of the sustainability of CDD interventions, three interrelated conclusions can be drawn from this paper. First, a project that appears to be a failure based on conventional criteria of sustainability may be considered a partial or even a total success if it forms an experiment from which useful lessons can be learned for future collective undertakings. Conversely, what appears to be a success may not be so if the project does not meet the priority needs of the targeted population but was accepted only to please the donor and obtain foreign funds that would not have otherwise been available. (After the donor's withdrawal, there is a risk that the project will be discontinued or, at least, neglected.) Clearly, sustainability evaluation techniques must not be confined to rigorous methods simulating outcomes of CDD interventions under various sets of quantifiable assumptions.

The second conclusion is that evaluation must go beyond the veil of reported facts and statements in an attempt to grasp the complex realities of power relations and social mechanisms. These realities are typically elusive to external eyes. To be elucidated, they demand a special kind of skill that can only be acquired through first-hand experience of data collection at field level. Unfortunately, in big international organizations such as the World Bank, too much importance is given to hiring people with impeccable academic credentials, thereby ignoring the sort of talents, experiences, and qualities that matter most for getting sound evaluations. Such qualities, that imply a "sense of the field," include the following: a natural ease in relating to people of radically different backgrounds comprising both community members and facilitators; a readiness to live in tough conditions during the time needed for effective fieldwork; a taste for multidisciplinary approaches; a great ability to listen to people and elicit answers; a reluctance to limit queries so that they fit into a well-defined conceptual framework; a good ability to devise indirect questions and adjust them in unexpected directions as the interview proceeds, in order to discover delicate facts and inadmissible behaviors; and a sharp sense of criticism with which to detect sheer lies or half-truths, and to build on them in a subtle manner with a view to probing into key events.

Third, it is difficult to see how sustainability could be effectively assessed in one shot upon the completion of a CDD project. The discussion in this chapter suggests that a series of evaluative steps are needed that take place at different times in the project's life cycle, as well as after the donor agency has withdrawn. Such an ongoing evaluation process should involve the intended beneficiaries so that any result is discussed, interpreted, criticized, commented, and acted upon by the people primarily concerned.

Notes

1. Stiles (2002).
2. The Bank's *World Development Report 2000/2001* duly reflected this shift in approach. Mansuri and Rao (2003).
3. Conning and Kevane (2002); Bardhan (2002); Mansuri and Rao (2003).
4. Carroll (1992); White and Eicher (1999), p. 33.
5. Bardhan (2002), p. 200.
6. World Bank (2003), p. 9.
7. See White, chapter 2 in this volume.
8. Source: personal field observations.
9. On the basis of data collected on 132 community-maintained infrastructure projects in Northern Pakistan, Khwaja (2002) has shown that increased community participation positively affects performance for non-technical project decisions, yet has the opposite effect for technical decisions. Infrastructure maintenance is also better in non-complex projects, or in those made as extensions of old ones.
10. Platteau (forthcoming).
11. White and Eicher (1999), p. 18; Isham, Narayan, and Pritchett (1995); Khwaja (2002); Mansuri and Rao (2003), pp. 27-28.
12. Vivian and Maseko (1994); Birch and Shuria (2001).
13. Laurent (1998).
14. Harragin (2003). A similar difficulty emerges from a study dealing with a CDD project designed to promote community-organized and funded schools in Kenya (Gugerty and Kremer, 2000). A more optimistic conclusion was reached in a study that found a good matching in rural Bangladesh between wealth-ranking judgments arrived at through a rapid rural appraisal technique, on the one hand, and judgments obtained by using standard socioeconomic indicators from a household survey, on the other hand (Adams et al., 1997).
15. Birch and Shuria (2001).
16. See also Lindahl and Catterson, chapter 6 in this volume.
17. Source: personal field observations.
18. Platteau and Abraham (2002, 2003).
19. Source: personal field observations.
20. Tang (1992), p. 133.
21. Conning and Kevane (2002), p.380.
22. Brett (1999); in the same vein, see Platteau and Abraham (2002, 2003).
23. Mansuri and Rao (2003), pp. 27-28.

24. Baland and Platteau (1998, 1999, 2003).
25. Platteau (2000), paper 5.
26. Fujita et al. (1999), p. 3; see also Lam (1998) for Nepal.
27. See, for example, Swantz (1997); Tendler (2000).
28. For an illustration, see Lindahl and Catterson, chapter 6 in this volume.
29. When the elite is opportunistic, they may adopt the following shrewd tactic: in order to please the donor, admit the poor in a village organization in the anticipation that they will have to leave it for lack of wherewithal once external support vanishes. In Kibera slum, Nairobi, there exist so-called investment (informal) groups whose rich members intended to raise the amount of member contributions so as to get rid of the poorest members. Abraham, Baland, and Platteau (1998).
30. See Baland and Platteau (1998, 2003, and forthcoming) for proof and details.

References

Abraham, A., J. M. Baland, and J. P. Platteau. (1998). "Groupes informels de solidarité dans un bidonville du Tiers-Monde: le cas de Kibera, Nairobi." *Non Marchand* No. 2, pp. 29-52. Brussels: Editions De Boeck Université.

Adams, Alayne M., Timothy G. Evans, Rafi Mohammed, and Jennifer Farnsworth. (1997). "Socioeconomic Stratification by Wealth Rankings: Is It Valid?" *World Development* 25 (7), pp. 1165-72.

Baland, J. M., and J. P. Platteau. (1998). "Wealth Inequality and Efficiency in the Commons, Part II: The Regulated Case." *Oxford Economic Papers* 50 (1), pp. 1-22.

_____. (1999). "The Ambiguous Impact of Inequality on Local Resource Management." *World Development* 27 (5), pp. 773-788.

_____. (2003). "Institutions and the Efficient Management of Environmental Resources." In K. G. Mahler and J. Vincent (eds.), *Handbook of Environmental Economics,* Vol. 1A. Amsterdam: North-Holland and Elsevier.

_____. (forthcoming). "Collective Action and the Commons: The Role of Inequality." In J. M. Baland, P. Bardhan, and S. Bowles (eds.), *Inequality, Cooperation, and Environmental Sustainability.* Available online at http://discuss.santafe.edu/sustainability/papers

Banerjee, A., D. Mookherjee, K. Munshi, and D. Ray. (2001). "Inequality, Control Rights and Efficiency: A Study of Sugar Cooperatives in Western Maharashtra." *Journal of Political Economy* 109: pp. 138-190.

Bardhan, Pranab. (2000). "Irrigation and Co-operation: An Empirical Analysis of 48 Irrigation Communities in South India." *Economic Development and Cultural Change* 48 (4): pp. 847-65.

_____. (2002). "Decentralization of Governance and Development." *Journal of Economic Perspectives* 16 (4), pp. 185-205.

Bergeron, Gilles, Saul Sutkover Morris, and Juan Manuel Banegas. (1998). "How Reliable Are Group Informant Ratings? A Test of Food Security Ratings in Honduras." *World Development* 26 (10), pp. 1893-1902.

Birch, Isobel, and Halima A. O. Shuria. (2001). *Perspectives on Pastoral Development.* Oxfam Development Casebook. Oxford: Oxfam.

Brett, E. A. (1999). "Participation and Accountability in Development Management." Working Paper, Development Studies Institute, London School of Economics and Political Science, London.

Carroll, Thomas. (1992). *Intermediary NGOs: Supporting the Link in Grassroots Development.* West Hartford, CT: Kumarian Press.

Conning, Jonathan, and Kevane, Michael. (2002). "Community-based Targeting Mechanisms for Social Safety Nets: A Critical Review." *World Development* 30 (3), pp. 375-94.

Dayton-Johnson, Jeff. (2000). "The Determinants of Collective Action on the Local Commons: A Model with Evidence from Mexico." *Journal of Development Economics* 62 (1): pp. 181-208.

Fujita, M., Y. Hayami, and M. Kikuchi. (1999). "The Conditions of Collective Action for Local Commons Management: The Case of Irrigation in the Philippines." Processed. Aoyama-Gakuin University, Tokyo.

Gugerty, Mary Kay, and Michael Kremer. (2000). "Outside Funding of Community Organizations: Benefiting or Displacing the Poor?" Working Paper 7896, National Bureau of Economic Research, Cambridge, Massachusetts.

Harragin, Simon. (2003). "Relief and an Understanding of Local Knowledge: The Case of Southern Sudan." In V. Rao and M. Walton (eds.), *Culture and Public Action*. Stanford: Stanford University Press.

Ilahiane, H. (2001). "The Ethnopolitics of Irrigation Management in the Ziz Oasis, Morocco." In A. Aggrawal and C. C. Gibson (eds.), *Communities and the Environment: Ethnicity, Gender and the State in Community-based Conservation*. New Brunswick, NJ and London: Rutgers University Press, pp. 89-110.

Isham, Jonathan, Deepa Narayan, and Lant Pritchett. (1995). "Does Participation Improve Performance? Establishing Causality with Subjective Data." *World Bank Economic Review* 9 (2), pp. 175-200.

Islands of Peace. (2003). Stratégie d'intervention des Iles de Paix en Afrique. Mimeo. Huy (Belgium): Iles de Paix.

Khwaja, Asim Ijaz. (2002). "Can Good Projects Succeed in Bad Communities? Collective Action in Public Good Provision." Working Paper. Cambridge, MA: Harvard University.

Lam, W. F. (1998). *Governing Irrigation Systems in Nepal: Institutions, Infrastructure, and Collective Action*. Oakland, California: ICS Press.

Laurent, Pierre-Joseph. (1998). *Une association de développement en pays Mossi: Le don comme ruse*. Paris: Editions Karthala.

Mansuri, Ghazala, and Vijayendra Rao. (2003). "Evaluating Community-driven Development: A Review of the Evidence." Development Research Group. Washington, DC: World Bank.

Platteau, Jean-Philippe. (2000). *Institutions, Social Norms, and Economic Development*. London: Harwood Academic Publishers.

_____. (forthcoming). "Community-based Development in the Context of Within-group Heterogeneity." In N. Stern and B. Pleskovic (eds.), *Proceedings of the Annual World Bank Conference on Development Economics 2003*. Washington, DC: World Bank.

Platteau, Jean-Philippe, and Abraham, Anita. (2002). "Participatory Development in the Presence of Endogenous Community Imperfections." *Journal of Development Studies* 39 (2), pp. 104-36.

_____. (2003). "Participatory Development: Where Culture Creeps In." In V. Rao and M. Walton (eds.), *Culture and Development*. Stanford: Stanford University Press.

Rao, Vijayendra, and Ana Maria Ibanez. (2001). "The Social Impact of Social Funds in Jamaica: A Mixed-methods Analysis of Participation, Targeting, and Collective Action in Community-driven Development." Development Research Group. Washington, DC: The World Bank.

Stiles, Kendall. (2002). "International Support for NGOs in Bangladesh: Some Unintended Consequences." *World Development* 30 (5), pp. 835-46.

Swantz, M. L. (1997). "Community and Village-based Provision of Key Social Services: A Case Study of Tanzania." WIDER Research Paper No. 41. Helsinki: World Institute for Development Economics Research, United Nations.

Tang, S. (1992). *Institutions and Collective Action: Self-Governance in Irrigation Systems*. San Francisco: ICS Press.

Tendler, Judith. (2000). "Why Are Social Funds So Popular?" In S. Yusuf, W. Wu, and S. Evenett (eds.), *Local Dynamics in an Era of Globalization*. New York: Oxford University Press.

Vivian, Jessica, and Maseko, Gladys. (1994). "NGOs, Participation and Rural Development: Testing the Assumptions with Evidence from Zimbabwe." UNRISD (United Nations Research Institute for Social Development), Discussion Paper No. 49.

White, Robert, and Carl K. Eicher. (1999). "NGOs and the African Farmer: A Skeptical Perspective." Staff Paper 99-01. Department of Agricultural Economics, Michigan State University, East Lansing, Michigan.

World Bank. (2001). *World Development Report 2000/2001: Attacking Poverty*. Washington, DC: World Bank.

_____. (2003). "Community-driven Development: Discussion Paper on Study Methodology." Washington, DC: World Bank Operations Evaluation Department.

14

Bayesian Approaches to Assessing Sustainability: Are There Lessons to be Learned from Approaches to Health Care Evaluation?

Andrew H. Briggs[1]

With high levels of public financing and provision of health care in all industrialized economies, and increasing pressure on health care budgets, there has been increasing recognition that health care interventions must demonstrate value for money rather than simply show evidence of efficacy. This has led to increasing interest in the past two decades in the methods of evaluation of health care programs. A number of bodies in individual countries now offer guidance on best practice for evaluating health care interventions.[2] In the United States, a panel of experts was convened and reported on the best practice for conducting cost-effectiveness analyses.[3] A key area of methodological development in recent years has been the way in which uncertainty in the evaluative process is handled.

Increasingly, health economic appraisals have been conducted alongside clinical trials, with the result that patient-level information is available on both the costs and effects of interventions. This has naturally led to the use of standard statistical approaches for handling the uncertainty that arises from sampling variability in resource costs, health outcome effects (often valued in terms of the ubiquitous quality adjusted life year [QALY]), and incremental

Department of Public Health, University of Oxford.

Figures 14.1, 14.2 and table 14.1 are reprinted from chapter 8 (pp. 172-214) of *Economic Evaluation in Healthcare: Merging Theory with Practice,* edited by Drummond, M. F. and McGuire, A. (2001). By permission of Oxford University Press.

cost effectiveness ratio (or ICER) in so-called stochastic cost-effectiveness analyses. However, most economic appraisals are still undertaken outside of a clinical trial and involve synthesizing evidence from a number of (usually secondary) sources. Furthermore, even when patient-level data on costs and effects are available, it is widely acknowledged that some form of modeling is still required to estimate lifetime costs and benefits of health care interventions.[4] The use of formal decision analysis type models for structuring economic appraisals based on secondary data and for extrapolating the longer-term consequences from short-term trials is now widespread. These model-based analyses are often termed deterministic cost-effectiveness analyses, because a given set of input parameters/assumptions completely determines the outputs of the model. For lack of primary data, the analysis of uncertainty for these deterministic models has predominantly been undertaken using univariate sensitivity analysis methods, based on looking at the effect on the model outcomes of varying the input parameters over "plausible" ranges.

More recently, many commentators and analysts have been advocating the use of probabilistic methods for assessing uncertainty. This involves specifying distributions for all the parameters of the model to represent uncertainty in those parameters. This uncertainty is then propagated through the model using Monte Carlo simulation and in this way the distribution over the outcome of interest from the model can been estimated. Some examples in the literature have paid little attention to the choice of the distribution of parameters, with the result that their analyses can appear somewhat arbitrary. However, there is a growing realization that through a careful choice of distributions for the input parameters of models, to reflect the underlying statistical uncertainty of the parameter estimates, the uncertainty about the outcome of interest can also be given some statistical credibility. This process of assigning statistical distributions to parameters and propagating uncertainty to examine the effects on output parameters makes most sense within the Bayesian statistical paradigm. Nevertheless, by adopting an evidence-based approach to parameter estimation, the method should also appeal to those who incline towards the classical approach to statistics.

The purpose of this paper is two-fold. The first aim is to illustrate the general approach of probabilistic modeling and its use in the context of the evaluation of health care programs. The second aim is to consider whether the general approach commonly employed in health care evaluation has anything to offer in the kinds of evaluation of development effectiveness undertaken at the World Bank—in particular with regard to the notion of sustainability of development efforts.

The paper is organized as follows. Section 1 outlines the decision-making context of economic appraisal in health care. Although cost-effectiveness analysis predominates where program costs are measured in monetary terms but health outcome effects are considered in generic health units (such as the

QALY), it is argued that the methodological approach could equally apply to cost-benefit techniques where the interest is in the ratio of program costs to program benefits measured in monetary terms. Section 2 begins with a general discussion of why probabilistic assessments are desirable in relation to standard sensitivity analysis methods and goes on to consider how parameter distributions should be chosen using standard (often Bayesian) statistical principles. Section 3 presents an example of a Markov model-based health care evaluation of beta-blocker treatment for congestive heart failure. Section 4 then considers the parallels between assessment of health care programs and the issues faced by World Bank evaluations in developing countries. Section 5 briefly summarizes and offers some conclusions.

1. Decision Making in Health Care Program Evaluation

The standard tool of evaluation for economists is cost-benefit analysis, with its roots in welfare economics.[5] Costs and benefits of a program are evaluated in the same units (almost always monetary), allowing the costs and benefits to be directly compared. In principle, programs that have higher benefits than costs (i.e., that have a positive net benefit) should be implemented. However, where there is a budget constraint on the implementation of programs, efficiency demands that programs be implemented in ascending order of their cost-benefit ratios.

In health economics, however, a slightly different tool has emerged through a desire not to have to measure health outcomes in monetary terms. Instead, health outcomes are measured in generic health units—most commonly the QALY—and the cost-effectiveness ratios of different programs can then be compared. While efficiency demands that programs be implemented in ascending order of their cost-effectiveness ratio, doing so would require full information on all currently provided and potential programs. In practice, it is common to find the cost-effectiveness ratio compared to a threshold or ceiling value of cost-effectiveness that is considered to represent some maximum acceptable limit on what society is prepared to pay for a unit of health gain.

In the evaluation of health care programs it is rare to find a true "do nothing" option in that almost all health conditions have some form of recommended treatment or care package. Therefore the importance of an incremental approach has been emphasized, with most evaluations of new programs undertaken in comparison to an existing agreed treatment program.[6]

Suppose that we are comparing a new experimental therapy (or treatment group) with some currently provided standard (or control) therapy, which represents the most cost-effective treatment available at present. Further suppose that we know both the true costs of the new therapy (C_T) versus the control therapy (C_C) and the true effectiveness (in terms of health outcome) of the new therapy (E_T) versus the control therapy (E_C). O'Brien and colleagues identify four situations that can arise in relation to the incremental cost and effectiveness of the therapies:[7]

(1) $C_T - C_C < 0$; $E_T - E_C > 0$;   *dominance*—accept experimental therapy as it is both cheaper and more effective than existing therapy.

(2) $C_T - C_C > 0$; $E_T - E_C < 0$;   *dominance*—reject experimental therapy as it is both more expensive and less effective than existing therapy.

(3) $C_T - C_C > 0$; $E_T - E_C > 0$;   *tradeoff*—consider magnitude of the additional cost of the new therapy relative to its additional effectiveness.

(4) $C_T - C_C < 0$; $E_T - E_C < 0$;   *tradeoff*—consider magnitude of the cost-saving of the new therapy relative to its reduced effectiveness.

These four situations are equivalent to the four quadrants of the cost-effectiveness plane that has been advocated for the analysis of cost-effectiveness results[8] (Figure 14.1). Note that the cost-effectiveness space illustrated in this figure is incremental, such that the comparison therapy (control treatment in this case) is the origin in the figure and the horizontal and vertical axes therefore relate to the effect and cost differences, respectively. Where one intervention is simultaneously cheaper and more effective than the other (situations 1 & 2 above and the SE & NW quadrants on the cost-effectiveness plane) it is clearly the treatment of choice since it dominates the alternative intervention. However, where one intervention is both more effective and more costly (situations 3 & 4 above and quadrants SW & NE on the cost-effectiveness plane) then the decision is no longer clear. Rather, a judgment must be made concerning whether the additional costs of the more expensive therapy are justified by the greater effectiveness of that therapy. To aid such judgment, an incremental cost-effectiveness ratio (ICER) can be calculated, which provides a summary of the cost-effectiveness of one intervention relative to the other. In terms of the notation introduced above, the ICER is given by:

(5) $$ICER \ = \ \frac{C_T - C_C}{E_T - E_C}$$

It is this ICER statistic that is estimated in cost-effectiveness analyses and compared to some threshold value representing willingness to pay for health

Figure 14.1
The Cost-Effectiveness Plane

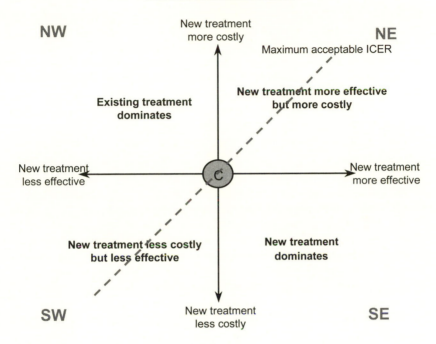

gain. This threshold can be represented on the cost-effectiveness plane as the slope of a straight line passing through the origin and dividing the plane into a cost-effective half and a cost-ineffective half.

2. Probabilistic Analysis of Cost-Effectiveness Models

The decision rules described above are based on the assumption that the average treatment cost and effect parameters for the eligible patient group are known with certainty. Of course, in practice this is never the case and it is therefore important to consider how uncertainty affects the results of the analysis.

In most cost-effectiveness analyses, costs and outcomes are not directly observed for patients following different treatment pathways. Rather, existing evidence is synthesized using a decision-analytic model in order to estimate the costs and health outcome effects of the different treatments under study. Such models require information to populate them, and these informational requirements are referred to as the parameters of the model. These parameters will relate to: probabilities (for example conditional probabilities for branching pathways in a model and transition probabilities for movement between model states over time); the resource use and health outcome consequences of the programs under evaluation; the data necessary to value those consequences (unit cost/price information for resource use and quality of life weights for cost-utility analyses); and parameters relating to treatment effects.

In traditional sensitivity analyses, analysts tend to report a range of values for parameters in their models and to use this range to consider the effect of altering a parameter value either individually (in a univariate sensitivity analysis) or in combination with others (in a multivariate analysis). More recently, however, there has been growing interest in the methods of probabilistic sensitivity analysis[9] as a way to handle uncertainty in cost-effectiveness models.[10] In probabilistic analyses, each parameter is assigned a distribution and the cost-effectiveness results associated with simultaneously selecting random values from those distributions are recorded in a Monte Carlo simulation of the model.

Parameters in decision models represent summary values related to the average experience across a population of (potential) patients. Therefore, the relevant uncertainty to capture in the formation of a distribution for the parameter is related to the sampling distribution of the parameter, not to the variability in the values observed in a particular population. Although an assumption of normality for parameters is widely used in statistics, it is worth remembering that the assumption is based on asymptotics (the central limit theorem) and that the normal distribution has no bounds on the values it can take. In practice, parameters of the model will have logical limitations on the values they can take. Consideration is given below to four different types of parameters commonly employed in cost-effectiveness models: probabilities, resource items, unit costs, and relative risks. For each, the nature of the data informing parameter estimates, the logical bounds on the parameter, and the way in which Bayesian methods can help to select distributions for parameters are outlined.

Probability Parameters

Probabilities for cost-effectiveness models are often based on the observed proportions of the event of interest, for example the number of successfully treated cases. At an individual level, a treated patient is either classed as a success or as a failure; therefore, the data can be considered as independent Bernoulli trials leading to a binomial form of the data likelihood. With such data it is natural to use the proportion of successful patients as the estimate of the corresponding probability in the model. However, in considering the distribution of that probability, note that the binomial distribution is a discrete distribution related to the sample size of the study generating the data, whereas it makes sense to model the distribution of probability in the model as continuous.

Standard frequentist methods for estimating a confidence interval for a proportion involve calculating the binomial estimate of variance and assuming a normal sampling distribution in order to generate the interval. While this approach gives a good approximation to the true confidence interval when the probability of an event is not close to zero or one, the assumption of normality is not appropriate for probabilistic sensitivity analysis. This is because the probability is known to be bounded on the interval zero-one, while the normal distribution will (eventually) generate values outside this interval in a Monte Carlo simulation, since it is unbounded.

Fortunately, Bayesian methods provide a straightforward option for moving from the discrete binomial likelihood to the continuous uncertainty concerning the probability parameter. The beta distribution is a continuous distribution on the interval zero-one and is conjugate to the binomial distribution. This means that if it is possible to represent prior belief using a beta distribution, then the integration of that prior belief with the binomial data has a closed form, with the result that the posterior distribution of the probability will also follow a beta distribution. Fortunately, by varying the two parameters of the beta distribution, a wide variety of possible shapes to the distribution over the interval can be obtained: skewed, symmetric, uniform, near normal, and even U-shaped.

Resource Item Parameters

All economic analyses are concerned with the use of resources. The numbers of resource items that a patient utilizes can be considered a count variable. The Poisson distribution with single parameter lambda (which gives both the mean and variance of the distribution) is often used to model count data. If we are interested in the distribution of the mean resource use for a group of patients we could use the Poisson estimate of variance to obtain a standard error for the mean resource use, relying on the central limit theorem to give a normal sampling distribution. However, this may be problematic for smaller samples, because of the non-negligible probability that the normal distribution could take a value less than zero, when it is clear that mean resource use cannot be negative.

Again, the Bayesian approach provides a solution. The gamma distribution is conjugate to the Poisson distribution, is constrained to be positive, and is fully continuous. Therefore, the gamma distribution for the mean resource use can be specified without fear of generating inconsistent values in a probabilistic analysis.

Unit Cost Parameters

Unit costs are applied to resource volumes in order to evaluate all resource use on a common (monetary) scale. Note that the unit of analysis for such costs differs from that for other parameters; unit costs are typically calculated across a broad group of patients. The unit cost of a surgical procedure or stay in a particular ward will typically be given at the level of the hospital or similar provider unit. By contrast, the unit cost of a drug or device may be set nationally or provincially and may not vary at all within the context of a country-specific cost-effectiveness analysis. Furthermore, the unit cost of a resource item is strictly continuous, unlike the data on resource use considered above. Since unit costs are constrained to be positive, then a gamma distribution could be used to represent uncertainty in these costs. However, unit costs are less likely to be highly variable than the resource items they are employed to value, which may mean that a normal distribution may be safely employed. It is perhaps telling that most economic analyses conducted alongside clinical trials treat unit costs as fixed rather than stochastic.

Relative Risk Parameters

It is very common for economic models to include relative risks as parameters. This mirrors the fact that relative risk is often the primary outcome in clinical trials. Methods for calculating confidence intervals for relative risk estimated in such trials assume that the central limit theorem will lead to the natural logarithm of relative risk (which is additive) being normally distributed, such that confidence intervals can be determined in the standard way. A confidence interval for a relative risk is then obtained by exponentiating the confidence limits on the log scale. This standard approach to confidence interval estimation clearly suggests an equivalent approach to specifying a log-normally distributed parameter for relative risk to be used in a probabilistic sensitivity analysis. Furthermore, since the normal distribution is self-conjugate (a normal prior and a normal data likelihood generate a normal posterior distribution), the application of Bayes' theorem on a normally distributed parameter is especially straightforward.

The General Appeal of the Bayesian Approach

In standard statistical methods (such as practiced in almost all clinical trials), the parameters to be estimated from the data are considered to have true values and do not vary. Probabilities attached to confidence limits relate to the long-run coverage probabilities of the intervals, were the same experiment to be repeated many times. In modeling the cost-effectiveness of interventions in a probabilistic analysis, parameters are considered to be random variables that can take a range of values defined by the chosen distribution. Such an approach is inherently Bayesian in nature. Explicit recognition of this fact allows analysts to exploit the existing Bayesian methodology in a way that is entirely consistent with the aims of a model-based cost effectiveness analysis.

Eddy and colleagues have outlined just such an approach to synthesizing data, based on empirical Bayes methods, that they term the "confidence profile" technique[11] for health technology assessment, and such methods are beginning to be applied to cost-effectiveness analysis modeling.[12] Attempting probabilistic analysis within a Bayesian framework should lead to more defensible assumptions (in terms of choosing appropriate distributions) than without adopting a Bayesian approach. By contrast, without the benefit of Bayesian methods, solutions to the same problem appear rather *ad hoc*.[13]

In summary, for those parameters of a cost-effectiveness model that could, in principle, be estimated from observed data, consideration should be given to the prior distribution of these parameters to reflect uncertainty. Where possible, this consideration should be based on the available data from existing studies, supplemented where necessary by expert opinion. The specified prior distributions should relate to second-order uncertainty rather than to the variability between individual patients, and care should be taken to ensure that the prior distributions chosen are consistent with any logical bounds on the parameter values.

3. Modeling Beta-Blockers for CHF

To illustrate a Bayesian approach to estimating the cost-effectiveness of health care programs an example of a probabilistic analysis of beta-blocker treatment for congestive heart failure (CHF) in Canada is employed. A brief introduction to the model follows; full details of the model can be found elsewhere.[14]

The use of beta-blocker therapy has recently been shown to be effective in reducing mortality in patients with CHF.[15] A U.S. study estimated the cost-effectiveness of a proprietary beta-blocker employing a Markov model to synthesize data from clinical trials of mortality benefit together with estimated costs of therapy and other treatment costs of CHF.[16] However, generic beta-blocker therapy is also available and emerging evidence suggests that some generics may also reduce mortality at a fraction of the cost of the proprietary therapy. In order to examine the relative cost-effectiveness of beta-blockers for CHF in Canada, a model was developed following the structure of previous models,[17] but updated to include Canadian prices and to include a generic as well as the proprietary beta-blocker. A meta-analysis of the literature on the mortality effects of the two compounds was undertaken to estimate the relative risk reduction for each treatment option. Benefits were estimated as life-years gained from treatment.

The Markov model is presented in Figure 14.2. Patients are classified by the number of CHF hospitalizations, which are represented by different Markov states, since patients' hospitalization history is assumed to influence their future risk of hospitalization and, therefore, death.

The Choice of Prior Distributions

The model involves four basic types of parameters: absolute risks of death and hospitalization among patients not receiving beta-blocker therapy; relative risks of death and hospitalization among patients receiving beta-blocker therapy; resource events; and unit costs of resource events. Table 14.1 shows the description of the parameters and the assumed distributions for the CHF model. Absolute risks were assumed to follow a beta distribution, which is constrained on the interval zero-one. Relative risks were assumed to be normally distributed on the log scale, with the measure of variance estimated directly from the random-effects meta-analysis conducted as part of the original study. The average number of resource events was assumed to have a gamma distribution, with coefficient of variation equal to 0.5. Finally, unit costs were assumed to have a normal distribution with coefficient of variation equal to 0.1.[18]

Figure 14.2
Markov Model of Congestive Heart Failure

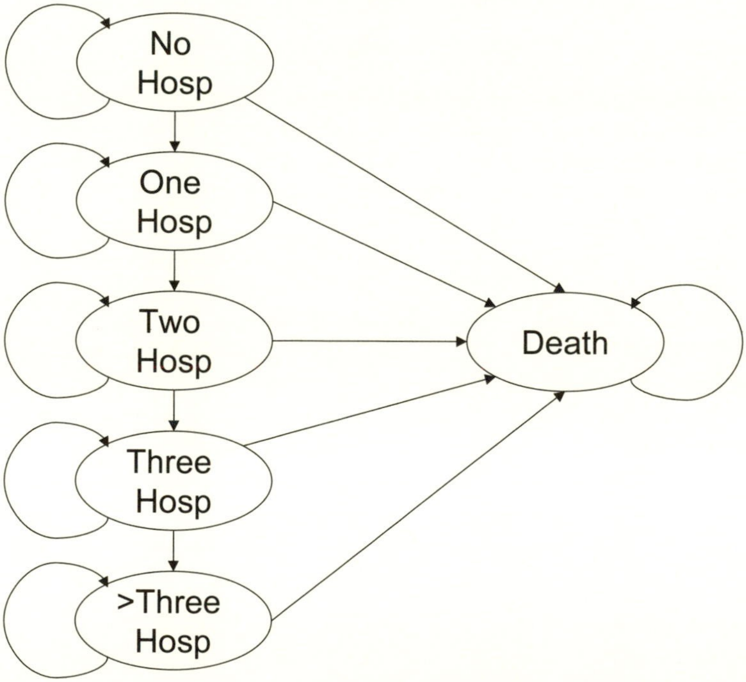

Note: States are shown as ovals and transitions between states as arrows. "Hosp" is the abbreviation for hospitalizations and states relate to how many times a patient has been in hospital. Transitions between the hospitalization states indicate a further hospitalization event while transitions to the same state indicate that no further hospitalization has occurred.

Table 14.1
Distributional Assumptions for the Parameters in the
Congestive Heart Failure Model

pDieHosp *probability of dying in hospital at age 45* Beta distribution with parameters: alpha 244 beta 1791	**pDieHome** *probability of dying at home at age 45* Beta distribution with parameters: alpha 183 beta 1852
InRRdieM *log of relative risk of death on Metoprolol* Normal distribution with parameters: Mean -0.35 SE 0.10	**InRRhospM** *log of relative risk of hospitalization on Metoprolol* Normal distribution with parameters: Mean -0.68 SE 0.43
InRRdieC *log of the relative risk of death on Carvedilol* Normal distribution with parameters: Mean -0.58 SE 0.19	**InRRhospC** *log of the relative risk of hospitalization on Carvedilol* Normal distribution with parameters: Mean -0.41 SE 0.17
ipHosp45 *probability of initial hospitalization at age 45* Beta distribution with parameters: alpha 251 beta 1784	**cpHosp23** *probability of third hospitalization* Beta distribution with parameters: alpha 95 beta 270
cpHosp12 *probability of second hospitalization* Beta distribution with parameters: alpha 288 beta 1768	**cpHosp34** *probability of four or more hospitalizations* Beta distribution with parameters: alpha 36 beta 70

Note: GP is the abbreviation for general medical practitioner.

Note that some parameters of the model were not given a distribution. For example, discount rates as methodological variables were not handled probabilistically. In addition, the prices of the drug treatments under evaluation were kept fixed at the current formulary reimbursement rates.

Results from the Probabilistic Analysis of the Congestive Heart Failure Model

Having chosen the distributions for the parameters of the model, values were selected from each of the distributions at random and the costs and life-years associated with each of the treatment options evaluated. This process was repeated 1,000 times and the results are presented on the cost-effectiveness plane in Figure 14.3. The results show that there is a clear difference in cost between the generic and the proprietary beta-blocker. While favoring the proprietary drug treatment, the difference in effectiveness between the two compounds is less clear. In terms of cost-effectiveness, the generic beta-blocker compared to no treatment had an ICER of Can$ 4,100 per life-year gained with a 95 percent credible interval, estimated from the simulation results of Can$ 3,300 to Can$ 8,700. The incremental cost-effectiveness of the proprietary beta-blocker over the generic is Can$ 8,400 per life-year gained, with an associated 95 percent credible interval, running from a lower limit of Can$

Figure 14.3
Results of a Probabilistic Sensitivity Analysis of Beta-Blocker Therapy for Congestive Heart Failure Presented on the Cost-Effectiveness Plane

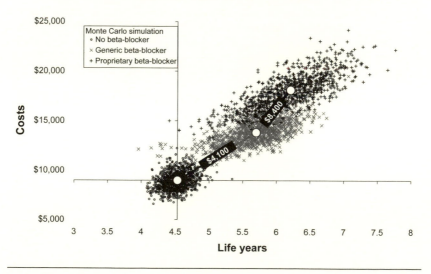

Notes: NT—no therapy; M—generic beta-blocker; C—proprietary beta-blocker

3,900 to an upper limit where the proprietary beta-blocker is dominated (that is, where it is less effective and more expensive than the generic). There seems to be clear evidence that beta-blocker therapy is cost-effective for patients with heart failure, but whether the use of the proprietary beta-blocker is justified is a more difficult decision.

Value of Information and the Importance of Uncertainty

The conventional trial-based approach to clinical decision making is that new treatments should only be adopted when the null hypothesis of no difference can be rejected at the $p<0.05$ level. However, this is widely acknowledged to be an arbitrary decision rule and may not lead to an economically efficient outcome. A number of commentators have begun to advocate a value of information approach for decision making in health care.[19] This approach can be broadly summarized as suggesting that the normative basis for decision making should be an expected value approach since this will maximize efficiency.[20] Arbitrary error rates are inappropriate ways in which to handle uncertainty; indeed Claxton (1999) has argued that conventional "inference" is irrelevant. Uncertainty is only important to the extent that reducing uncertainty (by increasing information) will add value. The value of information can be estimated by specifying a loss function relating to the consequences of incorrect decision making and integrating this loss function with the chances of incorrect decision making (as determined by a probabilistic model). Consideration of the expected loss, given a loss function specified by the threshold willingness to pay for health gain and the chances of incurring that loss for a specified population size and expected lifetime of the technology, allows the calculation of the expected value of perfect information (EVPI). The EVPI puts an upper bound on the returns to future research by giving the expected value for completely eliminating uncertainty.

In reality, of course, uncertainty can never be fully eliminated and there is a cost to acquiring further information. Actual research design should therefore proceed with regard to the expected value of sample information. The point at which the marginal cost of further information collection equals the marginal benefit of reduced uncertainty defines the optimal study size.

A complete description of value of information methods is beyond the scope of this paper, and practical examples are still rare. In theory at least, value of information methodology provides a framework for determining efficient research design by modeling the decision rather than the outcomes of the program. Nevertheless, it should be clear that a necessary requirement for a value of information analysis is a fully specified probabilistic model.

Extrapolation (or Sustainability) of the Treatment Effect

A key issue identified by the original authors of the congestive heart failure model was the duration (or sustainability) of the treatment effect. The relative risk parameters for the model were estimated from a meta-analysis of clinical trials as described above. However, the period over which the estimated treatment effect in those trials was observed was approximately one year, whereas the model itself was run for twenty years. A natural question was therefore whether the treatment effect observed in the trials could be expected to continue for the full twenty years of the analysis. The authors explored the effects of alternative assumptions concerning the duration of treatment effect using univariate sensitivity analysis. For the base case analysis described above, they assumed that the full relative risk reductions would be apparent for the first year, but that for the remaining nineteen years, the risk reductions would diminish exponentially. Two other scenarios were considered: an optimistic scenario, which assumed that the treatment effect estimated from the clinical trials was maintained over the full twenty years; and a pessimistic scenario which assumed that the treatment effect only lasted for the first year. The results of this analysis are presented in Table 14.2. Note that for each scenario, there is an expected value and an estimated 95 percent credible interval, indicating that although the uncertainty in the sustainability of the treatment effect has been handled using univariate sensitivity analysis, it has been applied in a hierarchical way such that a full probabilistic analysis is available for each scenario.

One of the great flexibilities of the Bayesian paradigm is the ability to attach degrees of belief to entities or states of the world for which there is no

Table 14.2

Exploration of the Sustainability of Treatment Effect in the Congestive Heart Failure Model

Duration of treatment benefit	Generic versus no treatment		Proprietary versus generic	
	EV	(95% CI)	EV	(95% CI)
Base case[a]	$4,100	($3,300 - $8,700)	$8,400	($3,900 -Dominated)
Optimistic scenario[b]	$1,600	($1,600 -$11,300)	$7,200	($1,700 -Dominated)
Pessimistic scenario[c]	$6,500	($4,200 -$19,800)	$29,500	($4,900 -Dominated)
Model averaged[d]	$3,800	($3,000 -$11,700)	$12,300	($3,400 -Dominated)

Notes: EV—expected value; CI—credible interval. [a]Assumes full treatment effect for one year and diminishing effect over remaining 19 years. [b]Assumes full treatment effect for 20 years. [c]Assumes full treatment effect for just the first year. [d]Model averaging using weights of 50 percent for base case, 30 percent for optimistic, and 20 percent for pessimistic scenarios.

long-run information. The often-quoted textbook example is the probability that a particular candidate becomes president of the United States. The Bayesian has no problem in assigning a probability to such an eventuality, but the frequentist must conclude that a probability cannot be assigned. In the Bayesian paradigm this flexibility means that probabilities can be assigned to the scenarios about which we are uncertain. As an illustration, the final row of Table 14.2 shows how it is possible to "average" over the three scenarios presented by assigning probabilities to each, where those probabilities reflect the degree of belief that those scenarios might occur.

4. Using Bayesian Methods to Model Sustainability?

Having outlined the use of Bayesian methods to form probabilistic models in the area of health care program evaluation, it is natural to ask whether these methods would be appropriate for representing uncertainty in the types of evaluations of development effectiveness undertaken at the World Bank. Evaluations of development effectiveness tend to be broader in scope than health economic evaluations of treatment interventions. Among development evaluations, it is worth distinguishing two broad types: those of discrete investments that most readily fit the treatment analogy of medical interventions, such as a rural roads program, school building, or textbook supply, and those of more diffuse interventions—such as institution building and support to policy reform—that are more difficult to fit into the treatment intervention model.

One of the criteria for the evaluation of an investment program is sustainability. The following definition is taken from World Bank Operations Evaluation Department (OED) website,[21] with emphasis added:

> OED's sustainability measure assesses the resilience to risk of net benefits flows over time by answering these questions: At the time of evaluation, what is the resilience to risks of future net benefits flows? How sensitive is the project to changes in the operating environment? Will the project continue to produce net benefits, as long as intended, or even longer? How well will the project weather shocks and changing circumstances? Sustainability reflects the resiliency to risks of a project as measured by the *likelihood* that its estimated net benefits will be maintained or exceeded over the project's intended useful life.

The mention of the term likelihood is important since it implies that there should be probabilistic quantification of sustainability.

In the evaluations of specific intervention projects that fit the medical intervention model, cost-benefit analysis is the commonly employed evaluative technique, with the cost-benefit ratio the outcome of interest. This is comparable to the ICER statistic commonly employed in health economic analyses, and the probabilistic methods outlined above could be used to represent the uncertainty in the parameters of that analysis. Such projects more naturally have a "do nothing" comparator (such as not implementing a program of rural road construction, or not building a new school) yet it should be clear that the evaluation is nevertheless fundamentally incremental and therefore amenable to a similar approach to that used widely in health care evaluation.

The flow of net benefits after the completion of a project, just as in the medical model, may be crucial to the judgment of whether or not a project is cost-beneficial. By definition (and again just as in the medical model) there may be no direct evidence on those flows. This lack of information, however, should not limit attempts to explore the sensitivity of the decision to how net benefit flows are estimated. Just as with the model of CHF treatment, it may be worth identifying scenarios in relation to the sustainability of the net benefits over time, and fully quantifying the expected value and uncertainty intervals for each of these different scenarios. Whether it is worth taking the next step— to quantifying the likelihood of those scenarios so as to generate an overall estimate of value for the program, with associated uncertainty—is less clear, and is discussed in more detail below.

The World Bank undertakes an increasing number of evaluations of the more diffuse type that are more difficult to fit into the treatment intervention model. In these evaluations the traditional cost-benefit approach is less prevalent since it is considered to be too difficult to reliably produce a convincing model. Instead, logical frameworks (or logframes) are sometimes used to link the program's inputs with its outputs and outcomes. These frameworks essentially provide a process by which the overall goal of the program can be achieved, based on a set of assumptions holding. In addition, potential risks to the success of a program may also be identified.

In essence, the set of assumptions required to relate the activities undertaken to the ultimate goal of the program describes a state of the world. What is not clear is the extent to which a given logframe also explores the possibility of alternative assumptions (leading to alternative states of the world), with associated alternative activities and corresponding outputs. Even when these alternative risks and assumptions together with their consequences are fully described, they are rarely quantified in terms of the likelihood that they will occur. Yet it should be possible to treat the overall framework in a similar way to a standard decision-tree analysis by attaching probabilities to different states of the world. The sensitivity of the decision of whether to implement a program could then be assessed in relation to the likely outputs of the program, given uncertainty over different states of the world.

It may be even more difficult to get a realistic view of the flows of net benefits for these more diffuse projects. However, these flows must surely depend on the goal of the project having been achieved (at least to some extent) and will therefore be a function of the different states of the world. Nevertheless, the very existence of the logframe approach and its rationale suggests that there has been some disappointment in the past with the level of benefits achieved from a program once assistance has been removed. This suggests that the flow of net benefits at least has some historical precedent. It may be that what is required is an assessment of the extent to which the very process of using logframes (which after all emphasize the process elements of implementing a program and measuring the consequences of implementation) results in improved net benefit flows.

As has been argued above, the Bayesian approach to probability analysis allows formal quantification and assessment through subjective degree of belief even in the absence of information. However, there is evidence to suggest that even "experts" are rather poor at estimating probabilities and it is fair to say that it is often the perceived "subjective" nature of formal Bayesian assessments that is most commonly cited against the use of the method. The potential solution to this problem, and one that is consistent with both the Bayesian approach and the normative basis of public policy decision making, is to assign a vague prior to parameters of unknown value. In a full Bayesian value of information analysis this has the likely result that it would be worth collecting information on this parameter before proceeding to make a decision.

5. Discussion

All evaluative techniques depend more or less on some modeling structure, whether that be a formal decision analytic type model or the logical framework adopted for some of the World Bank projects. Modeling methods particularly come to the fore when extrapolating beyond the period of data collection, as for example when considering the sustainability of medical treatment effects or the sustainability of net benefit flows.

Models will necessarily involve a number of parameters that form the inputs to the modeling process. How uncertainty in these parameters influences the outcomes predicted by the model can be tested through sensitivity analysis. The most commonly employed form of sensitivity analysis involves simply varying each parameter independently of the others in a univariate analysis. However, this is unrealistic and can lead to serious underestimation of the overall extent of uncertainty. More recently interest has focused on Monte Carlo methods for evaluating the consequences of uncertainty in all parameters simultaneously. The choice of distribution for parameters in such an analysis is much more straightforward in a Bayesian framework where the parameter distributions can be related to the type of data likelihood.

It is important to remember, however, that uncertainty goes beyond these probabilistic models. Uncertainty will also be a function of the modeling assumptions themselves; of particular interest in this paper is the concept of extrapolation or sustainability of program effects. In a powerfully argued paper, Draper (1995) suggests that many of the catastrophic failures of prediction models can be explained by the failure to consider the uncertainty that is due to the model as opposed to focusing on the uncertainty in predictions that are conditional on the model. In examples varying from the Challenger space shuttle disaster to the failure to accurately predict oil prices for the purposes of government policy, the problem is argued to be the choice of a single model on which to condition uncertainty estimates.

The proposed solution is to employ Bayesian model averaging, which effectively combines the predictions of a number of models in order to better represent not only uncertainty within the modeling process, but also that between different models. This is achieved by specifying the probability with which each model is considered to represent the "true" model—and it emphasizes the flexibility of the Bayesian view of probability in comparison to the classical frequentist view.

Yet Bayesian model averaging is not without its problems and is not uncontroversial. Many analysts prefer to present the results of different models in what is effectively the hierarchical use of univariate sensitivity analysis in order to better understand the consequences of model choice. Nevertheless, it is likely that model-averaging methods provide a better method than simply choosing the "best" candidate model and only representing uncertainty conditional on that model structure.

Estimates of sustainability of net benefit flows, whether generated from formal modeling methods or not, are likely to be made with very little information since by definition extrapolation beyond primary data is involved. However, it may be possible to make inferences from past projects. The UK Treasury has highlighted the problem of what it terms "optimism bias" in the evaluations of potential public sector projects.[22] In seeking funding approval for capital investment projects, applicants commonly understated costs and overstated the potential benefits of the projects—often considerably. Through knowledge of this the Treasury now adjusts early proposals for this bias and works with those presenting the evaluations to reduce the optimism bias, in a bid to ensure that public sector projects do not overrun their projected costs and achieve their stated outcomes. There seem to be a number of similarities between this process and that of the use of logical frameworks by the World Bank. This suggests that it may be possible to estimate, based on past experience, the reduction in net benefit flows after the support for a program has been removed, and that it may even be possible to assess the extent to which the wider use of a logframe approach has mitigated against reduced net benefit flows.

Perhaps a related issue is that having a great deal of uncertainty associated with an evaluation is often seen as a problem. Analysts and evaluators may be under some pressure to be able to make statements and recommendations that are clear, rather than ones that are associated with wide uncertainty intervals.

However, the accurate representation of uncertainty should be seen as an important characteristic of a well-conducted evaluation, not as a limitation. Only if uncertainty is accurately represented can future decisions regarding the potential collection of further data be truly fully informed.

6. Conclusion

It is important to recognize that the Bayesian approach is not a panacea for all the problems encountered in evaluations. Many of the judgments involved in conducting evaluations are difficult, and will remain so under a Bayesian paradigm. Nevertheless, the Bayesian approach to evaluation has much to offer the analyst. The Bayesian focus on modeling the decision-making process and the consequences of error, rather than employing arbitrary error rates (the practice that predominates in the clinical evaluation field) is compelling. The flexibility with which probabilities can be assigned to all entities of interest makes the Bayesian paradigm the natural choice for those concerned with decision making. In particular, Bayesian models can (and should) not only quantify uncertainty but also describe the appropriate way to handle that uncertainty, in terms of whether a decision should be made immediately, or whether a decision should be delayed while more information is collected to guide that decision.

Notes

1. I am particularly grateful to Howard White for help, guidance, and comments on this paper. Funding from a UK Department of Health Public Health Career Scientist Award is gratefully acknowledged. The usual disclaimer applies.
2. Canadian Coordinating Office for Health Technology Assessment (1997); National Institute for Clinical Excellence (2001); Pharmaceutical Benefits Advisory Committee (1995).
3. Gold et al. (1996).
4. Buxton et al. (1997).
5. Mishan (1988).
6. Note that this distinction is important. Evaluation of interventions relative to "do nothing" has been advocated by the World Health Organization. However, in choosing to describe such cost-effectiveness ratios as "average" they have created confusion between incremental analysis to a do nothing option and true average analyses where costs for one option are divided by the effects observed for that option—a practice that is clearly inappropriate.
7. O'Brien et al. (1994).
8. Anderson et al. (1986); Black (1990).
9. Critchfield, Willard, and Connelly (1986); Doubilet et al. (1985). Monte Carlo simulation methods have not been limited to the medical decision-making field and many early examples can be found in the operations research literature. However, it is fair to say that until recently this form of analysis has not been prevalent in practical applications of evaluative methods in the health care field.
10. Briggs (2000); Manning, Fryback, and Weinstein (1996); O'Brien, Drummond, Labelle, and Willan (1994).
11. Eddy, Hasselblad, and Shachter (1990).

12. Sendi et al. (1999); Fryback, Chinnis, and Ulvila (2001).
13. Lord and Asante (1999); Pasta, Taylor, and Henning (1999).
14. Levy et al. (2001).
15. Avezum et al. (1998); Heidenreich, Lee, and Massie (1997); Lechat et al. (1998).
16. Delea et al. (1999).
17. Delea, Vera-Llonch, Richner, Fowler, and Oster (1999); Paul et al. (1994).
18. Since no information was available on variance of mean resource event or unit cost the coefficient of variation was used to relate the variance to the mean value. A value of 0.5 was chosen for resource use to give a high variance (or vague prior). A value of 0.1 was chosen for unit costs to reflect that it was considered that unit costs were likely to be associated with less uncertainty than resource use.
19. Claxton and Posnett (1996); Felli and Hazen (1998); Claxton (1999).
20. As well as adjustments to simple expected value decision rules based on value of information methods described here, it might also be desirable to delay a decision seen as desirable under expected value if there are likely to be potential problems in reversing the decision. That is, the "option value" should also be included Palmer and Smith (2000).
21. *www.worldbank.org/oed/eta-approach.html*
22. HM Treasury (2002).

References

Anderson, J. P., J. W. Bush, M. Chen, and D. Dolenc. (1986). "Policy Space Areas and Properties of Benefit-cost/utility Analysis." *Journal of the American Medical Association* 255 (6), pp. 794-795.

Avezum, A., R. T. Tsuyuki, J. Pogue, and S. Yusuf. (1998). "Beta-blocker Therapy for Congestive Heart Failure: A Systemic Overview and Critical Appraisal of the Published Trials." *Canadian Journal of Cardiology* 14 (8), pp. 1045-1053.

Black, W. C. (1990). "The CE Plane: A Graphic Representation of Cost-effectiveness." *Medical Decision Making* 10 (3), pp. 212-214.

Briggs, A. H. (2000). "Handling Uncertainty in Cost-effectiveness Models." *PharmacoEconomics* 17 (5), pp. 479-500.

Buxton, M. J., M. F. Drummond, B. van Hout, R. L. Prince, T. A. Sheldon, T. Szucs, and M. Vray. (1997). "Modeling in Economic Evaluation: An Unavoidable Fact of Life." *Health Economics* 6, pp. 217-227.

Canadian Coordinating Office for Health Technology Assessment (CCOHTA). (1997). *Guidelines for Economic Evaluation of Pharmaceuticals*, 2nd ed. Ottawa: CCOHTA.

Claxton K. (1999). "The Irrelevance of Inference: A Decision-making Approach to the Stochastic Evaluation of Health Care." *Journal of Health Economics* 18, pp. 341-364.

Claxton K., and J. Posnett. (1996). "An Economic Approach to Clinical Trial Design and Research Priority-setting." *Health Economics* 5 (6), pp. 513-524.

Critchfield, G. C., K. E. Willard, and D. P. Connelly. (1986). "Probabilistic Sensitivity Analysis Methods for General Decision Models." *Computers and Biomedical Research* 19, pp. 254-265.

Delea, T. E., M. Vera-Llonch, R. E. Richner, M. B. Fowler, and G. Oster. (1999). "Cost Effectiveness of Carvedilol for Heart Failure." *American Journal of Cardiology* 83 (6), pp. 890-896.

Doubilet, P., C. B. Begg, M. C. Weinstein, et al. (1985). "Probabilistic Sensitivity Analysis Using Monte Carlo Simulation. A Practical Approach." *Medical Decision Making* 5, pp. 157-177.

Draper, D. (1995). "Assessment and Propagation of Model Uncertainty." *Journal of the Royal Statistical Society,* Series B, 57 (1), pp. 45-97.

Eddy, D. M., V. Hasselblad, and R. Shachter. (1990). "A Bayesian Method for Synthesizing Evidence: The Confidence Profile Method." *International Journal of Technology Assessment in Healthcare* 6 (1), pp. 31-55.

Felli, J. C., and G. B. Hazen. (1998). "Sensitivvity Analysis and the Expected Value of Perfect Information." *Medical Decision Making* 18, pp. 95-109.

Fryback, D. G., J.-O. J. Chinnis, and J. W. Ulvila. (2001). "Bayesian Cost-effectiveness Analysis: An Example Using the GUSTO Trial." *International Journal of Technology Assessment in Healthcare* 17 (1), pp. 83-97.

Gold, M. R., J. E. Siegel, L. B. Russell, and M. C. Weinstein. (1996). *Cost-effectiveness in Health and Medicine.* New York: Oxford University Press.

Heidenreich, P. A., T. T. Lee, and B. M. Massie. (1997). "Effect of Beta-blockade on Mortality in Patients with Heart Failure: A Meta-analysis of Randomized Clinical Trials." *Journal of the American College of Cardiology* 30 (1), pp. 27-34.

HM Treasury. (2002). *The Green Book: Appraisal and Evaluation in Central Government.* London: Treasury Stationery Office.

Lechat, P., M. Packer, S. Chalon, M. Cucherat, T. Arab, and J. P. Boissel. (1998). "Clinical Effects of Beta-adrenergic Blockade in Chronic Heart Failure: A Meta-analysis of Double-blind, Placebo-controlled, Randomized Trials." *Circulation* 98 (12), pp. 1184-1191.

Levy, A. R., A. H. Briggs, C. Demers, and B. J. O'Brien. (2001). "Cost-effectiveness of Beta-blocker Therapy with Metoprolol or with Carvedilol for Treatment of Heart Failure in Canada." *American Heart Journal* 137 (3), pp. 537-543.

Lord, J., and M. A. Asante. (1999). "Estimating Uncertainty Ranges for Costs by the Bootstrap Procedure Combined with Probabilistic Sensitivity Analysis." *Health Economics* 8 (4), pp. 323-333.

Manning, W. G., D. G. Fryback, and M. C. Weinstein. (1996). "Reflecting Uncertainty in Cost-effectiveness Analysis." In M. R. Gold et al. (eds.), *Cost-effectiveness in Health and Medicine*, pp. 247-275. New York: Oxford University Press.

Mishan, E. J. (1988). *Cost-benefit Analysis*, 4th ed. London: Routledge.

National Institute for Clinical Excellence (NICE). (2001). *Guidance for Manufacturers and Sponsors.* London: NICE.

O'Brien, B. J., M. F. Drummond, R. J. Labelle, and A. Willan. (1994). "In Search of Power and Significance: Issues in the Design and Analysis of Stochastic Cost-effectiveness Studies in Healthcare." *Medical Care* 32 (2), pp. 150-163.

Palmer, S., and P. C. Smith. (2000). "Incorporating Option Values into the Economic Evaluation of Healthcare Technologies." *Journal of Health Economics* 19 (5), pp. 755-766.

Pasta, D. J., J. L. Taylor, and J. M. Henning. (1999). "Probabilistic Sensitivity Analysis Incorporating the Bootstrap: An Example Comparing Treatments for the Eradication of *Helicobacter pylori.*" *Medical Decision Making* 19 (3), pp. 353-363.

Paul, S. D., K. M. Kuntz, K. A. Eagle, and M. C. Weinstein. (1994). "Costs and Effectiveness of Angiotensin-converting Enzyme Inhibition in Patients with Congestive Heart Failure [see comments]." *Archives of Internal Medicine* 154 (10), pp. 1143-1149.

Pharmaceutical Benefits Advisory Committee. (1995). *Guidelines for the Pharmaceutical Industry on Preparation of Submissions to the Pharmaceutical Benefits Advisory Committee.* Canberra: Commonwealth Department.

Sendi, P. P., B. A. Craig, G. Meier, D. Pfluger, A. Gafni, M. Opravil, M. Battegay, and H. C. Bucher. (1999). "Cost-effectiveness of Azithromycin for Preventing *Mycobacterium avium* Complex Infection in HIV-positive Patients in the Era of Highly Active Antiretroviral Therapy. The Swiss HIV Cohort Study." *Journal of Antimicrobial Chemotherapy* 44 (6), pp. 811-817.

Comments on the papers by Platteau and Briggs

Ruth Meinzen-Dick

Evaluating past performance is hard enough. Evaluating future performance—sustainability—is even harder. But it is very important that this issue has been raised. The long-term perspective is essential for determining internal rates of return for externally oriented impact evaluations, whether for the World Bank's Operations Evaluation Department, donors, or higher-level government officials deciding on the "success" of projects and returns on investments. But it is also at least as important for internally oriented impact assessments—for project staff and affected people to learn from what is going on in the project, reorient activities in that project, or reshape them for the next project.

Here it is important to go beyond impact assessment as "project justification" to ensure that internal learning takes place through the project—itself a factor in sustainability. Many impact assessment approaches stress the virtue of having outsiders conduct the studies, in order to increase (perceived) objectivity. By contrast, the evaluation field stresses involving project implementers and participants in the study, so as to tap into their understanding, as well as to make sure they understand, buy into, and benefit from the evaluation.[1] The latter approach seems particularly relevant to the issues of institutional sustainability: reviews of projects can themselves contribute to sustainability if they help the institutions that are involved in the project to reflect on and improve their performance. Platteau's paper makes the important point that in a comprehensive approach to community-driven development (CDD), for communities to make mistakes and even failures does not necessarily constitute a failure of the program, provided they can learn from their mistakes. Perhaps this principle should apply also to project management entities. Communities need to learn to work in new ways, but so do project managers. The question is how to increase the learning from mistakes. Can evaluations themselves play a role in this learning process?

Platteau's paper rightly points out the importance of institutions and of the distribution of benefits for project sustainability. Community-driven development has been a response to institutional failures of the state and private sector (markets), and is often presumed to be automatically more equitable in distribution. But proposing it as an alternative does not mean it will always work. Too much optimism has been placed on the ease of working through community institutions, based often on a few "successful" cases, without looking carefully at the factors that made them successful. The problem with bas-

---

Senior research fellow, International Food Policy Research Institute.

ing generalizations on a few cases is that not only may expectations be too high for CDD, but a few apparent failures can also cause the approach to be rejected. What is needed, rather, is careful comparative analysis of a larger sample of projects (and sites within projects) with different degrees of apparent "success," and some notion of how representative each may be.

Platteau's paper identifies some of the key challenges to institutional sustainability, and the nature of the outcomes of CDD. This is useful to counter simplistic notions that CDD will automatically give efficient, equitable, and/ or sustainable outcomes. I would add one further caveat on equity considerations. It is not only cash contribution requirements that might preclude the poor from participating in local organizations. Labor requirements and even the way meetings are run may prevent poor people or women from participating effectively.

We often hear that cooperation leads to further cooperation, or builds social capital. But conversely, the failure of local organizations set up by external programs can have negative repercussions that cause distrust and set back a community's capacity to cooperate in other areas. This aspect has been all too often overlooked in both research and implementation.

But lest we get too pessimistic, we must also remember the alternatives— states, markets, or even nothing—leaving existing institutions in place with no interventions. It is a common problem to compare the actual performance of one type of program to an assumed ideal performance of another. For example, if existing institutions are highly inegalitarian, then it is likely that the existing distribution of resources is concentrated. Thus, the alternative systems that are proposed may also not be desirable. The key question then to be addressed is whether these institutions get better or worse at distributing wealth when external resources are introduced, such as through a CDD program. On the one hand, if the project challenges existing power relations, it may be blocked, but if it does not challenge them it may not effectively reach the poor.

In fact, CDD is often held to an even higher standard than other types of programs, because it is expected to empower people as well as deliver services. Briggs' paper points out that new treatments should be compared to existing treatments, in terms of costs and effectiveness. A similar approach should be used in evaluating CDD. CDD needs to be compared with what would happen if the activities were entrusted to state entities or markets, which may be thin or poorly regulated.

The proposed Bayesian method of analyzing probability distributions of various influencing factors is intriguing, leading to consideration of how we might apply it to institutional performance. A growing body of knowledge on the factors affecting community-level institutions for collective action, based initially on case studies, but increasingly on larger samples of communities, allows testing of the effect of hypothesized factors in different contexts.[2]

It would be interesting and challenging for researchers to make this information more useful for evaluators to assess long-run sustainability. Some variables that should be included in the models have already been identified, such as group size, various types of heterogeneity, and length of time that groups have been functioning. However, the list of factors hypothesized to affect collective action is long, and may need to be sifted and adapted to particular project areas.

Of course, even more valuable than making this information useful for evaluators would be to make it useful for project design and implementation. For example, there are indications that the capacity for collective action may be greater in communities at greater distance from cities or market centers. These are also likely to be the areas where alternative state and market institutions perform less well. Thus, it might be possible to identify areas of comparative advantage for different types of institutions in delivering basic services.

There are promising signs in this direction. For example, recent studies in Burkina Faso[3] and Kenya[4] have developed indicators of collective action, and related them to various structural and performance variables in communities. Empirically, we find that the same factors do not play out the same way in every situation, and thus we cannot come up with universal variables or parameters. But awareness of the importance of institutions for sustainability would indicate, as Briggs states, that "it would be worth collecting information on this parameter before proceeding to make a decision." As Martin Ravallion stresses in his comments (following chapter 10 of this volume), understanding local institutions is critical for governments as well as the World Bank to adapt programs to their context. What this means is that we need to invest in understanding institutional performance in different situations, not just once and for all.

Notes

1.   Mackay and Horton (2003).
2.   For example, Baland and Platteau (1996); Ostrom (1990).
3.   McCarthy et al. (2002).
4.   Place et al. (2002).

References

Baland, J., and J. P. Platteau. (1996). *Halting Degradation of Natural Resources. Is There a Role for Rural Communities?* Oxford: UN Food and Agriculture Organization and Clarendon Press.

Mackay, R., and D. Horton. (2003). "Expanding the Use of Impact Assessment and Evaluation in Agricultural Research and Development." *Agricultural Systems* 78 (2), p. 2003.

McCarthy, N., C. Dutilly-Diané, and B. Drabo. (2002). "Cooperation, Collective Action and Natural Resources Management in Burkina Faso: A Methodological Note." CAPRi Working Paper 27. Washington, DC: International Food Policy Research Institute.

Ostrom, E. (1990). *Governing the Commons: The Evolution of Institutions for Collective Action*. New York: Cambridge University Press.

Ostrom, E., J. Walker, and Gardner, R. (1994). *Rules, Games, and Common-Pool Resources*. Ann Arbor: University of Michigan Press.

Place, F., G. Kariuki, J. Wangila, P. Kristjanson, A. Makauki, and J. Ndubi. (2002). "Assessing the Factors Underlying Differences in Group Performance: Methodological Issues and Empirical Findings from the Highlands of Central Kenya." CAPRi Working Paper 25. Washington, DC: International Food Policy Research Institute.

Comments on the paper by Briggs

William Stevenson

I will focus on Andrew Briggs' paper not because I deserve to be on the same stage with him as a practitioner of Bayesian Monte Carlo analysis, but rather to share my perspective on the extent to which these ideas could have application, at least for private sector practitioners, in multilateral development banks. Briggs makes the case that we should consider applying Bayesian analysis and Monte Carlo simulations to reach better-informed decisions, whether on the resiliency of debt service coverage, rates of return on projects, economic rates of return, or equity returns, all of which are day-to-day concerns for us.

This type of analysis is generally recognized as having "arrived" for corporate finance practitioners with a 1968 article by David Hertz in the *Harvard Business Review*, on the application of Monte Carlo analysis in capital budgeting decision making. By 1971, a mere three years later, Hertz's ideas had become pretty much mainstreamed at least in the major resource transformation companies (oil companies, forest products, and so forth).

My next encounter with this type of analysis as a professional was when I was working for a big construction company in support of the Channel Tunnel project's development company. By any measure, this involved the largest project financing up to that date, with a 1 billion pound equity initial offering that had the bad luck of entering the market one week after the October 1987 "Black Friday" stock market crash. Both the company and its lenders had layers and layers of consultants evaluating everything, who were expected to stand up, cross their hearts, and say "these are good projections" going forward. One of the consultants was a white-haired, sixty-eight-year-old engineer named Howard, from a highly respected U.S. engineering company. Howard said that he had done 10,000 Monte Carlo simulation runs around the base-cost estimate and had come to the conclusion that there was less than a 5 percent chance of more than a 10 percent overrun. We younger guys, not experts on construction costs by any means, offered the point of view that that

Director, Operations Evaluation Group, International Finance Corporation.

finding was prima facie implausible given the state of scope definition, engineering, and contract development for this green-field, first-of-its kind project, and that we might get laughed at if we put that on a slide. And he assured us that there was such conservative overlaying of contingencies in the base-cost estimate that it was a very good number...and that in any case, that was his expert opinion.

Well, as some of you may know, the final cost of the project came in at about 13 billion pounds, on a base cost-estimate of 4.8 billion; in fact, it was a 175 percent overrun. I've often wanted to ask Howard what his reaction would be to that outcome in light of his going-in assurances. I'm sure he would say "That just shows that it fell in that 5 percent probability range, right? I never said it couldn't happen, right?" That's the great advantage of probability analysis over deterministic: it always has an answer.

The question behind that little anecdote is as follows: In project finance, is the added analytical sophistication likely to lead to better decisions in the face of uncertainty, or—as my old cost-accounting professor used to put it—is the value of the information worth the cost of getting it? This is a very practical question. Whether the approach is worth applying in the operational work of the International Finance Corporation, for example, depends on the scope it offers for improving decision making over current practices.

In IFC as in many organizations that finance public- and private-sector projects, appraisal optimism turns out to be the norm. We did a market assessment study a few years ago, and found that in IFC appraisals, material optimism against outcomes in revenue and margin projections featured about 70 percent of the time. Material optimism was defined as over-estimates exceeding 20 percent. The materially optimistic cases outnumbered the materially conservative cases by a ratio of three to one. Not surprisingly, the materially optimistic cases turned out to feature disproportionately in failed projects. So to the question, Are there good returns on making better estimates? our experience yields an unequivocal *Yes*. But is there a better forecasting accuracy gain in trying to internalize probability assumptions in the projections, going forward?

When we looked at the sources of optimism, we found that the undisputed first was the incentive structure facing our staff: managers can track new approvals volumes on a yearly basis, and they have merit increases to give out at the end of the year, so it is really easy to find staff motivated to find reasons to say yes, not no, to new investments. (IFC has since made strides in shifting the incentive structure to a results- and outcome-based tracking.)

The second source of appraisal optimism was lack of systematic feedback of the variances of outcomes from expectations into the assumptions that influence new project decisions. The needed data simply had never been tracked before. We in the Operations Evaluation Group have provided such feedback in special studies, and we do it in our self-evaluation reports, project by project. IFC staff facing new decisions, involving a certain layering up of risks at the project level, need to be able to consider the historical, empirical, actuarial results of similarly stacked-up risks in past operations.[1]

Third, lack of actual knowledge of outcomes to inform new decisions has been another big factor in appraisal optimism. Up to now, we have not brought this kind of empirical analysis to bear on individual new decisions, in a readily available format mainstreamed into the operational decision process.

The fourth factor in appraisal optimism is an unsolvable problem: what I would call "un-modelable" *force majeure* events. How do you take on board the probability of a monsoon wiping out your shrimp farm? How can such events be modeled in aggregate, and how much probability do you assign to this event happening in a given year in a going-forward analysis? Or what about major currency devaluations? Most of the recent crisis countries were not rated as high-risk during the period just preceding their crisis. These are special challenges.

Finally, we make "most likely case" assumptions on a deterministic basis, but the reality is that on an expected value basis, each of those drivers of results has a downward bias in its probability curve. For example, the probability of having a cost *under*-run of 50 percent is much lower than the probability of a cost *over*-run of 100 percent. Or the probability of the capacity utilization being 20 percent, in year one of operations, against a base case assumption of 70 percent, is much higher than the probability of the capacity utilization being 150 percent, and so on. Overall, there are more ways to fall short than there are to do better, and as a result, the expected values around these most likely case assumptions tend to be to the low side if you're talking about debt service coverage or returns.

Thus, all of this seems to suggest that applying Bayesian and Monte Carlo simulation analysis would be worthwhile. Internalizing these factors in the model, in principle, would adjust both for the downside skew and give a cumulative probability of, say, the debt service coverage or equity returns exceeding a threshold for minimum acceptability. And in principle, we would then have a basis for better decisions.

But will it, in fact, cure the problem of appraisal optimism and improve decision making? Not necessarily, for several reasons.

If incentives to increase the volume of new business still drive the quality of the due diligence and the appetite of management to say no versus yes, in the face of demonstrably historically low outcome prospects, then we will not escape the problem and, as the professor used the words: we'll get garbage in, in the probability assumptions, and garbage out, in the numbers.

Another issue is, do we have the knowledge and skills to do such analysis? Our investment officers have not been hired for these skills, which might be expensive to obtain.

Further, we would still have the problem of coping with the *force majeure* risk, and the question of the selectivity of its application. Logically, one would want to apply this approach in large and complex projects, but there again, the ability to make better decisions has to be determined by some knowledge of the plausible ranges for those underlying parameters. That information may not be any more apparent just because they're large.

Will senior decision makers understand such analysis, especially if it ends up with a "no-go" set of cumulative probabilities? Certainly it will embarrass them. Board members don't tend to like being confronted with uncertainty, and will want to be assured that a project will succeed, because they're being asked to approve it in the post-Enron environment, where the unwelcome prospect of board accountability is suddenly on the agenda.

Such bureaucratic sociological implications would need to be thought through and confronted in deciding whether or not to try to take this on. Niccolo Machiavelli had useful advice in this context: "There is nothing more difficult to take on, more perilous to conduct, or more uncertain in its success, than to take the lead in the introduction of a new order of things. Because the innovator has for enemies all those who have done well under the old conditions, and lukewarm defenders in those who may do well under the new." In short, organizations need new business, and there may be strong associated counter-incentives to applying better tools that will strengthen the case for saying "no".

This said, let me share briefly with you a lessons-learned story from a man named Alain Enthoven. He was brought into the 1960s Pentagon by Defense Secretary McNamara as a whiz kid in quantitative decision methods to try to reduce the cost overruns in the weapons procurement program. Enthoven was both an expert practitioner and very persuasive in the face of pushback from the crusty generals, all veterans of many a procurement turf battle. He had the power of intellect and the backing of a powerful boss, and he prevailed on a lot of procurement decisions, one of the most famous of which concerned something called at the time the TFX fighter (which later morphed into the F-111B and saw service from Vietnam through the Gulf War). Over the objections of all the service branches, the TFX was to be an inter-service fighter-bomber that was designed to be able to serve the needs of the Navy, the Air Force, and the Marine Corps, an all-around, basic model that could then be slightly modified and save money compared to separate development programs geared to the needs of each service. And Enthoven had reams of analyses showing that it would be the least-cost solution to all their needs. The TFX fighter turned out to have a huge overrun compared to the existing norm of several hundred percent—and only the Air Force version ever went into service. Later, when Enthoven reflected on that experience, he ended by saying, "What I learned is that it's a lot better to be approximately correct than to be precisely wrong."

Now, I am not suggesting that using Monte Carlo analysis will lead us to be precisely wrong more often, but this story does show that what may appear to be qualitative "non-rational" factors such as incentives can easily render wrong what otherwise is good, quantitatively based decision making. That would argue for perhaps pilot-testing this approach in a big, complicated project to see what the numbers would show. Would it change the investment decision? I have no idea, but starting somewhere, and having an analysis whose efficacy you could evaluate later on, would be certainly an intelligent way to begin.

Note

1. For example, recently we looked at our agribusiness portfolio and determined that given the particularly high-risk nature of the agribusiness sector, if the projects at approval had featured three factors, each scaled on a risk scale of 1 to 3—be it sponsor risk, export market risk, or debt leverage risk—there was an 85 percent probability of the debt not being repaid on schedule.

Part 5

**Use of Evaluation Findings to
Improve Development Effectiveness**

15

Trends in the Evaluation of Efforts to Reduce Poverty

Sulley Gariba

Growing and deepening incidence of poverty, notably in Africa, has brought to the fore the question of development effectiveness, both in the allocation of domestic resources and in the application of aid. Demonstrating progress against the Millennium Development Goals, providing evidence of diminishing poverty, and addressing the challenges of sustainable development have become vital in maintaining support and resources for development, whether from donor sources or from the budgets supported by tax revenues of developing countries themselves. Meanwhile, concern about the level of utilization of evaluation results to increase development effectiveness has been at the center of discourse about the value of evaluation itself.

In principle, evaluation has a key role to play in enhancing the results of country-led development. It is integral to building capacity for development effectiveness—the abilities and functions that link the adoption of development policy on the one hand to the success of development efforts on the other. In the spaces between policy formulation, policy adoption, and policy implementation, improvements in the capacity to internalize proposed reforms and negotiate values become central topics for development evaluation. If development evaluation is viewed from this perspective, the stakes for utilization of evaluation are high.

In practice, the role of evaluation in improving development effectiveness depends greatly on who participates in the evaluation. The traditional para-

Executive director, Institute for Policy Alternatives, a public policy think tank in Northern Ghana; associate director of the Center for Interdisciplinary Research of the University for Development Studies in Northern Ghana; and president of the International Development Evaluation Association.

digm of evaluation as an independent assessment of program effectiveness and of impacts on development presupposes that evaluation is carried out by specialized evaluators, using means of measurement that are scientific and unbiased. But if evaluation results are to be used to effect needed improvements in poverty-reduction initiatives, the evaluation enterprise must involve the people who are most affected by these policies and programs. For this to happen, the requirements include not just a commitment to learning and policy reform from donors, but also a sustained mechanism for accountability and learning within developing countries themselves. Institutional mechanisms are needed that permit the use of evaluation findings, backed by a concerted demand for evaluation, particularly from independent bodies such as parliamentary committees or independent audit commissions.

What types of development evaluation are showing the highest propensity to be used? Examples of three approaches to the use of evaluation for improving development effectiveness are described below. It should be kept in mind that in these examples, important methodological challenges linger, and the institutional mechanisms for the utilization of evaluation are still undeveloped in most cases.

1. Practical Examples

The application of participatory monitoring and evaluation of poverty-reduction interventions in many developing countries has generated a significant shift towards what Shadish, Cook, and Leviton (1991) have referred to as the "instrumental use" of evaluation—whereby evaluation directly causes a change in a project, program, or development policy. This congruence between evaluation activities and their use for development effectiveness stems from:

- Participatory methodology that empowers all the stakeholders to be engaged in evaluation; and
- The incorporation of feedback into participatory monitoring and evaluation, as an integral requirement for the integrity of the evaluation function. Such feedback is not simply expressed in a report; rather it takes the form of an accountability forum that brings service providers into encounters with consumers, government with citizens, and public institutions and politicians (in the executive) with elected parliamentarians.

Use of MDG Evaluations for Refining National Poverty Reduction Strategies

All UN member countries have signed the Millennium Declaration, and the eight Millennium Goals (MDGs) with time-bound targets are being used in monitoring the development progress made in selected countries. The monitoring parameters used in individual countries are set both by the broad MDG indicators and by countries' own specific poverty reduction targets. The process of setting parameters involves a series of consultations with government and cross-sections of stakeholders, including organized civil society. In several countries these consultations have led to:

- Detailed overview of the historical context of development priority-setting in the country;
- Analysis of the policy trends that underpin the country's efforts to reduce poverty;
- A comparison of the country-set targets with the MDGs (where applicable);
- Assessment of the effects that policies are having on the attainment of both the immediate (country) targets and the MDGs.

Ghana is monitoring progress toward the MDGs, and applying the results to improve the policy coherence in the country's development agenda. The results are being used, first, to build awareness of poverty reduction initiatives and focus country--level debate on the implementation and monitoring of efforts in this area; and second, to evaluate the feasibility of the national targets spelled out in Ghana's Poverty Reduction Strategy (GPRS) and to recommend appropriate modifications. The GPRS serves as the primary framework within which to plan development priorities, from national through sectoral to local government levels. The relationship between poverty reduction targets and budget allocations is now scrutinized more closely, and both Ghana's national budget and its companion funding mechanisms—the Highly Indebted Poor Countries (HIPC) initiative and the multi-donor budget support—are closely aligned with the poverty reduction priorities set out in the GPRS. In the past, lack of detailed data on the incidence of poverty made the poverty reduction task more difficult. The Core Welfare Indicators Questionnaire now under way addresses this gap; it will yield more local-level data and permit the selective targeting of poverty reduction initiatives to socioeconomic groups who were previously missed.

Performance-Based Budget and Disbursements

Throughout the developing world, examples now abound of performance-based disbursements of funds earmarked for poverty reduction, either through direct budget support or through the channeling of debt relief funds to poverty-targeted development objectives. Evaluation is central to performance-based disbursement; it establishes performance-based indicators and provides the basis for applying performance--based rules.

In Ghana, efforts to reduce poverty in a sustained manner are increasingly linked to performance-based budgets and disbursements. For example, as a consequence of Ghana's adherence to the HIPC initiative and with the completion of the GPRS, a consortium of ten donors agreed to pool resources in a Multi-donor Budget Support mechanism, totaling an estimated US$ 250 million a year for three years of the implementation of the poverty reduction strategy. During a first-year evaluation of this mechanism, inconsistencies were found between the overall policy statements underpinning the poverty reduction strategy and the budget allocations earmarked for their implementation. The government reacted by realigning policy with budget priorities and using the evaluation as the basis for negotiating disbursement triggers with donor partners. Based on the lessons of these evaluations, Ghana's process of establishing indicators is now increasingly country-driven. Its performance-based disbursement arrangements have been fabricated using different country experiences.

Citizen Engagement in Assessing the Performance of Public Policies and Services

The fastest growing area of application of evaluation outcomes, and the one with the greatest potential for development effectiveness, is the engagement of citizens in promoting policy and institutional change.

Citizens transform Ugandan education sector. An expenditure tracking study, one of the first-generation evaluations conducted in Uganda in 1996, found that only 10 percent of funds allocated to school construction and operations ever reached the intended schools. A follow-up study in 2001 found that the figure had risen to 80 percent. At the same time, primary school enrollment had increased from 50 percent to 95 percent. What had happened in the interim? Two factors stand out. First, Uganda adopted a policy of transparency that made it mandatory to post public notices of resource allocations. As a result, parents would turn up at the doors of district administrators and school heads, demanding to know what was happening to the money given to their children's classrooms or teachers. Second, Uganda adopted a sectorwide approach to planning, budgeting, and donor liaison. In preference to stand-alone technical cooperation projects, donor funds are increasingly channeled through the government's own budgets and decision-making processes. Resource plans and strategies are prepared and reviewed by a sector working group, which meets twice yearly and brings together the education ministry, central agencies, NGOs, and donors. Increasingly, this process of learning is also heightening accountability, as the expenditure review process becomes fully integrated into the routines of doing business.

The Bangalore scorecard. In Bangalore, India, through an initiative of the Public Affairs Center, a system has been developed for systematically monitoring the perceptions of public service end-users. Based on interviews at the household or frontline facility levels, users are asked to rate the services they have sought or received. Ratings are given for waiting times, courtesy, responsiveness, and general satisfaction with health, environmental, and educational services. The ratings are published in newspapers and other media. Indications are that the surveys and their publication are making managers more responsive to client needs and providing better service as a result. The practice introduces direct accountability between the frontline service facility managers and their constituency of end-users, as well as serving as a means to mobilize citizen engagement in monitoring and evaluating the performance of public services.

Public perceptions of corruption: Ghana case study. In Ghana, a national survey of public perceptions of key public service institutions developed a corruption and transparency matrix, with dire consequences for some of the institutions evaluated. The judiciary was found to be among the highest in public perceptions of corruption; the Customs and Excise Services received scathing public criticism; and the water supply and electricity services were cited as inefficient and insensitive to the needs of consumers, especially the poor. Even the national Parliament was not spared; few people were found to understand what Parliament does. This report, published in 2000, triggered considerable national debate about the anti-corruption policy direction and subsequently spurred the formation of a Ghana Anti-corruption Coalition, with an elaborate action plan that included massive public education on the issues of corruption in public life, accountability, and efficient service delivery to the poor. Further, the evaluation report compelled Parliament to establish public hearings on corruption in the judiciary. Subsequently, the judicial service itself instituted an internal enquiry about corruption in the service.

2. Issues in the Use of Evaluation

Three issues in particular may hinder the use of evaluation to improve development effectiveness:

- Scope of participation—the challenge of who is involved, has access to the findings, and participates in using the findings. Civil society organizations are not involved in many evaluations that have high policy impacts and whose utilization affects the lives and work of many people. And in joint evaluations between aid-donor and aid-recipient organizations, the extent of country ownership raises enormous questions about how the results might be internalized and used to transform policies, budgets, and practices.
- Institutionalization is a major challenge for evaluation and its use for development effectiveness. In emerging democracies, the role of parliament is becoming increasingly significant in translating the demand for accountability into demand for evaluation. When constitutional bodies, such as parliament, demand an evaluation, the results of such evaluations have a much greater chance of being used.

- Timeliness of evaluation findings. Evaluation can be time-consuming and costly. Evaluators not only need to consider issues of methodological rigor but also the practical reality of delivering results when they are needed. Only thus can evaluation demonstrate its utility to decision makers.

References

Shadish, William, Jr., Thomas Cook, Laura Leviton. (1991). *Foundations of Program Evaluation: Theories of Practice.* Thousand Oaks, CA: Sage Publications.

16

The "Resource Restriction Condition" for Evaluation Effectiveness

> The incentives that are built into the institutional framework play the decisive role in shaping the kinds of skills and knowledge that pay off.—*Douglass North (1990)*

The organizers of this conference asked me to comment on the use of evaluation within the fiscal and budget contexts. I welcomed the invitation as an attractive conceptual challenge. It is not often that evaluation issues are elevated from the project, sector, or micro-institutional levels to the macroeconomic, fiscal, and budget levels, and yet—as will be seen—it is "up there" where key evaluative problems may have been seeded in the first place and where strategic macro-institutional rules and incentives ultimately determine the effectiveness of evaluation.

Within this context, I will suggest that the capacity of evaluation to enhance projects or sectoral programs at the micro level is seriously compromised unless these activities are subject to a tight budget constraint. In brief, I will posit that, if what I call the resource restriction condition (RRC) is missing, or is merely nominal, evaluation will be virtually powerless to change policies or access to resources.

First, I will comment on the budget conditions needed for evaluation to be effective at all stages of a budget process. Second, I will point out the main evaluation findings in relation to fiscal outcomes and budget processes in Latin America[1] at large, and offer possible explanations for those findings.

Former Minister of Finance, Colombia, and a former executive director of the World Bank.

Third, I will summarize the policy implications of the evaluation findings for the practice of evaluation in general, in developing countries and in multilateral institutions.[2]

1. The Objectives of Budget Frameworks

Most experts agree[3] that a well-designed budget framework needs to achieve and reconcile the following three basic objectives:

- Preserve macroeconomic stability by assuring policy consistency at the most aggregate level of public revenues and public expenditures.
- Establish strategic priorities for sectoral expenditures across programs and projects.
- Achieve process efficiency in the execution and evaluation of the budget itself.

At each of these levels there are evaluation tasks and challenges.

Most of the time, evaluation is accorded most importance at the third level—the budget-process expenditure level. Evaluations at this level focus on results of programs and projects.[4] Considerable attention tends to be given to inputs, to results-based management,[5] to efficacy and efficiency measurements, to outcomes, and even to the impact of given interventions.

However, the priority would be better placed at the macroeconomic and macro-institutional level.[6] For evaluations to be "real," and able to enhance efficiency at the second and third levels, they need to affect access to budget resources or to influence the policies that determine this access. If decisions on budget resources are taken independently of evaluation results, those evaluations will largely be perfunctory[7] and they will not significantly enhance the effectiveness of the evaluated projects, programs, or policies. Without a tight budget constraint at the macroeconomic level and for public sectors at all levels of government, it will be very difficult for evaluation to act as an incentive;[8] on the contrary, the lack of a tight budget constraint itself provides the "wrong" incentive. Under conditions of fiscal profligacy, the abundance of resources may prevent evaluations from inducing better results.

To explore these questions empirically, I take the case of Latin America, where during the 1990s, a soft budget constraint at the national and subnational[9] levels engendered growing fiscal deficits for public sectors at large and contributed to macroeconomic instability.

2. Latin America's Fiscal Experience

The data at the national level suggest that the region (except for Chile) has not had a tight budget constraint since the late 1990s and that its fiscal deficits have been growing since 1995 (Table 16.1 and Table 16.2).[10]

Table 16.1
Fiscal Balances, Selected Latin American Countries, 1990s
(Percent of GDP)

COUNTRY	TOTAL REVENUE			TOTAL EXPENDITURE			FISCAL BALANCE		
	1997	1998	1999	1997	1998	1999	1997	1998	1999
Latin America	23.3	21.3	22.4	24.7	23.8	25.4	-1.4	-2.5	-3.0
Argentina	17.2	19.0	20.3	18.6	20.4	22.0	-1.4	-1.4	-1.7
Brazil	28.9	32.1	34.4	34.1	40.0	43.9	-6.1	-8.0	-9.5
Bolivia	30.3	23.1	30.8	33.7	35.0	34.7	-3.4	-4.0	-3.9
Chile	32.0	23.6	23.1	31.2	23.2	24.5	0.8	0.4	-1.5
Colombia	33.6	29.5	32.5	36.7	32.9	37.1	-3.1	-3.4	-4.6
Costa Rica	29.8	12.9	13.1	31.3	15.4	15.4	-1.5	-2.5	-2.3
Mexico	23.0	20.4	20.7	23.6	21.6	21.8	-1.5	-1.2	-1.1
Peru	14.2	14.3	13.0	15.0	15.3	15.8	0.4	-1.0	-2.7
Venezuela	31.9	21.0	24.7	29.3	27.6	25.9	2.6	-6.6	-1.2
Ecuador	23.8	20.3	25.2	26.3	26.3	30.0	-2.6	-6.0	-4.8

Source: ECLAC, *Economic Survey of Latin America and the Caribbean 1999-2000*, December 2000, Table No. II. 1, p. 38.

Table 16.2
Fiscal Deficits, Selected Latin American Countries, 1990s
(Percent of GDP)

	1995	1996	1997	1998	1999	2000	2001
Fiscal balance	- 1.7	- 1.6	- 1.3	-2.2	- 3.0	-2.8	- 3.3

Source: CEPAL (2002) *Situación y Perspectivas,* Estudios Económicos de América Latina y el Caribe 2001-2002, p. 39.

3. Evaluation Effectiveness, Incentives, and Institutional Conditions

Evaluation effectiveness can be impaired by the lack of a tight budget constraint but also by the type of spending that budget resources finance. More specifically, evaluation effectiveness can be impaired by the institutional conditions and incentive environments[11] within which particular public expenditures take place.[12]

In Latin America, social spending grew faster than public spending as a whole. Table 16.3 shows that between 1990-91 and 1996-97, social spending grew from 10.1 percent to 12.4 percent of GDP. Most likely these percentages have continued to grow in the last few years. Transfers from the national to the subnational level to finance decentralization schemes[13] also grew very fast in the 1990s. Since most of these transfers responded to formulas and to resource transfer targets, evaluations of their results were not subject to the resource restriction condition.

Table 16.3
Latin America: Social Expenditures in Relation to GDP, 1990-97

COUNTRY	Social Expenditure/ GDP		Social Expenditure/GDP							
	Social Expenditure/ GDP		Education		Health		Social Security		Housing	
	1990-1991	1996-1997	1990-1991	1996-1997	1990-1991	1996-1997	1990-1991	1996-1997	1990-1991	1996-1997
Argentina	17.7	17.9	3.3	3.8	4.0	4.1	8.3	8.0	2.1	1.9
Bolivia	6.0	12.0	3.1	5.9	1.2	1.4	1.0	2.7	0.7	2.0
Brazil	19.0	19.8	3.7	3.4	3.6	2.9	8.1	10.1	3.5	3.4
Chile	13.0	14.1	2.6	3.3	2.1	2.5	7.0	6.7	1.4	1.7
Colombia	8.1	15.3	3.1	4.4	1.2	3.7	3.0	5.4	0.8	1.8
Costa Rica	18.2	20.8	4.7	5.8	7.1	7.3	4.4	5.5	2.0	2.2
El Salvador	5.4	7.7	2.1	2.6	1.8	2.8	1.4	2.0	0.2	0.2
Guatemala	3.3	4.2	1.6	1.7	0.9	0.9	0.7	0.7	0.1	0.9
Honduras	7.8	7.2								
Mexico	6.5	8.5	2.6	3.7			3.1	3.6	0.8	1.2
Nicaragua	10.3	10.7	4.9	4.3	4.2	4.4			1.2	1.9
Panama	18.6	21.9	4.7	5.5	6.1	6.8	5.8	6.6	2.0	3.1
Paraguay	3.0	7.9	1.2	3.9	0.3	1.2	1.1	2.6	0.4	0.2
Peru	2.3	5.8								
Dominican	4.5	6.0	1.2	2.3	1.0	1.4	0.4	0.7	2.0	1.7
Republic	18.7	22.5	2.7	3.0	3.2	3.7	12.4	15.3	0.3	0.5
Uruguay	9.0	8.4	3.4	3.1	1.5	1.1	2.4	2.9	1.6	1.2
Venezuela										
Simple average	**10.1**	**12.4**	**3.0**	**3.8**	**2.7**	**3.2**	**4.2**	**5.2**	**1.3**	**1.6**

Source: CEPAL (2000), *Equidad, Desarrollo y Ciudadanía*, Santiago de Chile, p. 158.

The growth of social spending within overall budgets is often justified in terms of poverty and equity considerations; after all, the market process, on its own, may miss financing some of the most critical public goods.[14, 15] However, simply spending more on social needs does not guarantee that equity will improve. What really matters is *how* the money is spent and who evaluates the results.

Social expenditures may place their emphasis on financing either the supply side or the demand side. The latter enhances consumers' choice.[16] In Latin America most governments have opted more for the former approach. This has led to the capture[17] of public resources by other public sector rent-seekers[18] and to the development of conditions adverse to "real" evaluations—i.e. evaluations that would change resource allocations[19] in response to different performance results.

Latin America's growing fiscal deficits, rising social expenditures, and decentralization transfers by formula were not propitious for "real" evaluations. After all, if resources are not subject to a tight fiscal budget constraint, why have evaluations? And, if most of the growth in expenditures occurs in sectors such as education and health, which are inherently difficult to evaluate, then the results of evaluations can hardly enhance the effectiveness of those expenditures.

4. The Political Economy Explanation and Context

There are three main explanations for the observed findings.

- Latin America as a whole has what James Poterba calls "a common-pool problem."[20] This means that there is access to a common pool of resources and countries can hardly control their public expenditures.[21]
- The political pressures for public expenditures are enormous.[22] Macroeconomic stability is not really perceived as a collective asset but, at best, as a remote public good. Politically, it is an orphan. Its protection yields meager political dividends. The attribution of its abandonment is diffuse and ambiguous.
- Excessive financing made be available, not least from short-term international capital markets as well as multilateral sources.[23]

Under these circumstances it is easy for policymakers and politicians to become confused and to think that financing "below the line" is equivalent to adjustment "above the line." They will postpone real processes of adjustment as long as financing permits them to avoid improving the quality of expenditures, reducing expenditures, or raising revenues, in that order. Under these circumstances, "real" evaluations are the exception.

5. The Evaluation of Results and the Results of Evaluations

Evaluation conferences, seminars, and articles often focus on the problems related to the evaluation process—on what theory of evaluation to apply; how to distinguish between processes, inputs, results, outcomes; how to approach sampling or use Bayesian statistics[24]; how to deal with problems of endogeneity and sustainability or triangulation. And many scholars invest considerable energy in trying to resolve problems dealing with what I would call the "left side" of the evaluation equation—that is, everything that takes place from the design phase of an intervention to the assessment of its results.

But often too little attention is given to the "right side" of the evaluation equation—to what happens as a *consequence of the evaluation results* obtained. How are those results used? Who is interested in using them? And why? What happens after the specific micro-interactions have been concluded? This right side of the equation is where the key explanatory variables, the real incentives that are at work, are probably to be found. These real incentives can be seen in the connection or lack of it between the results of evaluations and the change in availability of resources or the change in policies that takes place after the evaluation has been finalized.

Once this "right-side" of the evaluation equation is discerned, many of the traditional problems of evaluation effectiveness become secondary. They will, eventually, be largely resolved by the supply side of the evaluation market, because the demand for "real evaluations" will induce an increasingly efficient supply response. The specifics of that supply response do not need to be established ex ante; they will vary depending on the characteristics of each intervention. In brief, the market will arbitrate the incentive compatibility[25] that now exists between the demand side and the supply side of evaluations.

Policy Implications

The resource restriction condition has key implications for the practice of evaluation and does much to explain why evaluations are often less effective than theory would predict. Hence, the search for enhanced effectiveness in evaluation should begin by asking whether the RRC is met or not. If it is not met, it can give rise inter alia to what Osvaldo Feinstein[26] calls the "reported results distortion," which is the difference between "effects on actual results" and "effects on reported results." Acknowledging the possibility of a reported results distortion is crucial to prevent it.

What does this imply for policy?

At the country level in Latin America, it implies that to achieve more effective evaluations of projects, programs, and policies, the best place to begin is at the macroeconomic and budget level. Even so, countries should also worry about what happens at the subnational level; in the 1990s, as noted, some of the region's more serious macroeconomic problems originated in fiscal deficits at this level.

At the multilateral level, the policy implication is that institutions should insist on a macroeconomic and tight budget constraint.[27] They could consider applying the principle of no additionality in their lending operations—a promising idea that has received some consideration by Brazil and Chile. Under this principle, borrowers would not have, as an incentive to obtain a loan, the possibility of gaining access to additional resources, but only the gains from other positive externalities of loans.

6. Concluding Observations

When explanations are sought for the limited capacity of evaluations to enhance developmental results, the answer may be found in the fact that often evaluation results do not really influence resource availability. If the resource restriction condition is not met, then evaluation results will not change policies or affect access to resources and the effectiveness of evaluation will be impaired. This hypothesis is hardly without empirical support. Excessive spending, growing fiscal deficits, and profligate policies in developed and developing countries are now more the norm the exception. It is difficult not to consider this soft budget resource context as part of the answer to many of the troubles that currently afflict evaluation in general.

Evaluation results should be perceived as an incentive and as an instrument to gain access to more resources, or to preserve existing access. By taking this approach, those interested in getting resources will then demand—from the supply side of evaluation—evaluation results that are credible and that have the capacity to generate additional resources. This is the analytical framework underlying what is called demand-driven evaluation.

Notes

1. For a review of the restrictions limiting evaluation effectiveness in Latin America, see Wiesner (2000), p. 15.
2. For an analysis of the relationships between multilateral lending and evaluation effectiveness, see Wiesner (2003), p. 138, which posits that "the wrong incentives are relevant."
3. See Campos and Sanjay (1999), p. 235.
4. Results, in a broad sense, refer to the effects of a given policy program or a project, whether in terms of (1) "outputs" (specific products emerging from processing inputs after the completion of a process); (2) outcomes (the specific changes intended for a given development conditions); or (3) "impact" (the overall global effect of an intervention). UNDP Evaluation Office (2001), p. 39.
5. See Binnendijk (2000), for insightful clarifications on the nuances between performance budgeting, performance information, and managing for results.
6. According to Wiesner (1998), p. xiv, "Evaluation effectiveness can be judged in terms of its efficiency in identifying public sector institutional obstacles and in contributing to the productive mediation between the demands for and supply of the "right" institutional arrangements.
7. In several countries in Latin America, the normative framework regulating sectors like education and health contains references to the "evaluation of results." But, in effect, those evaluations have no significant input on resource allocations, which are earmarked in advance. See Wiesner (1997), p. 191.
8. See Joseph Stiglitz (1998) for a review of the role of incentives in enhancing evaluation results.
9. This was the case in Argentina and Brazil (Dillinger and Webb, 1999) and in Colombia (Partow, 2002, p. 160).
10. Although, in principle, public sectors should find it difficult to create unsustainable resources to finance unsustainable levels of expenditure, in practice they are often able, at least for a while, to have access to permissive central banks, to debt forgiveness (through the Highly Indebted Poor Countries Initiative and the like), to revenues from occasional export booms, and to all sorts of mechanisms to increase expenditures, even when those increases are not warranted by results.
11. Kenneth Arrow has called incentives "the most important development in economics in the last 40 years." See Laffont and Martimort (2002).
12. For an excellent review of the factors that limit the evaluation of social expenditure in Latin America, see Haussman (1996), p. vii.
13. According to Wiesner (2003c), p. 10, "the initial Latin America approach contained key conceptual and operational flaws that, in some countries, arose because officials gave priority to the parceling out of free resources instead of looking for a process and assuring the right incentives."
14. From a distributive justice perspective, spending more public resources to equalize initial conditions and opportunities is perfectly justified. According to Solimano

(2000) p. 32, "The modern theory of distributive justice distinguishes between "outside" (or morally arbitrary) factors (gender, race, initial assets, talent) and "personal responsibility" elements (effort, risk-taking attitudes) in shaping the level of income, wealth, and welfare of the individual in society. Social inequality is a reflection of individual differences in these two sets of wealth-creating factors."

15. Wiesner (2003c), p. 32, posits that the main objective of social expenditures is to ensure equal educational and health opportunities to the children of poor people.

16. For the importance of "choice" in public spending for education, see Hanushek (1994), who avers that "giving parents and students the ability to choose among a range of nearby schools is intended to give them, rather than school administrators, the power to define a "good" education and to shape the schools accordingly."

17. The concept of "capture" was developed by Stigler (1971), pp. 3-21.

18. Tollison (1997) defines rent seeking as "the socially costly pursuit of wealth transfers." The concept of rent seeking was introduced in economics by Tullock (1967), who describes it as "the welfare cost of tariffs, monopolies, and theft." See also Krueger (1974).

19. It should be noted that an effective evaluation would not need to change the total amount of resources allocated to social purposes. But it would change to composition or the distribution of that total. See Wiesner (2003a).

20. Poterba and Von Hagen (1999) p. 3.

21. Under the so-called "commons problem" there are no property rights regulating the use of an asset. Individuals and organizations competing for the use of a common property will reduce its value to zero. This process is known as the dissipation of rent. See Cheung (1991), p. 83.

22. For the case of Brazil, Giambiagi (2002), p.1, has found that "the total primary federal public expenditure grew in real terms in all the eight years–with no exceptions–of the two Administrations, at a yearly average of 6 percent, more than doubling the average of yearly GDP growth rate of 2.4 percent."

23. For a review of the relationships between international financing and evaluation effectiveness, see Wiesner (2003a).

24. Briggs, chapter 14 in this volume.

25. Incentive compatibility is a system of behavior in which each individual has a personal incentive to act in accordance with some overall interest. A classic example of an incentive-compatible system is that used by parents to divide a cake between two hungry children, in which one is allowed to slice the cake in two and the other is allowed to choose which slice to take." See Bannock, Baxter, and Davis (1999), p. 196.

26. Personal communication.

27. At the same time, they need to recognize that they may function under a "collective action problem" which limits the effectiveness of even their own evaluations, and despite their best professional efforts.

References

Bannock, Graham, R. E. Baxter, and Evan Davis. (1999). *Dictionary of Economics.* Great Britain: *The Economist* Books.

Binnendijk, Annette. (2000). "Results-based Management in the Development Cooperation Agencies: A Review of Experience." Proceedings of the Beijing Conference on Evaluation Capacity Development, October 27-28, 2000.

Campos, J. Edgardo, and Pradhan Sanjay. (1999). "Budgetary Institutions and the Levels of Expenditure Outcomes in Australia and New Zealand." In James Poterba and

Jürgen von Hagen (eds.), *Fiscal Institutions and Fiscal Performance*. Chicago: University of Chicago Press.

Cheung, Steve N. S. (1991). "Common Property Rights." In John Eatwell, Murray Milgate, and Peter Newman (eds.), *The World of Economics*. New York: W.W. Norton.

Dillinger, William, and Steven B. Webb. (1999). "Fiscal Management in Federal Democracies: Argentina and Brazil." Policy Research Working Paper No. 2121. Washington, DC: The World Bank.

Giambiagi, Fabio. (2002). "Do Deficit de Metas as Metas de Deficit: A Politica Fiscal do Governo Fernando Henrique Cardoso 1995-2002." BNDES.

Hanushek, Eric. (1994). "Making Schools Work." Washington, DC: The Brookings Institution.

Haussman, Ricardo. (1996). "Prefacio." "Cómo Organizar con Exito los Servicios Sociales." Progreso Económico y Social en América Latina. Washington, DC, InterAmerican Development Bank.

Krueger, Anne. (1974). "The Political Economy of the Rent-seeking Society." *American Economic Review* (June), pp. 291-303.

Laffont, Jean-Jacques, and David Martimort. (2002). *The Theory of Incentives: The Principal-Agent Model*. Princeton, NJ: Princeton University Press.

North, Douglass. (1990). *Institutions, Institutional Change and Economic Performance*. Cambridge: Cambridge University Press.

Partow, Zeinab. (2002). "Macroeconomic and Fiscal Frameworks." In Marcelo M. Giugale, Oliver Lafourcade, and Connie Luff (eds.), *Colombia: The Economic Foundation of Peace*. Washington, DC: The World Bank.

Poterba, James, and Jürgen Von Hagen. (1999). "Introduction." In James Poterba and Jürgen von Hagen (eds.), *Fiscal Institutions and Fiscal Performance*. Chicago: University of Chicago Press.

Solimano, Andres. (2000). "Beyond Unequal Development." In Andrés Solimano, Eduardo Aninat, and Nancy Birdsall (eds.), *Distributive Justice & Economic Development: The Case of Chile and Developing Countries*. Ann Arbor: University of Michigan Press.

Stigler, George. (1971). "The Theory of Economic Regulation." *Bell Journal of Economics and Management Science* 2, pp. 3-21.

Stiglitz, Joseph. (1998). "Evaluation as an Incentive Investment." In Robert Picciotto and Eduardo Wiesner (eds.), *Evaluation and Development: The Institutional Dimension*. New Brunswick, NJ: Transaction Publishers.

Tollison, Robert. (1997). "Rent Seeking." In Dennis Mueller (ed.), *Perspectives on Public Choice: United Kingdom*. Cambridge: Cambridge University Press.

Tullock, Gordon. (1967). "The Welfare Cost of Tariffs, Monopolies, and Theft." *Western Economic Journal* (now *Economic Inquiry*) 5, pp. 224-32.

UNDP Evaluation Office. (2001). "Glossary of Terms." In *Development Effectiveness: Review of Evaluative Evidence*. New York: United Nations Development Program.

Wiesner, Eduardo. (1997). "Evaluation, Markets, and Institutions in the Reform Agenda of Developing Countries." In Eleanor Chelimsky, William R. Shadish (eds.), *Evaluation for the 21st Century: A Handbook*. London, New Delhi, Thousand Oaks, CA: Sage Publications.

_____. (1998). "Introduction." In Robert Picciotto and Eduardo Wiesner (eds.), *Evaluation and Development: The Institutional Dimension*. New Brunswick, NJ: Transaction Publishers.

_____. (2000). "Función de Evaluación de Planes, Programas, Estrategias y Proyectos." Funciones Básicas de la Planeación, Cuadernos del ILPES No. 46, Santiago de Chile.

_____. (2003a). "The Role of Incentives and Evaluations in Enhancing Development Effectiveness." Conference Paper. Oxford University, September 25-26.

_____. (2003b). "Politics, Aid, and Development Evaluation." In Patrick G. Grasso, Sulaiman S. Wasty, Rachel Weaving (eds.), *OED: The First Thirty Years*. Washington, DC. World Bank, Operations Evaluation Department.

_____. (2003c). "Decentralization y Equidad en América Latina: Enlaces Institucionales y de Política." Archivos de Economía, Documento No. 227, Junio, Departamento Nacional de Planeación, DNP, Bogotá, Colombia.

_____. (2003d). *Fiscal Federalism in Latin America: From Entitlements to Markets*. Washington, DC: Johns Hopkins University Press for Inter-American Development Bank.

17

Use of Evaluation Findings to Improve Development Effectiveness: Panel Discussion

Robert Picciotto: Director, Global Policy Project, *Chair*
Sulley Gariba: President, International Development Evaluation Association
Nancy MacPherson: Head of Evaluation, International Union for the Conservation of Nature
Eduardo Wiesner: Former Minister of Finance, Colombia, and former executive director, World Bank

Picciotto: This is an event of ideas (and also of IDEAS, the International Development Evaluation Association). We aim at an interactive session. To set the stage, let me pose the question, Is it the responsibility of the evaluator to secure results from evaluation? To get the ball rolling, I will contrast the answers of two mythical evaluation gurus: Michael Patton and Michael Scriven.

First, Patton. He might say that evaluation adds value only if its results are used. This means that evaluators must guide decision makers toward the correct decision by helping them identify the right objectives of the program, assess its performance, select the right evidence, identify the proper methods, and so forth. From this perspective, policymakers and managers want to do the right thing. They know more about their programs than evaluators do. They will resist change if they are publicly embarrassed, criticized, or shamed. If the evaluator does her job, she will get results. If she does not get results, the chances are she has not done her job as an evaluator. Utilization-based evaluation is quality evaluation. It is the only evaluation worth doing.

By contrast, Scriven might say something like this: to make evaluators responsible for the use of evaluation results is wrong. It leads to supine evaluation, tailored to what the client wants to hear. Evaluators have a higher calling: they are mandated to assess the merit and worth of public policies and programs from the standpoint of the citizens, the consumers, the poor, and the voiceless. It is not their responsibility to run programs; to ask them to participate in decision making injures their independence. If evaluators are judged by the use of evaluation findings, they become sheep in sheep's clothing, to use Churchill's phrase. In other words, if evaluation is only about learning, it does not make authority responsible. If it must churn out lessons to justify itself, it will generate an oversupply of simplistic and pious exhortations and platitudes. Worse: evaluators that do not encourage accountability for results fail to provide incentives for learning.

MacPherson: I have clearly declared myself to be in the "Patton" side of the camp. I manage the evaluation work for a large environmental NGO—the International Union for the Conservation of Nature—where the evaluation function is situated in the program office. So I work with program managers, and part of my job is to get program managers to use evaluation.

As to how we would propose to support the improvement of the use of evaluation results, let me offer five key messages we have derived from our experience over the past seven or eight years.

1. Develop a culture of questioning, learning, and accountability in our own organization as well as in civil society. This goes way beyond the function that we would normally prescribe for ourselves as evaluators.
2. Match what we evaluate with what we want to learn. This may mean evaluating beyond the sphere of aid. Currently, evaluation results don't tell us what we need to know about effective development or how well our organizations inspire and lead development efforts. If our collective goal is equitable, sustainable development, then we need to look at what works and what does not work in the search for more equitable and more sustainable societies.
3. Work with program managers in organizations and citizens in society to use evaluation for their purposes as well as ours. I don't think the low use of evaluation is any mystery when evaluation is prepared for evaluators' purposes, not for decision makers. We need to make more effort to help operational people to use evaluative processes for their purposes and hope that those overlap with ours. We need to help bring expert systems and user systems together.
4. Design interventions to learn. Here, I'm speaking as someone who works with program managers to help them be much clearer about evaluability, and about what we are trying to learn from all of these interventions. This calls for explicit assumptions, testable hypotheses, and time and resources devoted to learning. You design things very differently if you want to learn than if you just want to execute projects and programs. We also need to seek to extend the learning to help practitioners avoid mindless replication. Context is incredibly important: a cookie cutter approach will not work in the development business, and I think evaluators have to be very careful with the application of their results in that regard.
5. Create the demand. This may apply more to NGOs than it does to governments and multilaterals, but for us in an NGO it is crucial to be clear on the role of our governing body—so as to know what data and synthesis they

need to carry out that role—and also to know what monitoring data our senior managers need. Feedback from regular monitoring is just as important as feedback from evaluation.

Other points I would stress are:

- Assess the impacts of the rich on the poor, globalization, trade, and the private sector. The Millennium Goals focus on the poor. But what about targets for improving the impact of the rich countries' policies on the poor?
- Self-assessment and organizational assessment; project and program evaluation tells us very little about how our organizations function. How well do we lead, manage, and inspire development efforts? We need to look at us as well as them. Organizational assessment and self-assessment processes help us to focus on our own performance.
- Involve all staff in self-assessments. Have them think about performance and their own role in it, not just that of senior managers and not just the governing body.
- Donors, for their part, need to negotiate more useful evaluations focused on learning and to ensure good design in the first place. This speaks to the tension between the need to disburse money and the need that NGOs have to do useful things with that money.
- Organizations should seek feedback from clients and members on a regular basis.
- Focus on intermediate outcomes. The gap between our goals and our interventions is huge. Managers don't feel responsible, and nor are they, for the big changes, but neither can they visualize the results of change clearly enough. We need to help managers visualize the medium-term behavioral changes that we expect to see in individuals and institutions: Who changes? How do they change? What do we look for? And we need to monitor and evaluate those changes—which calls for developing good indicators of capacity development. Millions of dollars go into building institutional capacity, but we rarely know what we're looking for in terms of intermediate changes.

Gariba: Some of the increasing demands for accountability in the development business are not satisfied specifically by evaluation. But two clear trends are emerging in the ways in which evaluation results are being used for accountability.

One is that the public, and their elected representatives in Parliament, are using evaluation results to demand accountability for the use of public budgets. In Uganda, for example, a series of evaluations starting in the early 1990s used public expenditure tracking to show that a significant amount of the budgets allocated to schools were not, in fact, reaching schools. The result was a fairly substantial change in policy, including the introduction of quite a transparent process for displaying budgets to schools. There is now a culture of demand for accountability in the education sector, and demands for accountability have been increasingly articulated in Parliament. And in my own country, Ghana, an evaluation of the multi-donor budget system has started an interesting debate about the accountability of government to Parliament.

Second, on the question of learning, evaluation results are being fed back into the design of poverty reduction strategies. In Ghana, for example, a country-focused evaluation of progress against the Millennium Development Goals has been undertaken, involving multiple stakeholders coordinated through UNDP. The results are being translated into revisions of Ghana's poverty reduction strategy, to make its targets more realistic.

As regards citizen engagement and local participation, evaluation results will not be used unless they have real meaning for the people upon whom the evaluation is done. Use of community scorecards for assessing the performance of services, especially municipal services, is becoming quite widespread; examples come from India, West Africa, and Uganda. The communities so engaged are in a position to provide the kind of feedback that is needed to change their own lives as well as to influence public policy.

I leave you with a major challenge. The language of evaluation has become so complex that we in developing countries miss a lot of the coded messages that are transmitted. And evaluation utilization can only be meaningful if the language is simplified, and if it is understood by the people who matter the most: the poor.

Participant: Evaluation methods need to be shaped with a view to getting grassroots feedback. If beneficiaries are to press for improvements in services or in accountability for the use of public money, more emphasis on participatory evaluation techniques would be helpful, so that evaluations address beneficiaries' concerns and so that beneficiaries own the evaluation results. More evaluations need to cast the beneficiaries in the role of participants in the evaluation, rather than as subjects of evaluation, to illuminate how a project or other intervention affects beneficiaries *in their view*. And if we are to measure stakeholder/client satisfaction, we need to make sure all stakeholders are represented in planning evaluations and defining evaluation questions.

Participant: It's important to broaden the base of input in defining the criteria, standards, and objectives for evaluation, as well as in deciding who does the evaluation.

Participant: Most of us want to feel that as evaluators we lead to some change in how things are done, compared to what would have happened without good evaluation work from us. But part of our failure in helping our institutions get better results is because we are so caught up in producing evaluations that we shortchange the "marketing" or communication of the results to decision makers who can use them. Communicating our results is not the same as taking responsibility for what decision makers do with the results, but certainly, it is our responsibility to make sure that decision makers know what the findings are, so that they have a chance to act on them.

Participant: It is crucial to ensure that the lessons learned are available at the right place at the right time. The European Bank for Reconstruction and Development has a system whereby staff proposing new projects receive information from evaluators about relevant past experience. Then, before a new project goes to the Bank's Board for approval, evaluators indicate whether the lessons have been taken to heart. And although the Bank's evaluators don't have veto power, they can delay a project's approval while better use is made of the lessons. I think unless you have such an institutionalized system you will never get evaluation lessons applied.

Participant: I would like to make two points on how we are communicating evaluation results in my country, Japan. One is that though evaluation is being used as a basis for policy changes, there is a long distance from evaluation to policy changes. We have set up the Japan Evaluation Society, and have found a lot of waste in public spending. Taxpayers are interested to know whether their taxes are being wasted or not, but evaluation reports are not written with them in mind and are not easily accessible. The mass media act as intermediaries between the evaluation professionals and the public—but, following the natural inclination of the media, they pick up only the failure stories. One of the reasons why Japan is now reducing its spending on official development assistance is not fiscal deficits, but taxpayers' unhappiness with the kind of evaluation results that are reported in the media.

My second point is that for members of Parliament, who are the decision makers, it is vital to have a responsible intermediary to translate evaluation reports into language that is readily understood. We as evaluation professionals must have that kind of mechanism if our work is to affect policy.

Participant: The literature shows cases where there is a set of robust, well-known, evaluation results, but no policy change follows. For example, in the United States, many cities still have rent control: even though a large number of studies have shown the disadvantages of rent control, the political stability of that policy keeps it in place. Similarly, in education, a fair amount of evidence about class size is resisted. And evaluation findings that contradict common sense or contravene common experience tend to meet tremendous resistance. But, essentially, I think the onus is on us as evaluators to deliver credible, high-quality results even though we realize that in some cases we're not going to overturn the policy in place.

Gariba: Learning from evaluation has to be intrinsically connected with both social and public accountability. Individuals, institutions, governments, can claim to be learning from evaluation. But the key questions are: (1) Are they accountable for their actions? and (2) To whom?

To achieve accountability requires improving the medium for communicating evaluation results both to the public and also to decision makers, so that citizens can demand that the failure of a program must result in the adjustment of either budgetary allocations or public policies. It is social and public accountability that is an important litmus test for whether an institution has learned from an evaluation result. Until learning translates back into accountability to the public, you cannot actually say that learning has occurred.

MacPherson: Looking at the whole learning cycle, it is striking how responsibility for implementation disconnects people from the research and evaluation communities—from learning from people who spend their time either on action research or on the kind of work that implementers need to learn from. To help address this problem in IUCN, we have found that using more action research techniques in the design of our interventions has helped implementers to stay connected with learning channels. Designing an intervention to learn looks very different from just designing an intervention to get things done. A second point, especially in science-based organizations, is that it is important to keep the humility to be able to say, "We don't know what works," rather than buying into the expert-driven way of doing things. In IUCN we have learned a great deal from Frans Leeuw's theory-based work, and we are now looking at what works with similar kinds of interventions in other organizations whose mandates are very different from our own.

Wiesner: All these issues, of lesson learning, accountability, methodological problems, randomization, should be looked at from the perspective of the financing available. Once people realize that they are accountable—that they must really use evaluation lessons to be effective if they are to get access to more resources—then they will demand and conduct better evaluations. The interesting hypothesis is that in the last three years or five years or eight years— you choose your period—over the whole range of institutions and countries, there has been excessive financing. In that environment, how can evaluation be effective? Why worry about quality if you can always get more money?

Picciotto: In Wiesner's view, evaluation will not have an impact without hard budget constraints. But can the causality work the other way? Could it be that without evaluation, we will never get a hard budget constraint? If so, what are the implications for the politics of evaluation and the role of evaluation in governance more generally? How should evaluation functions and processes be structured vis-à-vis budget processes? Does "the new public management" of which Eduardo Wiesner is a pioneer, provide an answer?

Wiesner: These questions are well put but why do we persist in futile, nominal evaluations when the funds keep coming? Governments keep resources flowing for political reasons, independently of the results of evaluations. We should therefore shift the emphasis of evaluations into the political arena. Then, eventually—it's going to take a long time—evaluations in the political markets will converge with evaluations in the economic markets, and evaluations in both will probably become more effective. The implication is that we must evaluate both the economic system and the political system.

Participant: Financial resources to work in development *are* scarce. Even all of the resources that the World Bank, bilaterals, multilateral organizations have are really scarce in the face of developmental needs. So from that perspective, I am struck by the lack of interest of evaluators in tackling issues of accountability and cutting resources, if cutting is needed. Learning from evaluation is very important. But given that the resources are so scarce to do development work, we cannot just keep wasting millions right and left with limited impact. So we need to focus more heavily on the two issues of accountability and resource availability for projects. Having the capacity in developing countries to begin to deal with this more formally will be very important. For this we need more training programs, and we need to focus on how to increase the evaluative capacity in developing countries, in such a way that it can be more effective. And maybe training courses could include components to help evaluators deal with the need to communicate their findings so that they are widely understood and better used.

Participant: On the issue of whether or not we should allocate money when the results of evaluation show poor outcomes, I think there is no clear-cut solution. For instance, I work in public health, where outcomes often depend on behavior. Take the transmission of HIV, where health providers can do their best, strictly following good procedures and guidelines, and educating people. But because of people's perverse behavior you may end with a very poor outcome. Is that a reason for the World Bank or any organizations to stop funding an AIDS prevention program, or an organization that is doing a very good job but is not achieving good results? I don't think so.

Participant: I'm not an evaluator. I work at the Inter-American Development Bank (IADB), on the entry side of projects and country strategies. I'm concerned about the shift in evaluations away from the project level to the country level. My first reason is that a lot of development operations still take the form of projects and we can still learn very important lessons at the project level. Many of the projects that we do at IADB—innovation loans, pilot loans, and multi-phased loans, for example—could yield information to make better decisions in the future. Here I would emphasize that staff incentives play an important role in achieving projects and programs that are invaluable. To motivate task managers and keep them motivated on this issue, one of the things we can do is appeal to their professional pride and give them technical resources.

My second concern about the shift to country-level evaluations is: Who really gathers the information at the country level? Who has the incentive to do so, especially as long as aid resources continue to flow in? Some countries such as Costa Rica do take very seriously performance evaluations for their ministries. But in most aid recipient countries it's going to take a while to build evaluation incentives into the real mainstream, the political mainstream.

My last point is that impact evaluations have the character of global public goods, and their funding arrangements should reflect this.

Picciotto: What comes out of this discussion is that evaluators and program managers have a *joint* responsibility to get results. First, evaluators should do no harm; they should avoid affecting behavior in the wrong way, creating excessive risks or excessive risk aversion. And second, when evaluators think they have found the right answer to the right question, it is their responsibility to make it known at the right time, at the right place, to the right people. They must do so with fairness, balance, and objectivity. They must highlight the limits of what they have found and provide the evidence on which the conclusions are based.

Those who are being evaluated have a responsibility, too. They have a responsibility for self-evaluation; for judging the relevance and the quality of independent evaluations for themselves; for deciding what they want to do about the findings; and for implementing what they commit to do in light of the evaluation.

Thus, evaluation is a principled partnership with shared objectives, reciprocal obligations, and distinctive accountabilities. But, of course, we do not always have this kind of partnership. And when this is not the case, evaluators themselves have a responsibility to nurture the conditions for greater learning and accountability (including the political system) by involving the civil society and the media—and to assess the conditions on which the legitimacy of authority rests.

So the answer to the question I posed at the beginning of this session is that there is room for both Patton and Scriven in the big tent of our great evaluation profession.

Conference Participants

Aalam, Nurul, United Nations Development Program
Abbott, Kerry, Agency for Relief and Development, USA
Abdelhamid, Doha, Ministry of Finance, Egypt
Aguilos, Maribel, University of Maryland
Ahluwalia, Montek, International Monetary Fund
Atema, James, UK Agency for International Development, South Africa
Batwala, Rebecca, Ministry of Local Government, Uganda
Boruch, Robert, University of Pennsylvania
Borwankar, Reena, Academy for Educational Development, USA
Breier, Horst, Federal Ministry for Economic Cooperation and Development, Germany
Briggs, Andrew, Oxford University
Britan, Gerry, U.S. Agency for International Development
Budhram, Dowlat, InterAmerican Institute for Cooperation in Agriculture, Costa Rica
Caldicott, Jonathan, InterAmerican Development Bank
Carlson, Bruce, U.S. Agency for International Development
Chauke, Phillip, Development Bank of South Africa
Chen, Xuean, Ministry of Finance, China
Chibba, Michael, Canadian International Development Consultants
Clapp-Wincek, Cynthia, U.S. Agency for International Development
Cole, Mary, International Development Association
Conly, Jonathan, U.S. Agency for International Development
Cooksy, Leslie, University of Delaware
Curtis, Caroline, InterAmerican Development Bank
Dabelstein, Niels, DANIDA
Dahele, Rebecca, United Nations Capital Development Fund, New York
De Crombrugghe, Dominique, Ministry of Foreign Affairs, Belgium
Deaton, Angus, Princeton University
Debazou, Yantio, Ministry of Agriculture, Cameroon
El-Noury, Dahlia, Social Fund for Development, Egypt
Feinsilver, Julie, InterAmerican Development Bank
Ferroni, Marco, InterAmerican Development Bank
Ficatier, Yves, Agence Francaise de Developpement
Franklin, Nadra, LINKAGES-AED, USA
Fujiki, Misato, Embassy of Japan, USA
Furman, Ricardo, Centro de Estudios y Promoción del Desarrollo, Peru
Gale, Steven, U.S. Agency for International Development
Gariba, Sulley, Institute for Policy Alternatives, Ghana; University for Development
    Studies, Ghana
Gaskin-Reyes, Camille, InterAmerican Development Bank
Goldsbrough, David, International Monetary Fund

Grisby, Elaine, U.S. Agency for International Development
Gruber, Wolfgang, European Bank for Reconstruction and Development
Gwaradzimba, Fadzai, United Nations Development Program, Nigeria
Habimana, Andre, Ministry of Finance and Economic Planning, Rwanda
Hangadoumbo, Saidou, Family Health International, USA
Hastings, John, InterAmerican Development Bank
Henderson, Stanley, Statistics of South Africa, South Africa
Hilde, Tom, New York University
Hildebrandt, Kadidja, International Atomic Energy Commission
Hirono, Ryokichi, Seikei University and Graduate Institute for Policy Studies, Tokyo
Hurley, John, U.S. Treasury Department
Inasaridze, Nino, Aid Effectiveness Virtual Exchange Center, Georgia
Kabell, Dorte, Royal Danish Ministry of Foreign Affairs
Kandiero, Tony, His Excellency, Ambassador of the Republic of Malawi to the USA
Kedowide, Corneille, World Conservation Union in West Africa
Killick, Tony, Overseas Development Institute, UK
Kirk, Colin, Department for International Development, UK
Kishmir, Maxim, International Equity Management, USA
Kiya, Masahiko, Embassy of Japan, USA
Klein, HeideMarie, Siemens Liaison, USA
Korfker, Fredrik, European Bank for Reconstruction and Development
Krall, Daniel, American Red Cross
Kremer, Michael, Harvard University; BREAD; The Brookings Institution; Center for
    Global Development; and National Bureau of Economic Research
Kruse Tietz, Lydia, Pan American Health Organization
Kruse, Stein-Erik, Center for Health and Social Development, Norway
Leeuw, Frans, Education Review Office, Government of the Netherlands; and University
    of Utrecht
Lindahl, Claes, Management Perspectives International, Sweden
Lippert, Thierry, Direction de la Cooperation au Developpement, Luxembourg
Lundgren, Hans, Organization for Economic Cooperation and Development
Macha, Arnold, Vocational Education and Training Authority, United Arab Emirates
Mackrandilal, Vijaya, Chow Engineering, USA
MacPherson, Nancy, International Union for the Conservation of Nature
Mateos y Lago, Isabelle Sophie, International Monetary Fund
Meassick, Mark, InterAmerican Institute for Cooperation in Agriculture
Meinzen-Dick, Ruth, International Food Policy Research Institute
Molo, Thioune Ramata, International Development Research Center, Senegal
Morrow, Daniel, Elliot School of International Affairs, USA
Mungania, Penina, University of Louisville
Navin, Robert, U.S. Agency for International Development
Nawar, Maria Elena, InterAmerican Development Bank
Ndiaye, Gouthia, Bank of New York
Ndongo Mebometa, Guillaume, University of Quebec
Nichols, Flemming, International Fund for Agricultural Development
Ntisme, Patrick, Development Bank of South Africa
Ocampo, Ada, Program for Strengthening the Regional Capacity for Monitoring and
    Evaluation of Rural Poverty-Alleviation Projects in Latin America and the Caribbean
    (PREVAL), Peru
Odhiambo, Karen, Kenyan Evaluation Association

Odutolu, Dr. Oluwole, Harvard School of Public Health AIDS-Prevention Initiative, Nigeria
Ogden, Suzanne, Northeastern University
Ojo, Oladeji, African Development Bank
Paredes, Maritza, Columbia University
Perdomo, German, Pan-American Health Organization
Picado, Xinia, University of Costa Rica
Picciotto, Robert, Global Policy Project
Pineda, Moisés A., InterAmerican Development Bank
Pitman, Paula, Campaign for Female Education and Development International, USA
Platteau, Jean-Philippe, University of Namur
Pulgar-Vidal, Max, InterAmerican Development Bank
Quick, Steve, InterAmerican Development Bank
Quiroz, Consuelo, FUNDATADI, Venezuela
Rahman, M. Saif, Ohio Wesleyan University
Ramirez-Ramos, Laura, InterAmerican Development Bank
Ramos, Mario, Global Environment Facility
Riley, Joel, InterAmerican Development Bank
Ritterhoff, Robin, U.S. Treasury Department
Robinson, Loly, Office of the Prime Minister, Madagascar
Rodriguez, Alejandro, Institute for Agricultural Development and Agribusiness National Council of Decentralization, Peru
Rogers, Peter, Harvard University
Rola-Rudzen, Fay, Muresk Institute of Agriculture, Australia
Ruiz, Adan, Brandeis University
Sanguinetty, Jorge, DevTech Systems, Inc., USA
Sartorius, Rolf, Social Impact, USA
Savvas, Laure, Sterling Merchant Finance Ltd., USA
Shao, Patrick, Department of Housing, South Africa
Sivagnanasothy, Velayuthan, Ministry of Policy Development and Implementation, Sri Lanka
Sonderhoff, Beatrice, Japan International Cooperation Agency
Steele, Roger, World Vision, USA
Stewart, Frances, Oxford University
Szabo, Charles, InterAmerican Development Bank
Tsikata, Tsidi, International Monetary Fund
Valencia, Carlos A., InterAmerican Development Bank
Van den Berg, Rob, Ministry of Foreign Affairs, The Netherlands
Vasquez-Colina, Maria, Nystrand Center of Excellence in Education, College of Education and Human Development, USA
Verwey, Tobias, Development Bank of South Africa
Wacek, Rick, SIL International, USA
Walter, Graham, African Development Bank
Wanjau, Elizabeth, IQ Solutions, USA
Wiesner, Eduardo, former Minister of Finance, Colombia and former Executive Director, World Bank
Willard, Alice, American Red Cross
Yang-Yang Chen, Patricia, International Monetary Fund
Zhong, Hongfei, Ministry of Finance, China
Zmitrovis, Patrice, Social Impact, USA

Index